India and the Traveller

India and the Traveller

Aspects of Travelling Identity

Edited by
Rita Banerjee

B L O O M S B U R Y
NEW DELHI • LONDON • OXFORD • NEW YORK • SYDNEY

BLOOMSBURY INDIA
Bloomsbury Publishing India Pvt. Ltd
Second Floor, LSC Building No. 4, DDA Complex, Pocket C – 6 & 7,
Vasant Kunj, New Delhi, 110070

BLOOMSBURY, BLOOMSBURY ACADEMIC INDIA and the Diana logo
are trademarks of Bloomsbury Publishing Plc

First published in India 2022
This edition published 2022

Bloomsbury Academic
An imprint of Bloomsbury Publishing Plc

ISBN: HB: 978-93-54355-91-2; eBook: 978-93-54355-15-8

2 4 6 8 10 9 7 5 3 1

Typeset in Minion pro by Manipal Technologies Limited
Printed & bound in India by Replika Press Pvt. Ltd.

Contents

Section 3: Self-Fashioning of Indian Travellers

Section 4: Travel and Fiction

List of Figures

List of Abbreviations

BBC	British Broadcasting Corporation
BHU	Banaras Hindu University
BJP	Bharatiya Janata Party
ICHR	Indian Council for Historical Research
ICS	Indian Civil Service
INA	Indian National Army
JNU	Jawaharlal Nehru University
JSPS	Japan Society for Promotion of Sciences
LTTE	Liberation Tigers of Tamil Eelam
NEFA	North-East Frontier Agency
NMML	Nehru Memorial Museum and Library
SAFIC	Sri Aurobindo Foundation for Indian Culture
UGC	University Grants Commission
UNICEF	United Nations Children's Fund
VMLT	Vande Mataram Library Trust

Acknowledgements

The idea of this book originated in a conference held at Nehru Memorial Museum and Library (NMML) in New Delhi, India, in August 2019. I express my deep gratitude to the then director of NMML, Shakti Sinha, who unfortunately passed away a few months back, for his encouragement and for making the conference possible with all necessary support and arrangements. I am also thankful to the NMML staff for necessary assistance.

However, since then, the theme of the conference has been considerably modified, new contributions have come in and the remaining ones have been substantially altered so that the current volume is a different work. I am thankful to some colleagues, like Pramod K. Nayar and Jyoti Atwal, who have given me useful advice. I also thank the anonymous reviewer of Bloomsbury for important suggestions and the copyeditor for carefully preparing the manuscript. Finally, I would like to thank R. Chandra Sekhar of Bloomsbury India for his continual encouragement, advice and support for making the book possible.

Introduction

Aiming to explore different facets of the travelling persona, this book brings together travel writings related to India written by travellers from many countries and periods of time and with diverse intents and purposes. It looks at European and Asian travel accounts of India as well as of regional travellers travelling within and outside India. The chapters in the collection demonstrate the differences between the non-Indian and the Indian persona, just as they show how European and non-European visitors are distinguished from each other.

Jan Borm defines a 'travel book' as 'any narrative characterized by a non-fiction dominant that relates (almost always) in the first person a journey or journeys that the reader supposes to have taken place in reality while assuming or presupposing that author, narrator and principal character are but one or identical' (2012, 4; italics removed). Although this may serve as a conventional working definition, there are many variations. For instance, the field of travel writing shows fictional and semi-fictional narratives flourishing alongside real-life travel memoirs. In this anthology, we seek to bring fictional and non-fictional accounts together for examining the figure of the traveller.

Since the objective of travel writing during certain periods was to provide information about a place and a society, fictional works often fulfilled that function. As Borm quotes Pierre Aurégan: 'No doubt, reading Balzac will teach us as much — if not more — about post-revolutionary society as the historians of his time — forgotten today — did' (cited in Borm 2012, 10). Therefore, any attempt to separate ethnographic, sociological or historical narratives from works of fiction as belonging to completely different domains is futile.

Travel narratives, whether non-fictional or fictional, may serve as studies in the culture of a people or region. Sometimes, a semi-fictional work based on history provides us with glimpses of a forgotten past. Amitav Ghosh's *In An Antique Land* (studied in Chapter 12 of this volume), for instance, brings together the memoir of the young social anthropologist Ghosh in 20th-century Egypt and the semi-fictional journey of the Jewish merchant Abraham Ben Yiju from Egypt to South India and back in AD 1148, thus showing the contrast between the two worlds. Ghosh draws on letters, legal documents like a deed of manumission, records of debts, and even scraps of paper for rough jottings to narrate Ben Yiju's journey from Aden to coastal India and his slave Bomma's travels to Aden to sell his master's goods and buy household and other stuff for Ben Yiju. The narrative relies a good deal on imaginary construction and invention. It interweaves semi-fictional glimpses of Ben Yiju's life in Egypt and Mangalore (Mangaluru) with Ghosh's experience of the people in Lataifa and Nashawy and his visit to Mangalore.

The major purpose of merging the two narratives is evidently to contrast the barrierless trading world of the 12th century, which made the Indian Ocean–Mediterranean trade useful and lucrative and brought Ben Yiju, Ashu (the local Nair woman married to Ben Yiju) and Bomma together in vibrant work-related and personal relationships, with present-day Egypt where this would have been impossible because of visa restrictions and war. The narrative contrasts today's Mangalore, which is no longer a port, with the 12th-century Mangalore, which had palatial mansions of expatriates from the Middle East.

However, startlingly, there are rare instances of the survival of some elements of the forgotten culture in the 20th century. The travelogue relates Ghosh's astonishing discovery of unlooked-for identities, like the recognition of the similarities in the dialect of contemporary Lataifa and the North African Arabic of Ben Yiju. Bobbariya-bhuta, the spirit of a Muslim mariner and trader worshipped by the Magavira fishing folks of Mangalore, is a reminder of the close ties once existing between the fishing community and foreign merchants. The survival of the spirit in the current Hindu Sanskritised shrines shows Ghosh the continuation of Bomma's beliefs in contemporary Mangalorean society. The comparison between the non-fictional and semi-fictional accounts, therefore, enlightens us about the cultures of the Malabar Coast and the Middle East, as existing in the 12th and 20th centuries, presenting lost, transformed and enduring features.

Some literary narratives also adopt journey as a theme. Beginning with the *Odyssey*, such literature of travel includes Joseph Conrad's *Heart of Darkness* and V.S. Naipaul's books, which, he claims, are not descriptions of 'routes' as in olden times but which narrate his journey of 'inquiry' on a 'theme' (cited in Borm 2012, 8). Conrad's *Heart of Darkness* may serve as an example of a travel narrative that constructs a parallel inner journey.

> Such narratives, propelled especially by the popularization of Freud's ideas on the unconscious, link interior and exterior, psychological and physical journeys. Critics tend to regard the linking of these aspects as a feature of modern travel writing that distinguishes it from the texts of earlier centuries. Graham Greene's *Journey Without Maps*

> (1936), which quotes Conrad and conjoins Greene's experiences of West Africa with his childhood developments in Britain, is seen as the classic example. (Das and Youngs 2019, 8)

For instance, in Chapter 11, M.V. Lakshmi shows how, in two Japanese fictional works, travel becomes more of a parallel internal journey that enables the travellers to find answers to questions, rather than an account of a physical journey.

Focussing on India, this volume encompasses accounts of travels chiefly to and within India but also includes a few chapters on Indians travelling abroad. The first section looks at European travellers to India — early modern, colonial and postcolonial — while the second section examines Asian travellers to India — Japanese and Chinese along with Arabs who journeyed to India for pilgrimage, tourism and acquisition of knowledge. The third section concerns Indian travellers, men and women, touring various places in India or travelling outside the country. The final section discusses fictional, semi-fictional texts along with non-fictional ones, covering spatial and temporal travel of people and ideas. In the volume, purposes of travel range from pilgrimages to tourism, colonial administration, accompaniment of relations, spiritual enlightenment, postgraduate studies, acquisition of ethnographic information and religious texts and survey of contemporary politics. The book's objective is to offer glimpses of the perspectives of various travelling selves, their attitude towards travel, self, development of one's self, the other, as well as the relation between the self and the other. The volume enables a comparative viewpoint by allowing scope for examining similarities and differences between identities, affinity, opposition, accommodation and self-exploration.

Jean-Didier Urbain writes of the need to differentiate between travel and physical mobility: 'Mobility is physical movement, whereas travel, before it chooses a specific place, is above all an idea' (2012, 37). He shows, for instance, how instead of travelling to distant lands, travel could mean a visit to catacombs, 'a 300-km maze of disused underground quarries', 'somewhere in Paris, hidden in the darkness of a disused railway tunnel running under a park' (35). Travel itself has manifold connotations; for instance, it does not merely connote spatial journeys but also temporal ones. As René Descartes had said, 'Entering into dialogue with people from other centuries is like travelling' (37). In this volume, travel encompasses, spatial as well as temporal journeys. For instance, in the final chapter of this volume, Nishat Haider demonstrates that the narrative of Qurratulain Hyder's *River of Fire* maps the travel of individuals and ideas between different 'spatio-temporal chronotopes' by employing characters appearing as various reincarnations in different historical eras.

Travel writing today has given rise to many controversies, for instance, to what extent it is Eurocentric and how this slant towards Eurocentrism can be corrected. According to Tabish Khair, 'current definitions of both travel and travel writing are embedded in a distinctive cultural and historical experience: that of the European age of expansion and colonization stretching from the fifteenth century to the twentieth' (Khair 2006, 5). The Eurocentric approach to travel literature led to the diminishing value of travel memoirs written by non-Europeans. The travel texts of non-Europeans, for example, those of Asian and African travellers, to parts of Asia were neglected and had acquired a marginalised status. Khair writes, 'Such has been the centrality of later European Self-Other perception that even obvious facts — like the porous borders between Asia, Africa and Europe from prehistory through the Greek civilization and the Moorish era in Spain to the present times — have been overlooked outside specialist circles' (15). This book aims to correct this imbalance by including chapters on non-European travel. The accounts of the journeys of Chinese pilgrims and Arab traders to medieval India, Japanese travellers and scholars to early 20th-century India, and the parallel journeys of the contemporary Indian traveller and the 12th-century slave from India to Egypt move away from this Eurocentric discourse towards alternative dialogues.

The tendency to view the traveller and the travelee through this lens of self-other perception has been the enduring legacy of colonial, postcolonial and Eurocentric discourse. According to Robert Clarke, the inclusion of non-Western perspectives in travel literature has led to the contestation of some of the 'central ideas that have developed in relation to colonial and postcolonial travel writing in the last two decades' (Clarke 2018, 11). 'These include the proclivity of many critics to view all instances of exoticism as necessarily linked to discourses of appropriation and commodification' (11). In my view, Western perspectives on travelogues also include a hierarchical relationship between the traveller and the travelee and the uncontested subject position of the former. Non-Western travel writing, on the other hand, often shows a more egalitarian relationship, a search for affinity instead of opposition. Especially in oral narratives, a plurality of voices and a lack of a dominant and unified subject can be observed. In Chapter 7, Sumit Kumar Barua argues that the Japanese scholar Kimura Nichiki's writings on India bring out his love for the Bengali language, literature and culture and a sense of oneness with the land of his long residence. He also displays a desire to share in the aspirations and ideals of India as a nation during the period of British colonisation. In Chapter 5, the narrative of the medieval Arab travellers shows a relatively neutral ethnographic relation of indigenous social practices and shared values, although, at times, their Islamic origin leads them to denounce what they see as immoral practices.

Moreover, the Western perspective of travel writing has led to some critics opining that travel writing 'as a genre can never truly free itself from its colonial heritage and, from this perspective, it will always remain a neocolonial mode that reproduces a dominant North Atlantic idea of "civilization" from which travel writers continue to consolidate a privileged position by classifying, evaluating, and passing judgment on other parts of the world' (Edwards 2018, 19). On the other hand, according to others, 'the genre of travel writing has the potential to embrace revisionist, critical, and subversive narratives, political positions, and innovative modes of representation' (19). Travel writing may subvert or even parody the privileged hierarchy and the stereotypical opposition between the superior civilised self and the inferior uncivilised other in various situations. In Chapter 8, we see an *apparent* replication of this opposition between the civilised and the uncivilised in the travelogue of the Western-educated, middle-class, Bengali colonial administrator Sanjibchandra Chattopadhyay. However, his view of the uncivilised 'wild west' (Palamou) is ambivalent, as Saugata Bhaduri shows that the devices of 'relativisation' and 'ironic humour' turn the critical gaze on the *bhadralok* author himself, while the political exploitation of the uneducated tribals is satirised.

This anthology addresses certain crucial issues related to the self in travel memoirs. While travel had, for a long time, been associated with material journeys to other lands and acquisition of knowledge of the external world, according to some, the rationale for interior journeys arises in view of the shrinking of unexplored space in today's world, leading to a desire to 'turn inward into their psyche and memories' (see Das and Youngs 2019, 8–9). It is the nature of the space one encounters that determines the urge to reflect or undertake an inner journey. While travels to urban, populated spaces encourage observation of people, activities and society, solitude and expanse typically inspire self-reflection and self-probing. As Roslynn Haynes observes in connection with deserts, 'the sense of immensity, of visual emptiness, the lack of temporal references in a seemingly changeless landscape, and the characteristic silence of deserts present a further psychological challenge, raising profound questions about identity and meaning' (2019, 315). While expanse and solitude arouse religious thoughts in some travellers, to many others, deserts appear as 'a personal challenge to survive and to be the first to reach a destination' (316).

In Chapter 9, Jayati Gupta shows how Swami Vivekananda and Sister Nivedita's journey to the Himalayas, which also symbolise immensity and solitude, inspires spiritual revelation or induces self-reflection, just as the physical difficulties and arduousness of the journey during the late 19th century pose a challenge to the travellers. Gupta demonstrates that the physical journey entailed a parallel journey of spiritual self-realisation. Similarly, Debendranath Tagore's journey also involved a spiritual quest in the domain of nature. The narratives provide an insight into the traveller's sense of being alone with nature and its effects on them. As Gupta avers, Debendranath Tagore and Vivekananda were 'pilgrim souls', though they did not visit temples or churches or sacred places. They sought the experience of the divine in nature. In some ways, these travelogues remind us of aspects of 19th-century Romanticism in England, especially the ideas of William Wordsworth. According to Richard Barber, 'it [a pilgrimage] is journey both outwards, to new, strange, dangerous places, and inwards to spiritual improvement, whether through increased self-knowledge or through the braving of physical dangers' (1991, 1).

The goals of inner voyages and self-probing lead to a different mode of self-fashioning of the traveller. Isolated places and natural surroundings away from people do not offer scope for the formulation of the self in opposition to the other. For instance, in Chapter 11, although M.V. Lakshmi discusses two fictional narratives, the chapter shows how a few Japanese travellers' journey to India and visit to Buddhist sites and the Ajanta caves led to their inner psychological transformation.

Even when journeys of the self are not internal, the nature of the self perceiving the external world is crucial for the narrative. According to Nandini Das and Tim Youngs, 'What inflects the nature of the travel text is frequently a matter of voice. Classical travel narratives are often third person accounts, descriptions of journeys undertaken by someone else, or treatises formed out of the information accumulated from such journeys. Medieval customs of pilgrimage, however, introduced a sense of individual experience as well as structure in such descriptions of travel' (2019, 3). Medieval notions of selfhood and the other in the Western and the non-Western traditions offer comparisons with later presentations of the travelling self. Mary B. Campbell finds two contrasting tendencies in European travel writing: 'one of absolute interest in the external world, as in *Wonders of the East* or *Mandeville's Travels*, and one exploring the subjective and autobiographical capacities of the form — *The Booke of Margery Kempe* or *Robinson Crusoe*' (cited in Das and Youngs 2019, 3). With the growth of science and emphasis on empirical knowledge, travellers in the 17th and 18th centuries sought to understand and collect information dispassionately and objectively about the alien worlds they visited.

However, even when they aim for objectivity, travel accounts are shaped and coloured by the diverse tastes and predilections of the viewer, suggesting that travellers' accounts differ according to their specific perspectives. So, the reality that the travellers view really depends more on their selves and specificities of perspectives rather than the space they perceive. In spanning centuries of travel in the book, we see how the pilgrim's vision, which selects sacred spots for exploration and looks for objects and landscapes of renown belonging to the legendary past, differs from that of the merchant's, whose needs are related to the market and procurement of merchandise. In the 17th century, the outlook of tourists like Thomas Coryate differed from that of the East India Company merchants, who often wrote of the goods that they sold, the difficulties of transportation of merchandise in a land infested with robbers and the lack of royal authority and the rule of law in the countryside. Merchants and traders to India during the 17th century were often entrusted with the task of collecting information about the flora, the fauna and the people and of supplying necessary data to scientists and organisations like the Royal Society of London. Travellers doubled up as botanists, zoologists and ethnographers.

According to Roy Bridges, travel writing is 'a discourse designed to describe and interpret for its readers a geographical area together with its natural attributes and its human society and culture' (cited in Khair 2006, 4). We often see that the various actors' personalities, objectives, situations and preferences colour and shape the reality that they describe. For instance, Hariprabha Takeda, a Bengali woman visiting Japan, perceives Japanese marriage ceremonies, culinary practices and the domestic duties of Japanese women, including their household goods, with curiosity and attention and describes them in detail. By contrast, Rabindranath Tagore, who also visited Japan about the same time, relates the love of beauty of the Japanese, the lack of prolixity and ornamentation in their poetry and painting, and the characteristic restraint and concision of the Japanese temperament (1976, 82–84). As a man of letters, his narration focuses on general abstract qualities of human nature and creative expression. However, Takeda, as a woman, shows her kinship with the concerns and activities of women as well as her awareness of material objects and practices associated with everyday living. According to Nandita Basu, Hariprabha's *Bangamahilār Japanyātrā* (studied in Chapter 10) provides more information about Japan than Tagore's *Japanjatri*, demonstrating that their agendas varied.

As Khair says, 'Travel writing also entails defining, consciously or unconsciously, the writer's relationship to a geographical area, its natural attributes and its society and its culture; and, just as significantly, the writer's relationship to his or her own society and culture' (Khair 2006, 4). One may include the writer's political ideology as well. In the travel writings of Rabindranath Tagore, we see him fashioning himself as a messenger of the East or Asia to the Western world; he sought to position himself, as an Asian poet, against what he calls the aggressive nationalism of the West, which was a form of imperialism. As an Asian poet, he finds affinity with Persian poets of olden times like the Sufi poet Saadi and Hafez (Tagore 1917), who sought to break the shackles of tradition. However, he was disillusioned with contemporary Japan, which, in his view, was seeking to ape the West, forgetting their Oriental heritage of amity and spiritual bonding (Tagore 1917).

Cultural encounters involve a range of complex interactions, sometimes resulting in partial identification with specific groups and distantiation from others. In Chapter 1, 'Outsiders and Insiders: European Perceptions of India and the Problem of Cultural Distance', Joan-Pau Rubiés argues, by looking at Moroccan travellers, Jesuit missionaries, enlightened European thinkers and elite Muslim patrons, that cultural distances must be analysed within a fluid system rather than adopting an inevitable oppositional paradigm. Despite his Muslim identity, the Moroccan traveller Ibn Battuta remained an outsider in many circles; he was especially ignored in the western and central lands of Islam and comfortable only among Arab-speaking Muslims. Again, in their efforts to Indianise Christianity to render it palatable for potential Indian converts, the Jesuits sought cultural accommodation by learning languages, adapting to local practices and adopting indigenous literary genres. Enlightened, rational thinkers like François Bernier, however, chose to ally with their elite rationalist Muslim patrons on the basis of shared values with the intention of rejecting what they considered as irrational — the Hindu monist philosophy.

It is the travellers' relationship to their own culture and society and the light they intend their society to appear in before their audience that induces a conscious self-fashioning at times. Chapter 2 shows how, during the 17th century, diplomats like Thomas Roe and independent tourists like Thomas Coryate fashioned their images at Jahangir's court to promote their country's and their own interests. Faced with competition from the Portuguese, the ambassador Roe tried to show England as a country of rare crafts and sought to please Jahangir with European curiosities to promote East Indian trade. The itinerant traveller Coryate, on the other hand, showered praises and flattery on Jahangir and fashioned himself as a poor religious mendicant (a fakir) to acquire a pecuniary gift from the Mughal emperor.

During the colonial period, the European traveller's colonial outlook shaped their view of the colony and the natives they visited. Chapter 3, 'Discovering the Other: Northeast India in Early 19th-Century British Travel Writing', shows the surveyor, administrator or the military official as the colonial traveller, conveying detailed information on natural resources like tea, timber and minerals that would help the government. Moreover, the colonial traveller portrays the colonised as lacking agency, setting up the colonial self in opposition to that of the natives.

William Dalrymple's *The Age of Kali*, discussed in Chapter 4, provides us a postcolonial travelogue that sees India from a completely different perspective from that of the coloniser. Dalrymple calls his novel 'a collection of peripatetic essays, a distillation of ten years' travel around the Indian subcontinent' (1998, Introduction). He relates how, for four years, he led a 'nomadic' existence, moving from 'the fortresses of the drug barons of the North-West Frontier to the jungle lairs of the Tamil Tigers; from flashy Bombay drinks parties to murderous Bihari blood feuds' (Introduction). The text displays an awareness about self, travel and travel writing while relating a multiplicity of stories about India, Indian politics, society, casteism, relics of the Portuguese colonial past and of the decadent Mughal era.

Dalrymple's narrative suggests a desire to understand and relate to the other. According to Das and Youngs, 'it is tempting to claim that late twentieth- and twenty-first-century travel texts are more cognisant of and sensitive towards other cultures', beliefs and outlooks, cautioning, however, that 'texts that empathise with the other or that experiment with alternative points of view are few and consumed by a minority' (2019, 9). What Justin Edwards says of M.G. Vassanji's *A Place Within* (2008) may be relevant here, that it draws on 'a poetics of place and ethnicity based on a synchronous foreignicity that embraces antithesis, polarity, and confusion' (2018, 27). 'Synchronous foreignicity' has been defined by Fred Wah as 'the ability to remain within an ambivalence without succumbing to the pull of any single culture' (cited in Edwards 2018, 32n20). Dalrymple writes in the introduction to *The Age of Kali*:

> Its subject is an area of the world I revere like no other, and in which I have chosen to spend most of my time since I was free to make that choice. From my first visit to the region as an eighteen-year-old backpacker, I was completely overwhelmed: India thrilled, surprised, daunted and excited me. (1998, Introduction)

Dalrymple's words suggest one's habitation in different cultures. The text represents a plurality of Indias and presents the travelling 'self within that multiplicity'[1]. According to Edwards, 'The postcolonial travel writer highlights his or her presence within the construction of the text and actively negotiates the multivalence of their lives' (2018, 27).

The organisation of *The Age of Kali* does not focus on a single narrative of the writer's journey to a place or places but consists of glimpses of multiple unconnected visits to individuals or groups in different spheres. Postcolonial texts appear to be fragmented. 'Rather than representing a subject's travels from one point to another, these texts embrace fragmentation and disruption' (Edwards 2018, 27). There is no single theme that links the episodes.

Nor is there a uniform subject position. Dalrymple appears as a journalist relating two sides of a conflict about a rape case in Rajasthan, a historian discussing 16th-century Portuguese conquistadors and Jesuit missionaries in Goa, a privileged interviewer of the queen mother in Gwalior as well as of prominent politicians from less-privileged castes like Lalu Yadav in Bihar, and a raconteur of the past glories of nawabi Lucknow. It is the travellee's opinions and experience that acquire importance in the multiple narratives, while Dalrymple's authority as a subject is reduced. His identity seems to be characterised by mobility, which Edward Said finds inherent in the traveller, who does not present a stable, consistent and continuous self to the world. Said suggests that he is 'at home' in movement. He writes,

> I occasionally experience myself as a cluster of flowing currents. I prefer this to the idea of a solid self, the identity to which so many attach so much significance. These currents, like the themes of one's life, flow during the waking hours, and at their best they require no reconciling, no harmonizing . . . they are always in motion, in time, in place, in the form of all kinds of strange combinations moving about, not necessarily forward, sometimes against each other, contrapuntally yet without one central theme. (Said 1999, 295)

Significantly, mobility dependent on conscious self-fashioning characterised the selves of many travel narrators who belonged to earlier periods. For instance, Thomas Coryate, the itinerant Englishman who is more at home travelling, appears in various roles suitable for

1 Edwards writes: Caryl Phillips's *Atlantic Sound* (2000) shows 'a single position in multiple places, thus representing the world as multidimensional and presenting the self within that multiplicity' (2018, 27).

the occasions. Again, in Abū Zayd Al-Sīrāfī's travelogues on India and China, we find a variant, a composite travelling identity constituted by several informants' selves who relate the details of everyday life, the society and political systems of the lands they visit, rather than a single stable self with settled inclinations and attitudes.

According to Colin Thubron, a journey can be seen as 'a metaphor for life, a voyage through time as well as space — time seen as a road' (2012, 58). The *River of Fire* (discussed in the final chapter of this book) shows individual actors travelling through time by being reincarnated in different epochs and narrative memory itself travelling, 'migrating' and 'circulating'. Quest narratives also show travel through time. Travel books take the form of a quest narrating the 'setting out with some theme or aspiration, passing through adventure and conflict, and ending in a kind of resolution and homecoming' (2012, 58).

However, travel memoirs (especially those belonging to the late 20th century or contemporary periods) do not always achieve a 'resolution or home coming'. Sometimes, they have loose ends, which do not show a conclusion to the quest narrative. 'The whole history of travel writing, then, is not simply an account of objective voyage and description. It is the history of an endless tension between the temperament and character of generations of writers and that of worlds they travel through' (Thubron 2012, 58).

Significantly, the myth of objective presentation disappeared in the 20th century. Since a traveller's view was by definition partial and subjective, visitors viewed a specific space from multiple perspectives, revealing its various facets. Thubron aptly uses a diamond image to convey the reality that the traveller seeks to depict:

> The notion that there is an objective reality for the travel writer to capture once and for all is, even if true, practically useless. Any object, however simple, might be compared to a diamond held up to multiple shafts of light. These shafts may be directed at it from countless angles, but no beam can discover the stone in its totality. Each one simply illumines a limited assemblage of facets, some brilliant, some blurring into dark. (Thubron 2012, 66)

The many Indias that are depicted in the narratives discussed here reveal its many facets, although none can be said to present a complete India. Nor can any one travel narrative claim complete objectivity of presentation for the self of the narrator always dominates the narrative.

In the process of presenting their encounter with India, the travellers reveal manifold aspects of their selves. The early modern European traveller seeks to adapt partially to the conditions that confront them in the East. The self becomes largely accommodative, while the colonial administrator constructs an oppositional self. In the fluid trading world of the 17th century, strategies of self-fashioning for the English depended on the specific requirements of the situation — profit and supersession of trading rivals. Significantly, the Mughal imperial paintings at different periods develop the counter-strategy of imaging the emperor in a higher and, therefore, superior position vis-à-vis the English. By contrast, Asian travellers manifest various degrees of affinity with and seek partially to identify themselves with the people and culture they encounter. The traveller who journeys in the solitude of nature aims to introspect, comprehend oneself and attain spiritual fulfilment.

Moreover, the chapters in this anthology often seek to interrogate the self-other paradigm in travel writing without reproducing it. Regional travel writing in colonial India replicated the self-other opposition for the purpose of parodying the concept. Women's journeys to the East in the early 20th century involved crossing cultural barriers and seeking identity with the alien and the exotic. Common gendered concerns enabled transcultural identification. In fictional, temporal journeys, reincarnated selves engaged in memory travel to invoke a syncretic past that had been free of conflict.

Overview of Chapters

Section 1 chiefly discusses European travellers to India from diverse periods of time, giving us accounts of travellers from the late medieval period to the 20th century. The first chapter draws mostly but not entirely on European travellers from the late medieval to the early modern era. Joan-Pau Rubiés interrogates the notion of 'inside–outside dichotomy' and argues that different degrees of distance separate various groups of foreign travellers and sets of local people of the country in different circumstances. While some, like Jesuit missionaries, endeavour to Indianise themselves and adapt to local conditions to further their mission of conversion, Western rational free thinkers share ideas and beliefs with unorthodox and enlightened Muslim elites and deride supposedly irrational Hindu believers.

Chapter 2, which has two authors, is divided into two parts. In the first part, Christian Feser looks at the strategies of self-fashioning of two English travellers with a shared cultural background at Emperor Jahangir's court in the early 17th century: one, an ambassador sent by King James and the East India Company, and the other an itinerant of limited means, known for his journeys across the world. Their variant objectives determined their respective self-fashionings.

In the latter part of the essay, Christoph Heyl looks at various Mughal visual representations which sought to downplay the position of English visitors at court, thereby reversing the self-fashioning strategies of the Europeans at different periods of time. The rise in prominence of the East India Company over the years led the Mughal painters to place British Residents within the crowded space of durbars and at a lower level than that of the emperor to lessen the importance the former actually possessed.

By contrast, the following chapter shows how the colonial travelogues of British surveyors and administrators in Assam presented the native Assamese as palpably inferior to the Europeans in civility, natural abilities and cultural values to justify the British rule. In Chapter 3, Nandana Dutta looks at three 19th-century texts by Robert Boileau Pemberton, William Griffith and John Butler on Assam to analyse how each represents the 'natural', overly emphasising natural objects and flora and fauna at the expense of the people, in their efforts to 'write the human Other out of the picture'. This chapter seeks to uncover 'the Other beneath strategies of repression that are camouflaged by the excess of natural description, which reveals both confidence and anxiety' (Dutta, Chapter 3). The colonial administrator, scientist or the surveyor to the 'Northeast' confronts the strange and the mysterious with a mixture of confidence and anxiety. Dutta uses Michel de Certeau's work to find the marks of the 'confidence–anxiety duality' and to discover 'the often silenced or repressed Other'.

In Chapter 4, Ajie George examines William Dalrymple's *The Age of Kali* (1998), a collection of short travel narratives based on journeys through the Indian subcontinent from 1989 to 1998, as a postcolonial travelogue. She shows the text crossing disciplinary and cultural boundaries and functioning as 'socially and politically sensitised narratives' (George, Chapter 4). George argues that Dalrymple's identity as a traveller/writer/historian exemplifies how travel in a globalised world and spatial and temporal motions help produce 'combinations of identity'.

Section 2 focuses on Asian travellers to India from Japan, China and the Middle East, belonging to different periods. The narratives demonstrate a difference from the European perception of India in that one finds here a search for affinity rather than difference and opposition. To the Buddhist Japanese and Chinese traveller, the land of the birthplace of the Buddha was a place of pilgrimage. India was a land from where Buddhism had spread to Japan. Buddhist texts found in India provided them with knowledge of the doctrines. As in the first section, the chapters in Section 2 largely follow the chronological order. Chapter 5 compares the Chinese pilgrim Yuan Chwang's (or Hiuen Tsiang's) visit to India in the 7th century with the Arab trader's oral narrative of the 9th century. For the pilgrim, visits to places of sacred miracles evoked memories of their legendary associations. However, Yuan Chwang also depicted ethnographical customs and the practices of other similar Indian religions like Hinduism, showing a certain degree of tolerance rather than abhorrence. The Islamic traveller, on the other hand, was primarily concerned with conveying ethnographic information through the many-voiced *akhbār*, which had a largely secular and neutral perspective despite its flaunting of Islamic supremacy. Rita Banerjee argues that while the Buddhist pilgrim finds affinity in the country of the birth of the Buddha, the Islamic narrator-compiler maintains neutrality in reporting other cultures without creating a self-other opposition in the travelogue.

Chapter 6 discusses the journey of the 20th-century Japanese missionary traveller, Fuji Nichidatsu, to India. Unlike the Buddhist pilgrims of the earlier period, the nationalist Buddhist Fuji believed in pan-Asian unity with Japan at the helm. For him, India was a country which needed to be reclaimed for Nichiren Buddhism and linked with Japan. His missionary zeal distinguished him from the Japanese tourist interested in sightseeing or the archaeological and architectural significance of the Buddhist sites. Ranjana Mukhopadhyaya argues that when Fuji witnessed unethical or immoral practices among Indians, he attributed them to the spread of Western commercial values in a subject country under British rule. The binary Fuji wished to construct was primarily between Asia and the West. His militant Buddhism led him to defend the wars waged by Japan in the early 20th century. However, after the Second World War, he became an advocate for peace, holding the principle of pan-Asian pacifism.

In Chapter 7, Sumit Kumar Barua discusses a different kind of Buddhist scholar and researcher from Japan, Kimura Nichiki, who stayed and taught in Bengal for a number of years, supporting the Indian Independence movement. Unlike Fuji Nichidatsu, he was tolerant of the rituals of Hinduism and studied them, despite his deep interest in Buddhism. As an ethnographer, he compared Indian social customs with Japanese ones, discussing similarities and differences and their causes without ascribing superiority to either. His love of the Bengali language and knowledge of Bengali literature showed his closeness to India. As a traveller, Kimura Nichiki explored affinity and difference between the two Asian countries without seeking to construct them in opposition.

Section 3 focuses primarily on Indian travellers travelling to different regions of India, although the last chapter of this section narrates a Bengali woman's journey to Japan. In these writings, the relation between the self and the other acquires new dimensions. In Chapter 8, Saugata Bhaduri argues that Sanjibchandra Chattopadhyay's *Palamou* (1880–1883) marks a new trend in Bengali travel writing, introducing a completely new conception of the travelling self. Bhaduri points to the emergence of a number of secular, first-person travel narratives, entertaining rather than informative in tone, from 1882. The chapter shows that Sanjibchandra's narrative strategy consists of digressions and disclaimers, his plot concentrates on insignificant episodes, while the conclusion concludes nothing. In his account of the 'wild west' of Palamou, Sanjibchandra, the colonial administrator and Bengali *bhadralok*, employs the device of relativisation and a 'self-deprecating ironic humour', which turns his travelogue into a political critique of the exploitation of tribals and leads him to discover the other within the self (Bhaduri, Chapter 8).

In the following chapter (9), there is an absence of the other because travel takes place in the solitude of nature. It is not so much people that the traveller encounters but landscape and natural objects. Jayati Gupta examines three texts, namely, Debendranath Tagore's *Autobiography* and Sister Nivedita's *Notes of Some Wanderings with the Swami Vivekananda* (1913) and *Kedar Nath and Badri Narayan: A Pilgrim's Diary* (1916) as pilgrimage narratives. Swami Vivekananda and Nivedita's pilgrimage was different from the customary visits to sacred sites of pilgrimage that one finds in traditional accounts. Building on Richard Barber's contention that the act of pilgrimage can be both an 'outward' journey to new or strange places and an 'inward' one to 'spiritual improvement', Jayati Gupta shows how Devendranath Tagore's autobiography records the search of the pilgrim soul for the 'Supreme Soul' in the depths of his own soul (cited in Chapter 9). In Nivedita's account of travel from Nainital to Almora and Kathgodam, and wanderings in Kashmir, the aesthetic delight becomes akin to a spiritual experience. However, while the beauty of nature gave Nivedita aesthetic pleasure, spiritual realisation was most important for her teacher, Vivekananda. It was especially the visit to Amarnath and the sight of the ice Shiva-lingam that transported Vivekananda and transformed him spiritually. Nivedita writes: 'To him, the heavens had opened' (cited in Chapter 9).

Chapter 10 examines Hariprabha Takeda's narration of her visit to Japan in *Bangamahilār Japanyātrā* (1915). One of the first Bengali women to travel outside India, Hariprabha shows her courage, love of the novel and different, and power of adaptation in undertaking a sea voyage to Japan at the time she did. Nandita Basu shows how Hariprabha's education and upbringing as a Brahmo woman, social activism and non-conservative outlook enabled her to view the country of her marriage with curiosity and openness. The glossary of Japanese words that Hariprabha provides indicates her identity and interests as a woman. Her references to the practices of Buddhism and descriptions of social practices like marriage show a desire to understand another religion and culture. Hariprabha's admiration and sympathy for Japanese women who work along with men and her appreciation of the Japanese practice of public bath for women (nearly revolutionary for Indian women at the time) suggest that her sense of identity with the Japanese women enabled her to cross national and cultural barriers.

The absence of a study on Rabindranath Tagore in the section might be regarded as an omission because of the sheer volume of his travel writings and the richness of the corpus. The objective of this volume, as I have mentioned earlier, is not a comprehensive study of any one period or dimension of travelogues related to India or a study necessarily of well-known works. The book focuses on varieties of travelling selves, and I have referred to facets of Tagore's persona in this introduction to bring out the manifold aspects of evolving travelling identities and to show his difference from other travellers.

The concluding section of the book analyses accounts of travel in fictional and semi-fictional works, on many occasions, juxtaposing them with non-fictional travel, and looks at temporal as well as spatial travel. One of the objectives is to explore the relation between the non-fictional and fictional accounts, and the first two chapters in the section bring together and compare texts from both spheres. In her study of Mishima Yukio's fictional tetralogy *Hojo no Umi* (1969–1971), Endo Shusaku's *Fukai Kawa* (1993) and Hotta Yoshie's non-fictional work *Indo de Kangaeta Koto* in Chapter 11, M.V. Lakshmi analyses the images of India that appear in the works, especially the authors' employment of the device of *utamakura*, which involves reiteration of past images in the new works. She argues that in the two works of fiction especially, and to an extent in the non-fictional text, travel is more an internal process for the authors and the characters in the works than an external exercise of discovering new places and people. Lakshmi shows that some of the characters, on certain occasions, construct India as the other from a Western perspective using stereotypical images, while others seek to discover a different India. Moreover, visits to Buddhist sites in India sometimes become a self-transforming experience.

In Chapter 12, Jaya Yadav shows Ghosh as recreating the figure of the traveller as ever shifting to meet the emergent concerns of a postcolonial world. In a postcolonial world, Ghosh's presence does not overshadow the histories of those around him in Egypt. His own thoughts are constantly challenged by the Egyptians he interacts with, differentiating his account of travel in the region from those of colonial anthropologists. Moreover,

Ghosh discovers the slave Bomma, who rises to prominence from a marginalised status to play an important role in Ben Yiju's narrative. The novel becomes a historiographical project, shedding light on Bomma as the interconnected link between various worlds.

In Chapter 13, Nishat Haider shows that in Qurratulain Hyder's fictional narrative *River of Fire*, people as well as ideas travel across spatio-temporal and sociocultural borders. The novel shows four similar stories that are set in the subcontinent during different historical periods — 4th century BC, late 15th and early 16th centuries, end of the 18th and the whole of the 19th century extending to the post-Partition era. The three principal characters of the novel, Gautam Neelambar, Champak/Champa and Hari Shankar, are reincarnated in many ages. As they travel through time, they carry their memory, which includes collective images and narratives of the past. Through the travelling memories, Hyder shows the past syncretic civilisation of India. 'The memories that travel from the mythic past are eventually incorporated into local repertoires' (Haider, Chapter 13). Mnemonic narratives are constantly hybridised and remixed in unusual ways. Characters that reappear in different eras get transformed, becoming more complex, evolved and nuanced, because 'they are inflected by their foregoing persona' (Haider, Chapter 13). Through flexible narratives of memory, the novel elaborates alternate histories and works them into the national consciousness.

Earlier Works in the Field and the Present Volume

I have tried to demonstrate in this introduction that this volume fulfils a need by drawing attention to a specific and sometimes overlooked area in travel writing — the fashioning of travelling identities. As I have said, the book does not profess to be a comprehensive or intensive study of any area of travel writing. A variety of travel memoirs have been selected from diverse spheres to engage with the multiple facets of the travelling selves, including identity and opposition. Although 'Europe and India' forms an important section, this anthology, seeking not to restrict itself to the Western self-other oppositional paradigm, has moved to the interrogation of the concept from various angles and examination of other modes of self-fashioning.

Moreover, the volume reaches out to a non-specialised audience without limiting itself to specific periods of time or travellers from a country or region. Studies that cover particular periods or limit themselves to places like Europe or the Middle East are likely to cater to a relatively limited audience with exclusive interests. This collection focuses on viewing and comprehending a variety of travelling identities in diverse situations over the years from various cultures and nationalities. In the volume, India features as a space reflected on and interrogated by others and also as people associated intrinsically with this space who move within and out of it.

I look at a few similar and related volumes here that have appeared in recent years to show the difference between them and the present collection. Somdatta Mandal's *Indian Travel Narratives* (2020) focuses on the issue of the Indian identity of travellers, but it covers a more restricted area, devoting itself to Indian journeys from the 18th century up to the present times. Shobhana Bhattacharji's edited collection *Travel Writing in India* (2008) is an illuminating study that deals with fictional and non-fictional works, presenting travel writings from diverse regions and states such as Assam, Tamil Nadu, Gujarat, Bengal and the Himalayan region. However, it is chiefly concerned with the travels of Indian writers. By contrast, this volume seeks to introduce travellers to India as well as from India and has a specific focus on an aspect of the genre. *Indo-Persian Travels in the Age of Discoveries 1400-1800* (2007) by Muzaffar Alam and Sanjay Subrahmanyam provides illuminating readings of Persian travelogues dealing with India and Central Asian regions. Although a brilliant study, it covers, like the other works, texts specific to a region.

Two significant studies concerned with Bengal deserve our attention. Simonti Sen's *Travels to Europe: Self and Other in Bengali Travel Narratives 1879-1910* (2005), although very usefully focussed on the construction of the self and the other, is restricted to Bengali travellers to Europe and caters to readers specifically interested in Bengal. Jayati Gupta's study *Travel Culture, Travel Writing and Bengali Women 1870-1940* (2020) also draws attention to Bengali women's travel writing from 1870 to 1940. It is an intensive study with depth and focus and introduces important excerpts from individual travel writings. However, the broader scope of the current volume, the variety of perspectives and the opportunity for comparison that it offers through selected coverage and specific and narrowed focus on the construction of the travelling self indicate the new terrain it explores. By engaging with various aspects of the travelling self and the other in relation to India, it aims to contribute to the ongoing dialogue about travelogues.

References

Alam, Muzaffar, and Sanjay Subrahmanyam. 2007. *Indo-Persian Travels in the Age of Discoveries 1400-1800*. Cambridge: Cambridge University Press.

Barber, Richard. 1991. *Pilgrimages*. Woodbridge: Boydell Press.

Bhattacharji, Shobhana, ed. 2008. *Travel Writing in India*. Delhi: Sahitya Akademi.

Borm, Jan. 2012. 'Defining Travel: On the Travel Book, Travel Writing and Terminology'. In *Travel Writing: Critical Concepts in Literary and Cultural Studies*, edited by Tim Youngs and Charles Forsdick, 1–14. Vol. 4: *Approaches to Travel*. London and New York: Routledge.

Clarke, Robert. 2018. 'Postcolonial Travel Writing: An Introduction'. In *Cambridge Companion to Postcolonial Travel Writing*, edited by Robert Clarke. Cambridge and New York: Cambridge University Press. Online Publication.

Dalrymple, William. (1998) 2012. *The Age of Kali: Indian Travels and Encounters*. London: HarperCollins.

Das, Nandini, and Tim Youngs. 2019. 'Introduction' to *The Cambridge History of Travel Writing*, edited by Nandini Das and Tim Youngs. Cambridge: Cambridge University Press. Online Publication.

Edwards, Justin D. 2018. 'Postcolonial Travel Writing and Postcolonial Theory'. In *The Cambridge Companion to Postcolonial Travel Writing*, edited by Robert Clarke. Cambridge and New York: Cambridge University Press. Online Publication.

Gupta, Jayati. 2021. *Travel Culture, Travel Writing and Bengali Women 1870–1940*. Abingdon, Oxford: Routledge.

Haynes, Roslynn. 2019. 'Travel Writing and the Desert'. In *The Cambridge History of Travel Writing*, edited by Nandini Das and Tim Youngs, 315–329. Cambridge: Cambridge University Press. Online Publication.

Khair, Tabish. 2006. 'African and Asian Travel Texts in the Light of Europe: An Introduction'. In *Other Routes: 1500 Years of African and Asian Travel Writing*, edited by Tabish Khair, Martin Leer, Justin D. Edwards and Hanna Ziadeh, 1–27. Oxford: Signal Books.

Mandal, Somdatta. 2020. *Indian Travel Narratives*. Delhi: Pencraft International.

Said, Edward. 1999. *Out of Place: A Memoir*. New York: Vintage Books.

Sen, Simonti. 2005. *Travels to Europe: Self and Other in Bengali Travel Narratives 1879-1910*. Delhi: Orient Longman.

Tagore, Rabindranath. 1917. *Nationalism*. New York: Macmillan.

———. 1976. 'Japan-Yatri'. In *Rabindra Rachanabali*, 291–363. Vol. 19. Calcutta: Visva Bharati.

———. 1987 [1393 BS; Rpt. 1353 BS]. 'Parasshey'. In *Rabindra Rachanabali*. Vol. 12. Calcutta: Visva Bharati.

Thubron, Colin. 2012. 'Travel Writing Today: Its Rise and Its Dilemma'. In *Travel Writing: Critical Concepts in Literary and Cultural Studies*, edited by Tim Youngs and Charles Forsdick. Vol. 1: *The Production of Travel Writing*, 57–69. London and New York: Routledge.

Urbain, Jean-Didier. 2012. 'I Travel, Therefore I Am: The "Nomad Mind" and the Spirit of Travel?'. In *Travel Writing: Critical Concepts in Literary and Cultural Studies*, edited by Tim Youngs and Charles Forsdick, translated by Charles Forsdick. Vol. 4: *Approaches to Travel*, 24–43. London and New York: Routledge.

Section 1

EUROPE AND INDIA

1

Outsiders and Insiders: *European Perceptions of India and the Problem of Cultural Distance*

Joan-Pau Rubiés

Travel writing is an invaluable source for analysing how people from different cultural backgrounds perceived each other. Sometimes, it provides our only documentary evidence for reconstructing changing perceptions from distant periods. However, the very opposition of 'observers' and 'observed', or what anthropologists have termed as views internal (emic) or external (etic) to a cultural system, often tends to generate simplistic dichotomies. Such dichotomies are particularly likely when we are engaged in precolonial or colonial studies because the significant cultural differences between, for example, Europe and India, tend to become reified and distorted according to needs and agendas generated by more recent political and cultural identities. For instance, although at the Mughal court in Jahangir's time, one might use the generic term 'Franks' to describe all Europeans (a use of Muslim Arabic origin), whether Portuguese or English, Catholic or Protestant, Europe was culturally as well as politically plural. So was, of course, India, with its variety of ethnic groups, languages and religions. In addition, this world was very distant from ours, which is dominated by the structuring agency of the nation state. We need a definition of 'culture' that avoids simplistic reification, includes internal diversity or complexity and captures the dynamics of change.

My aim in this chapter is to interrogate the inside–outside dichotomy through a number of examples of travellers to India — mostly but not exclusively European — from the late medieval and early modern periods. It is important to emphasise that much of what follows reflects the plural conditions of a society that, despite many localised experiences of military conquest and settler colonialism, had not yet seen the full-scale imperial subjection of the British Raj. However, it seems to me that cultural developments in the 19th and 20th centuries often reproduce patterns of hybridity similar to those that I shall describe here. In this respect, it would be fair to say that the project of provincialising Europe also means recognising how Europe, over the centuries, became part of India as travellers and their tales went back and forth. I shall take as my starting point the concept of cultural distance — the mental assumptions and the ideologically charged system of knowledge that separate, for example, an external observer like the Catalan Jesuit Antoni Montserrat (or Antonio Monserrate, as his name is usually found in Portuguese and Spanish documents) from his royal host, Emperor Akbar. In 1582, Montserrat described Akbar to his fellow Europeans, inaugurating a substantial tradition of European descriptions of the Mughal court.[1] My argument shall be that while cultural distances matter a great deal, they must be recognised and analysed within a fluid system rather than by assuming a dominant logic of cultural opposition, or even incommensurability and incompatibility. A careful analysis of travellers' perceptions, and of how these change through experience, helps explain how complex interactions drive cultural change, with the possibility of creating bridges of mutual understanding and reducing cultural distances. This is not to deny that culture inevitably involves education into particular forms of sociability. What may be shared between people from different backgrounds is, for this reason, always limited to some extent, and the process of social education (which is a continuous, lifelong process) will generate what we may call 'inner' and 'outer' circles: those who share a cultural code and those who do not. Hence, a cosmopolitan code can, in some cases, entrench its distance from local cultures. The same individual may, additionally, reach a degree of understanding of cultural differences in one context and develop more distance in another. Let us think of a European traveller like François Bernier, returning home to France after many years in India. As he addresses his home audience in his printed

---

1 Montserrat's manuscript 'relation of Akbar, king of the Mughals' of 1582, written in Portuguese, was widely copied, reached Europe quickly and became a fundamental source for many other historians, especially the Jesuit historians of their overseas missions. His most detailed account, in Latin, was only published in the 20th century. See H. Hosten S.J. '*Mongolicae Legationis Commentarius*, or first Jesuit Mission to Akbar, by father Antonio Monserrate S.J.', *Memoirs of the Asiatic Society of Bengal* III, no. 9 (1914): 513–704. For an English version, see *The Commentary of Father Monserrate S.J. on his Journey to the Court of Akbar*; trans. from the original Latin by John S. Hoyland, annotated by S.N. Banerjee (Oxford: Oxford University Press, 1922). The *Commentarius*, based on a detailed travel diary, included a pathbreaking map of north India, and testifies to Montserrat's intimate knowledge and positive appreciation not only of Akbar's personal qualities as a ruler, but also of Mughal court culture and Indian civilisation. For example, it comments on the expressive capacity of the Persian language, which Montserrat learnt with Abu'l-Fazl; the wealth of cities like Lahore; and the architecture of the new royal capital Fatehpur Sikri. It fully belongs to the Renaissance paradigm that made it possible to value positively a non-Christian civilisation according to European cultural norms inspired by the classical past.

letters or in the Parisian salon of Madame de la Sablière, he enters a new cultural circle, one for whom Bernier's Mughal friends remain outsiders.

The Traveller as Outsider: Ibn Battuta in India

For many centuries, what we call religion encompassed a wide range of legal and cultural practices and functioned as the main marker of identities. If we look closer, however, ethnic and social distinctions also become relevant. A good example of the primacy of religion for structuring identities is the Moroccan traveller Ibn Battuta, who composed — or, more precisely, dictated — in Arabic one of the most detailed foreign accounts of travels in India in the Middle Ages.[2] Throughout his travels, Ibn Battuta was always an insider within what may be described as the vast Islamicate world of the 14th century, which extended from Granada in southern Spain to the ports of Southeast Asia and China. However, he was also an outsider with respect to many local languages and cultures in the places he visited or lived, including significant differences amongst Muslims. For example, during his journey and stay in India, he differentiated between Arabs (including people of the Maghreb like himself), Persians, Turks, Afghans and natives of India (Hindu converts). This double condition of insider and outsider is powerfully manifested during Ibn Battuta's stay of many years (1334–1342) at the cosmopolitan court of the sultan of Delhi, Muhammad bin Tughluq, who welcomed many foreigners into his service as a matter of policy and employed them in important capacities. Ibn Battuta noted the dangerous political tensions between these foreigners (mainly Khorasanis) and people from India who, even though they were Muslim and part of the sultan's army, resented the privileges of the former.[3] His own condition as an outsider who was, nonetheless, able to join the political elites is also reflected in his eventful journey to South India and the Maldive Islands in 1342–1346, supposedly as part of an embassy on the way to China.[4]

2 All quotations are from Ibn Battuta, *The Travels of Ibn Battuta, AD 1325-1254*, ed. trans. and annotated H.A.R. Gibb and C.F. Beckingham, 4 vols. (London: The Hakluyt Society, 1958–1994).

3 Ibn Battuta, *Travels*, 3: 721–722, describing a series of rebellions c.1333, notably the rebellion of 'Ain al-Mulk ibn Mahir and his brothers. He was defeated because the 'foreigners' — Persians, Turks and Khorasanis — were strongly motivated to fight against the Indians, whom they feared.

4 Ibn Battuta had been appointed by the sultan to accompany a return embassy travelling to the Yuan emperor of China, but a shipwreck, which involved losing the royal present and his own goods, foiled his plans, and he stayed in South India. Ibn Battuta's claims of having nonetheless reached China some years later are not credible.

Ibn Battuta's long narrative follows the vagaries of his personal itinerary, taking full advantage of the positive valuation of travel in medieval Islamic civilisation. Noticeably, however, he often seems more interested in describing Muslim communities and even identifying by name learned individuals whom he met than in dwelling at length on the strange customs of more exotic peoples. For example, his observations about the customs of the 'infidels' of India are relatively sparse, considering their prominence. In North India, he offered a detailed account of sati (almost a genre of its own) and of pious sacrifices in the Ganges, but this pales into insignificance when compared to his extensive description of Delhi and the dynastic history of Muhammad bin Tughluq and his immediate predecessors. His detailed and often intimate knowledge of the sultan and his court (notwithstanding a few historical errors) reflects, of course, the nature of his social interactions over many years.[5] Concerning the Hindu kings of Malabar, he remains much more impersonal. He observes (as many other travellers did) that they transmitted their titles to the sons of their sisters whilst excluding their own children, a peculiar system of succession via the maternal line that Ibn Battuta had also observed amongst a tribe of Berbers in western Sahara, the veiled *Massūfa* (Tuaregs).[6] He also praised the strict justice implemented by the kings of the region and their respect for Muslims, although — he also noted — they would never share food with them. These few curious observations about the 'infidel outsiders' do not appear in a very systematic fashion and fall short of a detailed personal engagement. Far more intimate is his account of how he settled in the Maldives (only superficially Islamicised at that time), was employed as a judge, entered into various temporary marriages, and used his legal position to try to change some local customs according to stricter religious standards.[7]

Ibn Battuta's overall bias towards his own particular community of believers is, in reality, perfectly coherent not only with the fact that he joined the elites of a conquest state in India, but also with the underlying logic of the *rihla*, the Arabic genre of travel writing to which the book belongs. The *rihla* may be understood as the account of an extended religious pilgrimage within the lands of Islam, rather than a systematic

---

5 Particularly masterful is Ibn Battuta's elaborate portrait of the positive and negative qualities of the sultan, notably his liberality and sense of justice, but also his brutality. See Ibn Battuta, *Travels*, 3: 657–708. It was, no doubt, a personal experience of courtly life that combined privilege and terror.

6 Ibn Battuta, *Travels*, 4: 807.

7 Ibn Battuta, *Travels*, 4: 827–829. He was particularly keen on women wearing more clothes. He was more successful in insisting on the regularity of daily prayers and certain rules about inheritance and divorce.

geographical survey.[8] Another famous medieval traveller of a few decades earlier, the Venetian Marco Polo, by contrast, says little about himself after his arrival at the court of Khubilai Khan, and structures his account (as told in the third person by Rustichello of Pisa), precisely titled *Divisament dou Monde*, as a description of the lands and peoples he saw or heard about.[9] The *rihla*, on the other hand, depicted a pilgrimage of religious knowledge, one that went beyond the prescribed visit to Mecca and was also meant to be informative and entertaining; for this reason, the personal narrative was enriched with many curiosities and anecdotes. For Ibn Battuta, who dictated his travels from memory in 1353 after returning to Morocco, the focus on Islamic learning had a precise rhetorical value: mentioning by name a number of prominent men strengthened his religious authority as a man with knowledge of the law, a *faqīh*, who had been employed as a *qadi* in Delhi. It also gave a stamp of authenticity to his account of events. There is reason to believe that the reality was less glorious. In what was at that time the periphery of an expanding Islamic oecumene, Ibn Battuta was able to inflate his credentials, but apparently he was considered quite ignorant in the western and central lands of Islam.[10]

Belonging to the community of Islamic scholars did not rule out tensions with other Muslims. At some points, Ibn Battuta, for example, distances himself from what he considered to be the excessively brutal behaviour of the Turkic conquerors towards 'infidels' in the frontier regions of South India. In Madurai, he was horrified when the 'sultan' Ghiyath al-Din unnecessarily massacred everybody found in the jungles, including women and children.[11] However, while he disapproved of this inhuman behaviour, he continued to seek patronage and recognition as an expert in Muslim law. Even in his official capacity as a *qadi*, and often with local wives and children (during his travels, he collected quite a few, as well as numerous young female slaves), Ibn Battuta remained largely unable to communicate with the vast majority of the population of India and was only truly comfortable amongst Arabic-speaking Muslims.[12] Ibn Battuta was also largely a foreigner in the context of the mercantile

8 The classic narrative that served as a model for the genre was the *Rihla* by Ibn Jubayr (1145–1217), a writer and royal secretary originally from Valencia in Muslim Spain — in fact, Ibn Battuta's narrative often incorporated whole passages from him.

9 On Marco Polo's account of India, see Joan-Pau Rubiés, *Travel and Ethnology in the Renaissance: South India through European Eyes (1250-1625)* (Cambridge: Cambridge University Press, 2000), 57–73.

10 The fact that he belonged to the Maliki legal school, rare in India, and had a limited knowledge of Persian also made his job more challenging. His position as *qadi* of Delhi was entirely honorific, and he even complained to the sultan that he was not allowed to make real decisions.

11 Ibn Battuta, *Travels*, 4: 860. Ibn Battuta called those actions an abomination.

12 In many conversations in India, Ibn Battuta often relied on interpreters.

cosmopolitanism that characterised port cities like Calicut (modern Kozhikode) or Kollam, which operated as meeting points between local Malayali, Gujarati, Arabic and Persian traders from Cambay, Mecca or Hormuz, and even Chinese traders. The society of these entrepôts was full of outsiders who in many cases were, nonetheless, doing business with the local communities. Those local communities, on the other hand, were internally divided, not only by religion or even language but also by social barriers such as the caste system, which for example was very structured in Kerala.

To sum up, we could say that in Ibn Battuta's narrative, 'cultural distance' operated on two levels: in relation to the cultural varieties within the Muslim community, and through the author's general identification with the Muslims in opposition to the rest, displaying a remarkable reluctance to engage with the majority of Hindus and other religious groups. Thus, in his account of the history of the sultans of Delhi, Ibn Battuta displayed the suspicion of many foreign Muslims towards those Indian converts who were too sympathetic towards Hindu susceptibilities, for example, about the sacredness of oxen.[13] He was explicit that while Muslims and 'infidels' inhabited the same geographical space, they remained permanently at war.[14] His religious identity had allowed him to be socially integrated and even join the political elite in very distant lands, but the ability to act as a member of an urbane and pious community of Muslim learning was complementary with treating the so-called infidels found in India and elsewhere as complete outsiders. It was a narrow and exclusive form of cosmopolitanism, learned and courtly but also with a tendency to transform everyday cultural differences into exotic curiosities. In this respect, few local themes attracted as many comments as the willingness of Indian women to burn themselves with their deceased husbands. The Moroccan's lack of knowledge of many local languages (as we have seen, he seems to rely on Arabic and some Persian) makes him an extreme example of traveller-outsider par excellence, and not typical of those many Muslims who did settle in India for longer periods, let alone those who were ethnically local and probably looked with resentment at all those gifts that Ibn Battuta (not known for his austerity) received from the sultan.

13 Ibn Battuta, *Travels,* 3: 648. The reference is to the pro-Hindu Sultan Kushru Khan.

14 Ibn Battuta, *Travels,* 3: 741–742. As Ibn Battuta saw it, the Muslims had the upper hand, but the Hindus resisted effectively in the least accessible parts of the country, such as hills and forests of reeds. Ibn Battuta was not embarrassed to allude to the callous way female captives were treated and traded, himself included — they were cheap and "uncivilized".

Local Engagements: Portuguese Settler Colonialism and Its Missions

In contrast with Ibn Battuta, there were many Muslims who settled in India for longer periods, either as traders or as members of the religious and military elite, and, in many cases, also married locally. From the 13th to the 17th centuries, Persian became increasingly central to Indian court politics, and in many contexts it cannot be considered a foreign language. The Mughal dynasty is itself a remarkable example of this process of cultural indigenisation: compare the often distant attitudes displayed by Babur, who arrived as an outsider with a Timurid cultural heritage and whose first language remained Turkic, to the manner in which his grandson Akbar embraced the patronage of Indian literature and sought to integrate Hindu military elites, notably the Rajputs, into his empire. His successor, Jahangir, was himself Akbar's son by a Rajput princess. Interestingly, a similar duality can be appreciated when we consider the Portuguese, the first European colonial power in the Indian subcontinent: when they began to establish a presence in some southern coastal towns in the early 16th century, many quickly became settlers and *casados* (married citizens), and whilst the Portuguese language no less than Catholicism remained central to their cultural identity, many traders or soldiers also learnt local languages, such as Malayalam, Tamil or Konkani, through their social interactions. In most cases, their children had Asian mothers and grew up as Indo-Portuguese in the context of a colonial society increasingly permeated with racial hierarchies, where native blood, together with the local climate and diet, was understood to exert a degenerative influence.[15] Whilst we can emphasise the imperialist aspects of the Portuguese, who conquered Goa and embarked upon an aggressive policy of conversions and even temple destructions, we also need to consider the traders operating in areas like Cochin (Kochi) or Cannanore (Kannur), who had to negotiate with the local rulers and independent trading communities of Malabar. In that context, a few Portuguese agents, renegades and other adventurers (including a number of Jews or New Christians) specialised as interpreters.

15 According to the witness of an upper-class Venetian traveller who visited Goa in 1673, Ambrogio Bembo, the Portuguese from Europe had a low opinion of those dark-skinned Indo-Portuguese with mixed ancestry, and the latter retaliated with innate antipathy towards those from Europe. Ambrogio Bembo, *Il viaggio in Asia (1671-1675) nei manoscritti de Minneapolis e di Bergamo*, ed. Antonio Invernizzi (Alessandria: Edizionidell'Orso, 2012), 235.

A remarkable example of a successful 'go-between' known for his knowledge of local languages was Duarte Barbosa, a Crown official employed as *escrivão* (scrivener) in the commercial factory of Cannanore, and author of one of the most influential and insightful descriptions of India from this period, completed c. 1517, within twenty years of Vasco da Gama's first landing in Calicut.[16] Barbosa was particularly knowledgeable about the Malabar Coast, and his account of the caste system in Kerala is one of the earliest and most perceptive contributions to the analysis of a Hindu social system in the early modern period. Interestingly, he does not present the caste system as something completely 'other'. Instead, by exporting the Portuguese word *casta*, Barbosa seems to suggest that it was understood as largely analogous to the Portuguese concern with purity of lineage (which is what *casta* originally meant in Spanish and Portuguese).[17] The Iberian concern with purity of blood had, in fact, two elements: one religious, focalised in the rejection of Jewish and Muslim ancestry, which was understood to have the potential to contaminate the Christian faith, and another that had to do with aristocratic pretensions. This secular aspect was a little more flexible because the European concept of nobility had a meritocratic component, and there were no absolute barriers to sexual unions across social classes. We could say that in this period, the European social system sought a fine balance between the religious equality proclaimed by Christianity in its universal pretensions and the hierarchical principles made manifest in aristocratic privilege (it is for the first, not the second, reason that caste in India was perceived by missionaries as an obstacle to conversion).[18] From this perspective, Barbosa could perceive that stricter principles of separation operated in the distinctions between the eighteen *leis de gentios* of Malabar (eighteen separate lineages with

16 The manuscript exists in various versions. For an edition noting these variants, see Duarte Barbosa, *O livro de Duarte Barbosa: edicao crítica e anotada*, ed. Maria Augusta de Veiga e Sousa, 2 vols. (Lisbon: Instituto de Investigacão Científica Tropical, 1996–2000).

17 Thus, manuscript variants of the same passage could use indifferently 'casta de nayre' (Nayar caste) and 'linhagem de naire' (Nayar lineage). See Barbosa, *Livro*, 2, 113. In his Spanish dictionary of 1611, Sebastián de Covarrubias defined *casta* as 'noble lineage'; where a lower status was implied, as in the case of Moors and Jews, the preferred word was 'race'. The two words belonged to the same semantic field of (pure/impure) biological ancestry in animals and people. See '*casta*' in Sebastián de Covarrubias, *Tesoro de la lengua castellana, o española* (Madrid: Luis Sánchez, 1611), ed. Ignacio Arellano and Rafael Zafra (Madrid: Vervuert, 2006), 473.

18 Some of the fiercest critics of caste as a religious category amongst missionaries were themselves aristocrats like Alessandro Valignano and Roberto Nobili. The latter argued that it was fine for Christian Brahmins to maintain traditional social rules provided those rules were not understood to distinguish degrees of religious purity, which would involve idolatry.

separate religious customs), and he observed that the prohibitions of physical contact and food sharing enforced by the social elites, the Nayars and Brahmins, were far more radical than those common in Europe.[19] In other words, by combining outsider assumptions with local forms of knowledge, the caste system could be interpreted as an extreme form of something recognisable in any aristocratic society: the desire to avoid mixing blood with social inferiors. Barbosa's views represent an example of the possibility of cultural interpretation through linguistic learning and empirical ethnography. As I have argued in the past, such descriptions relied on analogies rather than crude oppositions: the stronger the analogy, the finer the distinction.[20]

Throughout the 16th century, as Goa became a consolidated hybrid colony, Portuguese and Catholic but ethnically diverse (especially on the female side), the effort to learn local languages was often most apparent in the case of missionaries operating outside the city.[21] Most instances we have of detailed efforts to analyse Hinduism from its literature, for example, come from Malabar, Madurai or Vijayanagara. An approach to their work based on linguistic learning and limited cultural accommodation was very clearly central to the way Jesuit missionaries understood their task. It is, therefore, not surprising that many of the earlier writings on Hinduism were produced by them. The most extreme examples, however, met with internal opposition, notably the case of Roberto Nobili in Madurai. In his efforts to operate within caste society and attract Hindu Brahmins to Christianity in areas beyond the control of the Portuguese, he clearly pushed the boundaries — to the point that he was perceived as a missionary gone native. Whatever the people of Madurai might have thought of his efforts to dress and act like a sannyasi (a religious ascetic) and distance himself entirely from the Portuguese, he was criticised by fellow Jesuit Gonçalo Fernandes Trancoso for having betrayed his own people, in effect becoming an outsider to his community in order to become an insider in the community of Tamil Brahmins of Madurai.

It therefore seems clear that despite its imperial claims, the Portuguese colonial system in India — politically peripheral, largely commercial

19 Barbosa, *Livro*, II, 2: 108–230. Hence, each 'law' (*lei*) or caste was so separate from each other that the majority did not touch each other under pain of death ('*cada ũa destas é tão apartada em tanto estremo uns dos outros que os mais deles não se tocam uns com outros sob pena de morte*', 108).

20 For an extensive discussion, see Rubiés, *Travel and Ethnology*, chap. 6, 201–222.

21 On the side of laypersons, we could also consider all those renegade Portuguese soldiers who migrated to the court of Bijapur and converted to Islam, but unfortunately, we have little evidence of how they perceived their host societies and how happily they were integrated. The evidence is richer for Christians in the Ottoman Empire.

and usually bereft of manpower — did not generate a simple opposition between Europeans and Indians, but rather a large diversity of in-between positions. Let us illustrate this variety by quickly considering two very different settings: Catholic missionaries at the Mughal court, and those working in the native villages under Portuguese control.

As we have seen, the cosmopolitan Islamicate oeucumene generated a court culture that integrated foreign elements with local ones, a process of partial indigenisation of conquest elites that culminated at the Mughal court under Akbar and Jahangir. This court, where Persian became the dominant language, welcomed the 'Franks' as traders, ambassadors, mercenaries and even a few Christian missionaries, despite the resentment of some Muslim ulamas. Mughal court culture thus offered a specific setting for cosmopolitan encounters, distinct in many ways to those that took place in the city ports of Calicut or Surat, because the court fostered a wide range of cultural exchanges centred on curious learning that went beyond the practical arrangements that allowed traders of different religions and ethnic backgrounds to do business. Royal and noble patronage facilitated an honourable position for religious missionaries and philosophical travellers, and made possible direct and usually friendly dialogues such as those between Emperor Akbar and the Jesuits Rodolfo Aquaviva and Antoni Montserrat; Jahangir and the English ambassador Sir Thomas Roe; Abd al-Sattar bin Qasim Lahori and Jerome Xavier (Jerónimo Javier); and Daneshmend Khan and François Bernier.[22]

Such intellectual dialogues, often accompanied by ritualised exchanges of precious objects, had important limitations: the existence of polite hospitality and a degree of cultural learning (including many valuable literary efforts and ethnographic insights) do not imply that these foreigners stopped being regarded as outsiders. On the contrary, elite Europeans were often valued precisely because they were exotic. For Akbar, for example, having learned Jesuits like Aquaviva and Montserrat at court alongside Muslims, Hindu Brahmins, Parsis and Jains validated his own Sufi-inspired political claims. His syncretic religious movement or 'religion of God' (*din-i ilahi*), which offended many orthodox Muslims, was, however sincerely experienced,

---

22 'Abd al-Sattar bin Qasim Lahori assisted Jerome Xavier in translating Christian works into Persian, but he was also instructed to learn Latin and the history of 'the Franks' for his Mughal patrons. On the complex nature of this dual relationship, see Muzzafar Alam and Sanjay Subrahmanyam, 'Frank Disputations: Catholics and Muslims in the Court of Jahangir (1608-11),' *Indian Economic and Social History Review* 46(4) (2009): 457–511; Corinne Lefèvre, 'The *Majālis-I Jahāngīrī* (1608-1611): Dialogue and Asiatic Otherness at the Mughal Court,' *Journal of the Economic and Social History of the Orient*, 55 (2012): 255–286.

pragmatically focussed on loyalty to his own person, in a manner consonant with the personal loyalty he demanded from elite subjects of different religious persuasions. It may be best described as a culturally flexible ideology of sacred kingship that proclaimed the ideal of 'universal peace' (*sulh-i kull*) in an imperial context. Thus, contrary to the Jesuits' expectations, what was distinctive of Christianity played no significant role in Akbar's eclectic religion (Jesus was, after all, a respected Muslim prophet too). Jahangir, driven by a mixture of curiosity and material calculations, was even more distant, showing no lasting favouritism to the rival European powers that entered his court: while the Jesuit Jerome Xavier witnessed the collapse of his mission in 1613, successive English envoys, from William Hawkins to Thomas Roe, struggled to seize the opportunity and gain any lasting advantages for the East India Company, in spite of the emperor realising that their maritime power was superior to that of the Portuguese. Mughal book illustrations depicting Rodolfo Aquaviva or Sir Thomas Roe participating in courtly events have become iconic, but they perfectly represent this subordinate role. An artist might even copy or adapt a European technique for the portraits of these exotic male visitors, but the cultural logic of these images is always imbued with the political language and meaning — or, we could even say, the language-game — of Mughal court culture and, in particular, the representation of royalty that each artist sought to depict. For example, in a depiction of Akbar presiding over a religious dispute in the *ibadat-khana* of Fatehpur Sikri, the presence of the two Jesuits with their distinctive garb and sacred book (the Christian gospels) alongside Muslims, Hindus and representatives of other religions, all carrying their own sacred writings, testifies to the reality of the universal pretensions of the Mughal emperor as the supreme judge of any such disputes, according to the ideology developed by Abu'l Fazl in the *Akbar Nama* (Figure 1.1).[23] Europeans performed their roles as outsiders according to an insider logic that they struggled to comprehend fully, just as their capacity to exert pressure remained severely limited.

23 The two Jesuits depicted in this illustrated copy of Abu'l-Fazl's *Akbar Nama*, now in the Chester Beatty Library in Dublin (Ms 3, f.263), were probably Rodolfo Aquaviva and the Persian Muslim convert and interpreter Francisco Henriques, representing a debate that took place in 1580 in the *ibadat-khana*, as painted by the artist Narsingh c. 1603–1605. Abu'l Fazl described a challenge of an ordeal by fire issued by Aquaviva against Muslim ulamas who claimed that the gospel was a corrupt text (the parallel version by the Jesuit Montserrat varies in some significant details). For a discussion of the image, see Amina Okada, 'The Representation of Jesuit Missionaries in Mughal Painting,' in *Goa and the Great Mughal*, ed. Nuno Vassallo e Silva and Jorge Flores (London: Scala, 2004), 190–199.

Figure 1.1 ***A religious debate presided over by Akbar with the Jesuit padres in the* ibadat-khana *(detail).***

Source: *Akbar Nama*, inscribed by Narsingh, Agra, c. 1603–1605. © The Trustees of the Chester Beatty Library, Dublin. Ms 03.263.

In contrast to a setting dominated by local power dynamics, Christian missionaries who could count on a degree of implicit coercion from the Portuguese *Estado da Índia* practised a very different kind of accommodation, one calculated to facilitate conversions from a relatively dominant position. Here we find a process of cultural learning within a logic that sets foreign, rather than local, limits to the capacity of an outsider to become an insider. Let us consider the case of Thomas Stephens, a Jesuit in Salcete (Goa) who authored a 'Christian Purana' in Marathi — a poem describing the Incarnation of Jesus Christ — and some catechisms in Konkani.[24] He picked up precisely where Rodolfo Aquaviva, having returned from Akbar's court to die a martyr in the village of Cuncolim, had left off, trying to spread Christianity in the villages under Portuguese jurisdiction surrounding Goa but taking care to avoid provoking violent

24 Marathi was the poetic vernacular language, while Konkani remained the popular language, in the land of Salcete, south of Goa. The *Kristapurana* (completed between 1609 and 1614) was titled in Portuguese *Discurso sobre a vinda de Jesu Christo*, that is, Discourse on the coming of Jesus Christ.

religious confrontations with Hindus.[25] The logic of accommodation behind his missionary work — learning languages, adopting literary genres, collaborating with local Brahmin converts, all in order to make Christianity Indian — was, nonetheless, profoundly paternalistic: at the same time that it sought to break unnecessary barriers, it consolidated a hierarchical relationship between the European missionary, teacher of the religious truth, and the native converts. The locals may indeed have been able to teach him many useful things, such as local languages and poetry, but they remained under his authority — and under the shadow of the Portuguese in Goa. And yet, we cannot deny that this effort at selective accommodation to some extent was successful: Stephens's literary work in Marathi, conceived for oral recitation in an elite village context and imbued with many local references, became popular and was appropriated by the educated Christians of Brahmin origins as their own literature.[26] The Jesuit outsider eventually became, for this particular community of Indian Christians, an insider figure as part of a sociocultural evolution.

We can complicate the picture even further. As Ananya Chakravarti recently observed, Stephens, as a Catholic Englishman, was already an outsider to his European community, both in England, which he had to leave to keep his faith, and in Portugal, where he was a foreigner.[27] In fact, Stephens was one of those many Jesuits of non-Portuguese origin who struggled to be fully accepted by the Portuguese establishment. In this respect, although the Jesuits were a remarkably cosmopolitan order, nationality reasserted its claims even amongst them. The role of foreigners in the Portuguese *padroado* was particularly resented in the late 16th and early 17th centuries, partly in reaction to the domineering leadership exerted for over three decades by the Italian Alessandro Valignano, Visitor to the Jesuit missions in Asia (1574–1606). While a few non-Portuguese, like the Catalan Montserrat, had spent many years in Portugal and were effectively 'indigenised' by the time they reached India, others, such as Valignano; the Castilian (from Navarre) Jerome Xavier; and two other Italians, Roberto Nobili and Antonio Rubino,

25 The martyrdom of Aquaviva at Cuncolim in 1583, soon mythologised by the Jesuits, was the result of his failed attempt with a few companions and native converts to calm down the armed local Hindus, who had seen their temples destroyed by the Portuguese authorities and perceived the erection of churches as intolerable. Thomas Stephens recounted the events to his superiors without hiding the reasons for the anger of the villagers and was keen to find a less provocative approach.

26 For an analysis of this work as a work of accommodation targeting Brahmin converts and their literary and ideological expectations, see Ananya Chakravarti, *The Empire of Apostles: Religion, Accommodation and the Imagination of Empire in Early Modern Brazil and India* (Oxford: Oxford University Press, 2018), 200–227.

27 Chakravarti, *The Empire of Apostles,* 179.

were perceived as arrogant foreign intruders by the Indo-Portuguese. An Englishman like Stephens, so untypical in a context dominated by Iberians and Italians, was an outsider in every way. This may help explain why he committed himself so wholeheartedly to his Marathi literary work: it allowed him to pursue his universalistic mission in the local context of the villages of Salcete, and it was here, with the children of Brahmin converts in the college of Margão and later Rachol, where he found his true vocation.

The tension between foreign Jesuits practising accommodation like Stephens or Nobili and the Portuguese establishment was not merely an internal ecclesiastical affair, and had a corollary in the growth of a cultural distance between European observers and the population of Portuguese India. This population, as we have noted, was subject to an inner racial and cultural tension: it was European in religion (in its Catholic variety) and language (speaking a romance vernacular) but ethnically very mixed, with a predominance of women of native extraction. The hybridisation of genes and phenotypes and quite a few everyday customs created an Indo-Portuguese society that was no longer alien to India, but which nonetheless aspired to a European identity that other Europeans increasingly denied. European 'outsiders' who travelled to Goa for relatively long periods such as the Florentine merchant Francesco Carletti, the Roman aristocrat Pietro Della Valle, and the Dutch Jan Huygen van Linschotten, who had lived in the city many years (1583–1588) at the service of no less than the archbishop before turning back to Protestant and rebel Holland, all suggested in their independent descriptions of Goa for a European audience (in a series of works composed between the 1590s and the 1620s) that the Portuguese living in India were quite different from those in Europe, and could be perceived as almost as exotic as the Muslims and the Gentiles. In particular, these authors — for example, Linschoten in his extremely influential *Itinerario* (1596), whose message was reinforced by original engravings — emphasised the decline of the Portuguese military spirit, despite the widely shared aristocratic pretensions of *fidalgos* and *casados*, and their luxurious lifestyle, indolence and lasciviousness. This process of cultural degeneration was partly explained by the tropical climate, partly by racial mixing.[28] The

28 Jan Huygen van Linschoten, *The Voyage to the East Indies, from the Old English Translation of 1598*, ed. de Arthur Coke Burnell and Pieter Anton Tiele, 2 vols. (London: The Hakluyt Society, 1935), I, 175–222; especially 175–222. For an analysis, see Arie Pos, 'A Stranger's Testimony. Some of Jan Huygen van Linschoten's Views on and from Goa Compared with Portuguese Sources', in *Rivalry and Conflict. European Traders and Asia Trading Networks in the 16th and 17th centuries*, ed. Ernst Van Veen and Leonard Blussé (Leiden: CNWS, 2005), 89–107. Carletti, in turn, emphasised the beauty and sexual passions of the Indo-Portuguese *mestizo* women of Goa: see Carletti, *Ragionamenti del mio viaggio intorno al mondo*, ed. Gianfranco Silvestro (Milan: Enaudi, 1958), 220–229. Della Valle described a society with few real Portuguese and many wretched naked slaves, but permeated with ostentatious, xenophobic and prudish attitudes. He was upset in particular that he was forced to live separately from his adopted Georgian

category of 'European in India' is, therefore, not straightforward, as various layers of identity emerged within the structures of settler colonialism.

Philosophical Distance and Cosmopolitan Sympathy: François Bernier

Having considered the complex insider–outsider dichotomies generated in India by Muslim conquest imperialism and European settler colonialism, let us turn to a third type of traveller, the philosophical observer writing for a home audience. In the case of 17th-century travellers like Pietro della Valle and François Bernier, whose writings on India helped shape a distinctive early modern orientalist discourse in the European Republic of Letters, the very idea of travel to the East was built around the idea of exploring the opposition between 'us' and 'them' through curiosity, philosophical analysis and antiquarian research.

François Bernier, a medical doctor imbued with modern philosophical ideas of Epicurean inspiration, and thus largely materialist, developed by his teacher Pierre Gassendi, offers one of the most perfect examples of a narrative built around the idea of defining the cultural distance between Europe and India. His *Voyages* — in reality, a composite work — first appeared in 1670–1671, but was the result of observations collected during many years living at the Mughal court (1659–1666). There, whilst working as a salaried doctor for his patron Daneshmend Khan, master of the horse under Shah Jahan and governor of Delhi under Aurangzeb, Bernier introduced recent works of European philosophy to him and helped translate them into Persian. In his travel writings, however, Bernier addressed a European audience in a European language and used European genres — whether his philosophical letters or his dramatic history of a dynastic civil war.[29] In his letters to European scholars and royal officials, in particular, discussing the cities and climate of India,

daughter: Pietro della Valle, *Viaggi di Pietro della Valle il Pellegrino descritti da liu medesimo in lettere familiari all' erudito suo amico Mario Schipano. Parte terza, cioe l'India, co'l ritorno alla patria* (Rome: Biagio Deversin and Felice Cesaretti, 1663), 119.

29 For a modern critical edition, see François Bernier, *Un libertin dans l'Inde Moghole. Les Voyages de François Bernier (1565-1669)*, ed. Frédéric Tinguely (Paris: Chandeigne, 2008). Bernier's account of the civil war that brought Aurangzeb to power had, in reality, some equivalents in the Timurid-Mughal courtly tradition of historical writing. The Frenchman was very close to primary sources of information (mainly oral reports within the Mughal court), but he was also free from any of the ideological conventions that constrained the practice of history writing within Mughal court culture. His rhetorical models were classical (especially Tacitus) and European, and he followed them with remarkable originality to create a hybrid between tragedy and historical reportage. This allowed him to offer a personal interpretation of the nature of Mughal politics. For a discussion, see the introduction by Tinguely in Bernier, *Un libertin*, 23–28.

the political economy of the Mughal state, and the religion of the Hindu 'gentiles', he set up some fundamental dichotomies between Europe and India. For example (as I have shown elsewhere), he is one of the authors responsible for the way the image of oriental despotism played out in the European Enlightenment.[30] His account of the civil war and 'revolution' that brought Aurangzeb to power was also meant to reveal cultural diversity: as he wrote in his preface to the *Histoire de la dernière révolution des États du Grand Mogol*, he aimed to depict the manners, customs and particular genius of Mughals and Indians through actions and events.[31] We could say that Bernier, whilst engaging in a sophisticated dialogue with a Mughal elite that required learning the Persian language and several courtly language-games, also kept his distance and analysed what he saw and learnt through the sceptical eyes of modern European philosophy. He became, in part, an insider in order to ultimately become the supreme outsider, the informed observer capable of creating a new narrative about the religion, politics and architecture of Mughal India.[32]

This subtle interplay between languages, cultures and identities, on the other hand, did not rely on a simple opposition between Europe and India. On the contrary, it exploited crucial fissures within both European culture and Mughal culture with clinical precision. In his European context, Bernier sided decisively with modern sceptical, empirical and materialist philosophy against Neoplatonic idealism and traditional popular superstition. In India, on the other hand, he sided with his 'enlightened' Muslim Mughal patron, a man known for his learning, against popular superstition and the philosophical fantasies of Brahmins and Sufis. In effect, Bernier and his patron Daneshmend Khan built a bridge between modern European philosophy and the Mughal rejection of particular aspects of Hindu and (to a lesser extent) Muslim religious culture, a tentative bridge defined by elite rationalist opposition to what could be perceived as a shared target of irrational beliefs — for example, that ridiculous fear of solar eclipses common to peasants in Europe and

30 Joan-Pau Rubiés, 'Oriental Despotism and European Orientalism: Botero to Montesquieu', *Journal of Early Modern History: Contacts, Comparisons, Contrasts* 9(1–2) (2005): 109–180. See also Sylvia Murr, 'Le "politique au Mogol" selon Bernier: appareil conceptuel, rhétorique strategique, philosophie morale', *De la Royauté à l'État dans le monde indien*, 'Purusārtha' 13 (Paris: Éditions de l'EHESS, 1991), 239–311.

31 Bernier, *Un libertin*, 40

32 Peter Burke, 'The Philosopher as Traveller: Bernier's Orient', in *Voyages and Visions: Towards a Cultural History of Travel*, ed. J. Elsner and J.P. Rubiés (London: Reaktion Books, 1999), 124–137; Nicholas Dew, *Orientalism in Louis XIV's France* (Oxford: Oxford University Press, 2009), 131–167; Joan-Pau Rubiés, 'Race, Çlimate and Civilization in the Works of François Bernier', *L'inde des Lumières. Discours, histoire, savoirs (XVIIe-XIXe siècle)*, 'Purushartha' 31 (Paris: Éditions de l'EHESSS, 2013): 53–78.

India.[33] When purportedly demolishing the monist philosophical ideas of the most famous Hindu pandits of Benares in his *Lettre à Monsieur Chapelain*, in effect, Bernier targeted a Neoplatonic philosophical system — the idea of a great world soul — with analogous manifestations in Christian, Muslim and Hindu cultures, a parallel that allowed Bernier to conclude that the human capacity for error and irrationality was universal. This critique was one of the key themes of the libertine (free-thinking) intellectual culture in 17th-century France; clearly, Bernier's most important target was very far from the river Ganges.

That a Christian rationalist who espoused the new atomist physics and empiricist astronomy, and a Muslim rationalist who was interested in science, could find common ground against the mysteries and mystifications of a deluded, and deluding, priestly caste did not require an open rejection of all religious belief, whether Muslim or Christian. Whilst Bernier objected to Muslim Sufism no less than to Christian Neoplatonist mysticism, he could agree with a Muslim monotheist that belief in a revealed divine providence should be separated from irrational fables and popular superstitions. In this, he was following the path of his teacher Pierre Gassendi, a Catholic priest who had reinterpreted the philosophical system of Epicurus as compatible with the Christian faith. The distinction between reasonable and irrational religious beliefs was especially useful if the latter led to objectionable social practices such as sati, and Bernier's attitude is symptomatic of this elite transcultural complicity.

In this respect, it is important to emphasise that reactions to the ritual of widow sacrifice illustrate how a recurrent topic of observation that often defined the cultural distance between outsiders and insiders to Hindu culture, one found in many authors in different periods, could, in fact, express a wide range of attitudes.[34] After witnessing the death of three satis in Amjhera (near Gwalior), Ibn Battuta nearly fell off his horse, in an almost physical rejection of a ritual simply perceived as hellish, in this graphic manner keeping a maximum distance.[35] Pietro della Valle, in a remarkably sympathetic portrayal, sought to humanise the figure of the sati he met in Ikkeri in 1623 by talking to her at length,

33 Thus Bernier began his letter to Jean Chapelain on Hindu superstition, comparing reactions to an eclipse he saw in France in 1654 with another he claims to have witnessed in Delhi in 1666. See Bernier, *Un libertin*, 301.

34 For a very recent discussion, see Rita Banerjee, *India in Early Modern Travel Writing. Protestantism, Enlightenment and Toleration* (Leiden: Brill, 2021), 173–198.

35 Battuta, *Travels*, 3: 614–616, 'Account of the Indians who Burn Themselves to Death'. Ibn Battuta's account is permeated by the association of the fire and the darkness of the pavilions where the sacrifices took place with a scene from hell. He has a sati speak in Persian, saying that she does not fear the fire — an unlikely use of the court language that suggests the existence of an intermediary.

recording her name and her words and praising her female virtue, however misguided (he thought) the belief system that sustained it.[36] Decades later, Bernier, in true rationalist fashion, tried to intervene from a position of absolute intellectual superiority. His description offers a clear case of cultural 'othering':

> At Lahore I saw a very pretty woman burn, who was extremely young — I think she could not have been more than twelve years of age. The poor little creature appeared more dead than alive when she approached the pit; she trembled and wept with huge tears; but three or four of these tormentors [the brahmins], assisted by an old woman who held her under the armpits, seated her on the wood, tied her hands and feet lest she should run away, stoked the fire and burned her alive. I found it difficult to control my anger, but I had to limit myself to dislike this horrible religion.[37]

In this instance, Bernier had little time for exploring an insider perspective. His human sympathy for the young widow was based on an external act of witnessing, in contrast with, for example, Pietro della Valle, who was particularly keen to clarify the freedom of the satis in the face of social pressures and gave them an individual voice. Both Europeans rejected the ritual and sought to explain it by means of the weight of custom and powerful social pressures, but only Della Valle placed the woman's perspective at the centre of his narrative. He attempted to persuade her to avoid the sacrifice, to no avail, but her honour and virtue were, for him, a transcultural reality.[38] On the other hand, Bernier, no less eager to intervene, believed that those who needed persuasion were Mughal officials, because the young widows were victims of years of psychological manipulation — an infatuation and self-deceit inscribed in their minds from a very young age to subject them to the needs of their husbands.[39] As we have seen, his views on sati and other 'irrational' aspects of Hinduism were largely in agreement with those of some Mughal officials under whose patronage he lived at the court of Aurangzeb. He thus appealed to their authority to stop some of these sacrifices. One of these attempts was even successful: Bernier was able to persuade the young wife of the chief clerk employed by Daneshmend

36 Della Valle, *Viaggi*, 201–203.

37 Bernier, *Un libertin*, 314–315.

38 Far from a simple dialogue across cultures and genders, in Della Valle's homage to the sati Giaccamà there was a degree of projection of Christian Stoic ideas about female virtue then current in Catholic aristocratic culture. For an analysis, see Rubiés, *Travel and Ethnology*, 366–368.

39 Bernier, *Un libertin*, 311.

Khan not to burn herself. To do so, however, he had to threaten her with leaving her children without a pension. Crucially, he also had the support of her parents, because the children were very young. Although, for political reasons, the Mughals tolerated a religious practice they considered cruel and superstitious, they also sought to discourage it, and on this particular occasion, Bernier's *agha* was able to exert additional pressure in his capacity as the husband's employer.[40] Whilst very distant from Hindu beliefs, which he judged a product of the human capacity for false opinion, Bernier was, therefore, to some extent, an insider if we adopt the perspective of Mughal officials like Daneshmend Khan, who also felt culturally distant from their Hindu subjects. Perhaps here we can talk about a triangle involving multiple Indian perspectives within a heterogeneous cultural system, rather than a dual opposition between Europe and India. In this triangle, not all sides were equal: the possibility of a transcultural form of cosmopolitanism was built upon a rejection of full-scale multiculturalism, as the constructed claims of rational humanity emerged as non-negotiable.

Conclusion: Exoticism, Cultural Learning and Cultural Distance

The main danger of analysing travel writing through an insider–outsider dichotomy is that it tends to reinforce an image of cultural homogeneity that is often misleading. In all the cases I have considered here, there cannot be a coherent analysis that simply pits a foreign observer against the single cultural reality of India. Whether we take as our main evidence the writings of a North African Muslim who felt largely (but not fully) at home at the court of the sultan of Delhi; the ethnographic work produced by Portuguese crown officials in the port cities of Malabar, in an early example of European settler colonialism that increasingly became culturally hybrid; the literary creations of Jesuit missionaries devoted to selective cultural accommodation targeting Brahmin converts; or the letters written by a philosophical traveller who rejected traditional religious culture as superstitious in France no less than in India; what we find is that neither the foreigner nor the local were culturally homogeneous. Observers from Europe, for example, could belong to different nations and social backgrounds, could be Catholic or Protestant, and could target with their observations about India particular audiences in Europe. In this respect, encounters with culturally distant peoples often proved valuable for rethinking religion,

40 Bernier, *Un libertin*, 306–309.

politics, lineage and race, or gender back at home. On the other hand, the plurality within India offers an equivalent challenge, not only because of its longstanding internal linguistic and religious diversity but also on account of successive imperial and colonial realities created by military conquest elites and trading nations, often militant in their Muslim or Christian identities. The category of 'Indian' is thus made highly complex: an insider in Goa could be an outsider at the Mughal court, and both the Portuguese from Goa and the Deccani of Iranian extraction would be outsiders in the imperial city of Vijayanagara. Even so, the category of outsider, ultimately, remains relevant, especially in relation to the more locally rooted traditions. If there is a common thread that connects Ibn Battuta, Duarte Barbosa, Thomas Stephens and François Bernier, it is the distance they all kept from Hindu religion and castes. They did so, however, with varying degrees of knowledge and proximity.

No less important than acknowledging the lack of homogeneous cultural systems is understanding the dynamic aspects involved in the processes of exoticisation and cultural learning. The rhetoric of travel writing was often geared towards identifying and emphasising cultural differences according to a simple us-them axis, but travel writers, like many other external agents operating in commercial, imperial and colonial contexts, were often participants in a learning process that could involve various forms of cultural hybridisation. In early modern India, those who found themselves 'in between' were numerous: the cultures of long-distance trade, diplomacy, courtly politics and religious proselytism fostered various experiences of personal movement, ethnic mixture and artistic and intellectual exchange. At this point, the concept that becomes central to a more nuanced analysis is that of the cultural distance separating particular historical agents: that distance which allows us to identify fundamentally different cultural assumptions, but also to measure the ability of individuals to find analogies between different cultural systems, learn languages and cultural codes easily or with difficulty, create a common language for trade and politics in a multicultural setting, maintain religious conversations that are less exclusive or confrontational, or engage in reasonably satisfactory intellectual and artistic exchanges. Whilst the key ingredient for interpreting all these processes of transcultural interaction and negotiation is the calculation of mutual interests, measuring the relative cultural distances between historical agents and understanding the possible mechanisms that they had at their disposal to reduce them are no less important.

All this does not nullify the importance of the concepts of outsider and insider but leads us to emphasise their relative value for each individual or community in each context. As we acknowledge that cultural distances are relative rather than absolute, we are able to capture the fluidity of the process by which the outsider may, or may not, become an insider. As seen in the very different cases of Ibn Battuta and François Bernier, we can also identify at which point the traveller's construction of a cosmopolitan identity diverges, rightly or wrongly, from the practice of multiculturalism. That no cultural interaction can be reduced to a simple us–them dynamic reflects the complex and hybrid nature of all cultural systems. It also encourages us to keep at bay two possible uses of representations of cultural otherness that characterise human history at its worst: to foster hostility towards outsiders, or to legitimise intolerance and repression towards internal diversity.

References

Alam, Muzzafar, and S. Subrahmanyam. 2009. 'Frank Disputations: Catholics and Muslims in the Court of Jahangir (1608–11)'. *Indian Economic and Social History Review* 46(4): 457–511.

Banerjee, Rita. 2021. *India in Early Modern Travel Writing. Protestantism, Enlightenment and Toleration*. Leiden: Brill.

Barbosa, Duarte. 1996–2000. *O livro de Duarte Barbosa: edicao crítica e anotada*, edited by Maria Augusta de Veiga e Sousa. 2 vols. Lisbon: Instituto de Investigacão Científica Tropical.

Bembo, Ambrogio. 2012. *Il viaggio in Asia (1671–1675) nei manoscritti de Minneapolis e di Bergamo*, edited by Antonio Invernizzi. Alessandria: Edizioni dell'Orso.

Bernier, François. 2008. *Un libertin dans l'Inde Moghole. Les Voyages de François Bernier (1565–1669)*, edited by Frédéric Tinguely. Paris: Chandeigne.

Burke, Peter. 1999. 'The Philosopher as Traveller: Bernier's Orient'. In *Voyages and Visions: Towards a Cultural History of Travel*, edited by J. Elsner and J.P. Rubiés, 124–137. London: Reaktion Books.

Carletti, Francesco. 1958. *Ragionamenti del mioviaggiointorno al mondo*, edited by Gianfranco Silvestro. Milan: Enaudi.

Chakravarti, Ananya. 2018. *The Empire of Apostles: Religion, Accommodation and the Imagination of Empire in Early Modern Brazil and India*. Oxford: Oxford University Press.

Covarrubias, Sebastián de. 2006. *Tesoro de la lengua castellana, o española* (Madrid: Luis Sánchez, 1611), edited by Ignacio Arellanoa and Rafael Zafra. Madrid: Vervuert.

Della Valle, Pietro. 1663. *Viaggi di Pietro della Valle il pellegrino descritti da liume desimo in lettere familiari all' erudito suo amico Mario Schipano. Parte terza, cioè l'India, co'l ritorno alla patria*. Rome: Biagio Deversinand Felice Cesaretti.

Dew, Nicholas. 2009. *Orientalism in Louis XIV's France*. Oxford: Oxford University Press.

Hosten, Henry S.J. 1914. '*Mongolicae Legationis Commentarius*, or first Jesuit Mission to Akbar, by father Antonio Monserrate S.J.'. *Memoirs of the Asiatic Society of Bengal* 3(9): 513–704.

Ibn Battuta. 1958–1994. *The Travels of Ibn Battuta, AD 1325–1254*, edited, translated and annotated by H.A.R. Gibb and C.F. Beckingham. 4 vols. London: The Hakluyt Society.

Lefèvre, Corinne. 2012. 'The *Majālis-i Jahāngīrī* (1608–1611): Dialogue and Asiatic Otherness at the Mughal Court'. *Journal of the Economic and Social History of the Orient* 55(2–3): 255–286.

Linschoten, Jan Huygen van. 1935. *The Voyage to the East Indies, from the Old English Translation of 1598*, edited by Arthur Coke Burnell and Pieter Anton Tiele. 2 vols. London: The Hakluyt Society.

Monserrate, Antonio. 1992. *The Commentary of Father Monserrate S.J. on his Journey to the Court of Akbar*, translated from the original Latin by John S. Hoyland, annotated by S.N. Banerjee. Oxford: Oxford University Press.

Murr, Sylvia. 1991. 'Le "politique au Mogol" selon Bernier: appareil conceptuel, rhétorique strategique, philosophie morale'. In *De la Royauté à l'État dans le Monde Indien*, 'Purusārtha' 13, 239–311. Paris, Éditions de l'EHESS.

Okada, Amina. 2004. 'The Representation of Jesuit Missionaries in Mughal Painting'. In *Goa and the Great Mughal*, edited by Nuno Vassallo e Silva and Jorge Flores, 190–199. London: Scala.

Pos, Arie. 2005. 'A Stranger's Testimony. Some of Jan Huygen van Linschoten's Views on and from Goa Compared with Portuguese Sources'. In *Rivalry and Conflict. European Traders and Asia Trading Networks in the 16th and 17th Centuries*, edited by Ernst Van Veen and Leonard Blussé, 89–107. Leiden: CNWS.

Rubiés, Joan-Pau. 2000. *Travel and Ethnology in the Renaissance: South India through European Eyes (1250–1625)*. Cambridge: Cambridge University Press.

______. 2005. 'Oriental Despotism and European Orientalism: Botero to Montesquieu'. *Journal of Early Modern History: Contacts, Comparisons, Contrasts* 9(1–2): 109–180.

______. 2013. 'Race, Climate and Civilization in the Works of François Bernier'. In *L'inde des Lumières. Discours, histoire, savoirs (XVIIe-XIXe siècle)*, 'Purushārtha' 31, 55–78. Paris: Éditions de l'EHESSS.

2

Durbar Personas: *Thomas Roe and Thomas Coryate at the Mughal Court*

Christoph Heyl and Christian Feser*

Introduction

When Sir Thomas Roe (1581–1644) first arrived in Ajmer on 22 December 1615, his entrance as the representative of King James I to the Grand Mughal Jahangir was not as awe-inspiring as he had probably intended. Indeed, the first royally appointed English ambassador to the Mughal court was severely ill at the time and had been 'past sence and given over for dead' just weeks before (Roe 1899, 1:100). Still unable to stand or even sit upright without assistance, he had to be carried in a palanquin. Exhausted and certainly frustrated by his inability to project any degree of poise and dignity, one can only imagine Roe's reaction when, in an encampment several miles outside the imperial city, he was welcomed by a group of Englishmen that included one cheerful and familiar face: Thomas Coryate (1577?–1617), the 'Odcombian leggestretcher' (Coryate 1616, 42). Coryate left England in October 1612 and arrived in Ajmer in July 1615. Even with Roe's state as poorly as it was, Coryate did not waste the opportunity to treat the ambassador to 'a long, eloquent oration' (Peyton 1615–1617, 27). There is no record of Roe's response. The fortunate convergence of their paths at Jahangir's court allows us to analyse the strategies of self-fashioning of two individuals with a shared cultural background but vastly different motives for gaining favour with the Mughal emperor. While Coryate came to India as a traveller for travel's sake and to satiate his own (and his readers') curiosity, Roe arrived as the envoy of a country that, as Mika Natif

* Christian Feser is the author of the section entitled 'Swords, Paintings and an English Fakir: Curiosities at Court', and Christoph Heyl is the author of the section 'From the Margins to Centre Stage: Englishmen in Durbar Paintings'.

points out, was politically irrelevant to Jahangir but of great interest to him as a source for works of art (2018, 109). This chapter offers a discussion of how Coryate and Roe were largely reliant on self-fashioning *by means of* and *as* curiosities and were themselves regarded as such at the durbar, the audience held by the Mughal emperor at court. It will also address both Roe's afterlife in the British historical imagination and the depiction and perception of Europeans in the context of durbar scenes in the visual arts.

Swords, Paintings and an English Fakir: Curiosities at Court

Thomas Coryate, whom Roe dubbed 'the unwearied walker', had travelled overland from Constantinople (Istanbul) to Ajmer, a feat that took almost three years (Roe 1899, 1:103). Endlessly curious and eager to record as much of the journey as possible, Coryate remained suspiciously reticent about any of the hardships he must have faced. On the contrary, in his letters home to England, he emphasised his perennially stellar constitution in exuberant terms: 'I do enjoy at this time as pancraticall and athleticall a health as euer I did in my life: & so haue done euer since I came out of England, sauing for three days in *Constantinople*' (Coryate 1616, 26). Indeed, when Coryate wrote his first batch of letters in Ajmer between September and November 1615 (published in 1616 by his friends in London in the shape of a pamphlet entitled *Thomas Coriate Traueller for the English VVits*), he planned to extend his sojourn abroad for another seven years (to draw level with Odysseus) and then to either continue eastward to China or search for the legendary Prester John in Ethiopia.[1] Coryate had already fulfilled his wish to ride an elephant in Ajmer — which he had done, he writes in a metatextual comment, so that he could have an image of himself on an elephant in a future publication (Coryate 1616). His London friends were more than happy to oblige. They had a woodcut made that shows Coryate atop the animal, holding a notebook (his travel notes?) in his right hand and clad in the dapper (and completely inappropriate) outfit of a London gentleman.[2] The woodcut appears not only as the frontispiece but also twice more in *Thomas Coriate Traueller for the English VVits*. Coryate's

1 If Coryate admits any signs of desperation and discomfort in his own writing, these are only found in his final letter, penned in Agra in October 1616 and addressed to his mother, Gertrude. He desires to return to England directly, and he asks to be remembered by friends and family (not by stationers, as in his previous letters). He also discourages any expectation of further correspondence. After Coryate had died of dysentery near Surat in 1617, Thomas Roe remarked that he had 'left enough written to fill the world with new relations, and to have made any printer an alderman' (Sainsbury 1870, 234). Unfortunately, the manuscripts mentioned by Roe have been lost.

2 For a discussion of this woodcut, see Aune (2005).

next ambition was to talk to Jahangir. Since he had already gained sufficient knowledge of Turkish, Arabic, Persian and Hindustani during his travels, this seemed entirely feasible.

Thomas Roe, whom Coryate knew through their mutual friends John Donne and Ben Jonson, also kept a journal of his travels, which survives in several editions. He also sent letters to his noble patrons and England's political elite. In so far as Roe's roles at the Mughal court were both royal ambassador *and* employee of the East India Company, we have to acknowledge that he addressed a variety of audiences with his letters and his journal (which he knew was eventually going to pass into the East India Company's possession). As Rita Banerjee has remarked,

> These letters and entries show a degree of candour and pragmatism, which seems to be missing in the narrative he writes for his elite, aristocratic audience. For instance, while he frankly acknowledges the poor quality as well as the paucity of the presents sent to the Mughal court in his correspondence with the Company, he shifts his stance in his letters to noble patrons and critiques the insatiable desire for novelty and possession that urges Jahangir to demand more and more gifts from … foreign diplomats. (Banerjee 2017, 148)

After a largely uneventful sea voyage, Roe's tribulations started immediately after his fleet's landfall near Surat in September 1615. There, he gained some first-hand experience of the anti-English attitude of Prince Khurram (later known as Shah Jahan), who was Jahangir's favourite son and direct superior to the governor of Surat. Roe and his party were searched, and some of their luggage and merchandise was seized. Roe was highly indignant at being treated like any other visitor to the empire. He was also resolute in his desire to start out for Ajmer, the imperial residence since 1613. Progress, however, was slow: a firman (or edict) issued by Jahangir allowing Roe and his suite free passage only arrived weeks later.

On arrival at the Mughal court, Coryate and Roe started to pursue their respective aspirations: Coryate sought spectacular experiences with a view to future textualisation, while Roe needed to gather knowledge about India for his employer(s) and, more directly, a firman granting exclusive trading rights to supersede Portuguese and Dutch commercial predominance over England on the subcontinent. The pivotal element to all of these endeavours was, of course, the person of Jahangir, and it was crucial to gain access to him. Thus, descriptions of Jahangir and courtly rituals feature significantly in both Roe's and Coryate's texts.

Every morning, according to Balkrishan Shivram, Jahangir appeared at the *jharoka*, a small balcony, from whence he was visible to the general public, a custom called *jharoka-i-darshan* — darshan literally meaning 'seeing' (2007, 337). 'From the *jharoka* Mughal emperor [sic] usually went to the *diwan-i-am* (hall of public audience) or durbar where they conducted the main business of their offices, giving justice, in civil and criminal matters, including official misconduct' (337). Roe informs us that there are several other occasions at which Jahangir would show himself in front of the nobility:

> At noone hee returns thither [the jharoka] and sits some howers to see the fight of Eliphants and willd beasts; vnder him within a rayle attend the men of rancke.... At afternoon he returnes to the *Durbar* before mentioned. At 8 after supper he Comes downe to the *Gazelcan*. (Roe 1899, 1:106)

The *ghuslkhana*, literally 'bath house', was Jahangir's private audience quarters, to which only close confidants and highest-ranking members of the royal household had access. It was a space for private discussions, with the emperor seated on a throne closely surrounded by attendants (Roe 1899, 1:106–107). Courtly rituals such as these were based on the diurnal visibility of the emperor's person. Roe is clearly intrigued by the fact that even the highest authority of the state was obliged to adhere to these rituals and infers that 'for all his Subjects are slaues, so is he in a kynd of *reciprocall bondage*, for he is tyed to obserue these howres and Customes' (1:107–108; emphasis added).

As Richmond Barbour has remarked, 'to establish credibility — his own and the nation's — was the initial charge of [Roe's] embassy', and it was a charge with which he struggled greatly (2003, 147). Roe might have been the first royally appointed ambassador, but he was by no means the first Englishman to claim this title at the Mughal court. Before him, William Hawkins, Paul Canning, Thomas Kerridge and William Edwards had all attempted to obtain trading rights for the East India Company, claiming to be ambassadors, and had failed in a more or less spectacular fashion. It was thus vital to Roe to project gravitas and authenticity, and Coryate was a potential threat to this mission: 'A welcome companion at table, Coryate could be an embarrassment at court' (Barbour 2003, 115). The following quote from Roe's journal describes his first time attending the durbar and seeing Jahangir in mid-January 1616:

> The Place is a great Court, whither resort all sorts of People. The king sitts in a little *Gallery* ouer head; Ambassidors, the great men and strangers of qualety within the inmost rayle vnder him, raysed from the ground.... This sitting out hath *soe much affinitye with a Theatre* —

> the manner of the king in his gallery; The great men lifted *on a stage as actors; the vulgar below gazing on*. (Roe 1899, 1:108; emphasis added)

Roe uses the stage metaphor to describe his first impressions of the durbar, a theme pervading most of his descriptions of Mughal governance as dissimulation and hollow spectacle.[3] This idea also ties in with his previous characterisation of the relationship between the emperor and his subjects as a sort of reciprocal serfdom. Later, in 1616, Roe offers a caustic assessment of the visit of a Persian ambassador, who 'appeared rather a Iester or Iugler then a Person of any grauety, running vp and downe, and acting all his woords like a mimick Player' (1899, 2:300). Here, too, Roe contrasts his gravitas with the show performed by the Persian. However, his acrimonious words reveal the frustration he must have felt with his lack of diplomatic results. His practice of physically approaching Jahangir as closely as possible during audiences frequently irritated court officials. Ill-considered gaffes such as these did not serve to endear Roe to the nobility or to ease tensions with European rivals at court. It did not help that Roe refused to conform to the standard rituals of reverence towards Jahangir (such as prostrating himself on the ground) and did not learn any of the languages spoken at court. This attitude made his mission vulnerable to sabotage: several times, Asaf Khan refused Roe's translator access to Jahangir, forcing Roe to rely on a translator hired by the Portuguese (see, for instance, Roe 1899, 1:144–148, 2:376–377). Two circumstances are striking about these passages: on the one hand, Roe's insistence, against all practical reasons and even Jahangir's insinuations, on not learning the court language and, on the other hand, not making more use of Coryate, his house guest, on such occasions. Coryate would have had a more than sufficient grasp of Turkish, Persian, Arabic and Hindustani to support the ambassador. More than anything, this affirms the assumption that Roe held Coryate to be little more than a learned buffoon who might make a spectacle of himself in front of Jahangir (as the Persian ambassador had done in his eyes) and damage England's already doubtful reputation.

In contrast to Roe, Coryate, being a traveller, happily did whatever he could to expand his range of experiences. Planning months ahead, he used the time he spent waiting for caravans in cities such as Constantinople, Aleppo and Isfahan to grow fluent in several languages and get accustomed to local habits. Thus, in Ajmer, he was able to converse with locals and — due to his shortage of money and his simple garments — could easily fashion himself as an 'English fakir'.

3 Rita Banerjee discusses the intriguing idea that, on the contrary, Roe holds a mirror up to 'the stage mockery' of King James (2017, 163).

Although the most stable facet of Coryate's persona was arguably his staunch Protestantism, he seems extremely impressed by Jahangir and his father, Akbar. Coryate is not only unfazed by the Mughal principle of religious tolerance but also, as Paul Stevens and Rahul Sapra have pointed out, 'effectively valorizes this principle … in a way that undermines the exclusivity of his own religious conviction' (2007, 409). Jahangir is no despotic oriental Other, either. On the contrary, he is 'a verie worthy person' (Coryate 1616, 20) and 'of a seemelie composition of bodie, of a stature little unequall (as I guesse not without grounds of probabilitie) to mine, but much more corpulent then my selfe' (21).

Apart from the wealth and splendour of Jahangir's court, Coryate repeatedly highlights Jahangir's charity. Since Jahangir, although a Muslim, practised various rituals borrowed from Hinduism and Christianity, Coryate considered him as 'beeing of none [religion] but of his owne making' (1625, 601). According to Coryate, Jahangir's acts of benevolence surpass the charity of many Christians, which begs the question as to who is more pious. 'Cracke mee this Nut, all the Papal Charitie vaunters,' Coryate asks — and insinuates that Jahangir is a better Christian than Catholics are (601). More importantly, the emperor is even depicted as an almost Christ-like figure: in a 'memorable pietie', the emperor cooks for the public on certain holidays, 'kindling a fire with his owne hands … and [making] Kitcherie for fiue thousand poore' (601). Here, Coryate certainly evokes the New Testament feeding of the five thousand, an astonishing appraisal of a Muslim ruler (Stevens and Sapra 2007, 409).

In his final letter, Coryate proudly reproduces the Farsi speech he recited in front of Jahangir. In accordance with his self-fashioning as a poor pilgrim, Coryate addresses the Grand Mughal in his ragged clothes at the *jharoka-i-darshan*. Interestingly, in the textual material, we find a transliteration of the speech first and its English translation afterwards. Here, Coryate not only delivers proof of his mastery of Farsi but invites his readership to try pronouncing the unfamiliar tongue. Thus, he creates a verbal curiosity for his readers to experience first-hand, despite being far removed from the time and place of the action, a taste of what to expect from him once he returns to England. In his speech, Coryate introduces himself as a '*fooker daruces*' (Coryate 1618, sig. B2^{v}), as a fakir and dervish, later translated as 'poore Traveller' (sig. B3^{v}), which shows that his self-fashioning works on several levels. He knows what fakirs and dervishes are (he has encountered them on his travels), and he has lived like one for the last couple of years. Therefore, he reasons that he, in his clothing and demeanour, should also approximate a fakir during his performance at the durbar. It seems that Coryate captivated Jahangir's attention for a little while. In his speech, he elaborates on the motives for his travels (namely, to see Jahangir) and his further plans. Eventually, Jahangir wraps up a hundred rupees in a sheet and drops it from the balcony (sig. B4^{r}–B4^{v}).

If Coryate had expected a longer conversation or a higher reward for his long journey, he hides his disappointment well. That Jahangir was not more generous just proves how convincing Coryate's appearance as a fakir/dervish must have been. The emperor apparently considered Coryate to be a genuine fakir — and fakirs, by definition, neither need nor expect much money. Coryate planned this appearance, as he confesses, in secrecy, 'for I well knew that our Ambassador would haue stopped and Barracadoed all my proceeding' (Coryate 1618, sig. B4^{v}). Ever the self-respecting Englishman, Roe would not have suffered Coryate to enter Jahangir's presence begging for alms. However, 'he was contented to cease nibling at me, neuer had I more need of mony in all my life then at that time' (sig. B4^{v}). It seems that Roe's anger diminished when he learned that Coryate was quite desperate for funds to continue his journey. Indeed, not long after, Roe consented to provide Coryate with a letter of recommendation to the English ambassador in Aleppo. After Coryate's health started to fail more rapidly, Roe offered him a passage back to London on an East India Company ship (Terry 1655, 73–74).

Roe and Coryate both needed to gain Jahangir's attention amidst the pomp and grandeur of court ceremony. Here, Roe had a material advantage: as an official ambassador, he came bearing gifts. Jahangir's curiosity and desire for English (or rather European or *Farangi*) art is clearly palpable in his journal.[4] The ambassador often reacted aptly, displaying unexpected acts of what Stephen Greenblatt terms 'improvisational power' (1980).[5] While Roe never formally acknowledged the failure of his gift-giving strategy, we can trace his frustrations about unsuccessful presents in his writings. Even before he had met Jahangir, on the way to Ajmer, he had

4 According to Mika Natif, in Mughal India, the 'principle of *sulh-i kull* (often rendered as 'absolute peace' or 'Universal Conciliation') enabled an atmosphere of openness and curiosity about other cultures that played an important role in the creation of a pluralistic artistic language' (2018, 22). While this principle, introduced by Emperor Akbar, was certainly influential, one should not confuse it with modern notions of religious and cultural tolerance. The same Akbar also 'challenged the Jesuits [he had invited to court] to prove the veracity of their faith by entering a fire and coming out unscathed' (Truschke 2016, 79).

5 Greenblatt defines it as

> the ability both to capitalize on the unforeseen and to transform given materials into one's own scenario. The spur-of-the-moment quality of improvisation is not as critical here as the opportunistic grasp of that which seems fixed and established.... What is essential is the Europeans' ability again and again to insinuate themselves into the preexisting political, religious, even psychic structures of the natives and to turn those structures to their advantage. (1980, 227)

sent back word to the East India Company that the embassy's gifts were 'extreamly despised by those who have seene them; the lyning of the Coach and Cover of the Virginalls scorned, beeing velvett of these parts and faded to a base Tawny' (Roe 1899, 1:97). Not even the customs employees and the governor in Surat were impressed by the coach and the musical instrument intended for Jahangir, which did not augur well. Even worse, Roe writes, Jahangir had expected Italian paintings, not at all the knives and other trifles the English had brought. The ambassador rightly feared becoming a laughing stock at court. As expected, the coach and the virginals (as well as the coachman and musician) were courteously received but quickly sent away (1:118–119). Instead, to Roe's own surprise, the most successful gift of the day was his own sword:

> He [Jahangir] sent to me, though 10 a clock at night, for a seruant to tye on his scarfe and swoorde the english fashion, in which he tooke so great pryde that he marched vp and downe, draweing yt and flourishing, and since hath never beene seene without yt. (1:119)

Quickly, however, the novelty of the sword had worn off, and Roe heard that Jahangir had inquired among the Portuguese at court about the reason for the low value of the English gifts. Roe concludes that 'raretyes please as well' (1899, 1:119). While jewels, holding an economic value, make for adequate gifts, European curiosities ('raretyes') possess a higher symbolic value at the Mughal court. As Anne-Valérie Dulac observes, the term 'curiosity' in this regard refers to the precision of the manufacturing, its rarity and the implied unique skill of the artisan. Thus, a curiosity holds a third value, namely a diplomatic one: the rarer and more curious the object, the higher the chances of gaining favour with the recipient (2014, §9).

Attempting to gain a more permanent good standing with Jahangir by providing such objects, Roe gave him a very small and intricately worked crystal box in March 1616. It piqued Jahangir's interest, and Roe, eager to please, promised 'that many Curiosityes were to be found in our Country of rare price and estimation' (1899, 1:146). Roe himself would have been familiar with the allure of 'rarities' and the well-established practice of collecting in cabinets of curiosities. European collections featured curiosities from Asia, Africa and the Americas, which held value because they were regarded as exotic. Smaller private collections in London, such as Walter Cope's, had already attracted visitors at the end of the 17th century, while the 1630s saw the establishment of the much larger Musaeum Tradescantianum (or 'Tradescant's Ark'), Britain's first public museum. We find a very similar practice at Jahangir's court. Roe reports that during Nowruz, the Persian New Year, there was a designated space in one of the durbar halls for the presentation and exhibition of such curiosities:

> At the vpper end were sett out the pictures of the King of England, the Queene, my lady Elizabeth, the Countesse[s] of Sommersett and Salisbury, and of a Cittizens wife of London; below them another of Sir Thomas Smyth, gouernor of the East India company. Vnder foote it is layd with good Persian Carpetts of great lardgnes.... Within this square there were sett out for showe many little howses (one of siluer) and some other Curiosityes of Price. (1:143)

These particular curiosities could be reasonably assumed to be those that Jahangir favoured the most, and Roe would have understood the value (diplomatic, symbolic and otherwise) of having an English gift displayed in such a prominent space. Roe does not elucidate whether only English portraits were exhibited or whether there were others. However, he explicitly links the presence of these English portraits to the grandeur of the Mughal court with its precious 'Persian Carpetts' and valuable curiosities. This passage can be read in a variety of ways: from subtle hints at his own dissapproval of the courtly gaudiness in England to the commodification of the English and their cultural artefacts as 'Curiosityes of Price'.[6]

In July 1616, a particular summons from Jahangir prompted one of Roe's bolder diplomatic moves. The emperor requested the services of an amateur painter in Roe's household, a merchant by the name of Robert Hughes, to which the ambassador agreed and 'neuer receiued so much grace and fauour from the King as at this tyme, which all men tooke notice off, and accordingly altered their fashions toward mee' (Roe 1899, 1:211–212). Realising that Jahangir might be enticed by objects of art with a personal, emotional value, Roe attempted a risky act of improvisation. The same night, he requested an audience with Jahangir and offered him one of his own miniatures, a work by Isaac Oliver 'of a frend of myne that I esteemed very much, and was for Curiositye rare, which I would giue his Maiestie as a present, seeing hee so much affected that art' (1:213). Roe drew specific attention to the symbolic value of the curiosity ('that I esteemed very much'). Jahangir, seemingly impressed by the miniature, now himself made an unexpected move. He called for his 'Cheefe Paynter' (possibly the miniature painter Abu'l-Hasan), who declared he could produce a work of the same quality (1:214). Thus, Jahangir offered a wager: his painters would create perfect copies of the miniature, and if Roe could not identify his original among them, he would

6 During the Nowruz celebrations in the following year, Roe again mentions seeing portraits of the English royal family displayed prominently (see, for example, Roe [1899, 2:396]).

have to remunerate the Mughal artist. Indulging the emperor, and risking the loss of his miniature, Roe agreed (1:213–214). Less than a month later, in August 1616, Jahangir sent for Roe late at night. The ambassador reports that at the *ghuslkhana*, Jahangir

> shewed me 6 Pictures, 5 made by his man, all pasted on one table, so like that I was by candle-light troubled to discerne which was which; I confesse beyond all expectation; yet I shewed myne owne and the differences, which were in arte apparent, but not to be iudged by a Common eye. But for that at first sight I knew it not, hee was very merry and ioyfull. (1:225)

As it turned out, Roe had miscalculated the value of the Oliver miniature. Jahangir demonstrated that his artists were able to easily replicate European artworks.[7] This meant that Roe's estimation of the miniature as unique was obviously misjudged and its symbolic value thus rather diminished. However, without knowing it, Roe had touched a nerve. Encouraged by Jahangir, the artists at the Mughal court were proud of their ability to adopt and adapt various foreign styles, including those of European Renaissance portraiture.[8]

A short but crucial chapter of Roe's 'curiosity strategy' is his offering of another miniature. In September 1616, Roe is called up at night and asked to bring Jahangir a certain miniature (Roe 1899, 1:253; intriguingly, according to Roe, he had not previously shown it in public — we are left to wonder how Jahangir knew about it). According to Michael Strachan, the miniature in question was probably of Lady Eleanor Beeston, a woman Roe had married in secret in 1614 (2011). The emperor 'confessed hee neuer sawe so much arte, so much bewty, and Conjured mee to tell him truly whither euer such a woeman liued' (Roe 1899, 1:254), and received the miniature to have copies of it made for his wives. It is not mentioned again, but one can assume that it was returned.

It seems that the ambassador believed the meetings with Jahangir involving Roe's personal miniatures to be of particular importance to his overall mission of procuring the firman. However, it would take Roe almost another three years to procure the desired documents. As mentioned initially, Jahangir was curious about European cultural artefacts, but the politics of their countries of origin were inconsequential

---

7 Nandini Das has convincingly argued that this episode ties in with many others in Roe's *Embassy*, which reveal a wide range of English anxieties towards imitation: from English travellers' imitation of foreign customs to Mughal imitation of English art (Das 2009, 114–128).

8 An illuminating discussion of the cross-cultural use of images, adoption of painting techniques and repurposing of iconographic elements at the court of Jahangir can be found in Natif (2018, 205–231, 242–260).

to him. One can also assume that Jahangir, for all his — as Roe perceived it — affable professions of admiration for Roe's miniatures, was not very interested in European artists but rather invested in his painters' artful combination of techniques, styles and iconography.

Ironically, Roe and Coryate considered their respective 'curiosity strategies' at the Mughal court (Roe's presenting of curiosities and Coryate's presenting himself as a curiosity, the 'English fakir') extraordinarily successful. After Roe's constant attempts to insinuate himself into court protocol (which he abhorred), he regarded Jahangir's interest in his miniatures to be crucial moments of his embassy. After all, the English thought of portrait miniatures as a genre for which they possessed a unique talent (Dulac 2014, §15).

As Jonathan Gill Harris argues, Coryate's travels had taught him not just the languages but also 'the theatrical bodily practices — of scant clothing, respectful prostration and pleading for alms — that he needed to master in order to be legible to Jahangir as a worthy supplicant' (2013, 457). However, his interaction with Jahangir, which was expected to yield a generous reward and was supposed to be the climax of his travels and his final letter, was short, meagrely remunerated and not particularly memorable as far as the emperor was concerned. That self-fashioning 'backfired' and established strategies failed testifies to the difficulties faced by the precolonial Englishmen at the Mughal court. Contrary to their expectations, Jahangir was not interested in commerce with a marginal island nation, and his interest in European cultural artefacts (such as the 'material and human' curiosities discussed in this chapter) was erroneously perceived as a particular appreciation of English art and culture. Indeed, neither of Jahangir's extensive journals, the *Tuzuk-i-Jahangiri* and the *Jahangirnama*, make any reference to Coryate or Roe. However, the latter — ironically — would himself live on in Mughal cultural imagination within the medium that he had erroneously considered crucial to his own success as an ambassador: miniature painting. Within the Mughal and Indian varieties of the genre, durbar scenes, in particular, would prove to be a distinctive indicator for the English rise to power on the subcontinent.

From the Margins to Centre Stage: Englishmen in Durbar Paintings

Sir Thomas Roe made an intriguing appearance in a Mughal miniature painting created by an unknown artist. He is one of the many figures shown in a durbar scene, c. 1616, which has been described as 'Jahangir investing a courtier with a robe of honour watched by Sir Thomas Roe, English ambassador to the court of Jahangir at Agra from 1615–18, and others' (BM 1933,0610,1.0).[9] We see Jahangir in an elevated position befitting his rank, enthroned under the parted awning of an elaborate garden pavilion of red sandstone and white marble. A powerful visual focus for the entire painting is provided by the horizontal structure of the pavilion (which is further elongated and thus emphasised by having a *chhatri* on top), as well as the bright red awnings with their green and gold fringes and the gold of the throne standing out against the white marble.

However, among the multitude of figures populating this miniature, there is another one that very much stands out in its own way, and that is Sir Thomas Roe. In his outlandish garb, he provides a secondary focus of attention. He is shown wearing the sort of outfit that would have astonished even the Mughal courtiers accustomed to seeing a broad variety of attire. Roe's bare head makes him the odd one out in a place where everyone else is wearing a more or less elaborate turban as a matter of course. The cut of his breeches and his jerkin, complete with a white ruff and lace cuffs, also make him conspicuous. In his right hand, he is holding a notebook or some such. The figure to the right of Roe (as the viewer sees it) is facing him, turning his back on Jahangir to keep his eyes on the exotic foreigner. We can only see the cover of Roe's notebook, but the man depicted right next to him might well be peering at what would, for him, have been an enigmatic, exotic script on its pages. Right behind Roe, there are two musicians, a percussionist and a tanpura player. Likewise, the man holding the tanpura appears to be peering over Roe's shoulder, perhaps also intent on looking at the object in his right hand.

The various degrees of proximity to or distance from the emperor were of obvious importance in such group portraits. To be placed in the two-dimensional space of the miniature was tantamount to being placed in a hierarchy. Physical proximity was also at the heart of the *khil'at*, the ceremonial investiture of a person with a robe of honour, which is in progress in this image.[10]

The semantic distancing of a European figure in the imperial iconographies created for Jahangir can also be seen in *Jahangir Preferring a Sufi Shaikh to Kings*, a miniature created by Bichitr, c. 1615–1618.[11]

9 Anon., British Museum, registration number: 1933,0610,0.1, painting on paper, 23.10 × 27.80 cm. For the description as well as a high-resolution reproduction, see https://www.britishmuseum.org/collection/object/W_1933-0610-0-1 (accessed on 8 March 2021).

10 The *khil'at* ritual and its significance is extensively discussed in Gordon (2003). See also Sharma (2013, 244).

11 Gouache, gold and ink on paper, 25.3 × 18 cm, Smithsonian Institution, Freer Gallery of Art, Washington D.C., accession number: F1942.15a. For a reproduction, see https://www.si.edu/object/jahangir-preferring-sufi-shaikh-kings-st-petersburg-album%3Afsg_F1942.15a (accessed on 22 March 2021).

In this painting, Jahangir is shown sitting on an extraordinary throne consisting of a giant hourglass. The design of this vastly enlarged object is clearly based on an hourglass of European workmanship. Jahangir is handing a book to the Sufi shaikh, that is to say, he is honouring him by bestowing a gift. Below the shaikh, Bichitr placed three more figures in a vertically descending sequence. First comes the sultan of the Ottoman Empire (a generic portrait, probably loosely based on portraits of Mehmet II that had emanated from Gentile Bellini's workshop) (Weekes 2018). While the sultan is shown in a respectful attitude to Jahangir, James I of England/James VI of Scotland, who appears below him, is shown en face, ignoring the emperor. The sequence is completed by a self-portrait of Bichitr occupying the lowest rung in this visual hierarchy.

The portrait of King James is unmistakably based on the quasi-official iconography defined by John de Critz and his followers (Weekes 2018). This likeness was based on what must have been a portrait brought from England that had been given to Jahangir, possibly by Roe as a diplomatic gift or earlier and through other channels. The presence of a copy of this portrait in Bichitr's painting can perhaps be understood in the wider context of the episode of the wager between Jahangir and Roe referred to earlier. In a similar vein, *Jahangir Preferring a Sufi Shaikh to Kings* can be read as a statement putting foreign powers and products in their place. The portrait of James I is painstakingly reproduced, demonstrating that Bichitr can do just as well as a European artist. At the same time, it is placed so as to show Jahangir's comparative disregard for James I.

The elaborate European-style hourglass is likely to be a carrier of multiple layers of symbolic meaning. Based on established European iconographical conventions of the period, an hourglass would clearly have pointed to the passing of time and hence the finite nature of all things. It would therefore immediately have evoked the interrelated topoi of *tempus fugit* and *memento mori*. However, it is a matter of doubt whether any of this is the case here at all. The Farsi inscription on the hourglass expresses the wish that Jahangir's reign may continue for a millennium (Weekes 2018). In his study of sacred kingship and sainthood in Islam, Azfar Moin has put forward a compelling reading of this image, rightly foregrounding the millennial aspect (2012, 220–222). However, it is also clear that the emperor's imperial backside rests on a splendid, bizarrely enlarged example of European craftsmanship. Like the portrait of James I, this object is thus put in its place, employing the simple but powerful principle of vertical ordering. This painting by Bichitr perhaps also served to put an image such as the durbar scene featuring Jahangir and Roe (BM 1933,0610,1.0) into perspective. In BM 1933,0610,1.0, Roe does indeed provide a secondary focus of attention but only in his capacity as a human curiosity, enhancing the splendour of the Mughal court. However, *Jahangir Preferring a Sufi Shaikh to Kings* makes it clear how low Roe's sovereign stands in Jahangir's estimation.

The iconography, particularly of durbar scenes created during the reigns of Jahangir and Shah Jahan, was adapted during the 19th century by Khairullah and Ghulam Murtaza:

> Composed by the Delhi painter Khairullah, court scenes played upon the metaphorical significance of the long lost Peacock Throne of Shah Jahan re-imagining it within the space of the later Mughal court — thus creating a formidable visual imperial identity for the veteran blinded emperor Shah Alam II. Furthermore, Khairullah's younger colleague Ghulam Murtaza Khan took this legacy forward using the shared knowledge of Western perspective and Mughal painterly hierarchy to create court scenes for Akbar II. (r. 1806–1836) (Sharma n.p.)

Shah Alam's and his successor Akbar Shah's power was progressively eroded by the East India Company. Being financially dependent on the Company, Akbar Shah needed to make up for the loss of actual power by using the visual arts to bolster his perceived authority. Durbar scenes could provide reassuring statements about his standing vis-à-vis the British. Akbar Shah's reign saw a further standardisation of an already established type of durbar scene. This included a conspicuous European figure, easily recognisable as the British Resident, that is to say, the representative of the East India Company:

> Delhi painters such as Ghulam Murtaza Khan subscribed to a close-knit stylistic network of figure drawings and decorative design, which was first formulated by Khairullah. Yet their approach to upholding Akbar Shah's pre-eminence within the Mughal darbar was complicated by a figure whose addition within the purview of Mughal court painting was prominent and lasting — the British Resident. An explicit visual acknowledgement of the British Resident, the sole representative of the East India Company at Delhi and the administrator of stipends to the Mughal court, would have posed a challenge to late Mughal court painters, and bore upon the diplomatic relations between the late Mughals and the British. (Sharma 2013, 94)

Yuthika Sharma discusses two durbar scenes by Ghulam Murtaza, which she calls 'Cincinnati Akbar II' and 'British Library Akbar II'.[12]

12 Cincinnati Art Museum, The William T. and Louise Taft Semple Collection, 1962.458, and British Library, Add.Or.342; see Sharma (2013, 105, 112, 127).

'British Library Akbar II' is a quasi-official representation of the ruler which was widely known through copies. One such copy, from the collection of the Toledo Museum of Art, is reproduced in Figure 2.1.[13]

Figure 2.1 ***Court school of painters led by Ghulam Murtaza Khan,*** **The Delhi Durbar of Akbar II,** ***c. 1829.***

Source: Courtesy of the Toledo Museum of Art, Toledo, Ohio, United States of America (object number 2004.55).

13 Another copy was sold through Christies in 2005; see https://www.christies.com/en/lot/lot-4490711 (accessed on 20 March 2021). *The Delhi Durbar of Akbar II*, Toledo Museum, Toledo, Ohio, United States of America, object number: 2004.55. The object is described as 'painting on ivory with carved ivory frame' on the museum website. However, given the dimensions of the painting (17.1 × 27.6 cm), it is probably on paper rather than ivory. See http://emuseum.toledomuseum.org/objects/58768/the-delhi-durbar-of-akbar-ii;jsessionid=BD4BCE18BC29379F7762606B90ADA800?ctx=279fed9a-38b9-4bfd-b472-2f1fcb37ba7a&idx=95 (accessed on 17 March 2021). See also Kumari (2016).

Both durbar scenes feature a British Resident at Delhi, the first one Charles Metcalfe and the second one David Ochterlony. Ochterlony, wearing European dress including a bicorne hat, is easily spotted in Figure 2.1. He is positioned in the first row of the crowd of courtiers on the left-hand side as seen by the viewer, about halfway between the emperor and the lower margin of the painting. The positioning of the Resident below the emperor places him in a visual hierarchy below the monarch and, in the case of 'British Library Akbar II', among his courtiers. Sharma argues persuasively that

> The ubiquitous presence of the British Resident in a large majority of paintings created for Akbar Shah affirm his importance as an arbitrator of all Mughal affairs; yet, these paintings do not project a vision of shared power. Instead, the visual field appears as an arena for the reconfiguration of Mughal authority and the subversion of British dominance at Delhi. (2013, 150)

The iconographic pattern created by Ghulam Murtaza Khan in his durbar scene of Akbar II had an interesting afterlife. The 19th century saw a transformation and commodification of Indian miniature painting. A new type of miniature was created for a market predominantly consisting of Europeans in India. In terms of format and materiality, this type conformed to European traditions of miniature painting. Indian miniatures such as those created by Bichitr or Ghulam Murtaza were miniatures in the sense that individual portraits were indeed painted on a very small scale. However, a durbar scene could easily feature more than fifty figures, all of them exquisitely portrayed. This means that, although composed of miniaturised likenesses, such a group portrait was a fairly substantial piece. These miniatures were painted on paper, and, as in the examples discussed here, tended to be rectangular in terms of shape.

European miniatures, on the other hand, were usually portraits of one single person. Various materials were used; ivory became an increasingly popular choice during and beyond the 18th century. Such miniatures were usually fitted into a small glazed frame or sometimes a locket. Due to their small format, they could be carried about the owner's person or worn as jewellery.

During the 19th century, Indian artists and craftsmen began to create increasing numbers of miniatures conforming to this model. Perhaps this began when Europeans commissioned copies of existing miniatures they had brought to India. Local artists would have realised the potential of an expanding new market, i.e., British people who wanted not only copies of European images but also miniature paintings more closely associated with India. These paintings, due to their small size, could easily be taken or sent back to Britain and would, therefore, make ideal souvenirs. Their subject matter was manifold, with many miniatures depicting a canon of sights such as the Taj at Agra and the Qutb Minar or the Red Fort at Delhi. Copies of older portraits (especially of rulers of the past), including group portraits such as the durbar scenes discussed earlier, were also popular.

The diffusion of quasi-official images of the ruler had always involved the production of multiple copies. Copying was, therefore, a well-established practice in the Mughal tradition of art. However, now the transfer of an existing image filling an entire sheet of paper to the new format of a much smaller miniature necessitated a further step of extreme miniaturisation. What is more, when an original image on a rectangular sheet of paper was copied onto a much smaller oval piece of ivory, there had to be some cropping. This could lead to further modifications, such as subtle rearrangements of the individual figures in a group portrait. This process of copying images from the Mughal tradition into a format following the European miniature produced a very popular new commodity. A large number of such pieces were produced. As Sharma has pointed out, these occupied an interesting position between bona fide late Mughal art and what may be called 'Mughalerie' (2013, 250–261).

The durbar scene created by Ghulam Murtaza (referred to as 'British Museum Akbar II' by Sharma [2013], here represented by the Toledo Museum copy, Figure 2.1) was compressed into the format described earlier by an anonymous 19th century artist (Figure 2.2). The space available to the copyist was minute, measuring just 40 mm across. The number of courtiers represented was significantly reduced. Whereas Ghulam Murtaza created beautifully executed portrait heads, making it easy to identify members of the inner circle at Akbar's court, these have been much simplified here as a space of no more than 2 mm across was available for each face. The two figures to the right of the emperor as seen by the viewer, the princes Mirza Jahangir Bahadur and Mirza Babar Shib,[14] have been amalgamated into one unidentifiable generic figure. The design of Mirza Babar Shib's garments as shown in Ghulam Murtaza's painting has been transferred to the second figure in the first row on the right in the miniature on ivory. However, the colours have been changed, so for instance, what had been a black sash to begin with now shows as a golden sash. To vary the colour of individual garments was part of copyists' working practices, as a comparison between 'British Museum Akbar II', the copy of this painting in the Toledo Museum of Art and another copy sold through Christie's in 2005 readily shows.[15]

14 For identifications, see the description of a copy of this painting sold through Christie's in 2005. See https://www.christies.com/en/lot/lot-4490711 (accessed on 30 March 2021).

15 https://www.christies.com/en/lot/lot-4490711 (accessed on 30 March 2021).

Figure 2.2 ***Anon., Durbar Scene, gouache on ivory, glazed gold frame with a pin attached to the back gold casing so as to form a brooch. Dimensions: 40 × 33 mm, probably Delhi, c. mid-19th century.***

Source: Author's collection (C. Heyl).

The cropping, simplification and compression of Ghulam Murtaza's durbar scene resulted in a significant repositioning of the figure wearing European costume, the East India Company's Resident at Delhi.[16] Now he appears very much in the foreground of the entire composition, being the figure closest to the beholder. As this oval miniature on ivory was produced principally for European buyers and according to European conventions in terms of shape and materiality, it is not surprising that the composition after cropping would turn the sole European present into a much more prominent figure. In this, the anonymous copyist in effect reversed Ghulam Murtaza's strategy of visually reducing the importance of the British Resident.

There is a connection between this miniature (Figure 2.2) and another cropped and otherwise modified copy of a durbar scene found in an

16 Due to the diminutive size of the portrait head, it is not easy and perhaps not even possible to identify this person with any degree of certainty. The costume with the distinctive bicorne hat makes it clear that this must be the British Resident.

album assembled by Sir Thomas Theophilus Metcalfe (1843; British Library Add.Or.5475).[17] The similarity between the rectangular miniature of the durbar scene in the Metcalfe album and the oval miniature on ivory (Figure 2.2) is striking. The visual focus provided by the Metcalfe album miniature is a portrait of the British Resident, probably Metcalfe himself.[18] He is positioned much closer to the beholder than any other figure in the scene. What is more, while Akbar II's glance appears to be directed at him, he is turning his back on the emperor, his three-quarter portrait facing the viewer. Although Akbar II is still positioned at the centre of the composition, Metcalfe seems to be the one who is really at the heart of this scene. He appears like an impresario who has put on a colourful show, which may well have conformed to his self-perception at a court that was, to all intents and purposes, dependent on the East India Company.

There is a clear connection between the small oval miniature on ivory (Figure 2.2) and the rectangular one in the Metcalfe album. The oval miniature on ivory was either derived from that in the Metcalfe album, or both of these images go back to a common visual source. In any case, the small oval ivory miniature is probably based on intermediate copies circulating among the artists and copyists of 19th-century Delhi. Either way, its existence points to an evolving tradition of copying and adaptation responding to a changing market and changing power structures.

Apart from the new prominence of the Resident, the most conspicuous feature of the oval miniature on ivory (Figure 2.2) is its extreme miniaturisation. This raises the question of its role in the context of social practices. How would it have been displayed, and how would it have been viewed? Some sections of the miniature have sustained damage through some form of abrasion, resulting in loss of colour. The damage is particularly evident in the pediment of the throne and the blue robe worn by one of the prominent figures in the first row on the left-hand side. This indicates that this piece has not always been mounted under glass and in a small metal frame as it is now. Prior to this, it must have been displayed for

17 The album contains pasted-in miniatures, many of which were painted by Mazhar Ali Khan, and Metcalfe's manuscript notes, not paginated. Manuscript notes below the pasted-in durbar scene: 'His Majesty the late Emperor Akbur [sic!] Shah holding his Durbar of full dress Court on the Jushun. The anniversary of his accession to the throne'. For a scan of the page, see http://www.bl.uk/onlinegallery/onlineex/apac/addorimss/a/largeimage55375.html (accessed on 14 March 2021).

18 Once again, it is not easy to tell extremely small portraits of Charles Theophilus Metcalfe and his predecessor as Resident at Delhi, David Ochterlony, apart. Both would have worn the uniform of the Resident in use at the time.

some time in a manner exposing it to a certain amount of wear and tear. Perhaps it had been set into the lid of a decorative ivory box or some such. When it was mounted under glass, this must have been done with a view to both protecting and displaying the piece. This was done in India, as the style of the metalwork is consistent with that found in other examples of oval miniatures on ivory produced in India during the 19th century.

The gold casing protecting the back of the miniature is fitted with a pin, which indicates that the miniature was meant to be worn as a brooch. This further begs the question by whom and how it would have been viewed and appreciated. Pinned to a garment, the brooch would have been seen by people interacting with the wearer in a social context. However, given the minute size of the image, to see it clearly would have meant to get into extreme physical proximity with the person wearing it. In order to be viewed properly, it would have been necessary to take it off and to hand it around, and maybe to admire it with the aid of a magnifying glass. It would, therefore, have been useful as a conversation starter, a curiosity promoting social interaction among the owner's peer group. As brooches increasingly came to be regarded as items of ladies' jewellery, it is most likely that the wearer would have been female, although this would not have been absolutely certain well into the first half of the 19th century.

The example of the miniature illustrated in Figure 2.2 shows how the iconography of the durbar scene was put to new uses as it was adapted under the influence of the British in India and, as far as the examples discussed here are concerned, particularly under the influence of the British in 19th-century Delhi. Modifications and transformations of the durbar iconography went on, reaching a notable new stage a long way from India in the 1920s. In 1927, William Rothenstein created a large painting entitled *Thomas Roe at the Court of Ajmir* (1927, oil on canvas, 304.8 × 422) (Figure 2.3). It was placed in the Palace of Westminster as one of a series of images of similar size illustrating what was regarded as significant stages in British history.

Rothenstein's painting is a remarkable product of the historical imagination, visualising the first significant diplomatic encounter between England and the Mughal Empire, the embassy of Sir Thomas Roe discussed earlier. Rothenstein's painting can, in some respects, be described as a pastiche incorporating a number of models and influences. The artist was acquainted with and indeed admired Mughal painting, and he had been to India:

> In January 1910 … with Walter Crane and Ananda Coomaraswamy, Rothenstein went to the Royal Society of Arts in support of Ernest Havell,

Figure 2.3 ***William Rothenstein*****, Thomas Roe at the Court of Ajmir,** ***oil on canvas*****, 304.8 × 422, 1927.**
Source: Palace of Westminster, courtesy of the Parliamentary Art Collection, www.parliament.uk/art.

> retired principal of the Government School of Art in Calcutta, who protested against the school's policy for teaching Indian students, whose training consisted of copying classical casts and mediocre European art to the exclusion of indigenous design and motifs. Sir George Birdwood, a former curator of the Government Museum in Bombay and a founder of the Victoria and Albert Museum in that city, declared that India had no fine arts and that the figure of the Buddha was no more spiritual than a boiled suet pudding. Outraged, Rothenstein, who was already interested in Mughal painting, founded, together with Havell, in 1910, an India Society to educate the British public about Indian arts. In the winter of 1910–11 he went to India with the painter Christiana Herringham.... In Calcutta he met the Bengali poet Rabindranath Tagore, whom he introduced to literary and artistic circles in London in 1912. Rothenstein was instrumental in the publication by the India Society of translations of Tagore's Bengali lyrics *Gitanjali (Song-Offerings)*, for which he was awarded the Nobel prize for literature in 1913, the first such award to an Asian. The influence of Indian art led to changes in Rothenstein's own painting: enamoured of the mass and solidity of Indian architecture, his own Indian scenes became heavier in style where formerly they had been light and delicate. (Lago 2013)

Thomas Roe at the Court of Ajmir features an architectural backdrop that is very much akin to a stage set. It consists of an assembly of formulaic quotations from Mughal architecture — a minaret, two chhatris and a remarkably dysfunctional array of seven four-centred arches which could be distantly derived from familiar Delhi landmarks such as Humayun's tomb or, indeed, from derivative structures such as those put up temporarily for the Delhi durbar of 1911. This painting also clearly draws on Mughal paintings, especially on durbar scenes. The courtier in a white *jama* coat with gold ornaments on the right-hand side (as seen by the viewer), carrying a *dhal* type of shield distinguished by its typical set of four decorative bosses, appears to be based on a Mughal miniature, a durbar scene of Shah Jahan in the collection of the British Library which Rothenstein could easily have consulted.[19]

19 Add.Or.3853, see https://imagesonline.bl.uk/asset/3374 (accessed on 22 March 2021). The figure in Rothenstein's painting would seem to be a composite of two figures in the foreground in Add.Or.3853, with the jama derived from the figure on the left and the *dhal* taken from the figure on the right. The ceremonial staff held by both figures in the 17th-century miniature of the durbar of Shah Jahan has been incongruously replaced with a straight European-style rapier, although this figure also carries a curved sabre (*talwar*). Could the conspicuous and otherwise enigmatic presence of the European weapon be in some way connected with the episode of Roe making Jahangir a present of his own sword (as described earlier)?

We have seen that, in the development of the type of durbar scene that includes a European figure, it was always significant how that figure was positioned vis-à-vis both the emperor and other courtiers. This also holds true for Rothenstein's painting. In his rendering of the encounter between Jahangir and Roe, they are clearly looking at one another, so that Roe is turning his back on the beholder. This makes him what, in literary theory, one would call a focaliser — a character in a story through whose eyes events are perceived and from whose perspective the story is being told.[20] Looking at this painting, a European viewer would have been most likely to identify with Roe, the only European figure in this image. Thus, the image would have invited the viewer to imagine what it would have been like to be in this place at this time, surrounded by members of sophisticated court society and facing its supreme ruler.

In Rothenstein's monumental painting, Roe is handing a rolled-up document to Jahangir. The handing over of a significant document is not something that is commonly found in the tradition of Mughal painting. It is, however, present in European depictions of Anglo-Indian encounters, such as Benjamin West's painting *Shah Alam Conveying the Grant of the Diwani to Lord Clive, August 1765*, c. 1818 (oil on canvas, 290 x 400 mm, accession number: F 29).[21] Rothenstein's strategic use of central perspective is both subtle and effective. The vanishing point found in this image, the point where the lines of perspective converge and to which the gaze of the beholder is drawn, is situated just underneath Jahangir's raised right hand. It is, in fact, where his hand would have been had it remained on one of his knees, as his left hand still does. The composition, therefore, serves to accentuate the dynamics of interaction between Roe and Jahangir. Jahangir's raised right hand corresponds with Roe's right hand holding up his document. The painting thus depicts (or rather, retrospectively imagines) a dramatic moment of interaction.

Rothenstein's version of a durbar scene includes some more elements that are not found in the Mughal tradition. The most conspicuous element of his painting in this respect is two figures on the left-hand side bowing down. Are they doing obeisance to the emperor or to the English envoy? Could this perhaps be a foreshadowing of British dominance? None of this is explicit, as this work of art, like all works of art, consists of a semiotic structure that is to a certain extent open. It all depends on

20 This term was introduced by Gérard Genette in 1972. See Genette (1980, 186).

21 For a reproduction, see https://artuk.org/discover/artworks/shah-alam-mughal-emperor-17591806-conveying-the-grant-of-the-diwani-to-lord-clive-august-1765-191206 (accessed on 22 March 2021), and https://www.rct.uk/collection/themes/publications/eastern-encounters/chapter-2 (accessed on 22 March 2021).

how we fill what, in literary theory, one would describe as the gaps and the blanks in this painting, about how we would read it.[22] And what about the trumpet-like brass instruments that can be seen on the left-hand side of Rothenstein's image? These are not found in Mughal durbar scenes either. They appear to mark the momentous appearance of a European on the scene, rather like a fanfare announcing the entry of an important character in one of Shakespeare's plays.

Rothenstein's painting has recently become subject to a major controversy. In the context of the Black Lives Matter movement, public monuments and paintings commemorating those involved in colonial exploitation — including, but not limited to, the slave trade — have come under severe criticism. As recently as 2017, this painting was featured on the Houses of Parliament's website as follows:[23]

> To mark the start of the UK-India year of culture 2017, January's Artwork of the Month depicts the reception of the first British diplomatic representative on the Indian subcontinent. The painting shows the English politician and diplomat Sir Thomas Roe MP (1581–1644) being received by the Mughal Emperor Jahangir in 1616. Painted by the distinguished artist William Rothenstein (1872–1945), it was unveiled 90 years ago this year as part of the Building of Britain series in St Stephen's Hall. The programme of large mural paintings charts British history through eight important events painted by eight leading artists. Roe's reception at the Mughal court was chosen because the Jacobean diplomat succeeded 'by his courtesy and firmness at the Court of Ajmir in laying the foundation of British influence in India'.

This perception of Rothenstein's painting is now very much under revision. The Speaker's Advisory Committee on Works of Art announced plans for a review of the Parliamentary Art Collection in October 2020.[24] This is how the mission of the committee has been described.

> As part of the response to the issues raised by the Black Lives Matter movement, the Speaker's Advisory Committee on Works of Art, fully

22 The terms 'gaps' and 'blanks' are key elements of Wolfgang Iser's groundbreaking reader reception theory. For an introduction to his approach, see Iser (1978).

23 At the time of writing, an archived version of this old website was still available online; https://old.parliament.uk/about/art-in-parliament/news/2017/january/artwork-roe/ (accessed on 22 March 2021).

24 https://committees.parliament.uk/committee/301/speakers-advisory-committee-on-works-of-art/news/119794/speakers-advisory-committee-on-works-of-art-announces-review-plans-of-parliamentary-art-collection/ (accessed on 22 March 2021).

supported by the Speaker, Rt Hon Sir Lindsay Hoyle, is introducing a package of measures for reviewing and updating the Parliamentary Art Collection — supporting its aim for the collection to become more representative of diversity.

It may well be that, as a result of this review, Rothenstein's painting will disappear from the Palace of Westminster. Can an artist such as Rothenstein, whose credentials as an Indophile are impeccable, be retrospectively identified as an imperialist? There is no easy answer to this, as the meaning of any piece of art is never entirely explicit — it is of necessity and to a considerable extent in the eye of the beholder. What is more, in Rothenstein's time, it would have been entirely possible to be both an Indophile and an imperialist. Rothenstein's painting can be seen as a continuation, an adaptation and a subversion of the traditional Mughal durbar scene. As all durbar scenes, it is fundamentally and ineluctably about power.

References

Primary sources

Coryate, Thomas. 1616. *Thomas Coriate Traueller for the English VVits: Greeting. From the Court of the Great Mogul*. London: W. Jaggard and H. Fetherstone.

———. 1618. *Mr Thomas Coriat to his Friends in England Sendeth Greeting.* London: J. Beale.

———. 1625. 'Certaine Observations Written by Thomas Coryat.' In *Hakluytus Posthumus, or Purchas his Pilgrimes*, part I, book 4, edited by S. Purchas, 600–601. London: H. Featherstone.

Metcalfe, Thomas Theophilus. 1843. 'Reminiscences of Imperial Delhi.' Album. Add.Or.5475. British Library.

Peyton, Walter. 1615–1617. Unpublished manuscript. *Journal of a Voyage to East India and back*. Accessed 24 March 2021. https://www.exploration.amdigital.co.uk/Documents/SearchDetails/BL_Add_MS_19276.

Roe, Thomas. 1899. *The Embassy of Sir Thomas Roe to the Court of the Great Mogul, 1615–1619*, vols. 1 and 2, edited by W. Foster. London: The Hakluyt Society.

Sainsbury, William Noel, ed. 1870. *Calendar of State Papers Colonial, East Indies, China and Japan, Volume 3, 1617–1621*. London: Her Majesty's Stationery Office.

Terry, Edward. 1655. *A Voyage to East-India*. London: J. Martin and J. Allestrye.

Secondary sources

Aune, Mark. 2005. 'Elephants, Englishmen and India: Early Modern Travel Writing and the Pre-Colonial Moment.' *Early Modern Literary Studies* 11(1): n.p.

Banerjee, Rita. 2017. 'Thomas Roe and the Two Courts of Emperor Jahangir and King James'. *Études Anglaises* 70(2): 147–166.

Barbour, Richmond. 2003. *Before Orientalism: London's Theatre of the East, 1576–1626*. Cambridge: Cambridge University Press.

Das, Nandini. 2009. '"Apes of Imitation": Imitation and Identity in Sir Thomas Roe's Embassy to India'. In *A Companion to the Global Renaissance: English Literature and Culture in the Era of Expansion*, edited by J.G. Singh, 114–128. Chichester: Wiley-Blackwell.

Dulac, Anne-Valérie. 2014. 'Miniatures between East and West: The Art(s) of Diplomacy in Thomas Roe's *Embassy*'. *Études Épistémè* issue 26: n.p. 20 paragraphs. Accessed 17 March 2021. http://journals.openedition.org/episteme/343.

Genette, Gérard. 1980. *Narrative Discourse: An Essay in Method*. Translated by Jane E. Lewin. Ithaca, NY: Cornell University Press.

Gordon, Stewart, ed. 2003. *Robes of Honour: Khil'at in Pre-Colonial and Colonial India*. New Delhi: Oxford University Press.

Greenblatt, Stephen. 1980. *Renaissance Self-Fashioning: From More to Shakespeare*. Chicago: University of Chicago Press.

Harris, Jonathan Gill. 2013. 'Becoming Indian'. In *Early Modern Theatricality*, edited by Henry S. Turner, 442–459. Oxford: Oxford University Press.

Iser, Wolfgang. 1978. *The Act of Reading: A Theory of Aesthetic Response*. Baltimore: Johns Hopkins Press.

Kumari, Savita. 2016. 'Art and Politics: British Patronage in Delhi (1803–1857)'. *Art of the Orient* 5: 217–229. Accessed 22 March 2021. https://crossasia-journals.ub.uni-heidelberg.de/index.php/ ao/article/view/8820/8683.

Lago, Mary. 2013. 'Rothenstein, Sir William (1872–1945), Artist and Art Administrator'. In *Oxford Dictionary of National Biography*. Oxford University Press; online ed. Accessed 21 March 2021. https://www.oxforddnb.com/view/10.1093/ref:odnb/9780198614128.001.0001/odnb-9780198614128-e-35842.

Moin, A. Azfar. 2012. *The Millennial Sovereign. Sacred Kingship & Sainthood in Islam*. New York: Columbia University Press.

Natif, Mika. 2018. *Mughal Occidentalism: Artistic Encounters between Europe and Asia at the Courts of India, 1580–1630*. Leiden, Boston: Brill.

Sharma, Yuthika. 2013. 'Art Between Empires: Visual Culture & Artistic Knowledge in Late Mughal Delhi 1748–1875'. Unpublished PhD thesis, Graduate School of Arts and Sciences, Columbia University, New York.

Shivram, Balkrishan. 2007. 'Mughal Court Rituals: The Symbolism of Imperial Authority During Akbar's Reign'. *Proceedings of the Indian History Congress, 2006–2007* vol. 67: 331–349.

Stevens, Paul, and R. Sapra. 2007. 'Akbar's Dream: Moghul Toleration and English/British Orientalism'. *Modern Philology* 104(3): 379–411.

Strachan, Michael. 2011. 'Roe, Sir Thomas (1581–1644), Diplomat'. In *Oxford Dictionary of National Biography*. Oxford University Press; online ed. Accessed 12 January 2021. https://www.oxforddnb.com/view/10.1093/ref:odnb/9780198614128.001.0001/odnb-9780198614128-e-23943.

Truschke, Audrey. 2016. 'Deceptive Familiarity: European Perceptions of Access at the Mughal Court'. In *The Key to Power? The Culture of Access in Princely Courts, 1400–1750*, edited by Dries Raeymaekers and S. Derks, 65–99. Leiden, Boston: Brill.

Weekes, Ursula. 2018. 'A Closer Look at Mughal Emperor Jahangir Depicted on the Hourglass Throne'. *The British Academy* (blog). 5 April 2018. Accessed 14 March 2021. https://www.thebritishacademy.ac.uk/blog/closer-look-mughal-emperor-jahangir-depicted-hourglass-throne/.

3

Discovering the Other: *Northeast India in Early 19th-Century British Travel Writing*

Nandana Dutta

As the modern traveller (by train, road or air) enters Assam, the change most often noted by those coming for the first time and by those coming home is the quality of greenery — miles of green fields or expanses of dense and dark forests that are brighter and clearer than those left behind in *mainland India*.

An equally strong, if not transparent, impression and rhetoric of difference founded on the natural is at work in how the region's inhabitants and their culture are perceived as different from those in the rest of India. This discourse of 'natural exceptionalism' — persistent and unchanging despite political attempts at inclusion (within other discourses) at different times in the region's colonial and post-Independence history — has its origins in the early writings of British travellers. I use the word *natural* to mean 'existing in or derived from nature' and also (because of the theological associations drawn from the Christianising mission that came with the collaboration between British administrators and missionaries) 'relating to earthly human or physical nature as distinct from the spiritual or supernatural realm' (Lexico, n.d.). The word in this sense makes its way into notions of the *indigenous* — of *being found* in a place as opposed to *arriving there* — as also in labels like *simple*, which attach to manner, food, clothing, intellect and psychology. Such tacit assumptions were part of what came to be established as a polarising discourse that worked at two levels with the accounts written about this region. First, 'having defined the dark race in opposition to civilization with industrial culture, the native was [therefore] perceived as being "purer, nearer to the origin of man"' (Hammerstein 2010, 299; also citing Vera 2001). However, a second polarisation was at work, apparent in the verbal and visual images of the tribals and their environment. These images were contrasted with the palaces, forts and tombs of the high cultures of most of India in an internal polarisation that has continued into cultures of perception in the present.

As we read these texts, the excess of the *natural* in both wild and cultivated forms emerges emphatically. The people are mostly categorised as *tribes* who live in and come down from the densely wooded hills, or 'mountains' as they are called in the texts, and who pursue ways of life closely embedded in nature. Arupjyoti Saikia, referring to the descriptions of Colonel F. Roberts and Colonel L.W. Shakespeare that emphasise beauty and greenery and winding rivers, suggests that 'such engagement resulted in the creation of an idea of Assam as a space synonymous with natural (sic)', ignoring complexities for the sake of easier comprehension (2011, 23). This chapter examines its three texts, Robert Boileau Pemberton's *The Eastern Frontier of India* (1835), William Griffith's *Journals of Travels in Assam, Burma, Bhootan, Afghanistan and the Neighbouring Countries* (1847) and John Butler's *Travels and Adventures in the Province of Assam, During a Residence of Fourteen Years* (1855) — for how this excessive emphasis on the natural serves as a way to write the human Other out of the picture. It speculates about how they might be read against the grain, in terms of the Other. It reads the texts to discover/uncover the Other beneath strategies of repression that are camouflaged by an excess of descriptions of nature, which reveal both the confidence and the anxiety of the traveller. This divided response is perhaps why so many accounts take the shape of what Mary Louise Pratt calls 'civic description' (1994, 20), removing the travellers with all their accidents, mistakes and difficulties from the text and leaving it sanitised, impersonal and statistically complete. The travel writing mode founded on what happened to the traveller while observing a new scene demands the intimacy of the anecdotal style, but Robert Boileau Pemberton and William Griffith both remove this element from their texts. Such a stylistic preference, conjoined with extensive descriptions of natural elements, points to equal degrees of confidence and anxiety — confidence in the conceptual frames that the travellers were armed with and anxiety about the Other. Butler's many anecdotes in *Travel and Adventures* reveal what is left implicit in the texts of the other two travellers: the cooperation/collaboration of the boatmen, porters and other support staff who accompany the travelling surveyor or administrator/military official. Their acceptance of the foreigner is as important to note as the foreigner's/coloniser's acceptance and recognition of them. However, as Butler's text proves, presence does not necessarily simplify the problem of the representation of the Other but, instead, complicates it.

The natural was incorporated into imperial designs that set the patterns for resource exploitation — tea, timber, minerals, animals — and such texts are mines of information on these. While travellers' accounts from the rest of India that have explored and constructed different regions have been the subject of a considerable body of research, the exceptionalism that is evident in the discursive production of the northeastern region appears to account for the neglect of this particular section of the colonial archive by scholars of travel writing. So, the correspondence between the old colonial–native binary and the newly emerging one between the northeastern region and the rest of India largely went unnoticed.

The nature of travel into this region was itself unique. The route was mostly riverine, along the Brahmaputra after a stopover in Bengal, a fact that encouraged both comparison (in Griffith) and the occasional doubt about the usefulness of the comparative approach (Jenkins [1835] 1995, 24fn8).

Expressions of relief at finally being able to enter 'a kingdom scarcely if ever trodden by Europeans before' (Dr J.P. Wade on Captain Welsh's expedition, 16 November 1792, in Bhuyan [1990, 307–308]) and the need to quickly 'avail ourselves of so favourable an opportunity to obtain good surveys and to acquire every information that may be possible' (Lord Cornwallis' Minute, 3 October 1792, in Bhuyan [1990, 202]) influenced ideas about mystery, impenetrability and difficulty, as well as the urge to make up for lost time.

Once travellers arrived and embarked on various official assignments, their main modes of travel were elephants, if on land, and boats both vividly described by Butler (2004, 2–10), though the great surveys, as in the case of Griffith, were often also undertaken partly on foot with coolies carrying necessities.

The perception of the traveller was determined by several factors. These included prior training in various disciplines, a period of orientation at Fort William College in Calcutta (Kolkata), learning about the regions they were posted to and acquiring basic training in languages (but apparently not in Assamese, which is not listed in the college curriculum reproduced in David Kopf's book on the Bengal Renaissance [1969, 64, 98–99]). The new arrivals were also familiar with the prevailing culture of observation that the 18th- and 19th-century travellers — naturalists, surgeons and administrators — learnt from the systematic observation and recording techniques of the discipline of botany and especially from the example set by Joseph Banks (Miller and Reill 2010). Two other disciplines that proved to be influential were geology and literary aesthetics.

Precolonial travellers have also left accounts of the region. Hiuen Tsiang, who stayed for a month, mentions it. Jean-Baptiste Tavernier devotes a chapter to Assam in his two-volume account, *Travels in India Between Years 1640-1676* ([1676] 2007, 2, 216–224). François Bernier briefly mentions it in *Travels in the Mogul Empire AD 1656-1668* ([1934] 2011, 171–173), and Shihabuddin Talesh, who accompanied the expedition of Mir Jumla, writes about the region in *Tarikh-e-Aasham* (2009). All these men saw a prosperous and well-administered land. The British, however, saw wild nature urgently calling out for intervention. From this period, negative perceptions of the region begin to appear, expressed in discourses of difficulty, desolation and wilderness in conjunction with natural excess. Kate Teltscher has observed that, by the early 18th century, 'many of the enduring Indian travel-writing topoi' were already referring to 'an unchanging land where the customs of biblical times persisted, where diabolical idols were worshipped, where men were effeminate and widows followed the rite of sati' (2002, 192). She traces a trajectory that begins from the mid-18th century when the British were firmly established as rulers, and 'travel writers followed in the wake of conquering armies, documenting the people, customs, topography, flora, and fauna of newly acquired territories' (192). She then goes into the conventions of the picturesque often seen in women's travel writing. 'The country was emptied of political threat through conversion into a series of picturesque set pieces: charming ruins were set in a gently variegated landscape peopled by an array of Indian types' (192–193). Such views have themselves become stereotypes of travel writing critique, with readings of the colonial accounts under tropes like 'imperial gaze', 'imperial sublime' and the 'rhetoric of empire' being only too common.

Pemberton, Griffith and Butler also gesture at this culture of writing about 'newly acquired territories' but are frequently brought up short by their subject. Butler, indeed, is much struck by the 'ruins of the old city of Dheemapoor' (modern-day Dimapur), especially the old fort, the still upright entrance gateway and the great sandstone pillars, lying fallen on the ground, with carvings of lotuses, peacocks, tigers, deer and elephants (24–25). He appears to want to go with the stock descriptions of buildings and ruins. Such rhetorical frames, though, are only partially useful for the writers of British travel texts from the Northeast. Factors like the nature of the ground, reception of the coloniser, ethnic composition, present attitudes to the idea of colonial exploitation by the Indian nation state and, above all, stereotyping of people in terms very similar to those of the British all determine their retrospective reconstruction.

Butler's two sketches (between pages 24 and 25) show that the surrounding vegetation has claimed the ruins, with trees growing out of the crevices in the pillars ([1855] 2004). Illustrations in the rest of this volume, as in the earlier one, *A Sketch of Assam* (1847), prove the natural to have been the strongest impression: there is one that shows a Kookie warrior in traditional gear (facing page 79), while the Konomah Fort ('one of the strongest forts' in Assam [199]) is shown in one illustration as two large, grassy mounds in the ground (facing page 193), followed by one of its cross-sections revealing the impressive underground fort (facing page 199).

Reading Travel Texts

This chapter examines its three texts by Pemberton, Griffith and Butler for the manner in which excessive emphasis on the natural served to write the Other out of the picture.

All three texts fall into the twenty-year period (1835–1855) of the consolidation of British rule, involving efforts to put down rebellious tribal groups in various inaccessible parts of the region or conducting surveys to evaluate exploitable natural resources and map the territory. The 'discourse of difficulty' noted in the 18th- and early 19th-century British travel texts in India (Nayar 2008) is occasionally heard. Aesthetic tropes like the 'picturesque' and the 'sublime' are used, as the late arrival of the British in the region becomes a crucial factor in the character of travel writing. There is wonder and surprise at new plants, animals and terrain, but the immediate agenda of appropriation and control determines how the fierce, *wild* human is seen (or left unseen) against the impenetrable forests and inaccessible hills. Such texts are early sources of present notions of belonging and identity as they give body to difference, division, racial character and behaviour, while elaborating on the nature of the terrain and indicating the use to be made of land and resources. The story of imperial control of the region through these means is, of course, not unknown.[1] Read in the present, this story is an

1 Perhaps this approach is the reason why, even in scholarly studies (Handique 2004; Saikia 2011; Sharma 2011; Misra 1980; Tamuli and Choudhury 2009), an overall idea about 'colonial exploitation continued in the present by the Indian nation state' has been difficult to shed. Sharma's book (2011), for instance, is about the transformation of waste land into the prosperous tea garden and its incorporation into the colonial regime and subsequently into the national entity. The assumption of exploitation is a given, which is illustrated and substantiated from colonial texts. The prefatory note by one of these scholars, Rajib Handique, to Francis Hamilton's *An Account of Assam* (republished in 2017) reiterates the common assumptions about such texts, situating it within the 'knowledge gathering initiatives of the imperialists, so very necessary before foraying into a new territory' and pointing to '"psychological realities" that shaped the thoughts of contemporary Assam' (Handique 2017, n.p.). One is a reading of the text's effect in its time, the other of its effect in the present — largely within the frame of how these texts created the terms and stereotypes that continue to be used in the present.

interesting source of many of the rhetorical devices used for clearly and effectively conveying an interpretation or idea and moving or convincing an audience or a reader. Through such devices, national discourse makes sense of the region and finds the terms of appropriation — or inclusion — through which to place it within its political, economic and cultural horizons.

Therefore, the problem of *what* the colonial text offers present readers and *how* is critical. The influence of colonial accounts on the colony (Pratt 1992) and the 'the survival of colonial discourse in the postcolonial era' (Spurr 1993, 61) are established postcolonial positions. Pratt raises the question 'How has travel and exploration *writing produced* "the rest of the world" for European readerships?' (1992, 5; emphasis in original) Pratt's question may well be adapted to ask: How has British (and missionary) writing produced the northeastern region for the rest of India? Pratt's study of the deployment of landscape aesthetics in Africa shows the panorama, the picturesque and the prospect to have been popular perspectives (1994). Pemberton, who travelled along the range of hills on the eastern frontier, is particularly fond of the panorama seen from a promontory. 'Indian desolation' was another convenient formulation caused by 'uncontrolled nature', the 'indolence of the natives' and 'despotism and war' (Nayar 2008, 71), allowing interpretations that enabled or justified appropriation and subsequent improvement. These modes also reduced or erased human presence.

While it is quite possible for a critic to use these frames and to locate these elements in Pemberton, Griffith and Butler as well as note their opposites through scenes of fertile, cultivated lands, industrious people and benign rulers — the setting of these texts and a need to understand and identify the means by which the Other was rendered invisible are crucial for discovering the Other in present discourses. As an alternative reading strategy, Michel de Certeau's work on the Other offers some possibilities.

Like the writers mentioned earlier, as well as Stephen Greenblatt (1991) and the contributors to *Visions of Empire* (Miller and Reill 2010), Certeau also mentions the modes of thinking prevalent in the traveller's home country as influencing representations of the new world (1991). However, Certeau's pinpointing of 'lapsus and witticisms' (borrowing the idea of 'return of the repressed' from Sigmund Freud) in the texture of the narrative suggests a specific method to uncover hidden and unexpected elements that the author may unconsciously or strategically be repressing. As the texts in this chapter demonstrate, such elements may well be the result of proliferation of descriptions of a particular kind and adoption of certain writing strategies. What is it that travel narratives imply, *do not say* or are compelled to say against themselves? In the three texts I use, grammatical usage (for instance, Pemberton's use of the passive form in much of his account), suppression of the traveller's mobility, the mode of description adopted for people and the authors' predominant focus on the natural are all deployed to marginalise the Other. The challenge that such texts offer is to discover how the Other is *hidden* in full view. Emmanuel Levinas writes of how the Other 'remains infinitely transcendent, infinitely foreign' through his or her irreducibility to a graspable entity (1979, 194). Locating this infinity in the face, he develops his reflection on the resistance offered by the face to 'my powers' to comprehend and take over (Levinas 1979, 194–197). The possibility Levinas envisages of engaging with the expression on the Other's face when 'the face speaks to me, and thereby invites me to a relation *incommensurate with a power exercised*, be it enjoyment or knowledge' (198; emphasis added), helps explain the absence of engagement with expressions or faces in all these texts. This sense of the Other is useful while engaging with Certeau's demonstration of the processes by which the Other may be revealed in the text.

Representing Nature and the Other

The texts in this chapter, with their emphases on routes and hills, rivers and passes (Pemberton), flora and fauna and diseases (Griffith), and journeys by land and river to quell rebellious tribes (Butler), all construct the region as *natural* and *wild* or 'jungly' (Griffith [1839], cited in Sharma 2011, 31), awaiting colonial intervention to realise their full potential. People and place are seen as set in a continuum, *mirroring* one another in this characterisation, as observation and documentation swept everything that was encountered into one large panoramic nature scene.

All three texts predate the systematic classification of races that followed Charles Darwin's *Origin of Species* (1859) since it was only from around 1850 that 'notions of racial difference and of the distinctive characteristics of so-called *castes* and *tribes* were becoming established' (Bates 1995, 238). So the depiction of people as tribes in these texts was caught up in other concerns. While each account seems to be dominated by one major discourse based on the natural world that overwhelmed them, they are actually made up of a 'mixture of personal, scientific, commercial and exploration discourses' (Youngs 2013, Kindle: 50). These discourses determine where and how the tribal Other is found and described, what impression is constructed about their culture and how the individual travel writer inadvertently exposes racial biases in the process of representing people in their locations.

Pratt uses the term 'civic description' (1992, 20) for the account of travel that is 'devoid of anecdote', offers exhaustive information and is a 'statistical work' in the sense of being 'an inquiry into the state of a country' (20–21). She traces the development from earlier 'survival literature, civic description, or navigational narrative' to 'the new knowledge-building project of natural history' (24). This style is a crucial part of how these texts continue to be read — as sources of information (or knowledge of a place and people) for the imperial government and, subsequently, for scholarship about imperial and contemporary practices. However, the elimination of anecdotes is revealing, telling us about the travellers and their reaction to people and places.

In what follows, I have selected some passages that indicate how the threat of the native is disguised or subsumed by the absence of face-to-face encounters and reported speech, the banishment of accounts of the tribal group to a single paragraph bordered off from the rich surroundings (as in Griffith) and the depiction of the tribal chief as simple and childlike by the superior British officer (as in the crowded narrative of Butler).

The Pemberton report, published in 1835, downplays actual travel, the narration of everyday activities and meetings with people. Instead, it systematically describes rivers and their courses, routes and passes through 'the great chain of mountains' and across to the Yunan and internal approaches and lines of communication (both existing and newly opened ones). The final aim of this great survey is 'to facilitate the rendering them [sic] either lines of commercial intercourse or military operations' ([1835] 2018, 1). It contains descriptions of the newly annexed territories of Cachar and the Jynteeah and Cossyah (modern-day Jaintia and Khasi) hills.

The report is divided into sections, each describing a particular territory. His survey of the region seems to have taken Pemberton over a considerable expanse of land. The sections or chapters of the report indicate this: from the 'Mountain Chain on Eastern Frontier' down into 'Muneepoor', 'Assam', 'Arracan' and the 'Kingdom of Pong' (seat of the Shan tribes). There is a separate section called 'Military and Commercial Routes', followed by brief sections on 'Cachar' and 'Jynteeah' and 'Cossyah Hills'. It is not just an account of his own observations but is supplemented by the brief reports of many others who seem to have visited these places before him. Unlike many subsequent narratives, Pemberton's is rich and dense, diverging into accounts of tribal feuds and of many local rajahs and their interactions with their people, with the British and with other rajahs. However, the sheer volume of natural description (which is, of course, the goal of the survey) drowns the nascent anecdotal mode. Subsection 2 of Section 1 on Assam is fairly representative of this underdeveloped style. Writing of Jaee Singh, Rajah of Muneepoor, who took refuge in Assam in 1774, Pemberton describes his route:

> He crossed the northern extremity of the great western range of Muneepoor, to the village of Tholang, and from thence travelled in a north westerly direction across the hills, until he reached the Dhunseeree river, and prosecuting his journey over its sandy bed, arrived at Joorhath. ([1835] 2018, 59)

Of a more personal experience of opening up a route, he writes, 'It was not until 1832, that the attempt was successfully accomplished by Captain Jenkins and myself' (59). That statement is all we get of this part of an extensive journey that results in the report. A description of how the routes themselves travel follows: they 'commence' and 'run' and 'cross' and 'reach' alongside a repeated use of the passive voice. A valley 'is reached', pebbles 'are found' and plantations are 'met with' (60–61).

Michel de Certeau, referring to the work of Linde and Labov on two kinds of description — the *map* (for example, 'The girls' room is next to the kitchen') and the *tour* (for example, 'You turn right and come into the living room' — writes that 'description oscillates between *seeing* (the knowledge of an order of places) or *going* (spatialising actions) … a *tableau* ('there are …') or *movements* ('you enter, you go') (1988, 119). Certeau is making a distinction between immobility and mobility in the description itself. In Pemberton, three things happen. First, the route itself is mobilised. Next, actual events — to quote Certeau, 'meals, battles, crossing of rivers or mountains' featuring the traveller and the people he met on the way — are swept 'into the wings', the itineraries erased (Certeau 1988, 120–121). However, little stories from past encounters with chiefs and rajahs dot the account. Finally, the tribes themselves feature as tableau: various parts of the region are 'inhabited by' them. For example, the 'Bor Abors occupy the more lofty and retired ranges', and the Duphlas 'border on the Abors' (Pemberton [1835] 2018, 78). Also, some unintended ironies point to an aspect of the description of the Other that Certeau speaks of elsewhere. Many of these powerful tribes 'levy contributions on the Assamese inhabitants residing below their hills' with no attempts having been made 'to check so serious an obstacle to the improvement of the country' (78). A couple of paragraphs later, Pemberton writes of 'intercourse with' the more friendly and amenable 'Cossyas and Garrows' and 'the revenue derived from the taxes levied upon them' (79) — a taxation practice that is legitimate because it is systematic and Western. The text itself exposes the blindness that marked colonial exploitative practices. Such details of the encounters are examples of the slips that appear in these texts, and their effect is emphatic when set alongside admissions that 'knowledge of them [the tribes]' was 'imperfect' (79).

Griffith's text, edited by John MacClelland (geologist for the expedition), begins with a brief biography and letters on his impressions of rivers and local flora. The main text follows and is in the form of journals from different stages of his journeys. Trained for the medical profession, Griffith also acquired knowledge and training in botany while at the University of London.

> In 1832 he came to India and was appointed Assistant Surgeon attached to the EIC. In 1835 he was attached to the Bengal Presidency, and was part of a deputation, consisting of Wallich and himself as botanists, and Mr. MacClelland as geologist, to visit and inspect the Tea-forests (as they were called) of Assam, and to make researches in the natural history of that almost unexplored district. (Griffith 1847, chap. 1).

This journey, the first of many that Griffith undertook, resulted in impressive collections of plants and insects.

One small section of these expeditions — the twenty days spent in Cherrapunjee (entry dated 30 October 1835) — is characteristic of his style. Unlike Pemberton, Griffith describes the journeys in search of plants, but the distinction between tour and map, discussed earlier, appears frequently. Rivers 'flow', valleys 'open out' and cascades 'fall', but they are also part of the static scenes that are 'there'. His companions — the coolies he mentions in the preparations for the journey — are invisible in his narrative.

During the period spent in the Cherrapunjee area of the Khasi Hills, Griffith describes the botanical variety, the geological character, the topography and the birds in a long, enthusiastic paragraph. The rivers, low mountains, waterfalls, ravines, valleys and precipices that often form amphitheatres are magnificent 'sights'; that they are seen as the traveller moves is suppressed in the telling. The existence of coal mines and the high quality of coke are noted. There is an occasional mention of the 'excursion' and something 'found … halfway to Mamloo' (Griffith 1847, chap. 1, under 'Churra Punjee, October 30th'). However, there are no encounters with people. Instead, 'the natives' are relegated to a stand-alone paragraph, separate from the descriptions of the beautiful surroundings — as if they are unsuited to the locale:

> Regarding the natives, I have little to say. They are a stout-built, squat, big-legged hill tribe: the women in regard to shape being exactly like

> their mates; and as these are decidedly ugly — somewhat tartarish-looking people, very dirty, and chew pawn to profusion — they can scarcely be said to form a worthy portion of the gentler sex. They appear to be honest; but that is a quality which, from the example of their European lords, they are said to be losing fast. They have no written character; everything being transmitted by tradition, and performed by the interchange of tokens. They drink like fish, and manufacture a bad kind of arrack.... They pay respect to their dead by the erection of a sort of kairns and large erect slabs of sandstone rounded off at the upper end. (Griffith 1847, chap. 1, under 'Churra Punjee, October 30th')

His language fails because it is unable to find terms to describe what is an absolute Other. The inadvertent reference to 'the example of their European lords' complicates both the binary and the negative assessment. There is no evidence of verbal communication. The terms of description are external — the attention to 'shape' and appearance drawn from the scientific methods of describing flora and fauna. The alienation is enforced by the absence of a written language. An oral culture, transmitted by tradition and based on 'tokens', is difficult to penetrate and represent without violence. This Otherness is further emphasised in unattractive personal habits — chewing paan or drinking 'like fish' — and in the disgust he feels at a 'bad kind of arrack'. The clearest estrangement, though, is evident in cultural markers and practices — in the reference to the commemorative practice for the dead and in the comment, from a slightly later entry of 1836, referring to tattooing among the Singpho women: 'all the legs I saw during the day, being ornamented with rings of tattoo' (Griffith 1847, under 'Upper Assam, Jan 15th').

Certeau, in the essay on Michel de Montaigne's 'Of Cannibals', shows us Montaigne's critique of colonialism's misunderstanding of 'barbarians' and 'savages' through an interpretation of cannibalism and polygamy. In Certeau's interpretation, these are, for Montaigne, modes of conducting an exterior relationship with respect to war, that is, cannibalism, and an interior one with respect to marriage, as an unselfish dedication to their husband's 'valor' and 'virtue', that is, polygamy (Certeau 1986, 67). They are modes by which the 'specificity of another society resist[ed]s occidental codifications' (Certeau 1991, 223). Such a reading, undertaken from the points of view of the victim of cannibalism and the wife in a polygamous relationship — 'Others' in these practices — suggests 'how the strangeness of the cultural Other [may] be conveyed' (Barbieri 2002, 25). Such practices are culturally specific to communities. They reveal a relationship with a community's interiority as seen in the rituals of commemoration, the marriage customs that are described in the many sections on tribes that these accounts contain or in the practice of tattooing. They may also be evidence of a relationship with its exteriority, as in the case of headhunting. The last is frequently mentioned by both Butler and Pemberton as a barbaric act, but it has a place within a tribe's notions about valour in war, and understanding its community-specific significance is a necessary step in the process of uncovering or discovering the presence of an Other and in reading these texts on the Other's terms.

Major John Butler of the 55th Regiment of the Bengal Native Infantry, appointed in 1844 as the assistant agent to the governor-general, North-East Frontier Agency (NEFA), travelled around in Assam for fourteen years. His *Travels and Adventures* records his arrival and journey up the Brahmaputra with his wife and small child and subsequent trips on new commissions, often with troops, to the hills where various tribes lived. Unlike the other two texts, this book is written as a travelogue. It is in three parts and combines day-by-day accounts of phases of the journey, accidents, meetings with tribal chiefs and descriptions of the customs and rituals of several tribes. Part I, titled 'The Expedition to the Highlands of Assam', describes several 'adventures' and demonstrates Butler's easy camaraderie with his servants and troops when he is thrown into their midst. He seems to have had no problems in communicating, sitting around a fire with them, rowing a boat down the Brahmaputra or appearing vulnerable against the elements. The second part is titled 'The Hill-Tribes of Assam', but instead of dry, impersonal information, he describes religion and customs, dress, funerals and manners with the help of actual visits to tribal villages and interactions with people. In the third part, 'The District of Nowgong', he emerges as an attractive and amiable personality (unlike the impatient Griffith or the businesslike Pemberton), happy to wander not just physically but in the organisation of the material of his text. He mixes up his mode and material, which is most evident in the second part where he meets tribes during several expeditions. He avoids the static mode that the other accounts adopt. Therefore, Butler's processes of marginalisation of the Other are more difficult to pinpoint. He makes no effort to disguise the dominance he exercises over the people who provide various services. However, while visiting with the tribal chiefs and encountering differences in food, clothing and manners, the attitude to the Other reveals itself. In the entry for 8 December 1845, Butler writes of the visit paid by several of the party to the chief of the village of Rojapo-mah:

> They were all treated with great civility, and the chief invited them into his house, and offered them, out of a trough placed in the middle

> of the house, a ladle of fermented liquor as thick as mud, the smell of which was quite sufficient to debar them from partaking of the proffered cheer. I was much amused by *the action and gesture* made by the chief on his being asked by me to allow his children to go to Now-Gong to be taught in our schools. He declined the offer, and said that he would rather part with his life than his sons, though I promised good treatment and plenty of handsome *cornelian beads, the first consideration with a Nagah*. The chief got up several times to reply to questions put to him through our interpreters, and evinced much fear of our having a design of kidnapping his sons. (Butler [1855] 2004, 30–31; emphasis added)

Such anecdotes appear quite often in this text (unlike in those of Pemberton and Griffith). While indicating a different narrative style and interest in people and their cultural differences, they are examples of early ethnography (behaviour that is unexpected and, therefore, sought to be explained by an emergent stereotype, the 'Nagah', food and drink that are unfamiliar and evoke revulsion), and sites of what Certeau calls 'lapsus and witticisms'. Butler is amused by the chief's agitation, which was expressed as 'action and gesture' and not verbally, and in that he 'got up several times'. (The outrageous equation of children with cornelian beads is followed by an amused and ironic comment, that the beads are 'the first consideration with a Nagah', a 'witticism' that also qualifies as a lapse or slip in the light of an earlier moment in the text when Butler expresses tender concern about his wife and three-year-old child (Butler [1855] 2004, 4, 11).

The passage reveals a deep, unconscious failure of understanding and communication, notwithstanding the presence of interpreters, which is founded in this instance on suspicion about the Other's capacity to have parental or familial feelings. It is structured around two states — fear and amusement, one producing the other — in a framing that is a strategy of containment of his own deeply repressed and ambivalent state of confidence-anxiety. In an amazing insight into how the travel text works, Certeau (in his reading of Montaigne's essay [1986] as also of Jean de Lery's travel account [2000]) shows us how signs of the 'repressed' Other 'return' (Certeau 1988, 4). Butler's description — 'It was pleasing to watch with what cheerful agility the Nagahs ran off with their peculiar yelling noise, skipping over the walls' ([1855] 2004, 36) — can be unpacked beyond its infantile stereotype to reveal the posture and movement of healthy, athletic bodies and speech that is incomprehensible to the European. As William A. Barbieri notes of such moments, 'descriptions and images that are used to quell the otherness of the savages' yield more than what is actually stated and are 'accompanied by the reverberations that reassert it' (2002, 35).

In his programme to study the writings of French travellers to Brazil (left unfinished by his death), Certeau sets them within his larger project of heterology (1986) but now charts out a particular reading practice based on a number of points:

> a) how the specificity of another society, for example, that of the Tupi, resisted occidental codifications; b) how the fragments of a particular historicity of other societies (with, notably, differing relations to time, to space, and so on), elements capable of inscribing these societies within a duration, a memory, and a space of their own, were first brought into use; c) how, in the text of the ethnographic project, oriented initially toward reduction and preservation, are *irreducible details (sounds, 'words,' singularities) insinuated as faults in the discourse of comprehension,* so that the travel narrative presented the kind of organization that Freud posited in ordinary language: a system in which indices of an unconscious, that Others of the conscience, emerge in lapsus or witticisms. (Certeau 1991, 223; emphases in original)

The first two points create the assumption from which it is possible to identify these irreducible details. As the excerpts from the three travel texts of Pemberton, Griffith and Butler show, such texts are singularly vulnerable when read with Certeau's illuminating insight into textual repressions. The critical practice planned for the Brazilian accounts had already been established in his reading of Montaigne in *Heterologies*, but the intentions outlined for the new project on French travel texts enables a continuing deconstruction through the faults contained in their actual textual fabric. Barbieri, commenting on the project, points out Certeau's 'distinctive mode of analysis of travel writing, a method focused more on the processes through which his subjects produced their scientific narratives than on the products themselves' (2002, 29). Attention to the processes, however, leads us back to the texts — texts that disguise the absolute and incomprehensible difference of the colonised. That there was neither pure domination nor pure abjectness is apparent everywhere in the accounts: the tribes are fierce and recalcitrant or friendly and cooperative, not necessarily subservient. Abjectness is in the mind of the traveller, not in the object of his scrutiny. Many things make the traveller vulnerable, and to disguise this vulnerability and retain the image of the ruler, the writer deploys techniques to downplay native presence, describing cultivated fields and prosperous lands as if they just happened on their own or marginalising people in houses hidden by forests or hills as also in textual nooks and crannies. The texts are filled with the Other, and yet, the Other is sought to be hidden by vivid verbal evocations of dense forests and difficult routes (the *natural* exaggerated in the form of picturesque scenes emptied of human presence). They are marginalised and reduced by being denied speech. The defining features of their societies are viewed with the contempt of ignorance, and their habits and appearance are considered repellent. These textual choices, however, fail to erase the Other, as inadvertent signs of awareness pepper the descriptions. Giveaway phrases and sentences that work their subversive magic by appearing simultaneously as signs of superiority and dubious 'knowledge' — the ridiculous quality of which is lost on the travel writer — once noted, refuse to disappear again.

Framing Northeast India

In the light of these revelations, the postcolonial reading of these texts may be seen as establishing the discursive processes that served the imperial government. Such a reading is useful groundwork as the scepticism towards the past inherent in standard postcolonial approaches can open up many disguised modes of domination. Beyond these now common reading processes, it is important to note how the travel text functions in a particular place at a specific historical juncture and what it tells us, through its own descriptive cultures and discursive choices, about our own time. Still partially within the frame of colonial critique (as in how the British used these accounts in their governance and policies), these texts also have a currency in the present. The text that observed, described and planned out the Northeast of India because it was also the expression of a relationship of power, is now itself a model for the present dynamics of power within which the region is caught. Levinas and Certeau appear useful at this point. In their theorising on Otherness, Levinas frames and establishes the Other's significance, while Certeau provides an arsenal for scrutiny and critique. Taken together, these approaches explain how the absence or invisibility of the Other is engineered/achieved or constructed in these British accounts. Such framing and critique show up practices of rendering invisible that have been internalised and highlight telltale signs of the invisible in the discourse. While all three British texts demonstrate many of these characteristics, the difference in the use of the travelling mode in the writing distinguishes their effect. The Butler text, while appearing full of friendly banter and camaraderie and rich with encounters, offers a wider field to discover these slips — as every encounter he writes of is an occasion for the characteristic attitude to give itself away.

The question I began with — What is the place of these texts in the present? — returns as a challenge to read the discursive construction of the Northeast by the rest of India: the political establishment as well as the people in the cities and towns who *know of* the region within certain negative constructs and who encounter its people with varying degrees of suspicion, apprehension and alienation, expecting and seeing the exotic. The process of discovery that reading these texts of the past for their unintended revelations suggests, offers a model to read the discourse of Otherness variously formulated and directed at this region in the present by another set of travellers (in the sense that all forays into knowledge are travel processes). These travellers see the Northeastern Other and wonder at the fact that they are mobile (they appear in the country's capitals as students and job seekers) and have fully formed cultures that are adequate, internally, *in themselves* and in exchanges with the external.

The signs of the Other in these texts appear in the form of the language of descriptions, depictions of alien elements of culture from a vantage point of superiority or speech reported as inarticulate sounds or 'yelling' (Butler [1855] 2004, 36). As Certeau says, 'The written discourse which cites the speech of the other is not, cannot be the discourse of the other. On the contrary, this discourse, in writing the fable that authorizes it, alters it' (1986, 78). Citing can also be a *speaking for* — a dubious and highly questionable practice in representations of the Other. The overall understanding derived from the scrutiny of the British travel text and identification of its slips is available while undertaking a re-examination of current discourses about the Northeast of India that hide, often unaware that they are doing so, the processes of interpretation and appropriation that keep the region always in a state of doubt about its place in the fabric of the nation.[2]

References

Barbieri, William A., Jr. 2002. 'The Heterological Quest: Michel de Certeau's Travel Narratives and the "Other" of Comparative Religious Ethics'. *Journal of Religious Ethics* 30(1): 23–48. Accessed 3 February 2022. https://www.jstor.org/stable/40017925.

Bates, Crispin. 1995. 'Race, Caste and Tribe in Central India: The Early Origins of Indian Anthropometry'. In *The Concept of Race in South Asia*, edited by Peter Robb, 219–259. Delhi: Oxford University Press.

2 This is a potentially rich area of work — the examination of contemporary discourses of all kinds that feature the Northeast, with the methodology used for reading the travel texts. It would require close textual reading — a literary approach — and attention to what is hidden beneath the surfaces of texts. I only indicate it in this chapter because it is a subject for more extensive research.

Bernier, François. (1934) 2011. *Travels in the Mogul Empire AD 1656-1668*. Translated and annotated by Archibald Constable. Revised Vincent A. Smith. Delhi: Low Price Publications.

Bhuyan, S.K. 1990. *Anglo-Assamese Relations*. Guwahati: Lawyers Book Stall.

Butler, John. 1847. *A Sketch of Assam*. London: Smith, Elder and Co.

———. (1855) 2004. *Travels and Adventures in the Province of Assam, During a Residence of Fourteen Years*. New Delhi: Munshiram Manoharlal Publishers. Page numbers cited are from the Munshiram Manoharlal edition.

Certeau, Michel de. 1986. *Heterologies: Discourse on the Other*. Translated by Brian Massumi. Minneapolis and London: University of Minnesota Press.

———. 1988. 'Spatial Stories.' In *The Practice of Everyday Life*. Translated by Stephen F. Rendell. Berkeley, Los Angeles, London: University of California Press.

———. 1991. 'Travel Narratives of the French to Brazil: Sixteenth to Eighteenth Centuries'. *Representations*, no. 33, sp. issue: The New World (Winter), 221–226. Accessed 3 February 2022. https://doi.org/10.2307/2928765.

———. 2000. 'Ethno-Graphy: Speech, or the Space of the Other: Jean de Lery'. In *The Certeau Reader*, edited by Graham Ward, 129–149. Oxford and Malden, MA: Blackwell Publishing.

Greenblatt, Stephen. 1992. *Marvelous Possessions*. Chicago: University of Chicago Press.

Griffith, William. 1847. *Journals of Travels in Assam, Burma, Bhootan, Afghanistan and the Neighbouring Countries*. Calcutta: Bishop's College Press. Project Gutenberg eBook. Accessed 3 February 2022. https://www.gutenberg.org/ebooks/15171.

Hammerstein, Katharina von. 2010. '"Imperial Eyes": Visuality, Gaze and Racial Differentiation in Texts and Images around 1900'. *Colloquia Germanica* 43(4): 295–317. Accessed 3 February 2022. https://www.jstor.org/stable/23981895.

Handique, Rajib. 2004. *British Forest Policy in Assam*. Delhi: Mittal Publishers.

———. 2017. 'Introduction: A Few Words'. In *An Account of Assam*, edited by Francis Hamilton. Guwahati: Powershift.

Jenkins, Francis. (1835) 1995. *Report on the North-East Frontier of India*, edited and introduced by H.K. Barpujari. Guwahati: Spectrum Publications.

Kopf, David. 1969. *British Orientalism and the Bengal Renaissance: The Dynamics of Indian Modernization*. Calcutta: Firma K.L. Mukhopadhyay.

Levinas, Emmanuel. 1979. *Totality and Infinity: An Essay on Exteriority*. Translated by Alphonso Lingis. The Hague, Boston, London: Martinus Nijhoff.

Lexico. n.d. s.v 'natural'. *Oxford English Dictionary*. Accessed 3 February 2022. https://www.lexico.com/definition/natural.

Miller, David Philip, and Peter Hanns Reill, eds. 2010. *Visions of Empire: Voyages, Botany and Representations of Nature*. New York: Cambridge University Press.

Misra, Tilottama. 1980. 'Assam: A Colonial Hinterland'. *Economic and Political Weekly* 15(32): 1357–1359, 1361–1364. Accessed 3 February 2022. https://www.epw.in/journal/1980/32/special-articles/assam-colonial-hinterland.html.

Nayar, Pramod K. 2002. 'The Imperial Sublime: English Travel Writing and India, 1750-1820'. *Journal for Early Modern Cultural Studies* 2(2): 57–99. Accessed 3 February 2022. https://muse.jhu.edu/article/504417/pdf.

———. 2008. *English Writing and India, 1660-1920: Colonizing Aesthetics.* Abingdon and New York: Routledge.

Pemberton, Robert Boileau. (1835) 2018. *The Eastern Frontier of India.* New Delhi: Mittal Publications.

Pratt, Mary Louise. 1992. *Imperial Eyes, Travel Writing and Transculturation.* London and New York: Routledge.

———. 1994. 'Travel Narrative and Imperialist Vision'. In *Understanding Narrative*, edited by James Phelan and Peter J. Rabinowitz, 206–208. Columbus: Ohio State University Press.

Saikia, Arupjyoti. 2011. *Forests and Ecological History of Assam, 1826–2000.* New Delhi: Oxford University Press.

Sharma, Jayeeta. 2011. *Empire's Garden: Assam and the Making of India.* Durham and London: Duke University Press.

Spurr, David. 1993. *The Rhetoric of Empire: Colonial Discourse in Journalism, Travel Writing, and Imperial Administration.* Durham, NC and London: Duke University Press.

Talesh, Shihabuddin. 2009. *Tarikh-e-Aasham.* Translated (from the original Persian) by Mazhar Asif. Guwahati: Department of Historical and Antiquarian Studies.

Tamuli, Jitu, and Saswati Choudhury. 2009. 'Relooking at Forest Policies in Assam: Facilitating Reserved Forests as De Facto Open Access'. MPRA Paper no. 29560. Omeo Kumar Das Institute of Social Change and Development. Accessed 14 June 2020. https://mpra.ub.uni muenchen.de/29560/1/MPRA_paper_29560.pdf.

Tavernier, Jean-Baptiste. (1676) 2007. *Travels in India Between Years 1640-1676.* Translated by Valentine Ball. 2 Vols. Second edition edited by William Crooke. New Delhi, Chennai: Asian Educational Services.

Teltscher, Kate. 2002. 'India/Calcutta: City of Palaces and Dreadful Night'. In *The Cambridge Companion to Travel Writing*, edited by Peter Hulme and Tim Youngs, 191–206. Cambridge: Cambridge University Press.

Vera, Yvonne. 2001. 'A Voyeur's Paradise ... Images of Africa'. In *Encounter Images in the Meeting between Africa and Europe*, edited by Mai Palmberg, 115–120. Uppsala: Nordiska Afrikainstitutet.

4

Witnessing and Recording Sociocultural Realities in the Indian Subcontinent: *William Dalrymple's* The Age of Kali

Ajie George

Travel writers of the latter half of the 20th century are credited with reinventing the genre, 'giving it both a new popularity and a new critical respectability' by raising pertinent questions about the 'politics of representation', the 'spaces of transculturation' and the 'economic and cultural implications of globalizing projects of modernity' (Duncan and Gregory 1999, 1). *The Age of Kali* (1998), a collection of short travel narratives that records journeys through the Indian subcontinent during the period 1989 to 1998 is one of the well-known works of William Dalrymple. A travel writer and historian, Dalrymple is at home both in India and Scotland and is very active in the contemporary Indian literary scene. In this chapter, I examine the significance of cultural variables, of the persona of the travel writer and of the evolving form of the genre while exploring the accounts in *The Age of Kali* as socially and politically sensitised narratives and as transcultural, transdisciplinary investigations.

The forces that initiate and sustain travel are many; novel ways of recording travel have ensured that travel writing is now recognised as 'a prominent place for the mixture of personal reportage and socio-political analysis' (Hulme 2002, 94). Contemporary texts embody the genre's versatility and reveal the changing cultural desires and anxieties of both the travel writer and the reader of travel narratives (Hamera and Bendixen 2009, 2). Mobility offers contemporary writers the opportunity to escape conventional definitions of nationality and identity. It is possible today to 'belong' to more than one nation, which may involve frequently travelling to another country or even spending long durations of time in a country that is not traditionally or politically considered your 'own'. Pico Iyer, in his TED talk 'Where is Home?', discusses this whole new generation of 'international and multicultural' people who are 'taking pieces of many different places and putting them together into a stained-glass whole' and for whom 'home has really less to do with a piece of soil than … with a piece of soul' (2013). A similar sentiment was expressed in the manifesto of the Tate Triennial held in 2009, which coined the term 'altermodernity' to represent the specified global context in which we live; it 'arises out of planetary negotiations [and]discussions between agents from different cultures' (Bourriaud 2009). Edward Said, in *Out of Place*, wrote of how he experiences himself 'as a cluster of flowing currents' (1999, 295). Justin D. Edwards comments that this experience includes 'motions in time and place that produce unique combinations of identity' (2018, 20). In the writings of such travel writers, ambivalence itself becomes a trope (Clarke 2018, 6). William Dalrymple's identity as a traveller/writer/historian reflects the position that Said enjoyed: 'the paradoxical continuity of a traveler who is not only multiply located but also multidirectional'. This position allows him to engage 'in a progressive politics of mobility whereby the traveler/writer is self-reflexive about his participation in the genre and responds through a series of experimentations in form and style' (Edwards 2018, 21). Dalrymple's position — as British and Indian, travel writer and historian, serious writer and popular writer — celebrates diversity and heterogeneity, refusing to be slotted or easily defined. Most of his works exhibit self-reflexivity: the author, well aware of the postcolonial, deconstructionist approach that he employs, involves the reader in 'constructing' the narrative. Writing travel, thus, becomes a process of negotiation between witnessing and the author's identity, rather than a recounting of authoritative accounts of experience.

Travel writing has traditionally favoured the form of the novel — the lengthy narrative with detailed descriptions of people, places and events. The beginning, middle and end are provided by the frame of the journey, either through the geographical space or through a time period. A majority of Dalrymple's works, too, exploit this form. However, in two of his works, namely *The Age of Kali* (1998) and *Nine Lives* (2009), he has used short, mostly unrelated yet immensely riveting sketches held together mainly by the frame of the journey undertaken by the author through those places in which his subjects are situated. This form of writing is typical of a trajectory of travel writing popular during the late 20th century — travel journalism. Travel journalism, unlike the literature produced by the tourism industry and typical media houses, fuels a sense of global identity, promotes a mode of cross-cultural engagement and offers an alternative to 'the expansion of a global capitalism that flattens all experience beneath the impetus to consume' (Creech 2018, 160). William Dalrymple, in *The Age of Kali,* records his interactions with various people in the Indian subcontinent in the context of the rapid social and economic changes that occurred during the last two decades of the 20th century. Most of these accounts are anecdotal in style. Travel writing has always exhibited flexibility, accommodating various discourses by 'travel writers [who] avail themselves of the several licenses that are granted to a form that freely mixes fact and fable, anecdote and analysis' (Holland and Huggan 1998, 22). *The Age of Kali*, in 'mixing' anecdote and analysis, the personal and the political, religion and livelihood, and tradition and modernity, exhibits a sense of witnessing and of involvement, of immediacy and of sociopolitical awareness. It can also be seen as attempting to counter the popular narratives about India that dominate the Western imagination, especially ones perpetuated by the tourism industry that recall 'colonial nostalgia and the invented memories of imperial rule' (Huggan 2001, 58).

The Age of Kali has six sections, each dealing with a specific geographical location in India, Pakistan, Sri Lanka and the Réunion Island and with issues that are endemic to particular regions in some cases and the result of sociopolitical changes in others. The accounts also highlight the effects of development in India post the liberalisation of trade — the curious, peaceful coexistence of tradition and modernity and sometimes the simmering tensions caused by the demands of changing values and ideas. No one frame of reference can be applied to define India or the subcontinent; every village, town and region is a microcosm with a unique social code. The author draws attention to this heterogeneity, especially at a time when some niche practices and customs seem to be facing a threat from the levelling forces of urbanisation and modernisation (Gidwani and Sivaramakrishnan 2003). In 'reporting' these, the author is at once an analyst of the socioeconomic and political environment and a commentator on cultural identities.

While national cultures are generally produced through institutions and traditions that draw their identity from age-old beliefs and practices in South Asia, the religious community and the cultural community are often considered homologous. Another marker of cultural identity in India is caste, which has always been problematic, considering the notions of hierarchical stratification it implies. In her essay 'The Secular Mode for India', Romila Thapar observes that 'the primacy of caste over religion is demonstrated in the fact that every religion of India, indigenous or imported, observes the distinctions between those of caste and the Dalits' (2013, 7). Generally, the implications of caste are stronger and more evident in rural areas than the urban, which could be attributed to economic development and its attendant factors (education, migration, common living spaces, and so on) that have acted as levelling agents in urban areas (Demerath et al. 2006, 3813).

In *The Age of Kali*, one of the predominant threads that runs through the narratives set in northern and western India is that of caste: the 'wars' between the Bhumihars and the Yadavs in Bihar and between the Rajputs, Gujjars and the Kumhars in Rajasthan are representative of the violent, caste-driven nature of life in some other parts of India too. Evidently, the author's focus is on interrogating the issue of caste-based injustice. He chooses to access these issues through newspaper reports. These reports (that have been filtered through newsrooms) provide not only a framework to the narrative but also an interesting contrast to the kind of 'reporting' that the author indulges in. The author is intrigued that most people he talks to dismiss caste-based violence as everyday incidents. In Rajasthan, a victim of caste violence explains to the author how caste differentiation exists in all spheres of social life and that if it was restrictive, it was reassuring too. It was 'a protection against anarchy' (Dalrymple [1998] 2004, 115). Dalrymple, in the role of a journalist, records the opinions of people belonging to different castes; he also discusses (for the reader's sake) sociopolitical issues and the consequences of policies adopted by the government to eradicate caste-based discrimination. These first-hand reports, in which the author does not take the stand of the educated, Western observer who denounces caste as a discriminatory practice, attempt to present the nuances of a social system that has directed life for thousands of years. The story of a village-level social worker in Rajasthan, who was raped for trying to change (and, therefore, challenge) the age-old social practice of child marriage is a case in point. After meeting the victim, the author interviews the family of the alleged rapists, other villagers and officials from the police department too, all of whom cast aspersions on her character and are angry that 'she had gone public and so brought ill repute' to the village (107). In the case of the victim and women like her, the narrative reveals, the forces of caste, gender, literacy and economics are all lined up against them. Despite efforts by government bodies and women's organisations to ensure equal rights and opportunities for women, Dalrymple's account reiterates the resistance towards change and attests that a violent reaction has 'emerged from the dark depths of our social body to prevent what is conceived as loss of control' (Bhattacharya 2014, 5). Sociologist Debjani Ganguly's study of the caste system in India questions the dominant narrative of 'normative modernity', which theorises caste as 'a social structure and a way of living that is not in tune with a kind of secular, progressive, rational way of being' and brands caste practices as backward and oppressive (Ganguly 2005, ix–x). Though she does not deny that caste practices have been and still are oppressive, she proposes a non-pedagogical sensibility that will recognise them as not being opposed to modernisation but as practices that are 'entwined with numerous ways of dwelling and belonging in Indian modernity' (Ganguly 2005, ix–x). Dalrymple's narratives use the journalistic approach to interrogate caste-based conflict. He does not vilify the perpetrators of caste-based violence. On the contrary, many of them, like Bhera Ram, are portrayed as good men otherwise. Yet, the author acknowledges that 'the strength of caste feeling can be horrifying' (Dalrymple [1998] 2004, 120). The tone of censure in his writing is often against the evil effects of caste rather than against the system itself. He concedes that 'in the West, as everywhere else in the world, there is a caste system of sorts, … what is different about the Indian model is its rigidity and its central place in Hindu philosophy' (115). The first-hand, empathetic accounts humanise the 'news reports' (which were his entry points into the events), highlighting the overt and sometimes covert ways in which the complex mechanisms of caste, religion, politics and gender fuel these incidents.

Evidently, *The Age of Kali* focuses on individuals; it is through them that the author engages with the effects of social change. The accounts are journalistic in their pursuit of factual information, but they are also personalised in that they allow room for various micro-narratives. This writing style could be said to have evolved from what has been termed 'narrative journalism', a form that combines the information-gathering methods of journalistic reporting with the narrative techniques of realistic fiction using a process called saturation reporting. In this process, a writer follows a subject over a period of time and writes about it from a personal perspective (Zdovc 2012, 242). This kind of writing displayed sociopolitical awareness, was sensitive to the problems of the individual or of a small group and ensured that emphasis was put on 'observing the external world and systematically recording and analyzing such observations' (Weaver and McCombs 1980, 481). Dalrymple exploits this style of writing when he studies the consequence of rapid political change on politically active persons like the *rajmata* of Gwalior. He draws the reader's attention to her personality traits, foregrounding her piety, charm, strength and resilience. Interestingly, the author, while discussing the *rajmata*'s right-wing sympathies, takes the opportunity to educate the reader (if briefly) on the formation and growth of the Bharatiya Janata Party (BJP). Shifting effortlessly between the roles of journalist, travel writer, sensitised observer and social commentator, Dalrymple here embodies the contemporary travel writer whose role has evolved to include ethical engagements with issues that raise moral questions.

Dalrymple, through various accounts, problematises the clash between tradition and the demands of modernisation. In 1987, Deorala in Rajasthan gained worldwide attention after a young widow, Roop

Kanwar, committed sati, a practice banned by the British in 1829. The researcher/historian in him considers it necessary to trace the history of this practice, which he observes was prevalent in ancient Europe and India, at least from the 1st century BC onwards. After detailed sketches of the day's events from different perspectives, Dalrymple comments on the irreconcilable nature of the debate between the traditional, religious and cultural significance of the practice and the modern, educated incredulity that condemns it:

> Most secular urban Indians, and especially the feminist lobby, have started from the assumption that in the late twentieth century no educated woman could possibly commit sati, and that Roop Kanwar's sati could only have been forced. The villagers of Rajasthan, male and female, have a very different perspective. ([1998] 2004, 129)

Here, again, the carefully balanced narrative highlights the layered nature of the issue: the forces of religion, tradition, power, politics and gender make the incident and any response to it complex. The onus is on the educated, urban, progressive reader to ascertain their stand. Another account that focuses on women is set in Vrindavan, where Dalrymple meets Kanakalatha, a widow who lives a life of abject poverty and humiliation with her ninety-five-year-old mother, also a widow. He notes that these women have no sense of security and no access to healthcare; they also have no skills to help them earn money. Studies have revealed that the factors responsible for the vulnerable position of women stem from 'cultural expectations and assumptions about women's sexuality, which intersect with economic factors' (Young 2006, 201). Dalrymple points out that many of these widows who have been abandoned by their families in the name of custom belong to 'relatively wealthy, high-caste, landowning families' ([1998] 2004, 51). Religion and cultural practice are so closely intertwined in this account that it risks being labelled a product of the 'colonial gaze'; yet, the author's focus is on the corrupt network of people who exploit these women and make a living off them. Human depravity, and not necessarily Oriental degeneracy, is denounced by the author, who seems to speak on behalf of the humane global community.

Dalrymple contrasts these accounts of aggressive power politics and those of gender violence with the almost whimsical accounts of Lucknow and Hyderabad. The complete degeneration of the richest and most decadent of Indian cities, Lucknow, is captured through the reminiscences of some of its oldest residents, Mushtaq Naqvi and Suleiman Mahmudabad, whom the author meets in the city. These memories are almost like fairytales, and they offer the author an opportunity to comment on (and, therefore, contrast with the present) the city's rich history and culture. Residents narrate real-life stories of once-rich families that today face starvation. Dalrymple's fascination for and knowledge of colonial Indian history and architecture transport the reader to a Lucknow whose 'restlessness and open-mindedness' placed it on 'the fault line between the East and the West, the old world of the Nawabs and the new world of the Raj' ([1998] 2004, 36). He attributes Lucknow's initial fall from grace to the 'increasingly self-righteous spirit of evangelical Calcutta', which would no longer tolerate the excesses of 'native' courtly Lucknow (36–37). The author believes that even after the terrible events of 1857, Lucknow remained a prominent city of the Raj and that it was the Partition of 1947 that destroyed it completely.

Dalrymple, in his writing, has always relied heavily on alternate sources of information, archival records, literature from the period and architecture to reconstruct history (as is evident in works like *White Mughals* [2002], *The Last Mughal* [2006], *Return of a King* [2013], among others). Lucknow's history, too, is recreated through memory, literary texts, newspaper reports and architectural evidence. The tone in this piece is one of admiration for a culture that was not only aesthetically advanced but also proud of its multicultural identity. As in *From the Holy Mountain* (2004), the author uses such evidence to create a link between the present and the past and also to advocate tolerance and syncretism.

In southern India, the past glory of Hyderabad is recounted by Mir Moazam Husain, a descendent of the prime minister of the government of the Nizam of Hyderabad: under the Nizam, Hyderabad remained the centre for 'Indo-Islamic culture and the flagship of Deccani civilization' (Dalrymple [1998] 2004, 199). Dalrymple records how the aristocratic culture has filtered down to the streets so that, as claimed by a shopkeeper in Hyderabad, the ordinary folk believe that they are 'little Nizaams' who 'like to take life gently' and who repose a lot of faith in witchcraft and sorcery even today (202). The 1948 invasion of Hyderabad by the Indian army is another example of the author using *petit récits* to present an alternate version of history. Nationalist history terms the invasion as 'police action', but Mir Moazam recalls that it was an unequal fight between the ill-equipped Hyderabad State and the mighty Indian army, which used air power to attack the military and civilians alike. In his essay 'Memory, Responsibility and Identity', Ross Poole avers that every memory has a counter-memory, 'a version of the events remembered that contradicts, undermines, or subverts the received account' (2008). He writes that there are often 'groups within the contemporary society that claim these repressed memories as their own, and propose a rewriting of national memory in order to find a place for them' (2008, 263–286). The accounts of Lucknow and Hyderabad question the metanarratives of nationalism.

They recall Dalrymple's earlier narratives like *White Mughals* and *The Last Mughal*, in which he focuses on rewriting the colonial experience. These narratives could be viewed as cathartic texts that convey respect to alternative versions of history and to 'other' cultures.

European colonialism and its cultural fallouts are the focus when Dalrymple studies the remnants of colonial Britain in Lucknow, of Portugal in Goa and of France in the Réunion Island. These sections could be studied as narratives that counter the accusations made against travel writers by critics such as Mary Louise Pratt (1992), Graham Huggan (2011) and Debbie Lisle (2006) of continuing the imperialist agenda. Lisle charges contemporary travel writers with not being emancipatory in their approach, of not dealing with 'intricate and ambiguous power relations' (2006, 9) and of returning to old ways of narration although the genre has the potential to 're-imagine the world in ways that do not simply regurgitate the status quo or repeat a nostalgic longing for Empire' (xi). While the argument holds true for much of travel literature, there are a number of socially and politically engaged travellers who, according to Robert Clarke, 'have used their accounts as vehicles to critique the persistence of colonialism and imperialism' and question 'the emergence of new modes of cultural, economic, and political dominance in the age of globalization' (2018, 1). The lingering shadow of the past that is 'accused of tainting contemporary travel writing, in fact, informs the writing strategy' of many contemporary writers (George 2018, 392). The postcolonial travel writer–critic, therefore, operates within the discourse of orientalism, and his/her role is not only to question the tropes of orientalism but also to record the fluctuating 'micropractices' that make them possible. In an account titled 'East of Eton', Dalrymple presents the La Martiniere School in Lucknow, which was modelled on the public schools in England. The school is depicted as having resisted change even after Independence, continuing to exist as 'an archipelago of Englishness' (Dalrymple [1998] 2004, 87). Ironically, the author acknowledges that La Martiniere was finally changing after the murder of one of the schoolmasters: the corruption and lawlessness that prevailed in the society outside had penetrated the bubble, thus ringing in, according to him, 'the final twilight of the Raj' (89).

The impact of colonisation on Goa is seen from the perspective of Donna Georgina, a Goan who asserts that 'the Portuguese never oppressed us' and 'when the Indians came to Goa in 1961 it was 100 per cent an invasion' (Dalrymple [1998] 2004, 232). Dalrymple observes that the long Portuguese rule of 451 years over Goa 'had forged uniquely close bonds between the colonisers and the colonised' (232) and that the integration of Goa with the rest of India was seen by the Goans as a forcible and deliberate erosion of their identity (233). The general feeling of loss with the departure of the Europeans and the subsequent commercialisation of Goa by politicians and the tourism industry offer a perspective on European colonialism that is unlike that of the rest of India. Though he does not overtly state them, the author's sentiments seem to mirror those of Donna Georgina when he briefly traces Goa's colonial history and laments the collapse of its architectural glory.

The section on the French colony of Réunion in the Indian Ocean, titled 'The Sorcerer's Grave', records French colonial impact on the Réunion Island that, according to Dalrymple, 'is modulated by Reunion's tropical geography and what the Reunionists call *metissage*: the racial intermixture that has made the island a model of melting-pot multi-culturalism' ([1998] 2004, 266). This multiculturalism and the extreme isolation of the island have ensured the survival of unique folklore and religious practices. The impact on language, too, is remarkable: while most of the inhabitants can speak conventional modern French, they also communicate in 'an impenetrable Creole patois which mixes Malagasy, Tamil and Arabic on a base of eighteenth-century nautical French' (268). European, African and Indian traditions, language and religion have intermingled to produce a people who are not only 'unusually tolerant and open-minded, but also deeply heterodox' (267). Here too, change is observed by the author, as the younger generation moves towards the coastal towns that are dominated by immigrants from France. These accounts read like conventional travel pieces — they contain evocative descriptions of the environment and a smattering of anecdotal history that provide a background to the unique cultures that are also described.

The accounts of Lucknow, Goa and the Réunion Island, while delineating the varied ramifications of colonisation, affirm the author's understanding of European colonisation as a multifarious, historical phenomenon the impact of which on peoples and cultures cannot be generalised.

In the narratives that focus on the cities of Bangalore and Bombay (now Bengaluru and Mumbai), Dalrymple studies the effects of rapid modernisation on urban Indians. He argues that the transformation of Bangalore from a retirement city to a fast-paced, cosmopolitan one can be attributed to the Western influence that crept in following the establishment and growth of software companies. This hyper-development of the city (India's Silicon Valley) has led to a fear, especially among the urban economically weak class, that presents itself as xenophobia and nationalism. An instance of intolerance was displayed when Hindu and Muslim right-wing groups joined hands to defend 'traditional Indian morality' (Dalrymple [1998] 2004, 165) against the 1997 Miss World contest that was to be held in Bangalore. The opening up of the economy in the 1990s introduced a kind of capitalism that India was unfamiliar with until then; however, it seems to have done little to check class-based, caste-based, region-based and rural–urban-based social inequalities (Bhambri 2013, 78). Dalrymple argues that xenophobia and nationalism were just fronts behind which lay 'a very reasonable fear of progress, a genuine disorientation in the face of massive change' ([1998] 2004, 167). Here, again, the author empathises with those facing the strains of modernisation; he discerns the burden of tradition as also the threat of being left behind that terrifies them.

More perspectives on the impact of economic liberalisation are offered in 'Two Bombay Portraits', which details Dalrymple's meetings with Baba Sehgal, whom he calls 'the world's first Hindi rap megastar', and Shobha De, 'the Jackie Collins of India'. The tone in these sections seems patronising, but one has to concede that the descriptions and analogies are in keeping with Dalrymple's typical style — veracious and humorous. He proffers a succinct summary of the slow awakening of the Indian middle class to relative economic freedom and its attendant luxuries. Both Sehgal and De are seen as pioneers who offered indigenous content in imported forms to a large body of consumers who had longed for these indulgences. They are representative of the interstitial space, the period of transition from one way of life to another. In these sections, the author seems to take on the role of an outsider, one who is able to comment authoritatively on a process that he is able to analyse objectively. However, the binary of the insider–outsider is not one of superiority and inferiority, but more of one in which the author, who is not personally affected by the change, is equipped to critique dispassionately its consequences on those he observes.

The sections on Madurai and Kerala, both in southern India, deal with religion, ritual and faith in relation to two principal temples: the Meenakshi temple and the Chottanikkara Devi temple respectively. These read as precursors to *Nine Lives* (2009), dwelling on regionalised worship practices and also, again, drawing attention to the prominent place held by religion and ritual in the lives of the average Indian. In his account of Madurai, titled 'At the Court of the Fish-Eyed Goddess', Dalrymple uses the conventional trope of travel writing in his description of the architectural beauty of the famous Meenakshi temple:

> The *gopuras* dominate the city as completely as the cathedrals of the Middle Ages must once have dominated the landscape of Europe. They rise in great, tapering, wedge-shaped pyramids — each layer swarming with brightly coloured images of gods and demons, heroes and *yakshis*

> — until three quarters of the way to their apex, they terminate in a crown of cobra heads tipped with a pair of cat-eared demon finials. (Dalrymple [1998] 2004, 177)

This and the subsequent account of the temple festival reveal an interest and understanding beyond that of the mere tourist. Historical records (one written by Megasthenes in 302 BC and another, *Periplus Maris Erythraei*, by 'an anonymous Alexandrian' in the 1st century AD) and ancient literary texts (like the Tamil Sangam era works — *Shilappadikaram*, *The Garland of Madurai*, *The Sacred Games*) are referred to in chronicling the glorious past of the city when it traded in spices, silk, ivory and pearls with kingdoms as far away as Greece and Rome (Dalrymple [1998] 2004, 183–185).

Again, at the Chottannikkara Devi temple in Kerala, Dalrymple witnesses the exorcism of possessed women, a common enough ritual at the Parashakthi temple. In documenting the practices of people whose unique cultural identities often tend to get swept under the metanarratives of the dominant culture, the travel writer merges the roles of the social historian and the anthropologist. The drumbeats, conches, trumpets, writhing and chanting that accompany the exorcism seem overpowering to the Western author, but he notices that young children in the group of onlookers don't even flinch. They seem bored (Dalrymple [1998] 2004, 223). In both these accounts, interestingly, the author introduces to the readers the personal perspectives of specific devotees: Bhaskar in Madurai and Venugopal in Chottanikkara, both highly educated men who hold respectable positions at work and are ardent devotees immersed in the ancient ritual and practice of their respective temples. The author here seems to point out that these men do not perceive a disconnect between rational modern education and personal religion.

Civil war and its consequences are the subject of the piece on Sri Lanka, entitled 'Up the Tiger Path'. Dalrymple travelled to the island in 1990 when the struggle for the Tamil Eelam was at its peak and the so-called Indian Peace Keeping Force was leaving after a disastrous spell on the island. In this piece, the author visits Sri Lanka in the role of a journalist (commissioned by the British Broadcasting Corporation [BBC]), and he displays here the doggedness, endurance and skill of a war correspondent who gathers information in risk-prone areas. The Tamil struggle for peace is briefly introduced by the author; the violence committed by both the Sinhalese and the Tamils and the current situation on the ground are all conveyed in a terse style. Based on his research before the trip, he summarises that the Liberation Tigers of Tamil Eelam (LTTE) were 'almost fanatically disciplined', had 'few internal disputes' and their leader, Prabhakaran, received 'near-religious obedience from his fighters' (Dalrymple [1998] 2004, 238). Dalrymple, through shrewd calculations of human behaviour and action — thereby revealing his skills as a journalist — manages to gain (limited) access to one of the training camps of the female wing of the LTTE, the Freedom Birds. His is a rare account of the regiment. Though he uses humour to describe them (he starts off by claiming that they 'are the stuff of Bond movies' and then discovers that they 'were buttoned-up as an order of cloistered nuns'), he makes the readers aware that they were as important a part of the force as the men were (248–249). He admires the fearlessness, discipline, tenacity and zeal displayed by the young female and male recruits. He expresses concern about the exploitation of children — teenagers who handled automatic weapons nonchalantly and who spoke of massacres with little emotion.

The role of the author is a composite one here. Officially, he is a political journalist covering the 'withdrawal of the Indian Army from Sri Lanka' (238), but his account includes the observations of the narrative journalist, the investigative journalist, the warzone reporter, the human rights observer, the social historian, as well as the humorous, entertaining essayist.

The last few sections in *The Age of Kali* focus on Pakistan with special attention paid to two famous Pakistanis — Benazir Bhutto, the prime minister then, and Imran Khan, the legendary cricketer. Moving from city to city and between the different regions, the author provides glimpses into the varied cultures that constitute Pakistan. Dalrymple's journeys through the country reveal that feudalism, ethnic differences and political nepotism continue to determine the Pakistani way of life. At the frontiers of Pakistan, he records that violence was 'a way of life, an obsession, a philosophy' in the region (Dalrymple [1998] 2004, 313). In one of the most evocative sections of the book, the author draws parallels between the harsh, bleak landscape and its cold and proud inhabitants — the Pathans. Here, he describes the unique political status that has been enjoyed by them: though they are 'technically within Pakistan, the writ of Pakistan does not carry into the heartland of their territories'. Tribal laws and rules have remained unchallenged here since their origins (314). In the marketplaces of Peshawar, Dalrymple identifies the different racial types that have intermingled as a result of invasions and migrations over the centuries. In Lahore, his visit to the city's railway station provides him with the opportunity to elaborate on the significant role played by the railways in the evolution of the subcontinent during the 19th and 20th centuries. He claims that it was the railways that made Indians aware of the fact that their country was a single geographical unit and that 'made India a nation' (339). The landscapes, ethnicities, and ways of life described by the author are varied, and in each of these, the reader identifies the travel writer's many avatars, especially that of the social scientist. This is evident, again, in the section titled 'Benazir Bhutto: Mills & Boon in Karachi', which contains accounts based on the author's meetings with various members of the Bhutto family with a special focus on, of course, Benazir, who was then the prime minister of Pakistan. Through a series of interviews with Benazir herself and her relatives, the author presents to the reader the complex nature of politics, especially that of dynastic power, in the subcontinent. They reveal the struggles of newly democratic governments that find it difficult to let go of traditional notions of leadership and power and of how power affects the human psyche.

The Age of Kali encompasses the subcontinent, even as it calls attention to the cultural, religious, political and historical nuances of specific regions. Some of Dalrymple's accounts, while recording the beliefs and practices of communities, reiterate the view that these beliefs 'represent the wisdom of the community' and that they have 'some functional value in terms of the survival of the community' (Joseph 1993, 807). Other accounts counter Lisle's accusations of escape into 'imagined pasts', negotiate established tropes of the genre and evince the evolving, multifarious role of the contemporary travel writer. They echo Carl Thompson's sentiment that travel writing has the potential to 'create images of other cultures which are complex, respectful and (where appropriate) sympathetic, whilst also remaining mindful of the "relationships of knowledge and power" that operate in the modern world' (2011, 167).

One of the risks that postcolonial travel writing and theory faces today is that these discourses still emanate from centres of power. In Pratt's afterword to *The Cambridge Companion to Postcolonial Travel Writing*, she argues that postcolonial scholarly and aesthetic inquiry has focussed primarily on European colonialism, and this, she claims, was achieved at the cost of 'a series of exclusions' (2018, 221). There is an urgent need to 'see' the world through other languages and cultures, to use non-Western paradigms of analysis and to recalibrate existing precepts (Lindsay 2016, 33). Contemporary travel and travel writing like *The Age of Kali* consciously attempt to move away from exoticism and the dialectics of Western dominance towards an ethical engagement with contemporary concerns, thus affording the genre some redemption from its colonial moorings.

References

Bhambhri, C.P. 2013. 'The Indian Transition.' *Social Scientist* 41(1/2): 69–85.

Bhattacharya, Malini. 2014. 'Can Law Help Women to Survive?' *Social Scientist* 42(1/2): 3–12.

Bourriaud, Nicolas. 2009. 'Altmodern Explained — Manifesto'. Tate. Accessed 8 May 2017. www.tate.org.uk/whats-on/tate-britain/exhibition/altermodern/altermodern-explain-altermodern/altermodern-explained.

Clarke, Robert. 2018. 'Toward a Genealogy of Postcolonial Travel Writing'. In *The Cambridge Companion to Postcolonial Travel Writing*, edited by Robert Clarke, 1–15. Cambridge: Cambridge University Press.

Creech, Brian. 2018. 'Postcolonial Travel Journalism and the New Media'. In *The Cambridge Companion to Postcolonial Travel Writing*, edited by Robert Clarke, 157–172. Cambridge: Cambridge University Press.

Dalrymple, William. (1998) 2004. *The Age of Kali: Indian Travels and Encounters*. Gurgaon: Penguin Books India.

———. 2002. *White Mughals: Love and Betrayal in Eighteenth-Century India*. New Delhi: Penguin Books.

———. 2004. *From the Holy Mountain: A Journey in the Shadow of Byzantium*. New Delhi: Penguin Books.

———. 2006. *The Last Mughal: The Fall of a Dynasty, Delhi, 1857*. New Delhi: Penguin Books.

———. 2009. *Nine Lives: In Search of the Sacred in Modern India*. London: Bloomsbury.

———. 2013. *The Return of a King: The Battle for Afghanistan, 1839–1842*. London: Bloomsbury.

Demerath, N.J., Loren R. Demerath and Surinder S. Jodhka. 2006. 'Interrogating Caste and Religion in India's Emerging Middle Class'. *Economic and Political Weekly* 41(35): 3813–3818.

Duncan, James, and Derek Gregory, eds. 1999. *Writes of Passage: Reading Travel Writing*. New York: Routledge.

Edwards, Justin D. 2018. 'Postcolonial Travel Writing and Postcolonial Theory'. In *The Cambridge Companion to Postcolonial Travel Writing*, edited by Robert Clarke, 19–32. Cambridge: Cambridge University Press.

Ganguly, Debjani. 2005. *Caste, Colonialism and Counter-Modernity: Notes on a Postcolonial Hermeneutics of Caste*. London and New York: Routledge.

George, Ajie. 2018. 'Negotiating the Tropes of Travel Writing: William Dalrymple's *From the Holy Mountain* as a Counter-Narrative'. *Studies in Travel Writing* 22(4): 389–405.

Gidwani, Vinay, and Sivaramakrishnan K. 2003. 'Circular Migration and the Spaces of Cultural Assertion'. *Annals of the Association of American Geographers* 93(1): 186–213.

Hamera, Judith, and Alfred Bendixen. 2009. 'Introduction: New Worlds and Old Lands — The Travel Book and the Construction of American Identity'. In *The Cambridge Companion to American Travel Writing*, edited by Hamera and Bendixen, 1–9. Cambridge: Cambridge University Press.

Holland, Patrick, and Graham Huggan, eds. 1998. *Tourists with Typewriters: Critical Reflections on Contemporary Travel Writing*. Ann Arbor: University of Michigan Press.

Huggan, Graham. 2001. *The Postcolonial Exotic: Marketing the Margins*. London and New York: Routledge.

Huggan, Graham. 2008. *Interdisciplinary Measures: Literature and the Future of Postcolonial Studies*. Liverpool: Liverpool University Press.

Hulme, Peter. 2002. 'Travelling to Write (1940–2000)'. In *The Cambridge Companion to Travel Writing*, edited by Peter Hulme and Tim Youngs, 87–101.Cambridge: Cambridge University Press.

Iyer, Pico. 2013. 'Where is Home?' *TED Talks*. 17 July. Accessed 5 September 2015. www.youtube.com/watch.

Joseph, Sarah. 1993. 'Identity, Culture and Community'. *Economic and Political Weekly* 28(17): 807–809.

Lindsay, Claire. 2016. 'Travel Writing and Postcolonial Studies'. In *The Routledge Companion to Travel Writing*, edited by Carl Thompson, 25–34. New York: Routledge.

Lisle, Debbie. 2006. *The Global Politics of Contemporary Travel Writing*. Cambridge: Cambridge University Press.

Poole, Ross. 2008. 'Memory, Responsibility, and Identity'. *Social Research* 75(1): 263–286, Collective Memory and Collective Identity.

Pratt, Mary Louise. 1992. *Imperial Eyes: Studies in Travel Writing and Transculturation*. London and New York: Routledge.

———. 2018. 'Afterword'. In *The Cambridge Companion to Postcolonial Travel Writing*, edited by Robert Clarke, 217–230. Cambridge: Cambridge University Press.

Thompson, Carl. 2011. *Travel Writing*. New York: Routledge.

Said, Edward W. 1999. *Out of Place: A Memoir*. London: Granta.

Thapar, Romila. 2013. 'The Secular Mode for India'. *Social Scientist* 41(11/12): 3–10.

Weaver, David H., and Maxwell E. McCombs. 1980. 'Journalism and Social Science: A New Relationship?' *Public Opinion Quarterly* 44(4): 477–494.

Young, Kate. 2006. 'Widows without Rights: Challenging Marginalisation and Dispossession'. *Gender and Development* 14(2): 199–209.

Zdovc, Sonja Merljack. 2012. 'Zeljko Kozinc, The Subversive Reporter: Literary Journalism in Slovenia'. In *Literary Journalism Across the Globe: Journalistic Traditions and Transnational Influences*, edited by John S. Bak and Bill Reynolds, 238–259. Amherst: University of Massachusetts Press.

Section 2

ASIAN TRAVELLERS AND INDIA

5

Chinese Pilgrims and Arab Traders in Medieval India

Rita Banerjee

This chapter looks at the account of India by Yuan Chwang[1], the learned Buddhist pilgrim from China who travelled to India in the 7th century, and the narrative of two Arab travellers in the 9th century. While Yuan Chwang's narrative, *Records of Western Lands of the Great T'ang Period*, was written with painstaking labour, the 9th-century Arabic text, *Accounts of India and China,* was an oral version. It is very likely that several travellers had contributed to it apart from Abū Zayd al-Hasan al-Sīrāfī (or Abu Zayd Ḥasan Ibn Yazīd Sīrāfī) and an anonymous writer who were its recognised authors. As a Buddhist pilgrim, Yuan Chwang came to India in search of sacred Buddhist texts and primarily explored Buddhist monasteries and their organisation, sites known for miracles wrought there by the Buddha and holy places connected with Buddhist legends. However, he also wrote about the everyday lives, social customs and political history of the people he saw. By contrast, the Arab Islamic travellers to India and China viewed with curiosity and interest the physical features of the land and the people, their religions, social practices, justice and revenue systems and political

1 According to T.W. Rhys Davids, 'Yiian-Chwang is the correct presentation of the present Pekinese pronunciation. What would be the correct presentation, in English letters, of the way in which the pilgrim himself pronounced it, is not known' (1904, Preface). 'The pilgrim's family name was ^, now pronounced ch^en, but more anciently ch'in' (Thomas Wade cited in Davids [1904, Preface]). 'In modern Pekinese', the name would read as '1 hsuan chuang 2 yiian chuang' (Preface). Tracing the pronunciation of the first part of the pilgrim's name through various language systems, Davids arrives at the conclusion: 'But the vowel following the initial letter is like the German ti, or the French u, so that YUan would, for Indianists, express the right pronunciation of this form of the word' (Preface). He says that the above is 'only one of two apparently equally correct Chinese forms of writing the first half of the name' (Preface). The name has been spelt variously as Hiouen Thsang, Huan Ohwang, Yuen Chwang, Hiuen Tsiang, Hsiian Chwang, Hhiien Kwan (Preface). 'The latter half of the name is quite simple for Indianists. Using c for our English ch and i) for our English ng (n or m or m), it would be simply cwai)' (Preface).

governance and noted them, providing a comparative perspective. The two travelogues are shaped by the specific inclinations, objectives and religious views of the authors.

This chapter argues that the respective identities of the travellers determine their choice of and emphasis on subjects. The nature of the authorships shapes the organisation, and the variant voices determine the tone of the narratives. However, while the Buddhist pilgrim seeks affinity and the Islamic trader exoticises customs, neither seeks to adopt the oppositional stance in the way European travelogues do. Significantly, although Yuan Chwang was the sole narrator while the Arab narratives utilised multiple narrators, the impersonal third-person narrative voice appears in both works. The pilgrim's individual reaction to any sight or event is not apparent in the translations of the work.

Yuan Chwang's Visit

Yuan Chwang's book is titled *Ta-T'ang-Hsi-yu-chi*, translated as *Becords [Records] of Western Lands of the Great T'ang Period* (Watters 1904, 1). The use of 'Great T'ang' helps the reader to identify the 'dynasty within which the treatise was composed', and the work is distinguished from others with 'the same general name' (1). The title page of the *Hsi-yu-chi* indicates that it was 'translated' by Yuan Chwang and 'redacted' or 'compiled' by Pien-chi (1).[2] However, 'translation' in this case signifies that Yuan Chwang obtained the information in the book from 'foreign sources' (2).

Yuan Chwang was commissioned by the emperor to write his narrative. He gave the first draft of the work to the emperor in AD 646, although the work was completed in AD 648. By contrast, as we shall see, the absence of official sanction gives a very different shape to the Arab narrative. Yuan Chwang's 'Dedication' of his work to his royal patron is highly eulogistic and suggests flattery. Generous praise is showered on the reigning sovereign,

2 The preface to *On Yuan Chwang's Travels in India* mentions that 'Mr. Watters left behind him a work, ready for the press, on the travels of Ylian-Chwang in India in the 7*[11] Century a. d.' (Davids 1904, Preface). According to Davids, because of Thomas Watters's extensive knowledge of Chinese Buddhist literature, Sanskrit and Pali, he was very well qualified to 'write an authoritative work on the interpretation' of Yuan Chwang's 'records' (Preface). He argued that it would be superior to the earlier translation of Samuel Beal (I refer to both texts here). Davids states in the preface that have 'we have thought it best to leave Mr. Watters's Ms. untouched, and to print the works as it stands'.

T'ai Tsung had assigned to Pien-chi, a 'learned Brethren', the task of giving 'literary form' to the translated Buddhist texts brought by Yuan Chwang. However, he had later earned bad repute and, Watters conjectures, that 'the utmost that can be claimed for him' is that he organised Yuan Chwang's 'descriptions into a connected narrative' (2).

namely T'ai Tsung. For instance, he writes: '[His Majesty] has made the six units of countries into one empire and this his glory fills' (24). Tracing the king's genealogy, Yuan Chwang writes: 'He is a fourth to the Three Huang and his light illumines the world' (24). Watters suggests that the writer really means the emperor's son when he ostensibly refers to the father. Although Yuan Chwang 'uses the term Ta T'ang, yet the context shews he had in his mind only, or chiefly, T'ai Tsung' and not 'the founder of the T'ang dynasty', who had few qualities to recommend him (26). T'ai Tsung, on the contrary, was remembered as a wise and very capable emperor who quelled rebellions, restored peace and security to the borders of the empire and worked for the welfare of the people.

The dedication indicates an officially authorised work, which does not have signs of improvisation and maintains a formal tone, unlike the oral report of the Arab travellers. It largely follows a coherent organisational pattern and demonstrates the qualities of a fixed, permanent text intended for a limited number of designated readers. The official commission and its preservation suggest that it was intended for perusal in later ages. Generally, Yuan Chwang begins the description of a place by stating the approximate area, informing his readers about the climate, agricultural land and products and portraying the characteristics of the people. Then he goes on to discuss the number of Buddhist monasteries (often also referring to temples of other religions) and disciples. Next, he elaborates sites of interest along with any legends associated with them.

The writer's identity is emphatically religious and Buddhist, as is amply shown in the descriptions of monasteries and their organisations and the retellings of Buddhist legends and miracles associated with a place. As Watters says, 'Yuan-chuang in his travels cared little for other things and wanted to know only Buddha and Buddhism' (1904, 15). His key work was the translation of sacred Buddhist texts into Chinese, running into several volumes. The major part of the travel memoir is devoted to visits to monasteries and pilgrimage sites. He claims that the 'narrative which I have now composed is based on what I saw and heard' (25).

Sites of Pilgrimage and the Buddhist Persona

Towards the beginning, Yuan Chwang relates the Buddhist cosmography: 'In the ocean, resting on a gold disk, is the mountain Sumeru composed of four precious substances: along its middle the sun and moon revolve and on it the Devas sojourn' (Watters 1904, 31). His description of the universe and celestial bodies and elements of nature show the Chinese pilgrim's knowledge of Buddhist treatises and mythology. Yuan Chwang is primarily a scholar, well versed in the intricate theories of the religion's conception of the universe, the Buddha's ascent from and descent to the earth and their implications, and specific miracles. His knowledge is derived from Buddhist sacred books rather than what he actually sees or observes or learns from conversations in everyday life.

The pilgrim's geographical knowledge is also linked with Buddhist mythology. For example, he states that the rivers Ganges, Indus, Oxus (Amu Darya) and Sita[3] originate from the lake Anavatapta, which means 'unheated', as the 'Dragon King' that dwelt in the lake was 'exempt from the fiery heat, the violent storms, and the fear of the garudas which plagued other dragons' (Watters 1904, 34). Such details suggest an imaginary lake. As Watters writes: 'We must regard the "Unheated" Lake as a thing of fairyland, as in the Earthly Paradise or Garden of Eden' (34–35).

He visited many monasteries, and there are descriptions of various statues of the Buddha. On his way to India, he visited 'Fo-ho' (Balkh) country, which extended to the river Oxus in the north. To the south-west of the capital city, known as 'Little Bajagriha city', was the Na-fo (Nava)-Sangharama or the new monastery 'built by a former king of the country' (Watters 1904, 108). Not only was the image of the Buddha in the monastery made of 'precious substances', the halls were also decorated with expensive items. As a result, 'chiefs of the various states' looted the monastery (108). Yuan Chwang described the relics present there, the Buddha's tooth and broom, with specific details: 'a tooth of the Buddha an inch long and 7 io"" of an inch broad' and 'his broom made of kdia grass above two feet long and about seven inches round, the handle being set with pearls' (108). It was believed that on festival days, 'the relics moved by the "thorough sincerity" of a worshipper may emit a brilliant light' (108).

As a pilgrim, he sought sites and sanctified relics. For instance, the travel narrative provides very clear details of the location of a monastery (about 20 li east of the capital of the 'Kah-pi-Pa [Kapitha]'[333][4] country)

---

3 It is difficult to identify the river Sita. But, according to Yuan Chwang, Sita ran underground for some distance until it emerged at the 'Accumulated-rocks' Mountain, where it gave rise to the Yellow River of China (Watters 1904, 34).

4 According to Watters, a note informs the reader that 'the old name of Kapitha was Seng-Jca-she . . . This is a transcription of the name which is given as Sanka^ya or Sangka^ya (in Pali, Sankassa)' (1904, 335).

where the Buddha descended to the earth on golden stairs, accompanied by Brahma and Indra[5]:

> The Ju-lai had ascended from Jetavana to Heaven and there lodged in the 'Good-Law-Hall' ... at the end of three months he was about to descend. Then Indra by his divine power set up triple stairs of precious substances, the middle one of gold, the left one of crystal, and the right one of silver. The Buddha descended on the middle stair, Brahma holding a white whisk came down with him on the right stair and Indra holding up a jeweled sunshade descended on the left stair. (Watters 1904, 333–334)

According to the belief of the pilgrims, not only did these heavenly stairs exist at one time in reality, but they also lasted for a long time, although they had disappeared some centuries before Yuan Chwang's pilgrimage: 'Then certain kings on the site of the original stairs set up the present ones of brick and stone adorned with precious substances and after the pattern of the original stairs' (334). Actual stairs were built to conform to the appearance of the legendary stairs.

> The present stairs were above 70 feet high with a Buddhist temple on the top in which was a stone image of the Buddha, and images of Brahma and Indra were at the top of the right and left stairs respectively and these images like the originals appeared to be descending. (Watters 1904, 334)

The pilgrim-traveller evokes his faith to endorse a divine object that apparently had once existed but was no longer visible by using its replacement, constructed later, to imagine it. Yuan Chwang reports other miracles that had similarly disappeared, although disappearance does not provoke disbelief. The site's existence at the precise location serves to root the event to reality. Just as the original stairs had ceased to exist in this instance, so had the luminous image of the Buddha, left by him in the 'Shadow Cave' to convert the dragon Gopala, become nearly invisible. In a cave found in the country of Nagar (Nungnehar) (Watters 1904, 184), on the east bank of a ravine, Yuan Chwang tells us, the Buddha's likeness, 'once a clear and perfect resemblance', was 'only dimly visible and only at certain times and to certain persons' at the time of the pilgrim's visit (184). However, the cave's existence in that specific location was proof of the miracle, which induced pilgrims to visit the site.

5 Throughout the *Records*, we find references to the gods of the Brahminical religion, such as Brahma and Indra, who had merged with the devas of the Buddhist tradition.

In almost every religion, pilgrims look for sacred sites and preserved relics. Christian pilgrims to Palestine sought to identify sacred spots by the landmarks in the Bible. According to Jas Elsner and Joan-Pau Rubiés, 'in the case of the Holy Land, the Christians possessed a guidebook which they used to redefine the actual places and landmarks they found on the terrain in relation to their dominant mythology, namely the Old and New Testament' (1999, 16). Pilgrims were less interested in the contemporary landscape of Palestine than in the biblical associations of the place. Similarly, the actual landscape mattered less to the Buddhist pilgrim than the religious legend associated with it. Near the stairs 'was a tope [stupa] where the Ju-lai had taken a bath: beside this was a Buddhist temple where the Julai had gone into eamadhi' (Watters 1904, 334). The stupa was important not for its own sake but for the divine actions associated with it.

In fact, existing material objects are recognised by their supposed religious associations. At the side of the temple mentioned earlier was 'a large stone platform 50 paces long and seven feet high where the Julai had walked up and down, all his footsteps having the tracery of a lotus-flower: and on both sides of it were small topes erected by Indra and Brahma' (Watters 1904, 334).

Significantly, these sacred places are sometimes the site of punishment for non-believers in Buddhism. From Yuan Chwang's account, it appears that there was rivalry between Buddhism and Hinduism during those days. His relation of the misdoings of Brahmins attempts to show that Brahminism was inferior to Buddhism and that the propagators of the former indulged in fraudulent practices.

In *Si-Yu-Ki: Buddhist Records of the Western World,* Hiuen Tsiang refers to some ditches or gulfs associated with the wrong-doings and punishments of such miscreants like Dêvadatta, Kukâlî and Chanścha. The ditches, named after them, are 'unfathomable in their depth', and even during summer and autumn rains, they 'show no signs of the water standing in them' (2007, 20). We read of a Brahmin's daughter who 'calumniated Tathâgata' and 'went down alive into hell' in the ditch called 'Chanścha' (2017, 19). That the slanderer was the daughter of a Brahmin indicates enmity between the believers of the two religions. When the Buddha was preaching about doctrines of law before a huge congregation, this woman, 'a female follower of the heretics', 'thought thus with herself, "I will this very day destroy the good name of this Gautama, in order that my teacher may alone enjoy a wide reputation"' (Hiuen Tsiang 2007, 19). She fastened a piece of wood to her body and went to the garden of 'Anâthapindadat', where the Buddha was preaching. She vilified him by saying that the Buddha 'has had a private intercourse' with her and had impregnated her so that she was bearing the 'offspring of the Sâkya tribe' (20). Some believed her, while devout followers refused to accept her story. However, Śakra[6], 'the king of Dêvas', took the form of a white rat and, by gnawing at the 'bandage' that tied the wooden pillow to her body, unfastened it so that the wood fell to the ground. The falseness of her accusation was made known to everybody through Śakra's means. After this public exposure, 'she went down whole into the lowest hell of Avtchi, and received her due punishment' (20). That Śakra helped the Buddha suggests that the gods of the Brahminical religion were in league with the Buddha, although the Brahmins are designated as heretics who disbelieved the Buddha. Tathagata, as the Buddha was called, was 'honoured by men and Dêvas' (18), that is, by humans and gods.

On another occasion also, the devas aided in the exposure of some conspirators. A short distance behind the *saṅghârâma* of '*Anâthapindada*', some *brahmacharins* (celibate, dedicated and trained students in Brahminical religion) killed a courtesan and hid her body to accuse the Buddha of adultery and murder. When her body was found in the "Jêta-vana", they proclaimed that the Buddha had an illicit liaison with the woman and killed her to silence her (Tsiang 2007, 18). However, 'the Dêvas then in the sky joined together their voices and chanted, "This is a slander of the infamous heretics"' (19). The deities are shown as aiding the Buddha against the non-Buddhist Brahmins whom the pilgrim views as a threat to Buddhism.

However, that Yuan Chwang holds the Buddha as superior to the 'Brahmanical gods' is evident in his description of a *vihāra* and an adjacent temple: 'Farther east is a Dêva temple of equal size with the *vihâra*. When the sun is rising, the Dêva temple does not cast its shade on the *vihâra*, but when it is setting, the *vihâra* obscures the Dêva temple' (Tsiang 2007, 20). Nevertheless, the pilgrim's positive reference to Hindu temples suggests the merging of the two traditions to an extent and his tolerance of an allied religion. For instance, in his description of the 'city na-fo-H-p^o-ku-h (Navadevakula)', which was 'a journey of above 100 li south-east' from Kanyakubja (Kannauj), he mentions 'a *magnificent* Deva-Temple' on the 'east bank of the Ganges' (Watters 1904, 352; emphasis added).

The Pilgrim's Engagement with People, Society and Customs

Although he primarily focuses on Buddhist sites and legends, Yuan Chwang also portrays the people and society of India in his memoirs. He

6 In Buddhist cosmology, Śakra is the ruler of *Trāyastriṃśa* Heaven. 'Śakra' is a Sanskrit word meaning 'mighty' or 'powerful' and is used as an epithet of Indra in hymn 5.34 of the *Rigveda*. (Wikipedia) This would suggest the merging of two traditions of Hinduism and Buddhism. Deities from the Vedas form a part of Buddhist cosmology.

reveals his identity as a scholar by his long discussion of the etymology of various words like India, *varsha* (rainy season) and so on. He not only learnt Sanskrit and Pali but also studied the origin and development of words and the Indian educational system. He also describes the curricula of the students and the subjects taught, such as logic, medical sciences and astronomy, in detail. The more academic and scholarly nature of his treatise distinguishes it from the 9th-century narrative. However, his academic interests also suggest a relatively secular bent of mind.

The pilgrim generalises about the nature and appearance of the people, who inhabit the four divisions of Jambudvipa ruled by four lords or sovereigns: the 'Lord of Precious Substances', the 'Horse-Lord', the 'Man-Lord' and the 'Elephant-Lord'. As he explains, 'Now mankind difier [differ] in the quality of their natural dispositions and in their speech, the difference being partly due to local climatic circumstances and partly caused by continued use' (Watters 1904, 36). For instance, the northern people (the land is very cold there) are 'migratory herdsmen', 'wild' and 'fierce' by nature and apt to commit crimes (36). China, which is in the east, where the climate is congenial, is inhabited by well-mannered people educated in social virtues. They have organised political systems, while Buddhism, 'the system of religion which teaches purification of the heart and release from the bonds [of folly] and which instructs how to escape from birth and death flourishes in the country of the Elephant-Lord (India)' (36).

Complaining about the lack of records and information about India, Yuan Chwang says that while travelling as a pilgrim, he noted down the physical features of the land and the ethnological characteristics of the people, thereby indicating that his primary purpose was pilgrimage. However, although he claims to have personally seen and reported these customs, occasional errors (for example, incorrect information about the mourning ritual of a few tribes between China and India, as Watters points out) indicate that some of his information might have been second-hand and unverified.

In Yuan Chwang's portrayal of cities and people, their clothing and their social practices, a secular attitude and curiosity about human society and material objects are apparent. He describes the architecture of houses of various classes of people and Buddhist monasteries, introducing a comparison with China. Some houses are 'thatched with common grass', the walls are 'ornamented with chunam' and 'the floor is purified with cow-dung and strewn with flowers of the season' (Watters 1904, 147). He distinguishes this from Chinese practices: 'In these matters they differ from us' (147). However, he finds similarities with China in other respects. The 'halls and terraced belvederes' of some houses 'are of extraordinary height, and in style like those of China' (147). He especially praises the architecture of Buddhist monasteries, which have 'a tower at each of the four corners of the quadrangle and three high halls in a tier. The rafters and roofbeams are carved with strange figures, and the doors, windows, and walls are painted in various colours' (147).

Yuan Chwang also describes the clothes of the people. He distinguishes between varieties of material — kinds of cotton, 'Kausheya' or 'silk made from the cocoon of the Bombyx Mori', linen, encompassing 'fabrics' (or clothing made from the *kshuma* or flax, the *sana* or jute, and the *bhanga* or hemp) and 'woollen cloth' or 'blanket' (Watters 1904, 149). The clothing of non-Buddhist religious men is described 'as varied and extraordinary'. While 'some adorn themselves with a necklace of skulls', 'some are quite naked', and yet others 'cover the body with grass or boards. Some pull out their hair and clip their moustaches' (148).

Moreover, the pilgrim gives a brief and, what may be described as, an official exposition of the caste system. According to Watters, Yuan Chwang loosely defines castes as 'four orders of hereditary clan distinctions' (1904, 168). The Brahmins, the 'first order', 'keep their principles and live continently, strictly observing ceremonial purity'. The Kshatriyas, or the 'second order', are kings and aim at the virtues of 'benevolence and mercy'. The 'Vaisyaas', forming the 'third order', are traders who 'pursue gain', while the last, the 'Sudras', are 'agriculturists' or cultivators. He refers to practices like intra-caste marriages, the taboo on incest and women's remarriage. The ideas seem to be mainly drawn from Manu. Although the Buddhist scriptures place the Kshatriyas above the Brahmins, Yuan Chwang, following Brahmin sources, elevates the Brahmins above the Kshatriyas (168).

While drawing theories about the caste system from treatises, Yuan Chwang appears to rely on personal observation for specific details of meal habits and caste practices. Ethnographic details include the people's habits of washing themselves frequently, discarding utensils made of pottery or wood after meals, chewing 'tooth-sticks' after meals and smearing their bodies with 'sandal and saffron' (Watters 1904, 151–152). He describes the communities of outcastes thus: 'Butchers, fishermen, public performers, executioners, and scavengers have their habitations marked by a distinguishing sign. They are forced to live outside the city and they sneak along on the left when going about in the hamlets' (147).

The Supernatural

As we have seen in the case of the stairs from heaven and the descent of the Buddha, Brahma and Indra, Yuan Chwang makes liberal use of the supernatural. For instance, he intersperses his work with anecdotes about demons, their birth and rebirth as a consequence of sin and expiation in a matter-of-fact way, without showing any awareness of the miraculous. As in earlier instances, he combines sketches of actual locations with verifiable details and reports of miraculous events that took place there to give us a sense of reality. He refers to an 'Asoka tope', 'three or four li north of the monasteries' in the city Navadevakula, which 'marked the spot at which 600 hungry demons, having come to the Buddha and attained an understanding of his teaching, exchanged the demon state for that of devas' (Watters 1904, 352). Elsewhere, we read of 500 hungry demons who, as 'lay Buddhists' in their past life, had abused *bhikshus* and committed a sin. When they asked for the Buddha's pity, he 'enlarged' their 'needle-throats' to help them swallow their food. After 'having eaten, they burst, died, and went to Heaven' (353).

Kanyakubja and Harshavardhana

A central point of Yuan Chwang's narrative relates to the Buddhist king Harshavardhana, who welcomed and treated him with great courtesy and distinction, and his prosperous city, Kanyakubja. The city's prosperity is a result of the good governance of the king. The city was 'strongly defended', with 'lofty structures everywhere' (Watters 1904, 339). The city abounded in 'beautiful gardens and tanks of clear water, and in it rarities from strange lands were collected' (339). The pilgrim refers to the material and financial conditions of the people, their appearance and dress, knowledge, learning and religion:

> The inhabitants were well off and there were families with great wealth.... The people had a refined appearance and dressed in glossy silk attire; they were given to learning and the arts, and were clear and suggestive in discourse; they were equally divided between orthodoxy and heterodoxy. (Watters 1904, 340)

The prosperity and cultural refinement of the people of Kanyakubja testify to Harshavardhana's good governance and promotion of learning.

It might be seen as a measure of the king's religious tolerance that both monasteries and temples flourished in Kanyakubja. Just as Yuan Chwang lists Buddhist monasteries as a hundred in number 'with more than 10,000 Brethren' from both Mahāyāna and Hinayāna sects, he also estimates the number of temples as two hundred and 'the non-Buddhists' as 'several thousands in number' (Watters 1904, 340).

The king, Harshavardhana or Siladitya, is portrayed as being reluctant to take up kingship initially. Apparently, following the counsel of the

Bodhisattva Avalokitesvara, he accepted kingship, which was the result of 'his good karma', and the duty of salvaging 'Buddhism from the ruin into which it had been brought by the king of Karnasuvarna', 'a persecutor of Buddhism' (Watters 1904, 343). However, the king did not sit on the throne or adopt the title 'Maharaja'. The pilgrim narrates that on becoming the ruler, Siladitya not only successfully avenged his brother's murder but engaged in 'incessant warfare' until he 'had brought the Five Indias under allegiance' (343). However, after that, Siladitya governed peacefully for thirty years and built a great kingdom.

Apart from Siladitya's military acumen, Yuan Chwang testifies to his administrative abilities, devotional sincerity and furtherance of the cause of Buddhism:

> He was just in his administration, and punctilious in the discharge of his duties. He forgot sleep and food in his devotion to good work. He caused the use of animal food to cease throughout the Five Indias, and he prohibited the taking of life under severe penalties. He erected thousands of topes on the banks of the Ganges, established Travellers Rests through all his dominions, and erected Buddhist monasteries at sacred places of the Buddhists. He regularly held the Quinquennial Convocation; and gave away in religious alms everything except the material of war ... he furnished the chapels and liberally adorned the common halls of the monasteries. He brought the Brethren together for examination and discussion, giving rewards and punishments according to merit and demerit. (Watters 1904, 343–344)

That Yuan Chwang emphasises the actions of Harshavardhana that establish the latter's credentials as a devout Buddhist indicates his preference for shared religious values and the urge to seek affinity with fellow believers.

Yuan Chwang relates how Harshavardhana observed fairness and promoted the cause of Buddhism by treating the members according to their respective merits. He honoured and rewarded 'those Brethren who kept the rules of their Order strictly and were thoroughly sound in theory and practice' by 'elevating' them to '"the Lion's Throne" and from these he received religious instruction' (Watters 1904, 344). He only formally honoured the monks who observed the 'ceremonial code' but 'were not learned in the past' (344). He banished from the country those disciples of Buddhism who did not even observe the ceremonial codes and were immoral in their conduct.

Harshavardhana rewarded merit where he found it among his neighbouring princes and statesmen by treating them as his 'good friends' and shunned the presence of those 'who were of a different character'

(Watters 1904, 344). In Yuan Chwang's delineation of Harshavardhana, we find signs of a mutually appreciative relationship and see a fellow Buddhist's admiration of the virtues of a Buddhist king. Although India was an alien country with its own history and culture, Yuan Chwang's narration suggests his desire to find affinity with people of the same faith and cherish similar values.

Unlike the European reaction to differences as opposition, Yuan Chwang's description of India at a time when national barriers were not in place suggests an Asian Buddhist traveller's quest for affinity in the land of the Buddha. Primarily a pilgrim, he looks for sacred spots, recalling mythological associations of wonders enacted by the Buddha. As a scholar, he spared no effort to learn alien languages and derive knowledge from books. In his ethnographic reports, we see acceptance of transcultural variety, comparisons with China and existence of shared values.

Travellers from Arabia

Date and Authorship

Unlike the *Records of Western Lands*, there are controversies related to the authorship of *Accounts*. According to Abū Zayd, the author of Book 2, Book 1 was 'written in the year of the *Hejra* CCXXXVII [237]', which would be equivalent to DCCCLI (851) of the Christian era (2018, 40).[7] According to the second author then, the first book was written at 'a time when maritime business still ran on an even keel, on account of all the toing and froing overseas by merchants from Iraq' (Mackintosh-Smith 2014, 88). Tim Mackintosh-Smith says that 'there is no reason to doubt this date, and internal evidence supports it' (11). Book 2 'was obviously being written well after the end of the Huang Chao rebellion in China, suppressed in 271/884, and some considerable time into the ensuing decades of anarchy' (12). Almost at the beginning of Book 2, Abū Zayd discusses the 'causes of the Revolution', which led to the ruin of the country, the division of the

7 This edition is a reprint of an anonymous 1733 English translation of *Ancient Accounts of India and China by Two Mohammedan Travellers, Who Went to Those Parts in the Ninth Century; Translated from the Arabic, by the late Learned Eusebius Renaudot, With Notes, Illustrations and Inquiries by the same Hand* (London: Sam Harding, 1733). According to Tim Mackintosh-Smith, 'Sauvaget judged Renaudot's version to be good for its period though marred by "too many errors in reading and interpretation"' (2014, 13). Following Mackintosh-Smith, I use Abū Zayd (full name Abū Zayd al-Hasan al-Sīrāfī) in the text as the name of the second and principal author of this book as well as the version in *Ancient Accounts of India and China* (2018).

empire and the interruption in voyages to China (2018, 40). He relates how a high officer of the name of Baichu, though not of the royal family, rebelled against the State. He collected 'a Multitude of Vagabonds and abandoned People, whom he formed into a considerable Body of Troops', and laid a siege on Canfu, a port frequented by many Arab merchants (41). He conquered the city 'and put all the Inhabitants to the Sword' (41). Baichu's uprising and the siege took place in the 'Year of the *Hejra* CCLXIV, and of *Christ* DCCCLXXVII' (that is, 264/877; 41). The rebel not only killed many Chinese but also massacred 'one Hundred and twenty Thousand *Mohammedans*, *Jews*, *Christians*, and *Parsees*, who were there on Account of Traffic' (42). Abū Zayd, therefore, seeks to situate his narrative historically, giving dates of the events he relates. Moreover, one can say that the second narrative was compiled after this period, that is, AD 877.

Unlike Yuan Chwang's narrative, which was primarily written by a single author who was assigned the task by royalty, this narrative was an oral reproduction of the contributions of several informants. Abū Zayd's authorship is established by his claim in Book 2. However, since the first few pages of Book 1 are missing, where the author's name was possibly mentioned, surmises have lighted upon names like Sulaymān al-Tājir on the basis of the attribution of some of the texts to Sulaymān by Ibn al-Faqīh. In consequence, Sulaymān had been rather doubtfully credited with the authorship of the whole of Book 1 (Mackintosh-Smith 2014, 11). Significantly, in Book 2, Abū Zayd does not mention the name of the writer of Book 1: 'I have carefully examined the Book I have been ordered to peruse, that I might confirm what the Author relates' (2018, 39). He refers later to the latter merely as 'the person from whom that First Book was taken down' (Zayd 2014, 12). In another place in Book 2, we have a similar mention of the writer of Book 1: 'The Author, in his Book, notes some Customs and Laws of the *Chinese* ... Adultery' (Zayd 2018, 45). Even here, Abū Zayd avoids mentioning the name of the author of Book 1. Possibly, as Tim Mackintosh-Smith says, he did not know the name of the author (2014, 11)

More importantly, Abū Zayd and the anonymous author of Book 1 were compilers of the oral version or *akhbār*, rather than authors. '*Akhbār*, then, are supposedly verbatim oral reportage, a secular parallel to the literature of hadith, which records the sayings and doings of the Prophet Muhammad and his Companions' (Mackintosh-Smith 2014, 16). Following the geographer Al-Masūdī, Mackintosh-Smith refers to two types of oral report: 'those that are on everybody's tongues and those that have been passed down a chain of narrators' (cited in Mackintosh-Smith 2014, 16). *Accounts* bears the imprint of many narrators, and this composite authorship marks its contrast with the Chinese narrative.

As narrator-cum-compiler, the anonymous author and Abū Zayd had to establish their credibility. The latter professes that he is averse to fabrication and wishes to report truth: 'I have avoided relating any of the sort of accounts in which sailors exercise their powers of invention ... I have also restricted myself to relating only the true contents of each account' (Zayd 2014, 172). Often, the text refers to credit-worthy informants' relation of a circumstance. For instance, Abū Zayd recounts a meeting between his predecessor and a 'Man of undoubted Credit' and the latter's correction of a report (2018, 40). Moreover, the genre, by definition, is based on facts:

> Reality and solidity are what are implied by the first word of the title: *akhbār*, accounts, are reports from credible witnesses. And each *khabar*, each account, fits in with the others to be assembled into a jigsaw picture of a world not unlike our own, a world on the road to globalization. (Mackintosh-Smith 2014, 10).

Khabar suggests a report of facts. According to Mackintosh-Smith, '*akhbār*, like journalism today, were seen as the first draft of history — and, in the case of *Accounts of China and India*, of geography, ethnology, economics, zoology, and much else besides' (2014, 16). In all likelihood, many of the informants were traders or merchants. "Soliman" (or Sulaymān 2014), the merchant, has been mentioned as an informant (Zayd 2018, 7). Ebn Wahb appears as another informant. This was a world without national barriers. As Mackintosh-Smith says, 'the Asianization of the Arab-Islamic polity under the Abbasid dynasty from the mid-second/eighth century on — had thrown open an eastward-facing window of trade and travel' (2014, 13). Trade was free, welcomed and facilitated while the safety of traders was assured. 'The hemiglobal scope of commerce comes across in the diversity of goods described in the *Accounts*' (14). That many of the informants were connected to trade and commerce is evident in the way the ruin of the silk trade in China was reported. In addition to killing many people (Huang Chao rebellion), the report runs, the Chinese rebel also cut down trees, especially mulberry trees that bred silkworms. As a result, the silk trade was badly affected: 'This devastation is the Cause why Silk has failed, and that the Trade which us'd to be driven with it, in the Countries under the *Arabs*, is quite stagnated' (Zayd 2018, 42).

As oral accounts, 'most of the text has the feel of having been told and taken down directly', creating a sense of 'immediacy', improvisation, fluidity and, even at times, abruptness (Mackintosh-Smith 2014, 16). One often notices a sudden switching of subjects. For example, after relating the custom of the people of the 'Islands of Sila' of sending presents to the

Chinese emperor to ensure rainfall in their country, the author apologises for the dearth of information and ends abruptly with a completely unrelated point: 'They have white Falcons' (Zayd 2018, 38). Similarly, the description of the staple food of the Indians and the Chinese shifts unaccountably to the practice of circumcision (35).

The oral nature of *Accounts* has led to the occasional use of non-standard syntax, grammar and spellings in the manuscript.[8] Despite the improvisational tone, however, as Mackintosh-Smith points out, it is likely that the informants' stories had been revised with respect to vocabulary and syntax by the authors and 'acquired a polish in the telling and retelling' (Mackintosh-Smith 2014, 17). Yuan Chwang's written narrative with its complex and correct sentences would differ from the oral travelogue with its colloquial diction and non-standard grammar. However, since I am relying on translations here, I cannot comment at length on the language of the two texts.

An oral story differs from a written narrative with its sense of fixity, permanence and orderliness. Moreover, *Accounts* lacks the consistency and the rigidity that a single authorial voice produces. Rather, 'it weaves the threads and fragments of many journeys together into a text' (Mackintosh-Smith 2014, 17). Mackintosh-Smith points out two contradictory statements about Indian kings' payment of their army in Book 1. Like the Arabs, Balhara, an Indian king, pays his troops. Later, however, we read: 'The king of India has many troops ... they go to war at their expense and at no cost at all to the king' (85).

Like *Records*, *Accounts* reads like a report, conveying information on various topics. On the whole, one does not hear the first-person narrator's voice conveying their impression of and reaction to what they see or hear in the text, although there are a few exceptions. For instance, Abū Zayd's account resorts to the speaking voice and anecdotes sometimes, as in the merchant's story of the oyster and the fox: 'I was going along, said he, by *Saman*, in the District of *Bahrein* ... and upon the Sand I saw a dead Fox, with something, at his Muzzle, that held him fast' (Zayd 2018, 97). Here, the informant is given a voice and the opportunity to tell his story.

Accounts imparts information on subjects ranging from the flora and fauna to people and their appearances, currencies of exchange,

8 The manuscript, titled *Akhbār al-sīn wa-l-hind,* exists in the Bibliothèque Nationale de France, Paris. It dates approximately 'towards the end' of the 6th/12th century AD.

Since the book was compiled in about the 9th century, it was copied 300 years after that. 'It has an air of authenticity: its syntax, grammar, and orthography are not always strictly standard' (Mackintosh-Smith 2014, 24). As Tim Mackintosh-Smith says, 'It seems that little attempt has been made by copyists to force the text into a more literary mould' (24).

clothing, cleanliness, marital, sexual and religious practices, justice and administrative systems, including punishments of the guilty, and warfare. The perspective is comparative, entailing comparisons between Chinese and Indian customs.

Book 1 describes the Chinese and the Indian people, their dresses and food:

> The *Chinese* are more handsom than the *Indians*, and come nearer to the *Arabs*, not only in Countenance, but in their Dress, in their way of Riding, in their Manners, and in their processional Ceremonies. They wear long Garments, and Girdles in form of Belts, or Baldrics.
>
> The *Indians* wear two short Vests; and the Men as well as the Women wear golden Bracelets, adorned with precious Stones. (Zayd 2018, 38)

> Rice is the most common Food of the *Indians*, who eat no Wheat; whereas the *Chinese* eat of Rice and Wheat indifferently. Circumcision is practised neither by the *Indians* nor the *Chinese*. (34–35)

The writer's reference to the similarities between the appearances of the Chinese and the Arabs and their differences with the Indians points to his critical attitude towards some racial traits of ethnic groups. For instance, he describes the people of Andaman as 'quite naked' and of black 'Complexion', with 'frizled' hair, 'frightful' eyes and face and very large feet, 'almost a Cubit in length' (Zayd 2018, 4). He characterised them as cannibals who ate 'Human Flesh quite raw' and were liable to 'devour all the Passengers' of ships they 'could lay Hands on' (4). Often, ships which anchored on 'this barbarous Coast' to refill water sometimes lost 'their Men, but most escape' (4–5). This passage in Book 1 may resemble many later European descriptions of Asian ethnic groups. The exaggerations and emphasis on barbarity suggest a racist attitude, missing in the Chinese narrative. However, this is a many-voiced reportage, and the second author's narrative is relatively free from such descriptions.

The travelogue includes sketches of the flora. In Book 1, we find a description of coconut trees and their uses in certain islands. The writer relates how the people make 'whole Shirts, all of one Piece, Sleeves, Gussets and all, as also half Vests [or Jacquets]' out of the fibre (2018, 2).

The writers seem to focus on living habits, social customs, commerce and governance without describing branches of knowledge or educational systems in detail. In Book 1, we have: 'Physic and Philosophy are cultivated among the *Indians*, and the *Chinese* have some Skill in Medicine; but it almost wholly consists in the Art of applying hot Irons, or Cauteries. They have also some smattering of Astronomy; but therein the *Indians* surpass the *Chinese*' (2018, 37). This cursory description contrasts with the systematic knowledge and presentation of the educational curricula in India by Yuan Chwang.

While the Chinese pilgrim's narrative focussed on religion, especially Buddhism, the Arab writers make casual references to Indian and Chinese religions, which they consider as primarily idolatrous and characterised by a belief in metempsychosis. The author of Book 1 maintains that the Chinese religion is 'derived from the *Indians*', and 'both the one and the other believe the *Metempsychosis*' (2018, 36). Similarly, Abū Zayd writes, 'all the Kings of the *Indies* and of *China* believe the Metempsychosis or Transmigration of Souls, and make it an Article of their Religion' (2018, 69), and illustrates his statement with an anecdote.

Since the writers' emphasis is on social practices, they relate other customs which draw on religious beliefs as well. Discussing the practices of old people in India, Abū Zayd erroneously states that 'it is a customary Thing for Men and Women, of the *Indian* Blood, to desire those of their Family to throw them into the Fire, or drown them, when they are grown old' (2018, 82). The certainty that their souls would migrate to other bodies motivates this act.

The Islamic narrator distinguishes the Arabs from the Indians and the Chinese. As a believer in Islam, Abū Zayd often declares the truth and supremacy of the religion, especially as inspiring morality among the believers. He particularly condemns the immorality of women and speaks of prostitution as an institution in both China and India. Speaking of the customs of the devadasis (he refers to them as '*Women of the Idol*' [2018, 88]) in India, he associates Hindu religious practices with immorality by showing prostitution as prescribed by religion. According to him, the devadasis openly practise prostitution, and 'this Debauchery is made lawful'. He writes: 'She prostitutes herself at a certain rate, and delivers her Gains into the Hands of the Idol's Priest, to be by him disposed of, for the use and Support of the Temple. We praise the Almighty and Glorious God, who hath chosen us to be free from the Sins which defile the Men involved in Infidelity' (Zayd 2018, 88). In Abū Zayd's understanding, the temple thrives on money gained from the prostitution of the devadasis, and this practice is permissible as well as lawful. By contrast, Islam is free from such practices.

Similarly, Abū Zayd also narrates the practices of some Chinese women who do not marry but voluntarily prostitute themselves for pleasure and gain. They declare their intention before the 'commanding Officer of the Garrison in the City', and they are registered as public women by the concerned official, who puts down their particular details (Zayd 2018, 46).

> In the Evening these Women walk abroad in Dresses of different Colours, without any Veil, and prostitute themselves to all new comers that loved Debauchery; but the *Chinese* themselves send for them to their Houses, whence they depart not till the next Morning. Praised be God, who hath rescued us from the like Infamy. (Zayd 2018, 47)

In the text, Islam is characterised by an absence of immorality, which is associated with the Indian and Chinese religions and social customs.

Sometimes, the narrator seeks to differentiate the common practices of the Muslims from those of the Chinese and Indians. To distinguish between the two sets of people and their practices, the author of Book 1 states, 'Neither the one nor the other kill their Meat by cutting the Throat, as do the *Mohammedans*, but by beating them on the Mouth till they die' (2018, 35).

The text disparages the social practices of other lands on some occasions, and, often, all other religions are considered as wanting in comparison with Islam. Mackintosh-Smith argues that the Islamic and Arabic culture is a directing presence in the book: 'It orients the traveller to what he sees, how he sees it, and how he reports it, and the reader to how he receives the report' (2014, 17–18).

However, it would be wrong to say that the narrative is emphatically coloured by the Islamic view of things. On the whole, the form of reportage of social customs and economic and political systems produced by collaborative effort engenders a certain amount of neutrality and demonstrates a secular interest in non-religious activities. The description of activities is often free from any markers of contempt, sarcasm and denunciation. For instance, he does not condemn the Indian practice of ordeal by fire, which proved an accused person's guilt or innocence. The narrator describes how, in a case he had witnessed, the accused man was required to take out a ring from a cauldron of boiling water to prove his innocence. 'I saw one who did this, and receiv'd no manner of Hurt' (Zayd 2018, 31). The accuser 'in this Case' had 'to pay a Man of Gold' (31).

Moreover, sometimes we see a positive assessment of a system, which suggests the narrator's impartial credentials. For instance, the description of the Chinese system of taxation clearly indicates a favourable attitude towards the system:

> They have no Impost upon their Lands, but are subject only to a Poll Tax, which is levied upon Men only, and that, according to their Condition and Capacity. When any *Arabs*, or other Strangers are in this Country, the *Chinese* tax them in proportion to their Substance. When any Dearth makes Necessaries very dear, then does the King open his Storehouses, and sell all Sorts of Provisions much cheaper

> than they are to be had at Market; and hence no Dearth is of any long Continuance among the *Chinese*. (Zayd 2018, 24)

The passage suggests that the ruler is fair and impartial in taxing not only his own people but also foreign merchants, for he taxes them according to their 'Capacity' or 'Substance' (24). Moreover, the ruler makes his storehouse available to all in times of scarcity, selling at a rate much lower than the market price. Therefore, the ruler takes care of his people and ensures that they do not suffer on account of the scarcity of food. This positive assessment is based on shared values of good governance, a sense of justice and a ruler's responsibilities towards subjects. Elsewhere, Abū Zayd praises the Chinese administration of justice, maintaining that they appointed 'Men of Sincerity, zealous in the Cause of Justice' to 'their Tribunals' (2018, 73).

Sometimes, however, the cruelty or negative traits of Indians and Chinese are implicitly condemned. The portrayal of punishment for theft, for instance, suggests a tacit criticism of disproportionate punishment, but there is no overt reference to the superior values inculcated by Islam:

> Theft is always death, as well in the *Indies* as in *China*, whether the Theft be considerable or inconsiderable; and particularly in the *Indies*, where if a Thief has stolen but the value of a small Peice of Money, or a thing of greater worth, they take a long, strong, and sharp Stake, which they apply to his Fundament, and thrust it through, till it comes out at his Neck. (Zayd 2018, 34)

Despite condemnation of practices like prostitution, the travel narrative does not set up alien groups like the Chinese and the Indians in direct opposition to the Arabs, nor does it resort to hierarchical categorisation. The Islamic persona of the authors, although apparent, does not perennially intrude to shape the narrative.

These two medieval travel writings from different sources demonstrate the purposes and the personae of the authors. Yuan Chwang's stable and fixed persona as a Buddhist pilgrim determines the organisation and presentation of his material as well as his tone. The predominance of religious miracles and legends and scholarly interests distinguishes his pilgrimage narrative, although, like the Arabs, he includes ethnographic sketches of people and society also. The many-voiced, oral report of the Arab traders, on the other hand, demonstrates a more secular interest in commerce and ethnography, a fairly neutral perspective in the portrayal of other cultures and an improvisational tone. While the Buddhist pilgrim seeks kinship with the religion of India and demonstrates solidarity with his fellow Buddhists, the Islamic traveller distinguishes his religion from the idolatrous practices of India and China. However, tolerance of diverse cultural practices and the presence of shared values preclude hierarchical categorisation and an oppositional stance.

References

al-Sīrāfī, Abū Zayd. 2014. *Accounts of China and India*, edited and translated by Tim Mackintosh-Smith. In *Two Arabic Travel Books: Accounts of China and India, Mission to the Volga*, edited by Philip F. Kennedy and Shawkat M. Toorawa. New York and London: New York University Press.

Davids, T.W. Rhys. 1904. Preface. In Thomas Watters. *On Yuan Chwang's Travels in India 629-645 A.D.*, edited by T.W. Rhys Davids and S.W. Bushell. London: Royal Asiatic Society.

Elsner, Jas, and Joan-Pau Rubies. 1999. Introduction to *Voyages and Visions: Towards a Cultural History of Travel*, edited by Jas Elsner and Joan-Pau Rubiés, 1–56. London: Reaktion Books.

Mackintosh-Smith, Tim. 2014. Introduction to *Accounts of China and India*, edited and translated by Tim Mackintosh-Smith. *Two Arabic Travel Books: Accounts of China and India, Mission to the Volga*, edited by Philip F. Kennedy and Shawkat M. Toorawa. New York and London: New York University Press.

"Śakra (Buddhism)." Wikipedia. Accessed 2 May 2022. https://en.wikipedia.org/wiki/%C5%9Aakra_(Buddhism)#.

Sīrāfī Abu Zayd Ḥasan Ibn Yazīd. (1733) 2018. *Ancient Accounts of India and China*. New Delhi: Gyan Publishing House.

Tsiang, Hiuen. (1884) 2000. Digitalised 2007. *Si- Yu-Ki: Buddhist Records of the Western World. Translated From the Chinese of Hiuen Tsiang (A.D. 629) by Samuel Beal.* Vol. 2. Abingdon, Oxon: Routledge.

Watters, Thomas. 1904. *On Yuan Chwang's Travels in India 629-645 A.D.*, edited by T.W. Rhys Davids and S.W. Bushell. London: Royal Asiatic Society.

6

In Search of the Buddha in India: *Travelogues of Fuji Nichidatsu, a Buddhist Monk from Japan*[1]

Ranjana Mukhopadhyaya

India, as the birthplace of the Buddha and the land of origin of Buddhism, is a revered place for Buddhists all over the world. Pilgrimage to Buddhist sites in India is a dream cherished by all Buddhists. Buddhist monks, scholars, pilgrims and now tourists from Southeast Asia and East Asia have travelled to India to visit Buddhist sites such as Bodhgaya, Sarnath, Kushinagar, Vaishali and the like. The narrations of their journey to India, whether preserved in folklore, historical records or self-written accounts such as their travelogues, not only describe their visits to the sacred Buddhist sites but also give an account of the topography, history, culture and customs of the people they met and the political situation during their visit to India.

One such traveller from Japan was a Buddhist monk called Nichidatsu Fuji (1885–1985) who belonged to the Nichiren school of Japanese Buddhism and was the founder of a Buddhist organisation called Nipponzan Myohoji. He arrived in India in 1931 and lived there for about seven years. From 1931 to 1938, he travelled to various Buddhist sites in India, Nepal, Sri Lanka and Myanmar. He collected the Buddha's relics, worked for the revival of Buddhism in India and undertook restoration work at Buddhist sites. He met Mohandas Karamchand Gandhi in 1933, becoming one of the few Japanese monks to have done so. Fuji's travel writings show less interest in the sights, customs and culture of the people than in the sacred sites for Buddhist pilgrims. However, his was

1 This chapter is the outcome of the research conducted under the India-Japan Bilateral Joint Research Project Grant of the Indian Council for Historical Research (ICHR) and Japan Society for Promotion of Sciences (JSPS) (2016–2018). The author is thankful to ICHR and JSPS for the research grant.

a pilgrimage with a difference, for his missionary activities were aligned with his political aims. Fuji envisioned a pan-Asian unity achieved by Japanese Buddhism, and he visited India to accomplish this objective. As he was inspired by Nichiren's prophecies, his motivation was essentially religious, but his later experiences made him political.

After the Second World War, Nichidatsu Fuji became a Buddhist peace activist of international repute. He claimed to be guided by the pacifist ideology of Gandhi and the teachings of Nichiren Buddhism. The Buddhist organisation founded by him, Nipponzan Myohoji, spearheads various international peace movements such as anti-nuclear protests and peace marches. However, a little-known fact about this Buddhist organisation is that before the Second World War, Fuji and his disciples served as military chaplains in the Japanese Imperial Army, strongly advocated Japan-centric pan-Asian ideologies and supported the colonial expansion of Japan in Asia. As discussed later in this chapter, Fuji's meeting with Gandhi and his experiences in India were an important factor in the transformation of Fuji and his followers from being supporters of militarism and the war efforts of the imperialistic Japanese State to becoming an ardent advocate of pacifism and non-violence after the Second World War.

Fuji Nichidatsu Writings on India

Fuji's travel diaries and the letters written by him from India to his disciples and associates in Japan are now part of *Fuji Nichidatsu Zenshu* (Collected works of Fuji Nichidatsu) published from 1994 to 1999. This chapter will focus on Fuji's *Seiten Kaikyo Nisshi* (Accounts of preaching in the western heaven), *Busseki Junrei* (Pilgrimages to Buddhist sites) and *Wardha Nikki* (Wardha diaries), which are collections of his writings about his visits to Buddhist sites, missionary activities in India, his interactions with Gandhi in Wardha and, later, the exchange of letters between the two. His autobiography, titled *My Non-Violence: An Autobiography of a Japanese Buddhist,* written along with Tetsuo Yamaori, a Buddhist scholar and writer, gives an account of his experiences in India. The title of his autobiography reveals the significance of his meeting with Gandhi and the profound impact that it had on his life and his future missionary and peace activities. In addition to these, Fuji has written in the periodicals published by his organisation, such as *Tenku* and *Sarvodaya*. Fuji's letters, accounts of his travels to India before and after the Second World War and India's Independence, and lectures that he delivered during these visits to India have been extensively published in Japanese as well as translated into

English, such as *Waga Seiten Kaikyo* (My proselytisation in the Western heaven) and *Dokku* (Poisonous drum) in Japanese or *Buddhism for World Peace*, *Tranquil in this Realm of Mine* and others in English.

This chapter focuses on Fuji Nichidatsu's writings and tries to examine the significance of 'India' in the world view of Japanese Buddhists. Their construction of India derives from readings of Buddhist texts and visits to pilgrimage sites and is found in their travelogues and letters.

Fuji Nichidatsu's Life and Faith

Fuji was born on 6 August 1885 in the Kumamoto prefecture of Kyushu, the southern island of Japan. In 1903, at the age of eighteen, he became a monk of the Nichiren school of Japanese Buddhism. Fuji displayed fanatical faith in the teachings of the *Lotus Sūtra* and the prophecies of Nichiren, the 13th-century prophetic Buddhist monk and the founder of his sect. As discussed later, Fuji's overseas missionary activities, especially his strong desire to travel to India and to preach and revive Buddhism in India, were motivated by Nichiren's prophecies.

Nichiren Buddhism preaches absolute faith in the *Lotus Sūtra*, the main text of this sect. Nichiren, the founder, prophesied the advent of *Mappo* or the 'Age of Dharma Decline' based on his reading of the *Lotus Sūtra*. The complete degeneration of 'true dharma' or the teachings of Buddhism, resulting in political unrest and natural calamities, is predicted in this scripture. The prophesies and the writings of Nichiren extrapolating them are equally important teachings of this sect. One of Nichiren's major works is *Rissho Ankoku-ron* (Treaties for Righteous Teaching to Safeguard the Nation), in which he predicted the occurrence of natural calamities, epidemics, internal conflicts and civil wars. He perceived these events as signs of 'national crisis' (*kokunan*) that would afflict Japan. In this work, Nichiren 'admonishes the ruler', referred to as *Kokushu Kangyo,* for the country's misfortunes and holds him responsible for the protection of the nation. He preaches that the ruler should believe in 'true dharma', the *Lotus Sūtra*, to avert disasters and protect the nation. Therefore, preaching the *Lotus Sūtra* to the political authority and converting them into believers was the mission of a Nichiren follower. Fuji's purpose of meeting Gandhi, the leader of India's independence movement against British colonial rule, was motivated by this teaching of Nichiren.

Seiten-Kaikyo: 'Propagating the Dharma in Western Heaven'

Another major prophecy of Nichiren was that during the era of *Mappo*, Buddhism would return to its place of origin, India. In '*Kangyo Hachiman-*

sho' (*Admonishing of Hanchiman*), Nichiren writes that as the sun rises in the east and goes to the west, in the age of *Mappo*, Buddhism would go from Japan to India. Nichiren prophesies:

> The moon goes from west to east — a sign that the Buddhism of *Gasshi-koku* [Land of the Moon, referring to India] must progress eastwards. The sun rises in the east, signifying that the Buddha Dharma of *Fuso-koku* [Land of the Sun, that is, Japan] must return to India.... The light of the sun is brighter than that of the moon, signifying the illumining of the long darkness of the fifth [period of] 500 years [the beginning of the Age of Dharma Decline or Mappo]. (Nichiren 2003, 257–280)

In Nipponzan Myohoji, this return of Buddhism to India signified westward (from Japan) propagation of dharma and, therefore, is referred to as *Seiten-Kaikyo*, that is, 'propagating the dharma in the western heaven' where Seiten or 'western heaven' refers to India.

In his prophecies, Nichiren not only predicts the global spread of 'Buddhism of the Land of the Sun' but also preaches the superiority of Japanese Buddhism over Buddhism as practised in other countries, including India. Inspired by these prophecies of Nichiren, Fuji embarked on his overseas missionary activities to propagate Japanese Buddhism, that is, Nichiren Buddhism, in the Asian continent and India. Fuji's missionary zeal came from a sense of cultural and spiritual superiority that he derived from Nichiren's teachings, which placed Japanese Buddhism and the teachings of the *Lotus Sūtra* above all other doctrines or schools of Buddhism.

Fuji writes in 1930 before embarking on his voyage to India:

> I desire to take the initiative in realizing the auspicious omen of the Buddhism of Japan returning to the Western Heavens (*seiten*), India, as it is prophesied. I desire to regenerate the spiritual civilization of Asia, the Orient, and subdue the sixty two kinds of people with false views. [referring to sixty-two non-Buddhist schools of philosophy in India at the time of Buddha] I desire to deliver equally all humanity from the murderous civilization of the Europe and United States *asuras*, the inferno of confusion consolidated with strife. Follow me, one after another, to beat the *dokku* (poisonous drum) at the Himalayas, and let the rain of the dharma pour into the stream of the Ganga. If this dharma does not return to the Western Heaven, the prophecy of our great master (Nichiren) shall become falsehood. (Fuji 1997a, 38–39)

Fuji's criticism of Western civilisation, especially capitalism and modern materialism, became even more pronounced after his visit to

India, especially after his interaction with M.K. Gandhi, who was then spearheading the struggle against the British (Western) imperialism in India.

In 1917, at the age of thirty-three, Fuji set out on an overseas propagation of faith to China, with India as the final destination. The first temple of Nipponzan Myohoji was established in Liaoyang in Manchuria (China) in 1918 and then subsequently in Dalian, Tianjin and other places. Fuji planned to expand his missionary activities to Russia also, but when he heard of the Great Kanto Earthquake (1923), he perceived it as a 'national crisis'. He immediately returned to Japan and began his missionary activities there.

After the demise of his mother in 1930, Fuji decided to re-embark on his foreign mission. On 1 September 1930, he set sail from the Kobe port in Japan. On the way to India, he stopped at Dalian, Tianjin, Shanghai and other places in mainland China for his missionary activities. Finally, via Hong Kong, Singapore and Burma (Myanmar), Fuji reached India on 16 January 1931, landing at the Calcutta (Kolkata) port.

Fuji in India (1931–1938): Pilgrimage to Buddhist Sites

Like any other Buddhist pilgrim visiting India, Fuji, too, set out on a pilgrimage to various Buddhist sites in India such as Rajgir, Bodhgaya, Sarnath, Kushinagar and Lumbini. *Busseki Junrei* (Pilgrimage to Buddhist sites) is a collection of his travel diaries and letters that tells us about Fuji's travel itineraries, journey routes and his experiences of visiting the Buddhist places in India. On 10 February 1931, Fuji departed from Howrah station of Calcutta, and obviously, Rajgir was the first Buddhist site that he visited. At Rajgir, sitting on top of a rocky mountain called Vulture Peak (*Gadhrakuta*), Shakyamuni Buddha is said to have preached the *Lotus Sūtra*, the principal scripture of the Nichiren sect. In his first round of trips to the Buddhist sacred sites, he covered all of them within a week, starting from Rajgir and proceeding to Bodhgaya, Sarnath and Kushinagar. He then crossed over to Nepal to visit Lumbini. Fuji planned his trip to Buddhist sites keeping in mind the important dates in the Buddhist calendar; for instance, he reached Kushinagar, the place where the Buddha died, on 15 February, the day of the Buddha's nirvana. Similarly, later when he visited Lumbini, he chose to be there on the day (8 April 1931) observed as the Buddha's birthday in Japan.

Fuji went on pilgrimage to the Buddhist sites in India as a devout follower of Buddhism and maintained his distance from Japanese tourists who came to India on group tours organised by travel companies for pleasure trips to the sites. As a zealous missionary, he distinguished himself from the tourist. It was not curiosity for places of interest that inspired his travels. Nor was he interested in the archaeological or architectural significance of these Buddhist sites as he showed no interest in the excavations going on at the time. The imagery of these sites, as described in the Buddhist scriptures, was important for Fuji.

> As formally seen in the text of the *Tripitika*, the places of birth, death, nirvana, meditation, and preaching of Shakyamuni Buddha, which I visited by beating the drums and chanting the *Lotus Sūtra*, I uphold the grandeur and the solemnity of the gathering of the Buddha's disciples, revered Bodhisattvas and the Arahats at these places. That is the image and joyous feeling that I really want to seek from my pilgrimage. (Fuji 1997b, 10)

Fuji was also critical of Japanese monks and Buddhist scholars who had visited India for scholarly pursuits such as searching for Buddhist scriptures and to learn Sanskrit or Pali. His writings show him as a devout Buddhist on a mission to revive Buddhism in India by preaching and propagating Japanese Buddhism. In most Buddhist sites, Fuji stayed in the guesthouses run by Ceylonese (Sri Lankan) or Burmese (Myanmar) monks and admired them for constructing temples and lodges for pilgrims and safeguarding the sacred sites in a foreign land far away from their countries. He felt ashamed that he could not find a single monk or layperson from Japan who, despite seeing the devastated ruins of the Buddhist sites, had attempted to restore these sites. The persona of the missionary distinguishes him from the other Japanese.

While visiting Bodhgaya on 13 February 1931, he mentions in his diary the struggle between the Hindu mahants (priests) and the Buddhists over the management of the Mahabodhi Temple and the support given by Japanese Buddhists to Indian and Sri Lankan Buddhists in their attempts to regain control of this temple complex. He writes,

> The Mahabodhi temple is being controlled by the Hindu *mahants*. It should obviously be controlled by the Buddhists as written by many Japanese. But in this place, where is the Buddha Dharma? Only the Great Tower [referring to the pinnacle of the Mahabodhi temple] remains. Where are the Buddhists who can maintain this place? The same could be said for the Lumbini Garden in Nepal, which is also controlled by the Hindus there. Till there is Dharma prevalent in these places, even if there is Buddha statue or temple, it is like a carcass. (Fuji 1997b, 50)

As a zealous missionary, he criticises even those Buddhists who had visited India earlier but did not do enough for to restore Buddhist sites.

Fuji's travel to India was almost self-funded. Unlike other Japanese Buddhist monks who had visited India at this time, he was not officially dispatched by the headquarters of the Nichiren sect to visit India. Therefore, he got no support or sponsorship from his sect or temple in Japan. He travelled in India on a shoestring budget and was very thrifty in spending money. He writes that in order to save money, he would walk wherever it was possible, rather than renting a vehicle. Despite not knowing the local languages and the difficulty in locating the Buddhist sites, which were in dilapidated conditions, isolated and relatively less visited by tourists at the time of Fuji's visits to these places, he travelled alone to these Buddhist sites as he did not have money to hire local people as guides. In some places, he did not even get a porter and carried his luggage on his back. As stated earlier, Fuji stayed in guesthouses run by foreign monks, free of cost or by offering nominal donations. In his autobiography, *My Non-Violence*, Fuji narrates,

> When I landed at Calcutta, I was in such poor health that I weighed less than one hundred pounds. I thought my days were numbered. Wishing to die in India if I had to in the immediate future and to have my ashes buried in the Lumbini-Garden where Shakyamuni was born, I planned to go on a pilgrimage to this sacred place in Buddhism. But the journey was difficult. I had to ride on oxcart through paddies and roadless fields. When crossing streams, the oxcart was sometimes all but carried away. The holy place was so inaccessible that it took me another overnight oxcart ride after getting off the train at the nearest station. (Fuji 1972, 68)

Besides the arduousness of his journey, Fuji's travel diaries also mention the cultural shocks and other problems that foreign tourists in India usually face. While Fuji's inability to communicate well in English or Hindi was a major handicap for him, it was the behaviour of the local people, which he perceived as being devious and uncivil, that troubled him even more. He writes about being cheated of his money by tour guides and lodge owners, arguing with porters in the railway station for overcharging him, being misled by people posing as local guides, being accosted by street children begging for money, not finding a proper place to stay and so on. Fuji regretted that even in sacred places associated with the Buddha, contrary to his expectations of meeting pure-hearted people, he was duped or mistreated by the local people. These unpleasant experiences led him to question the ethical standards of Indian people. In his travel diaries, Fuji laments that Indians were driven by greed, which had made them morally degraded. Even for petty benefits or financial gains, they could stray away from the path of morality, betray their country or even kill their brethren. He saw the low ethical standards of Indians as signs of *Mappo*. Moreover, he attributes this moral degradation of Indians and their greed for money to the monetised, capitalistic economic system that was introduced in India by the British colonisers. This system, according to Fuji, had led the Indians to seek monetary benefits in their dealings with other people. Unlike the Western colonisers who construct the Indians in opposition to their Selves, as an Asian and a Buddhist, Fuji attributes the negative aspects of Indians to the incursion of Western values and the decline of the true religion of Buddhism. The binary that he constructs is ultimately between the West and the East and not between India and Japan. He states that the only way Indians could be made to give up their greed was not by imposing stricter laws but through inner spiritual development, which was only possible through the revival of Buddhism in India (Fuji 1997b, 100–101). Thus, Fuji associated his mission to revive Buddhism in India with the spiritual upliftment of the people here. His condemnation of Western colonialism and capitalism, which he held responsible for the decline of India and the rest of Asia, remained a persistent theme in his writings.

In *Busseki Junrei*, Fuji writes:

> Buddhism has declined in India and has degraded and become ineffective in China. Japan is the only place in Asia where Buddhism had reached its peak and is still flourishing. As a person born in Japan, I will have to strive hard to revive Buddhism in India, for the sake of the unity and prosperity of Asian fellowmen. (Fuji 1997b, 10–11)

He also laments the conditions prevalent in colonised India.

> In India, the period of true dharma is over, and the India which was the cradle of civilization, land of sages who have given profound philosophies to mankind, is now a land of poor and deprived people who are now politically controlled by a foreign race. (Fuji 1997b, 10–11)

Since Fuji associated the decline of Buddhism in India with the colonisation of Asia by Western powers, he believed that the revival of Buddhism was indispensable for the freedom of India. Therefore, the restoration of the Buddhist sacred sites in India, which he found in a dilapidated state, became an integral part of his seiten-kaikyo mission, that is, his vow to revive Buddhism in India. Fuji sees the decline of Buddhism and the colonisation of Asia by Western powers as signs of *Mappo* and emphasised the role of Japanese Buddhism in restoring both Buddhism and Asian nations to their former stature of glory. These were also dominant themes in the discourses on nationalism and pan-Asianism by Japanese Buddhists prior to the Second World War.

Fuji was disillusioned by his visits to dilapidated Buddhist sites, which were difficult to access. He also did not find any significant religious zeal in these sacred sites. Fuji had enthusiastically planned his visit to Lumbini in Nepal on the day of the birth of Lord Buddha, which is observed in Japan with great fervour as *Hana-matsuri* (flower festival). However, when he arrived at the Queen Mahamaya Temple in the Lumbini Garden, the site of the Buddha's birth, he was disappointed to see that no ceremony was being held there to observe this important religious day. The temple was surrounded by wilderness and farmlands with cattle grazing around it. Fuji says that he alone went round the temple, beating his handheld drum and chanting the *Lotus Sūtra*. The pond near the sacred tree in the Lumbini Garden, where Queen Mahamaya had given birth to Prince Siddhartha, had completely dried up. Fuji believes that when Buddhism is revived here, 'pure water, melted from the snow would spring up again' in this pond and wishes for it earnestly (1997b, 106). The diary entry, dated 16 April 1933, mentions a letter he had handed over to the Japanese consulate in Calcutta to pass on to the Nepalese government. In the letter, he had urged the latter to take up the restoration of Queen Mahamaya Temple and the Lumbini Garden, offering to donate money and raise funds from the Japanese living in India and disciples and monks in Japan. He had also suggested that if the Nepalese government was unable to take up the restoration work of Lumbini, they should handover the Lumbini Garden and the Mahamaya Temple to the Japanese Buddhists who were willing to restore and maintain this holy Buddhist site (119–120).

While Fuji was opposed to the idea of visiting the Buddhist sites for touristic pleasure, he considered it necessary to develop these sites to make them more accessible to Buddhist visitors from Japan 'for the future destiny of Japan and for the revival of India's future which is also related to the future of Eastern people' (Fuji 1997b, 11). Fuji insisted that it was a responsibility and obligation that Japan could not shun because it was a repayment of the debt to Buddhism, which had contributed to the development of Japanese civilisation for over three hundred thousand years. He says that the development of Buddhist sites 'holds the secret keys to solving the problems of Asia later after one hundred years' (Fuji 1997b, 8–9). He also called upon the Indo-Japanese Association (*Nichi-in Kyokai*) and the shipping and trading companies that were doing business in India to support the restoration and development of the Buddhist sites, urging the companies to waive or reduce the cost of transportation for Buddhist pilgrims from Japan to India (Fuji 1997b, 8–9).

Besides the restoration of Buddhist sites in India and Nepal, Fuji also aimed to construct a temple of Nipponzan Myohoji in India. From May 1932, he had started preaching from a makeshift hut-like temple built on the Japanese cremation grounds in Mumbai. In building the first temple of Nipponzan Myohoji in Calcutta (1935), Fuji received unexpected support from a non-Buddhist — Jugal Kishore Birla, noted industrialist, philanthropist and supporter of Indian philosophy, whose family had built large Hindu temples. Birla was willing to provide funds for building a Buddhist temple. In his diary, dated 13 December 1933, Fuji writes about his meeting with Birla and his generous donation:

> The Tataghata has indeed dispatched his messengers as well as men and women of pure faith for the sake of the revival of Indian civilization and Buddhism of Japan to return to the Western Heaven. Those who do the Buddha work are not necessarily Japanese or acquaintances. Only those who believe and receive, as well as those who can perceive the orders of the World Honored One, the Tataghata, can achieve the Buddha work. (1997a, 77–78)

These remarks show a tolerant Fuji discovering affinity with non-Buddhists among Indians who aid the spread of Buddhism.

Fuji's travels to Sri Lanka (1933) and Myanmar (Burma; 1934) resulted in his collection of Buddhist relics. He is overjoyed and feels assured of his special role:

> The attainment of my *seiten-kaikyo* has indeed been assured by the sovereign and transcendent power of the various buddhas that protect. It has now become sure that the dharma shall return to the homeland of Sakyamuni Buddha's teachings, India. Through the manifestation of a marvelous phenomenon, he proved that I shall be the messenger of the Tataghata sent by him. (Fuji 1997a, 73)

Fashioning himself as a man with a mission, Fuji aims at the triumph of Japanese Buddhism in India and a strong link of religion tying the two countries. Later, these relics played a significant role in Fuji's military chaplaincy during the Second World War. Fuji presented these relics of the Buddha to military leaders who were serving in China and Korea and urged them to build stupas to enshrine these relics.

Meeting with Gandhi: 'Wardha Diary'

The turning point in Fuji's life and his missionary activities in India was his meeting with M.K. Gandhi. Fuji met Gandhi on 4 October 1933 in Sevagram Ashram, a hermitage in the small town of Wardha (located in the state of Maharashtra in western India), where Gandhi had shifted after his release from the Pune jail. He had been arrested for organising the Dandi March (from 12 March to 6 April 1930) against the monopolistic salt laws of the British government.

Fuji's meeting with Gandhi has been recounted in his 'Wardha Diary' ('Wardha Nikki'). His disciple Okitsu Tadao had sought an appointment for a meeting with Gandhi. Finally, on 2 October, Fuji received a letter from Gandhi informing him that he could meet them on 4 October at 4 pm for only 15 minutes. Fuji was keen to meet Gandhi to impress upon the latter his mission to revive Buddhism in India. 'I shall meet him [Gandhi] as the representative of the Indian people who are the descendants of the Buddha. Being a messenger of Japanese Buddhism, I shall fulfill a part of my mission, my mission which must be revealed to the Indian people' (Fuji 1997a, 46). On the morning of 4 October 1933, Fuji arrived in Wardha with his disciple Okitsu, who also served as his interpreter as he could speak English and a little Hindi. At the time of their appointment, they were ushered into a room where Gandhi was sitting surrounded by people and spinning cotton yarn with his charkha (a type of spinning wheel). Okitsu introduced Fuji and gave Gandhi a box of Japanese rice crackers and a round fan. Fuji writes that while receiving these gifts, Gandhi sceptically asked them whether Japan wanted to 'conquer' India using goods and merchandise. Okitsu replied that since they were monks, they knew nothing about business and that these gifts were not samples of Japanese merchandise but tokens of their gratitude. Fuji feels that Gandhi was sceptical of Japanese goods because the British colonised India by trade. Gandhi enquired whether Fuji could speak English and if he had learnt Sanskrit or Pali as other Buddhist scholars usually did. Okitsu replied that Fuji had studied Buddhism only in Japanese and had not learnt Pali or Sanskrit as he was not an academician or a scholar but a religious practitioner. Gandhi then recommended that Fuji study Hindi so that they could speak to each other.

Gandhi asked about the hand drums that Fuji was carrying with him and when he was told by Okitsu that it was a tradition of the Nichiren school of Japanese Buddhism to beat this kind of drum, he also enquired about their sect. Okitsu spoke to Gandhi during this 20-minute interview while Fuji chanted the *Lotus Sūtra*. Fuji describes his emotions during this first meeting with Gandhi:

> During all this time, I had my hands clasped together in a prayer with my eyes closed, thanking this utmost valuable and rare opportunity. Rather than expecting to get something out of the conversation, I wished to grasp Gandhi-ji himself by this meeting. I did not intend to hear any opinion, nor did I wish to make him understand any of my views. (Fuji 1997a, 53)

Later in the evening, both Fuji and Okitsu joined Gandhi in a prayer meeting held in the ashram.

As Fuji could not converse with Gandhi due to linguistic barriers, he decided to write a letter to him. The letter, titled a 'Letter to Gandhi' (dated 4 October) and written in Japanese, was translated into English by Okitsu with the help of the secretary of Jamnalal Bajaj, industrialist and follower of Gandhi, and handed over to Gandhi on 7 October.[2]

Fuji begins the letter by emphasising the Buddhist linkages between India and Japan and the contribution of Buddhism transmitted from India towards the civilisational and spiritual development of Japan. Fuji writes, 'Indian Buddhism is the womb of the civilization of Japanese people' (1998, 132). However, he then expresses his disappointment about the decline of Buddhism in India. He regrets that he has not come across any Buddhist in India in his three years of stay, and he sometimes wonders if it is the same India about which he has read in Buddhist scriptures.

In this letter, Fuji also touches upon the Manchuria Incident and the condemnation that Japan had to face from the international community, including India, due to its military aggression in China and its subsequent departure from the League of Nations. Fuji defends the creation of Manchukoku as Japan's efforts to 'spread its religious and civilization benefits to Asia as envisioned in Nichiren's prophecy' (1998, 133). According to Fuji, the real intention behind the Japanese invasion of Asia was to spread the 'enlightenment of Buddha and create a Pure land or Buddha-land in this World' (133). He argues that India and other countries failed to understand the true form of Buddhism that was followed in Japan (133).

Fuji quotes from a book written by Gandhi where the latter had apparently stated that there cannot be true patriotism without religious faith. Fuji asserts that Japan's militarism was an expression of its patriotism, and for Japanese people, patriotism had become a form of religious faith. He appeals to the Buddhist connections between India and Japan for dispelling the misconceptions of Japan and for deepening

2 Only the Japanese version of this letter remains, which is included in 'Wardha Diary' in Fuji (1998, 132–140).

the mutual understanding between the two countries. Fuji explains that his purpose in visiting India was 'to reveal the truth of Japan to the people of India by spreading Japanese Buddhism in India' (Fuji 1998, 133–135). He conveys to Gandhi the prophecies of Nichiren regarding Buddhism returning to its place of origin and his teachings that advised the following of the true dharma for the deliverance of the nation and its people from their sufferings. He ends his letter by reiterating his resolve to revive Buddhism in India and offers himself for this mission, even if it required spending his life in India. (Fuji 1998, 132–140)

The obvious intention of Fuji's letter to Gandhi was to convey to him his purpose of coming to India and to receive his understanding and support for his missionary activities in India. However, Fuji, eager to change Gandhi's attitude towards Japan, is evidently trying to convince him about the righteousness of Japan's military campaigns in Asia by giving a Buddhist explanation for Japanese aggression.

Gandhi's reply to Fuji's letter was published in the *Hindu* on 12 October 1933. Avoiding any reference to the Manchuria Incident or Japan's colonial expansion in Asia, Gandhi writes that Buddhism has been incorporated into Hinduism and preserved in India in its purest form, while it has deteriorated in countries where it was adopted. He advises Fuji to study Sanskrit and Pali to enhance his knowledge of Buddhism and to learn the language of the locals, Hindi, to carry out religious activities in India. Finally, Gandhi emphasises that religious revival can best be done through daily life practice of religion (1973, 56). In this way, Gandhi expresses a subtle disapproval of Fuji's mission to revive Buddhism in India and his attempt to justify Japan's militarism.

However, 8 October 1933, the day Fuji and Okitsu went to collect their letter from Gandhi, became a momentous day in Fuji's mission of seiten-kaikyo. Gandhi had displayed a keen interest in Fuji's handheld drum, called taiko in Japanese and also referred to as 'celestial drums' (*tenko*) in the Nichiren sect. Whenever Fuji and his disciple came to meet Gandhi, they would enter the ashram beating the drums and chanting the *Lotus Sūtra*. Gandhi told Fuji that he liked the sound of his drums and asked him to come back again and beat the drums in the ashram. Fuji quotes Gandhi as saying, 'It has become a pleasure of mine to hear your courageous drum beat every day at 4:00. I also like the sound of the drum' (Fuji 1997a, 62). Okitsu presented a drum to Gandhi. Gandhi took the drum and started beating it. He also chanted the *Odiamoku* (the title words of the *Lotus Sūtra*), repeating after Fuji. Fuji saw this gesture of Gandhi as an accomplishment of his mission of seiten-Kaikyo. He writes:

> At last Nipponzan's *Gyakku-Senryo* [practice of beating the drum and chanting the Lotus Sutra] has received the good friendship, echo and joy extended by the great leader of the Indian independence movement, the single sage of today, and the very representative of the Indian nation, the descendent of Sakyamuni Buddha. Ah…my genuine vow of Saiten-Kaikyo has finally found its time. The voice of the 300 million people rejoicing the sound of Dharma was now heard through the melting voice of joy that passed Gandhi-ji's lips here at the ashram of Wardha. (Fuji 1997a, 61)

Fuji writes that while Gandhi was sceptical about gifts from Japan, he had readily accepted a religion of Japan. This chanting of the *Lotus Sūtra* and beating of drums by Gandhi was also seen by Fuji as *Kokushu Kangyo*, that is, converting the ruler to 'true dharma'. Fuji believed that the acceptance of the *Lotus Sūtra* by Gandhi would pave the way for India's independence. Fuji writes in his *Wardha Diary*:

> Today was the day we presented the Dharma-drum to Gandhi-ji. Today was the day we beat the great Dharma-drum on Gandhi-ji's stage. Today was the day the *Tenku* (celestial drum) in prayer for *Rissho-ankoku* presented from Japan resounded itself in the Indian independence movement. From now on, *Seiten-kaikyo* will be as today's extension. Indeed, today was the day of '*shinsui-shogo*' (awaken from delusion and seek for the father, the Buddha) for the Indian nation. The deep darkness of night that had long covered the Indian sky shall now begin to clear. (1997a, 65)

Wishing to stay in close proximity to Gandhi, Fuji, who was staying in the residence of Jamnalal Bajaj, sought Gandhi's permission for staying in the ashram. Gandhi agreed, on the condition that he had to follow the rules of the ashram and also learn Hindi and Sanskrit. Fuji asked permission to use the drum to chant the sūtras during his stay in the ashram. Gandhi not only agreed but also said that he would join him in beating the drums (Fuji 1998, 39–46).

The diary entries of the two months of Fuji's stay in Wardha reveal how he settles down in the ashram and adapts to the monastic-like, disciplined lifestyle of other ashram inmates. His religious practice of beating the drum and chanting the *Lotus Sūtra* becomes an integral part of the morning and evening prayers of the ashram. On 14 November, Fuji writes that Gandhi left the ashram and set out on his nationwide movement for the Harijans (term used by Gandhi to refer to the untouchables in India) by beating the dharma drums, and Fuji saw him off at the gates of the ashram by beating his drums (Fuji 1998, 84–86).

Fuji also learns to spin cotton yarn with the charkha. Fuji was amazed that in an age when nations were fighting with modern machinery and armaments, Gandhi was determined to carry out his struggle against British imperialism through non-violent means and by advocating economic self-reliance symbolically represented by the spinning of the charkha. In his diary entry dated 17 October, Fuji compares Gandhi's spinning of the charkha to the Buddhist parable of Prince Nose's (previous life incarnation of the Buddha) devoted act of drawing water from the ocean with a shell to retrieve the magical pearl from the *Nagaloka* (dragon palace) (1997a, 68–69). He writes: 'When India's independence is spun out from this spinning wheel, I must awaken to its power which is beyond thought or discussion, for this spinning wheel would be a far greater miracle than that of today's spinning machine. This is the secret of Gandhi-ji's enlightenment' (69). Fuji's anti-materialistic and anti-capitalist views were further strengthened by his observation of the frugal lifestyles of the ashram inmates.

As promised to Gandhi, Fuji started learning Hindi. He wrote his first letter in Hindi and presented it to Gandhi on 7 November, along with bundles of cotton yarn that he had spun with the charkha in the ashram. He received a reply from Gandhi, also in Hindi, on 29 November, appreciating Fuji's efforts (Fuji 1998, 77–78, 103–104).

On 10 December, Fuji left Wardha for Calcutta to meet Jugal Kishore Birla and undertake the construction of his first temple in India. Gandhi's letter of 11 December 1933, written in Hindi to Fuji after he had left Wardha, urges him to return to Wardha and continue with his study of Hindi. Gandhi wrote that he longed for the sound of Fuji's drums and that he should always consider the ashram as his home (Fuji 1998, 1). Despite their differences of opinion regarding Japan's imperialistic expansion in Asia, Gandhi had high regard for Fuji as a devout, religious man.

Fuji's Religious Nationalism and Buddhist Pan-Asianism

After Fuji returned to Japan in 1938 and the outbreak of the second Sino-Japanese War (1937–1945) (which Fuji saw as a national calamity), he continued to exchange letters with Gandhi. He sent his disciples to Wardha. They resided in the ashram, and through them, Fuji continued to communicate with Gandhi. That the interaction between Fuji and Gandhi was a meeting between two great pacifists of Asia is a popular misconception. A study of the letters that were exchanged between Fuji and Gandhi reveals their differences of opinion about imperialism, freedom and the future of Asia, which became even wider after the outbreak of the second Sino-Japanese War.

Fuji represented a form of pre-war Buddhist nationalism in Japan, referred to as *Nichirenshugi* or 'Nichirenism', based on combining faith in the *Lotus Sūtra* with emperor worship (the belief that Japanese emperorship is a sacred entity). This idea was at the core of the nationalistic ideologies prevalent in Japan during the World Wars. The fusion of nationalistic and Buddhist teachings helped Japanese Buddhists develop an ethnocentric nationalistic narrative that not only gave religious legitimacy to the militarism and ultra-nationalism of the Japanese State and its people but was also used by Buddhist monks to justify their involvement in the war of the Japanese State during the Second World War. Therefore, despite Fuji's close interactions with Gandhi and his support for India's freedom struggle, his Japan-centric ethnonationalism remained unaltered as it was based on a world view derived from such Buddhist nationalistic ideologies. This world view prompted Fuji and his disciples to join the Japanese army as military chaplains during the Second World War. They were involved in the military campaigns of the Japanese army in Burma, Manchuria and other places in Asia (Mukhopadhyaya 2010, 388–399).

According to Tetsuo Yamaori, Fuji's support for Japanese imperialism and militarism could be attributed to his visions of Buddhist pan-Asianism, which was created out of his understanding of Nichiren Buddhism that preached the supremacy of its teachings over all others and also emphasised Japan's role in spreading the 'true dharma' and creating Buddha-land in this world. Moreover, anti-Western thoughts and anti-capitalism were at the core of Fuji's pan-Asianism. Therefore, paradoxically, Fuji was able to justify Japan's colonial expansion in Asia on the one hand and support Gandhi and India's freedom movement against British colonialism on the other (Yamaori 1973, 4–10).

Fuji's Post-war Pacifist Transformation

Drawing on their association with Gandhi, Fuji and his disciples transformed themselves to become staunch believers in 'absolute non-violence' after Japan's defeat in the Second World War. The promotion of *sekai heiwa* (world peace) became a major slogan in the post-war transformation of Nipponzan Myohoji. The two major peace activities of present-day Nipponzan Myohoji are peace walks and the construction of peace pagodas (Shanti stupa/*Heiwa-to*) as symbols of peace in different places in the world. Nipponzan Myohoji's peace walk combines the tradition of *Angyo* (walking while chanting and beating the drums) of the Nichiren sect and Gandhian principles of non-violence and pacifism (Mukhopadhyaya 2014, 358–362).

In 1953, Fuji received the Buddha's relic from the first prime minister of India, Jawaharlal Nehru, which led to the construction of peace pagodas by Nipponzan Myohoji in Japan, India, Sri Lanka, Nepal, the United Kingdom, the United States of America and various other places in the world. In his autobiography, *My Non-Violence,* Fuji writes that he was invited to the Buddha Jayanti festival in 1959, organised by the Indian government to commemorate the 2500 years of the nirvana of the Buddha. After this event, a committee for the restoration of Buddhist sites was set up by Nehru with himself as its chairperson. Fuji was invited to this committee and got involved in the construction of the peace pagoda. In 1969, the work was completed, thus marking the success of Fuji's seiten-kaikyo in India. Later, he was also involved in the construction of a peace pagoda in Kalinga in Orissa (Fuji 1972, 97–117).

In his speech on 19 January 1979, on receiving the Jawaharlal Nehru Award for International Understanding, Fuji talks about his mission of revival of Buddhism in India, which had remained unchanged over the years:

> The revival of Buddhism will not remain merely a spiritual movement within India which is requisite to establishment of a peaceful nation, it is also the most indispensable spiritual movement in order to create universal peace in today's world.… The reason for reviving Buddhism in India and disseminating Buddhism to the whole world is to bestow the seal of fearlessness to all the living creatures who are exposed to the menace of the murder machines, weapons of destruction which possess the capacity to over-kill the humankind of this saha-world. (1997a, 34)

Evidently, anti-capitalism and anti-materialism and, therefore, anti-Western ideology remained ingrained even in Fuji's post-war pacifist ideology.

Conclusion

Fuji's travel diaries and writings about his pilgrimage to India should be read in the context of the geopolitical dynamics of Asia in the 20th century. The opening up of Japan to foreign diplomacy and trade after the Meiji Restoration (1868), Japan's victories in the first Sino-Japanese War (1894–1895) and Russo-Japanese War (1904–1905) that led to the increase in its political and military might in Asia and its colonial control over various parts of the Asian continent facilitated overseas travels by Buddhists from Japan to different countries in Asia to proselytise their brand of Japanese Buddhism. The mention of Japanese shipping or cotton companies doing business in India in Fuji's diaries and his close interaction with prominent Indian industrialists like Bajaj and Birla indicate their role in Fuji's missionary activities in India.

Fuji's vision of Buddhist revivalism and his post-war pacifism bear the imprint of the dominant political ideologies and intellectual currents of his time. As stated earlier, Fuji's mission to revive Buddhism in India not only reflected his sense of religious superiority derived from the prophecies of Nichiren but also revealed a Japan-centric pan-Asianism, a prominent ideology among wartime Japanese intellectuals. Before the Second World War, the Japanese idea of pan-Asianism, which called for unity among Asian countries against Western imperialism, bestowed upon Japan a prominent role in Asia by virtue of its economic and political prowess. However, after its defeat in the Second World War, when Japan denounced militarism and adopted a pacifist constitution renouncing its sovereign right to wage war, Fuji, too, became a strong advocate of pacifism. His post-war pacifism combined Buddhist teachings of ahimsa (non-violence) with new interpretations of the teachings of Nichiren Buddhism and adopted the Gandhian method of non-violent resistance in his anti-war peace movements.

References

Fuji, Nichidatsu. 1972. *My Non-Violence*. Edited and translated by Tetsuo Yamaori. Tokyo: Shunjusha.

———. 1994–1999. *Fuji Nichidatsu Shonin Zenshu* [*Collected works of Reverend Fuji Nichidatsu*]. 10 vols. Tokyo: Jyobunkan, Tokyo.

———. 1996. *Seiten Kaikyo Nisshi* [Accounts of preaching in the Western paradise]. In *Collected Works of Reverend Fuji Nichidatsu*]. Vol. 3. Tokyo: Jyobunkan.

———. 1997a. *Buddhism for World Peace*. Translated by Yumiko Miyazaki. New Delhi: Sterling Publishers Pvt. Ltd.

———. 1997b. *Busseki Junrei* [(Pilgrimage to Buddhist sites)]. In *Collected Works of Reverend Fuji Nichidatsu*. Vol. 4. Tokyo: Jyobunkan.

———. 1998. *Wardha Nikki* [Wardha diary]. In *Collected Works of Reverend Fuji Nichidatsu*. Vol. 5. Tokyo: Jyobunkan.

Gandhi, Mohandas Karamchand. 1973. 'Advice to Japanese Buddhist Priests'. *Hindu*; 12 October 1933. In *Collected Works of Mahatma Gandhi*. Vol. LVI. New Delhi: The Publication Division, Ministry of Information and Broadcasting, Government of India.

Mukhopadhyaya, Ranjana. 2010. 'Fuji Nichidatsu: Seiten [Indo] Kaikyo no Taiken' ['Fuji Nichidatsu: The Experience of Proselytizing in Western Paradise (India)']. In *Kindai Nihon no Bukkyo: Ajia Taiken to Shiso no Henyo* [*Buddhists of modern Japan: Their experiences of Asia and ideological transformation*], edited by Masamichi Ogawara. Tokyo: Keio University Publication.

———. 2014. 'Fuji Nichidatsu to Nipponzan Myohoji no Kaigai Fukyo: Seiten-Kaikyo kara Sekai Heiwa Undo he' ['Overseas Missionary Activities of Fuji Nichidatsu and Nipponzan Myohoji: From Proselytizing in Western Paradise to World Peace']. In *Kingendai no Hokkekyo Undo to Zaikei Kyodan* [*Contemporary Lotus Sutra Movements and Lay Buddhist Organizations*], edited by Nishiyama Shigeru. Series Nichiren 4. Tokyo: Shunjusha Publications.

Nichiren, Shonin. 2003. 'Kangyo Hachiman-sho' [Remonstration with Bodhisattva Hachiman]. In *Writings of Nichiren, Shonin: Doctrine 1*, translated by Kyotsu Hori and edited by Jay Sakashita. Tokyo: Nichiren-shu Overseas Propagation Association. USA: University of Hawaii Press.

Yamaori, Tetsuo. 1973. 'Fuji Nichidatsu-ron: Indo taiken-kata Ajiashugi no ichi tenkei' ['Theory of Fuji Nichidatsu: A Typical Example of Indian Experience based Asianism']. *Ajia Keizai* (Asian Economies), 14(9): 2–19. Tokyo.

7

India in the Eyes of Japanese Travellers: *Kimura Nichiki in Bengal**

Sumit Kumar Barua

Indo-Japanese Relationship over the Years

The friendship between India and Japan dates back to the 6th century AD. To date, there have been no major political disputes between the two countries. Both the countries share a common intellectual discourse and a rich cultural, literary and religious linkage (Singh 2014). The first interaction between these two countries began during Emperor Kimmei's reign (AD 539–571) (Brewster 2010). Soon after the arrival of Buddhism in Japan from India, via China and Korea, it became the state religion of Japan under the rule of Prince Umayado (AD 593–622) (Nag 1926). Buddhism played a pivotal role in the exchange of art and culture between the two countries. The influence of India's art and culture disseminated so deep in Japan that well-known Japanese scholar Hajime Nakamura commented, 'Without Indian influence, Japanese culture would not be what it is today' (1961).

This strong bonding between the two countries is a result of the visits of various Japanese travellers and scholars who came to tour Buddhist sites and learn about Buddhism and Indian art and culture. They have contributed immensely towards building friendship between the two countries. The contributions of Nanjō Bunyū, Kitabatake Dōryū and Okakura Kakuzō are well known and well researched.

However, a few scholars, such as Kimura Nichiki, who practically devoted their lives to the task of building Indo-Japanese friendship have not received the attention they deserve. During his long stay in India for about twenty-five years, Kimura assimilated to the Indian way of life,

* The author is grateful to Masahiko Togawa for many helpful discussions and constructive suggestions and to Mriduchhanda Chattopadhyay for her translation of some original works of Kimura Nichiki from Japanese into English. All translations from Bengali into English are by the author.

learnt several Indian languages, associated himself with places of learning as a student, researcher and teacher and compiled comprehensive and highly scholastic volumes on Mahāyāna Buddhism. He was associated with institutions such as the Bengal Buddhist Association (Bauddha Dharmānkur Sabhā) and tried to introduce the common people to the life and culture of Japan through his articles in Bengali periodicals. Moreover, upon his return to Japan, Kimura tried to present India, as he had perceived it, to the Japanese through his various articles. Also, he actively supported the Indian freedom struggle, and his memoirs stand as evidence of his deep respect for the Indian freedom fighters.

In this chapter, we will focus on Kimura's role in consolidating the Indo-Japanese relationship and his portrayal of India — Indian history, ethnography, religion and social customs — for Japanese readers. His works show his respect for India and his love for the cross-cultural way of life in the two countries. Although Kimura's books cannot be termed travel narratives, his works on the history of religions in India, well-known individuals, the political situation in India and the society and culture of Bengal and India are akin to travelogues in their representation of the culture, politics and society of India.

Indo-Japanese Cultural Exchange and Kimura Nichiki

This section gives a brief overview of the cultural exchange between Japan and India and the visits of Japanese scholars to India. During the medieval and early modern period (1185–1860), Japan was isolated. There was no immigration or emigration except for Chinese and Dutch traders. This period also witnessed the fiercest suppression of Buddhism (*haibutsu kishaku*[1]) in the history of Japan, beginning with the downfall of the Tokugawa regime and the resuscitation of imperial rule in Japan.

Japan underwent a metamorphosis through comprehensive social reforms during the modern period (1868–1912), after the famous and progressive Meiji Restoration in 1868. The country went on a paradigm shift from 'national isolation' to embracing modernisation. The wave of westernisation swept Japan during that time, and the country opened up for foreigners. The introduction of the Iwakura Mission in the 1870s facilitated the travel of the Japanese to other parts of the world, mainly for higher studies, so that they could contribute to the development of the

1 In the history of Japan, *haibutsu kishaku* refers to the practice that advocated the expulsion of Buddhism during the medieval and early modern period. This resulted in the destruction of Buddhist temples, images and texts and also compelled Buddhist monks to return to secular life.

nation on completion of their studies and return to Japan. During this period, the assault on Buddhism diminished as well. Japanese Buddhists were induced to travel abroad to the United States, Europe and Southeast Asia to revive the respect that Buddhist practitioners commanded and enjoyed in ancient times in Japan. The objective of these travellers was to reconstruct Buddhism that would flourish in Japan.

Nanjō Bunyū, who travelled to Europe for studies in 1876, spoke of the importance of travelling to India for Japanese Buddhists as that would help them to recover the supposedly original Buddhism (Jaffe 2019). Kitabatake Dōryū, belonging to the *Jodo Shinshu* sect of Buddhism, was the first Japanese to reach the Mahabodhi Temple at Bodh Gaya in 1883. In Kitabatake's travel writings, we find some disrespect for India, probably owing to the prevailing poverty and backwardness of the country. He often sarcastically refers to Indians by their skin colour as *kokundo* or *kuronbo* (blacks) (Jaffe 2019). The number of Japanese travellers to India improved steadily in the years before the First World War. The religious exchange inspired many Japanese students to come to India to understand and study Indian art, culture and philosophy apart from Buddhism.

An important visitor was Okakura Kakuzō, an avid scholar of Japanese and Indian art. Okakura played a pivotal role in establishing the cultural relationship between India and Japan. During his visit and stay in India, Okakura came into contact with great Indian personalities like Swami Vivekananda, Sister Nivedita and Rabindranath Tagore.

Two long-term visitors were Kimura Nichiki and Kawaguchi Ekai. Motivated by his interest in Buddhist textual studies and the desire to find valuable Tibetan sūtras, Kawaguchi Ekai was the first Japanese to embark on a journey to Tibet, travelling through India and Nepal in 1897. Ekai's travelogues present an account of Tibet from the Asian perspective. A student and, later, a priest of the Nichiren Buddhist sect, Kimura Nichiki stayed in India for twenty-five years and served thirteen years as a faculty at the University of Calcutta, exploring the tradition, culture and values of India.

Kimura Nichiki: A Brief Life History

Kimura Shōzaburō, known by the name Ryukan Kimura, was awarded the position of a cleric in the Nichiren[2] Buddhist sect in Japan in 1896.

2 Nichiren Buddhism is a branch of Mahāyāna Buddhism based on the teachings of the 13th-century Japanese Buddhist priest Nichiren. It focuses on the *Lotus Sūtra* doctrine that all people have an innate Buddha nature and are, therefore, inherently capable of attaining salvation in their current form and present lifetime. The religious movements of the Nichiren sect went a step further as a social movement with a message to alleviate the sufferings of the poor working-class people in Japan.

He changed his name to Kimura Nichiki in 1931 (Jaffe 2019). After completing the preparatory course and one year of university education, Kimura came to India as an overseas student in 1907 to Chittagong (Chattogram).

He also got the opportunity to know Bengali culture more closely because of the amiability of the residents of Chittagong. He gained expertise in fluently speaking the Bengali language in the regional dialects of Chittagong.[3] Nichiki studied Buddhism for nearly three years under the supervision of Dharmavangsha Mahāsthavira, the president of the Chittagong Buddhist Association.

After completing his studies in Chittagong in 1911, Kimura moved to Calcutta (Kolkata), entering the Sanskrit College. There, he 'commenced to study various subjects of ancient culture under Indian scholars' (Kimura 1959). Kimura studied with Bidhusekhar Shastri at the Department of Asian Studies in Sanskrit College till 1914. Then, he started his research on Buddhism, Sanskrit and Indian epigraphy under Haraprasad Shastri (Azuma 1992). Kimura's proficiency in Indian languages, as well as his research, won him many accolades and awards (Azuma 1992).

After a brief interlude in Japan in 1917, Kimura 'went again to India to study further on various branches of Indian philosophy under Prof. H.P. Shastri' (Kimura 1959). Later, in 1918, he joined the newly established Department of Pali of the University of Calcutta as an assistant professor of Indian Buddhist History and Mahāyāna Philosophy, holding the 'post for about fifteen years, giving lectures on the subjects of Buddhist philosophy and history of Buddhism' (Kimura 1959).

Apart from that, he also taught the Japanese language at the University of Calcutta and supervised researches on the comparative study of Mahāyāna and Theravāda Buddhism. The presence of educated Japanese like Kimura in Calcutta was of great assistance to many of his compatriots residing there. Thus, Kimura's role in Indo-Japanese relationship deserves special mention.

After returning to Japan in 1929, Kimura joined Rissho University, becoming *Senmonbu Bucho* (divisional head) there in 1931. He also took up the position of chief at the Buddhist Nihonji Temple in Chiba (Jaffe 2019). He retired in 1955 from the university and breathed his last in 1965.

---

3 Depending on the pronunciation and phonology, linguistics has classified the Bengali dialects into six main categories: Rarhi, Bangali, Varendri, Manbhumi, Rangpuri and Sundarbani (Chatterji 1926; Sen 1942). The dialect of Chittagong, known as Chatgaya or Satgaya, is a variation of Bangali dialect (Hoque 2015).

Kimura and Sociocultural Life in Bengal

The Buddhist revival movement was in progress in India under the leadership of Anagarika Dharmapala and Kripasarana Mahathera when Kimura visited the country. The contribution of the Bengal Buddhist Association (founded by Kripasarana in 1892) to the movement in India is often eclipsed by that of the Mahabodhi Society of India (founded by Dharmapala in 1891), although the role of the former was immense (Barua, forthcoming). Sir Asutosh Mukherjee and several other distinguished scholars and personalities of Bengal, such as Satishchandra Vidyabhushan and Abanindranath Tagore, actively supported this association (Barua 2015; forthcoming).

During his stay in Calcutta, as a faculty at the University of Calcutta and a close supporter of the Association, Kimura came in contact with several luminaries of Bengal, notably Rabindranath Tagore and Ramendrasundar Trivedi. We will review some of his associations with such distinguished scholars and their significance as revealed through his writings.

Kimura's memoir about Ramendrasundar Trivedi, who was a scientist and a litterateur, titled 'Ramendrasundar', was published in the periodical *Sāhitya* (1919). Although not travelogues, such works focussing on knowledgeable and versatile Bengali personalities show the Japanese interest in the cultural life of Bengal. Kimura mentioned that he was attracted by Trivedi's appearance and scholarly ability and gained from their interactions. According to him, 'Remembrance of ancient India can be still visible in such forms' (Kimura 1919, 459). In this article, Kimura refers to Trivedi as his *śikṣādātā* (educator) and later as his *śāntidātā* (patron of peace) (1919, 461–462).

When Kimura inquired about Hindu religion, philosophy and tantra, Trivedi politely acknowledged his dearth of knowledge on those topics, which initially rendered Kimura suspicious of the extent of Trivedi's scholastic abilities. However, he was enamoured of Trivedi's knowledge and scholarship about *vaidic yajña* (offering and sacrificial rituals). Being a student and a researcher of ancient Indian cultures, Kimura was interested to know about *yajña*, a ritual of sacrifice, devotion, worship and offering. Kimura was particularly grateful to Trivedi for explaining *yajña* to him, as reflected in his memoirs:

> After many topics, the topic of vaidic yajña was mentioned. Offerings or Yajña may refer to various things. Honestly, it is very difficult to describe them unless it is seen by their own eyes. However, it is unfortunate that India apparently has forgotten about the ancient culture and custom of

> the yajña, and we need to depend upon scholars if we wish to learn or explore it. Ramendrasundar was one such scholar. (Kimura 1919, 461)

Kimura writes that he visited many scholars for information, but none helped him except Ramendrasundar:

> Actually, Ramendrasundar explained the complicated and complex concepts of Brahminical texts with so much ease that he drew my utmost respect. He started to teach me the evolution of the concept and the relationship between the theory and practice so finely that I realised his great scholastic ability and that his teachings are much beyond textbook knowledge. (Kimura 1919, 463–464)

The persona of Kimura that emerges here is that of a traveller interested in knowing and learning about Indian practices, probing them in depth and exploring their religious significance. He is a knowledge-seeker, occasionally doubtful about his contacts but trusting and sincere.

One may question why Kimura, a Mahāyāni Buddhist, was so keen on learning about Hindu rituals like the *yajña* — whether this reflects his interest in the mingling of religions or his role as a cultural historian. Interestingly, while Kimura had served as a chief priest of the Nichiren sect, he was also the founder-president of the Vedanta Society of Japan, a branch of the Ramakrishna Mission from 1958. Often in his writings, preserved in the archives of the Vedanta Society of Japan, we see that Kimura tried to spread the ideals and philosophies of the religious harmony of Ramakrishna Paramhamsadeva and Swami Vivekananda in Japan. Thus, instead of focussing on religion from an orthodox perspective, Kimura's works and actions reflected his acceptance of various religions, unorthodox tolerance and desire to synthesise spiritual thoughts. His works on India are characterised by such tendencies. He was more than a cultural historian, as will be discussed later.

Like his predecessor, Okakura Kakuzō, Kimura was drawn into the orbit of Rabindranath Tagore. He mentions his regular interactions with the poet in several places:

> It was the days of the eminent poet Tagore who was very famous. I read his poems with interest and respected him as my revered teacher of Bengali. He also loved me and I called on him at his Jorasanko home every day; sometimes several times in a day from my boarding house. (Kimura 1959, 38–39)

Kimura helped the poet in his visit to Japan in every possible way, acting as his interlocutor and translating the poet's remarks and conversations from Bengali and English to Japanese for the benefit of the audience. Kimura writes:

> 1915: Next year, he [Rabindranath] told me that he had long cherished a desire to go to Japan and that he would like to visit Japan by all means within one or two years. He requested me to accompany him to act as his interpreter and also asked me to make all necessary arrangements beforehand. So, I returned to Japan at the end of March 1915 after a lapse of 8 years to arrange for his trip in 1915. (Kimura 1959, 39)

That Tagore entrusted Kimura with the job of his interpreter indicates the poet's trust in Kimura, just as it shows Kimura's knowledge of Bengali and his competence. By being completely at home in the Bengali language, Kimura shows his oneness and close acquaintance with the alien land.

Tagore was heartily welcomed by the scholars and intellectuals in Japan, including university faculties, successors of the neo-art movement initiated by Okakura Kakuzō, higher dignitaries of Buddhist communities and other scholars. On 13 June 1916, a grand felicitation programme was arranged for Tagore at the historical Kan'ei-ji shrine at Ueno, Tokyo, where Kimura served as Tagore's interpreter, simultaneously interpreting Tagore's poetry in Bengali, 'Matribhashar Spandan'. Tagore was delighted with Kimura's deft expertise in interpretation. All the Japanese present at the ceremony were astonished to see Kimura's expertise in the Bengali language, his ability to translate impromptu the lectures and verses of the poet and his close relationship with Tagore. Kimura's expertise in learning Bengali and reading, translating and interpreting Bengali literature shows his involvement and identification with the alien literary culture of Bengal. By learning the language and speaking it, he becomes one with the people. His is not the distanced, detached Western persona commenting on and representing an alien culture. Instead, Kimura's is a committed, kindred personality, with his own interpretation of and personal interactions with the language, literature and culture of a people aligned with them. Kimura's interactions with the contemporary poets and writers of Bengal like Tagore reflected not only his deep reverence for Indian scholars but also his affinity with the Indian temperament and spirit.

Kimura Nichiki and the Indian Independence Struggle

When Kimura visited India, the Indian freedom struggle against British imperialism was at its peak. Kimura writes, 'It was just in the midst of the second furious revolutionary movement in India; that is to say, it was the time in the virulent conditions of anti-British movement' (1959, 38).

Since Kimura actively supported the Indian nationalist movement during his stay in India and after his return to Japan, his works present a valuable account of the Indian freedom movement and his deep reverence for Indian freedom fighters, particularly Rash Behari Bose. Kimura's profound respect for Bose is expressed in his writings:

> He [Rash Behari Bose] was not only a respectable Indian gentleman, but also a man of patriotic spirit with fervent soul. I paid my highest respect to his sincerity and knew the high value of his true heart.... Although he had been in Japan for more than 30 years as an Indian refugee, he was always thinking of Indian Independence. He never forgot of the independence of his mother country ... the brilliant and distinguished services rendered by Mr. Rashbehari Bose to his mother country will remain forever in the histories of Japan and India. (Kimura 1959, 40, 41)

The last quoted sentence suggests the union of the histories of Japan and India and ties the interests of both countries together. Rash Behari Bose, an Indian patriot, becomes one equally remembered in Japan. Kimura implicitly endorses the ideal of 'One Asia' here and implies the common interests of two countries, thus erasing the sense of alienness. Apart from that, the second-person narratives also demonstrate Kimura's opposition to British oppression and his active support of the Indian nationalist movement.

Hailing from a land that has never been colonised by foreign countries, Kimura was deeply pained to see the oppression that Indians faced at the hands of British rulers. In the memoir about Kimura written by Kazuo Azuma (1992), the author relates an incident that he had heard from the nephew of Kimura's teacher in Chittagong (Chattogram) about Kimura's anti-British stand. Later, he also heard about it from another Japanese historian, Mr Kase.

> The then British commissioner in Chittagong would go out for a stroll in the morning every day with a stick in his hand. Everyone, including the local people, aware of his arrogant nature, would move away from his way during his stroll. One morning, when the commissioner was taking his regular morning walk, Kimura, who was also doing the same, crossed the path from an opposite direction. Kimura, unaware of the nature of the commissioner, did not move away from the road. This incident enraged the commissioner, who furiously started flogging Kimura. Deeply insulted by this cruel act, Kimura immediately protested by resisting the cane with his hands. While the passers-by stared in astonishment, the commissioner was immensely embarrassed, and was forced to publicly apologise to Kimura. On

> that day, Kimura was wearing a kimono, and his uncommon attire grabbed the attention of everybody. The people of Chittagong became awestruck by the great courage and morale of Kimura in resisting the tyranny of a British official and that too barehanded. The news spread fast, turning him into a legend in Chittagong. (Azuma 1992, 81–82)

Kimura's aversion to imperial Britain was reflected in his other actions as well. For example, he mentions that he tried in vain during the 1910s to help a Bengali 'terrorist group' smuggling arms from Japan to India (Kimura 1943; Nakazato 2016). Many of Kimura's colleagues in India looked upon him as a Japanese spy on observing Kimura's active support to the nationalist movement during his stay in Calcutta (Jaffe 2019). *Tomar Pataka* (Your flag) (1965) by Sachindranath Bandyopadhyay briefly mentions Kimura assisting revolutionaries like Lala Lajpat Rai and Rash Behari Bose during the initial days in Japan.

Upon his return to Japan, Kimura penned the book *Indo-shi no Kaibo to Dokuritsu Mondai* (1943) to introduce the people of Japan to the contemporary Indian freedom struggle. This book documents the Indian struggle for independence, starting from the Sepoy Mutiny (1857) to the Quit India Movement (1942). Kimura writes:

> In India, the first rebellion movement was in 1857 [historians often refer to it as the Revolt of the Sepoy (Soldiers)]. The second radical revolutionary movement was in 1905 and the third was the non-cooperation movement in 1921. These three Indian movements had invaded the English rule in the past 169 years that marked exploitation. India has sacrificed thousands of patriots and numerous great men in this freedom struggle. (1943, 5)

When this radio book was first published in 1943 by Nihon Housho Shuppan Kiyokai (Japan Broadcast Publishing Association), Japan was already embattled against the Allied forces in the Second World War. Therefore, one may infer that through this book, Kimura was trying to make the common Japanese people aware of the Indian struggle for independence against their common enemy at that time — the British.

In a public lecture about Indian independence and Japanese support to the cause in the spring of 1942, Kimura repeatedly made statements in support of the 'Greater East Asia Co-prosperity Sphere' (Nakazato 2016). He explained why Japan must support the Indians in their war of independence by referring to the Bhagavad Gita as well as history. His references to the Bhagavad Gita were used to justify why the Indians should fight the British: 'The path of righteousness must defeat evil at all costs. A warrior must sacrifice his life in order to defeat evil. This is what

I insist on. Protect the right way. Protect the good' (Kimura 1943). In his view, the imperialist British were 'bad', and hence, the Indians have the right to fight with them to gain their independence. Unlike other Buddhist pilgrims and scholars, he did not scruple to draw supporting evidence from Vedantic Hindu texts. Thus, Kimura's identification with the cause, both during his stay in India and after his return, shows the affinity of his self, as an anti-imperialist traveller from the East, with the Indians.

Kimura set his feet on independent India only once in 1956 under the patronage of the prime minister of India, Pandit Jawaharlal Nehru, to attend the 2500th anniversary of Lord Buddha — Buddha Jayanti. In his memoirs, Kimura glorifies India's freedom from subjection: 'Now that India has gained her Independence, I see before my eyes India's magnificent figure of independence' (Kimura 1959).

Kimura Nichiki and the Buddhist Revival Movement in India

Kimura was more of a Buddhist scholar than a pilgrim. His contribution to the revival of Buddhism in India was probably the most significant among the Japanese Buddhists in India. The annual reports of the Bengal Buddhist Association in 1911, 1913 and 1922 record that Kimura was an honorary member of the association, was deeply involved with its activities and often published articles (mainly in Bengali) in *Jagajjyoti*, the association's journal (Azuma 1996).

Kimura's contribution to the Buddhist revival movement can be considered as an intellectual one, as will be discussed in this section. During his stay in India, Kimura published a series of books and articles on his researches on Indian Buddhism. Some of Kimura's celebrated works on Buddhism are *The Original and Developed Doctrines of Indian Buddhism in Charts* (1920), *Introduction to the History of Early Buddhist Schools* (1925) and *A Historical Study of the Terms Hinayāna and Mahāyāna and the Origin of Mahāyāna Buddhism* (1927) to name a few. Kimura's work on Buddhism, published in India, may be viewed as an effort to spread the history of Buddhism from a Japanese perspective to an English-speaking audience (Jaffe 2019). Although Kimura used Indian historical sources, archival materials and Western translations of Indian philosophical and religious literatures and Chinese accounts similar to those used by Western researchers, Kimura's works about Buddhism were unique and free from Western or Chinese influence. Through his works, Kimura made several arguments that highlighted the general difference between Eastern and Western thinking and illustrated the broader context of Buddhism in India. According to him, Buddhism in India was not only considered as a religion but also influenced the economy and politics in ancient India (Stewart 1988). For example, contrary to V.A. Smith (1904), Kimura (1920) writes that Buddhist educational centres such as Nālandā were also political and, therefore, undoubtedly commercial centres. The impact and interaction of commercial, political and religious communities then would have been dynamic.

In the book *The Original and Developed Doctrines of Indian Buddhism in Charts*, Kimura skilfully presents an indispensable genealogical guide to the complex original Indian Buddhist doctrines. His concern was to provide a simple and easily understandable guide for students. He writes:

> The want of a comprehensive manual has made it more difficult for the students of Buddhism to obtain a clear idea of the Buddhist doctrines as promulgated in diverse Buddhist Philosophers. I have found it essentially necessary that some convenient and at the same time effective method should be adopted to teach students of Buddhism. About the beginning of the last session I prepared some of these charts in order to see whether the students can profit by them in any way and whether I can thus base my lectures on them.... Some eight different sets of doctrines have been summarized here for the present. They are — (i)The Original doctrines of Buddha, (ii) The Sthaviravādin doctrines, (iii) The Mahāsānghika doctrines, (iv) The doctrine of Aśvaghosa I, (v) Those of Harivarman, (vi) Those of Nāgarjuna, (vii) Those of Asanga and Vasubandhu, (viii) Aśvaghosa II. (Kimura 1920, Preface)

This book serves as a convenient and effective method to learn about the history and philosophy of Indian Buddhism even today. Kimura's desire to present the material comprehensively and coherently for the benefit of the students shows him as a painstaking, careful scholar and teacher of the religion.

Perhaps Kimura's most celebrated book on Buddhism is *A Historical Study of the Hinayāna and Mahāyāna and the Origin of Mahāyāna Buddhism* (1927). This book holds critical documentation of the history of Indian Buddhism, starting from the days of Lord Buddha till the Pāla dynasty, which may be considered to be the golden era of Buddhism in India. Kimura writes:

> Since my appointment as a Post-Graduate teacher in the Department of Arts of the Calcutta University, it has been my intention to write a proper history of Indian Buddhism from the time of its founder up to the Pāla dynasty, or more properly speaking, up to the Mahomedan conquest of Eastern India, and also a history of Buddhist Philosophy bearing on the Original and Developed forms of Buddhism. (Kimura 1927; Preface)

In the writing of the history of Buddhism in India, Kimura's religious and scholarly persona is discernible. Buddhism is a common thread linking India and Japan, which bred affinity rather than distance and opposition. Religion is a part of the cultural life of a society, and his book shows his involvement as an Asian and an Eastern writer in the cultural life of Bengal.

Kimura's book *A Historical Study of the Hinayāna and Mahāyāna and the Origin of Mahāyāna Buddhism* described the lineage of Buddhism in India and its classification into Hīnayāna and Mahāyāna from the Mahāyāna perspective of the lineage. It also provided a detailed genealogy of the terms *Hīnayāna* and *Mahāyāna* (Jaffe 2019). Kimura writes that the terms Mahāyāna and Hīnayāna carry the sense of 'superiority and inferiority' and 'praise and depreciation'. It is unlikely that the followers of the Hīnayāna school would have introduced this sense. Hence, the terms *Mahāyāna*, *Hīnayāna* and other allied terms occurred in *Mahāyāna Sūtra* and the Śāstras many times, but there is not a single instance of them in Pāli Nikaya (Kimura 1978).

Kimura Nichiki's Indological Outlook

Among his various scholastic endeavours, during his stay in India, Kimura penned a series of articles in Bengali titled 'Japane Samajik Protha' (Social customs in Japan) under the name Shri R. Kimura, and they were published in the periodical *Bungabani*. In these articles, he tried to introduce Japan to the common people in Bengal. These articles serve as a testimony to Kimura's desire to introduce a foreign country to Indians and his expertise in Bengali language.

After his permanent return to Japan in 1931, Kimura published a series of articles mainly in Japanese where he focussed on providing what he believed was the foundational knowledge required for understanding Nichiren Buddhism as well as many works concerning Indian thought (Jaffe 2019). Since understanding India remains incomplete without understanding its glorious history and culture, Kimura tried to present India's culture, history and society to the Japanese readers in his articles. Some of his most celebrated articles on Indian history, philosophy and culture are 'Bhagavadgītāni gen hareta Saṃkhya-yoga shisō' (Samkhya-yoga thought that appeared in the Bhagavad Gita, 1958), 'Jinseirisō no shimokuhyō to Indo rinri no tokushu-sei' (The four goals of life and the uniqueness of Indian ethics, 1953), 'Bengaruvaishnavaekigyō no tokushu-sei' (The uniqueness of Bengal Vaisnava, 1962), 'Daijōbukkyō to Bhagavadgītā to no kankei' (Relationship between Mahāyāna Buddhism and Bhagavad Gita, 1958), 'Indo niokeru Butsuzō-zō no rekishi' (History of Buddhist statues in India, 1935) and 'Indo no kyōtsū-tekikokuminsei to tokushu-tekikokuminsei' (India's common nationality and special nationality, 1965).

In this series, Kimura often refers to Indian cultures and customs to make the Japanese customs more familiar to the Bengali readers. For example, in some articles, Kimura discusses the Japanese marriage system, drawing a parallel with the ancient Indian marriage system:

> The main criterion of marriage in Japan is the eligibility of the youth (both male and female), the second is the family and descent, and third is the society and country. Marriage is the thing that fulfils an individual; marriage makes both man and woman complete. The ideal of ancient India is also applicable to Japan as well. (Kimura 1923a, 55)

Kimura demonstrates that Japanese marriage rituals are similar in many respects to that of Indians, although there are also salient differences between the two:

> In Japan, too, parents take the initiative for the marriage, and after the affirmation from their son/daughter, they confirm the marriage through the matchmaker (nākhād). In India, the priest plays an important role in the marriage, which is considered to be a religious ritual. But in Japan, marriage is just a 'social ritual' that does not require any priest. The nākhāds perform all the rituals.... When Buddhism came to Japan from India via China and Korea, it was preached as the religion for spirituality and outwardly upliftment. Since then, the Japanese perceived that this religion is not related to their day-to-day activities. Thus, they do not consider marriage to be a religious ritual. If required and/or wished, some individuals may get married in front of a priest according to their religious views. In Japan, the parents of the bride need to send various things such as regular clothes, special dresses for traditional events like festivals and events, white dress for mourning and different goods (Jisandougu) for the household to the house of the in-law. But, unlike India, in Japan, the bride and her family comes to the house of the groom to get married. The Japanese consider marriage to be a 'serious' event, so, it is conducted in a serious tone, unlike in India where the groom comes with music, dance and grandeur in a happy mood. Despite the feeling of a sacred event, the bride's family feels that after marriage, the bride will not return to her original unmarried form. Her spinsterhood will perish, which is equivalent to her death. As the bride will go to the in-laws' house as a 'wife', which is as a new human being, her head is covered with a white cloth that is usually used to cover the dead body. (Kimura 1923b; 499–500)

To point out the difference between the rituals of Japanese and Indian marriage, Kimura adds:

> On the other hand, the rituals of chanting Vedic mantra (hymns) and making an offering to the fire, which is common in Indian marriages, are not found in Japanese marriages. Japanese marriages lack the religious rituals or chanting of mantras. The main thing about Japanese marriages is the drinking of sāke. After drinking sāke, the couple sings a particular song for well-being, along with the relatives and the match-maker. If necessary, then the priests make the couples promise to maintain the sanctity of the marriage. In India, putting sindoor (vermillion powder) on the parting of the bride's hair by the groom is considered as the main symbol of marriage. Similarly, getting the hair tied in a particular bun by the bride is considered to be a symbol for being newly married. (1923b, 500)

In these articles, Kimura shows his close acquaintance with Hindu rituals and social customs as well as an ethnographer's curiosity. His efforts to compare Japanese and Indian rituals and explain Japanese practices in terms of Hindu rituals suggest his desire to make Japanese customs intelligible to Indian readers. However, he makes no attempt to suggest the superiority of Japanese customs and practices.

By and large, however, we do not find him presenting Indian social customs to the Japanese lay readers in this way. In Japan, Kimura published these articles mainly in journals suitable for academicians. Therefore, we can conclude that Kimura had faith in Okakura Kakuzō's concept of 'Asia is one'.

Kimura tries to give a holistic view of the historical development of Indian ethnicity and culture during his stay in India. While discussing the cultural history of India, Kimura relies on the classifications recommended by Sir William Jones for categorising the geographical regions. The first region he describes is:

> the region surrounding the Indus river in western India that was the home of Vedic Aryans; but non-Vedic Aryan people were also inhabitants of that area. After the invasion of the 'Macadenians' during the first century BC and fourth century AD, people of mixed race are found in this region but they still uphold the Vedic Aryan characteristics like straightforwardness, courageous innocence and righteousness…. Due to their strength and warrior-like nature, these people form an important part of the army in British India and, at the same time, these people are daring and are also part of the Indian revolutionary movement. (Kimura 1965, 115)

Kimura describes the central and southeastern region of India as the home of mixed races and non-Vedic Aryans but 'a region that is the birthplace of some of the greatest authors, scientists, artists, musicians and dramatists since ancient times. Great people like Vyāsa, Vālmīki, Kālidāsa, Bhababhuti are from this region' (Kimura 1965, 115).

Describing southern India, Kimura mentions that southern India was originally inhabited by the Dravidians who retained their ancient culture. However, Aryan tribes advanced to the south of the Vindhya Mountains during the 6th and 7th century BC. Kimura comments:

> A historical look at Ramayana certainly suggests this southward progression. Prince Rama of Ayodhyā was living in the Vindhya hills where villain Rāvaṇa abducted his wife, Sītā, to Ceylon Island. Rāma in alliance with people from the southern foothills advanced to southern India to go to Ceylon and bring back his wife. (Kimura 1965, 116)

Kimura's portrayal of Ramayana was from a neutral stand point, testifying to the movement of the Aryans from northern to southern India. His portrayal was based on archaeological and historical facts. In the article, Kimura did not mention the Aryans as conquerors or Dravidians as losers, reflecting the neutrality of his stance towards Brahminical dominance.

During the time Kimura spent in Bengal, there were various sociocultural movements taking place in India with their centre of activity at Calcutta. Thus, his long-term stay in Calcutta helped him to study the cultural heritage of Bengal more closely. He writes:

> Especially Bengal has uniqueness in this region. As mentioned before, this area has been the home of the Non-Vedic Aryans since ancient times. However, after the invasion and migration of the people from the west and Mongolians, many races got mixed.... The people here are patriotic and Bengal has been the birthplace of different movements like Chaitanya's Vaishnava movement, First revolution of 1857 [Sepoy Mutiny], Buddhist Revival Movement and Radical Revolution of 1905 (Bangabhanga Andolan). (Kimura 1965, 115–116)

Interestingly, Kimura mentions the spread of female education in Bengal: 'The number of girls studying in higher educational institutions in Bengal is amazingly high' (Kimura 1965). Notably, although female education until middle school was rising, the number of female students in higher educational institutions in Japan in the 1920s was quite low (Saito 2004). Hence, although this remark was merely a cursory comment made by Kimura in his article, it may be seen as his perception of the progressiveness of Bengali society at that time.

According to Kimura, the knowledge about India remains incomplete without the knowledge of Indian religious faiths. To record the history and status of different religious faiths in India during the 1st and 2nd centuries, Kimura mentions:

> From numismatic and epigraphic evidence as well as from various Hindu literatures, we come to know that the popular Hindu religions which are known under the names of Vaiṣṇavism, Śaivism and Śāktism were in a very flourishing condition in the time of Nāgarjuna. In my opinion, these are, also, not of Vedic origin, but originally belonged to the religious ideas of Outlandic Indo-Aryans. However, I think that the great Buddhist propaganda under king Asoka led the Vedic priests to Brahmanise the religious ideas of Outlandic? Indo-Aryans in order to start a counter-movement against it. (Kimura 1927, 25)

Here, it may be noted that Kimura possibly referred to the Aryans as foreigners and, hence, used the term 'Outlandic'.

In a few of his articles, apart from Buddhism, Kimura discusses various other religions in India like Vaiṣṇavism, their sociocultural impact and also their inter-relationships. For example, in a discussion on the relationship between Mahāyāna Buddhism and Hinduism in ancient India, Kimura says that it is difficult to isolate or compartmentalise one path from other. 'Instead, they progress in spiral and influence each other' (Kimura 1958, 206). Thus, Kimura was a true believer in the Indian ethos of harmony of all religions — *sarvadharmasamanvaya* — as has been reflected in his aforementioned works as president of the Vedanta Society of Japan. His persona is characterised by tolerance towards all religions.

Kimura's articles on Vaiṣṇavism essentially present an integral part of Indian religion and culture to the Japanese. 'This religion (Vaiṣṇavism) has a variety of names but it is essentially a religion of Bhakti or Love and Faith' (Kimura 1927, 25). In his articles, Kimura discusses the evolution of Vaiṣṇavism as a religion and then its context in literature:

> Indian philosophy teaches us to suppress emotions in order to protect the 'self' from the evil trend. On the other hand, Vaiṣṇavism teaches us to refine the feelings so that supreme state is achieved. This refinement can be achieved through training. Chandīdāsa displayed this proverb, saying, 'The human being is the highest and there is nothing higher'. (Kimura 1962, 118)

Controlling and channelling 'love' is also an important part of Vaiṣṇavism, where achieving transcendental love (*Mahābhāva*) is the only goal. Kimura mentions the concepts of *svakiyā* and *parakīyā* in this regard. He says that parakīyā refers to loving somebody else's wife or husband, but it holds two kinds of significance. It is a symbol of love, and at the same time, it is a training of controlling love. To give an example of parakīyā, he mentions the love of Radha and Krishna as parakīyā, but 'it is the most sacred transcendental love' in Indian culture (Kimura 1962, 119). He writes that the poetry of medieval Bengali and Maithili poets Chandidas and Vidyapati contained the essence of parakīyā love. In this context of parakīyā love, Kimura mentions the marriage system in India as he perceived it:

> The marriage in India is set by the parents at the age of both men and women. It is not a marriage where two people loved one another. There are couples who love each other by chance, but some couples do not find love for the rest of their lives.... In such a case, the man is the husband of another, and the woman is the wife of another. In that sense the love in India was sometimes parakīyā. (Kimura 1962, 119)

In this interpretation, religious doctrine has been interestingly connected with an actual social practice.

According to Kimura, the second phase of Vaiṣṇavism went forward from spiritual upliftment to the social reform movement in India, initiated by Sri Chaitanya. Since the Nichiren sect in Japan always worked for the upliftment of the socially downtrodden, Sri Chaitanya's attempt to bring social harmony and equality in the Indian society of the time was hugely praised by Kimura:

> He (Sri Chaitanya) and his disciples Nityānanda and Advaitachārya are considered three great men (in Vaiṣṇavism). This phase is the most prolific part of Vaiṣṇavism, worshiping Rādha-Kṛṣna, extending help and support to all, not recognizing class, equalizing humanity, and doing *namsankrityan* (combining chorus with a drum instrument). (Kimura 1962, 121)

This provides an interesting insight into a religious leader's influence on accepted social practices, leading to their modification. Such descriptions and comments show Kimura's persona as enlightened, unorthodox and egalitarian.

Conclusion

The persona of Kimura Nichiki that emerges from this brief study of some of his works on India and his activities there shows the Japanese scholar as seeking affinity and alliance with the country he visited. Although he showed exemplary scholarship in the study of the origin and doctrines of

Buddhism, he never attempted to proclaim that Buddhism was superior to Indian religions. On the contrary, he showed equal interest in Vedic rituals and Vaiṣṇavism. His intensive knowledge and love of the Bengali language and poetry and his closeness to Rabindranath Tagore show his sense of oneness with Bengal and India. His comparative discussions of the customs and social practices of India and Japan indicate an ethnographer's interest in the people and their manners without suggesting any sense of superiority of the one over the other. Whereas Europeans sought to construct India as the Other, Kimura sought to identify himself with the country of his residence, demonstrating his deep involvement with the culture, religion and society of India and closely allying himself with Indian aspirations for freedom from the shackles of British rule.

References

Azuma, Kazuo. 1992. 'Bharat o Japaner Setu R. Kimura' (R. Kimura, the bridge between India and Japan). In *Hundred Years of the Bauddha Dharmankur Sabha*, 80–94. [In Bengali.] Calcutta (Kolkata): Bengal Buddhist Association.

———. 1996. 'R. Kimurar Kotha' (About R. Kimura). In *Ujjwal Surja (The Glittering Sun)*, 32–53. [In Bengali.] Kolkata: Subarnarekha.

Bandyopadhyay, Sachindranath. 1965. *Tomar Pataka* (Your Flag). [In Bengali]. Calcutta (Kolkata): Sankar Publishers.

Barua, Kanak Baran. 2015. 'Legacy of Karmayogi Kripasaran Mahathero for Resurgence of Buddhism in Indian and Abroad.' Accessed 6 June 2021. https://www.researchgate.net/publication/326265323_LEGACY_OF_KARMAYOGI_KRIPASARAN_MAHATHERO_FOR_RESURGENCE_OF_BUDDHISM_IN_INDIA_AND_ABROAD.

Barua, Sumit Kumar. 2021. *Bismrito Yatri Nichiki Kimura*. [In Bengali]. Kolkata: Spark Publication.

———. Forthcoming. 'Indo-Japanese Friendship: A Narrative Exposition of the Works of Kimura Nichiki in India.' In *Buddhism in Shaping India-Japan Relations*, edited by Masahiko Togawa and Ranjana Mukhopadhyaya. New Delhi: Routledge India.

Brewster, David. 2010. 'The India-Japan Security Relationship: An Enduring Security Partnership?' *Asian Security* 6(2): 95–120.

Chatterji, Suniti Kumar. 1926. *The Origin and Development of the Bengali Language*. Calcutta: Calcutta University Press.

Hoque, Muhammad Azizul. 2015. 'Chittagonian Variety: Dialect, Language, or Semi-Language?' *IIUC Studies* 12: 41–62.

Jaffe, Richard M. 2019. *Seeking Sakyamuni: South Asia in the Formation of Modern Japanese Buddhism*. Chicago and London: The University of Chicago Press.

Kimura, Shri R. 1919. 'Ramendrasundar'. [In Bengali.] *Sahitya*.

———. 1923a. 'Japane Samajik Protha' (Social Customs in Japan). [In Bengali.] *Bangabani*, 2nd year Vol. 2.

Kimura, Shri R. 1923b. 'Japane Samajik Protha' (Social Customs in Japan). [In Bengali.] *Bangabani*. 2nd year Vol. 4.

Kimura, Ryukan. 1920. 'The Shifting Centre of Buddhism in India.' *Journal of the Department of Letters* I:12–47.

———. 1927. *A Historical Study of the Terms Hinayāna and Mahāyāna and the Origin of Mahāyāna Buddhism*. Calcutta: Calcutta University Press.

———. 1978. *A Historical Study of the terms Hinayāna and Mahāyāna and the Origin of Mahāyāna Buddhism*. Patna: Indological Book Corporation.

Kimura, Nichiki. 1943. *Indo-shi no Kaibo to Dokuritsu Mondai* (Dissecting Indian history and the question of independence). [In Japanese.] Tokyo: Nihon Housho Shuppan Kiyokai

———. 1958. 'Daijōbukkyō to Bhagavadgītā to no kankei' (The relation between Mahāyāna Buddhism and Bhagavad Gita). [In Japanese.] *Journal of Religious Studies* 154: 403–404.

———. 1959. 'My Memory about the Late Rasbehari Bose'. In *Rasbehari Bose, His Struggle for India's Independence,* edited by Radhanath Rath, 38–44. Calcutta (Kolkata): Modern Indian Press.

———. 1962. 'BengaruVaishnava ekigyō no tokushu-sei' (Characteristics of Vaisnavism of Bengal). [In Japanese.] *Indogaku Bukkyōgaku Kenkyū*' 10(1): 118–121.

———. 1965. 'Indo no kyōtsū-tekikokuminsei to tokushu-tekikokuminsei' (India's common national character and special national character). [In Japanese.] *Indogaku Bukkyōgaku Kenkyū* 14(1): 114–117.

Nag, Kalidas. 1926. 'Greater India'. *Greater India Society Bulletin* 1: 1–44

Nakamura, Hajime. 1961. *Japan and Indian Asia, their Cultural Relations in the Past and Present.* Calcutta: K.L. Mukhopadhyay.

Nakazato, Nariaki. 2016. *Neonationalist Mythology in Postwar Japan: Pal's Dissenting Judgment at the Tokyo War Crimes Tribunal.* Lanham: Rowman& Littlefield.

Saito, Y. 2004. 'Gender Equality in Education in Japan'. *Educational Science Journal of the Faculty of Education and Human Sciences* 6(2): 145–162.

Sen, Sukumar. 1942. *The History of Language.* [In Bengali.] Calcutta: Eastern Publishers.

Singh, Sudhir. 2014. 'Indo-Japan Relations: Deepening Bonhomie and New Security Equilibrium in the Asia Pacific'. *International Journal of East Asian Studies* 3(2): 13–26.

Smith, V.A. 1904. *Early History of India.* Oxford: Clarendon Press.

Stewart, M.L. 1988. *Nalanda Mahavihara: An Historiographic Study of Its Art and Archaeology, 1812-1938.* United Kingdom: University of London, School of Oriental and African Studies.

Section 3

SELF-FASHIONING OF INDIAN TRAVELLERS

8

The *Bhadralok* and His 'Wild West': *Reading Sanjibchandra Chattopadhyay's* Palamou

Saugata Bhaduri

This chapter is a study of the curious and rather short travelogue, *Palamou* (1880–1883)[1], by Sanjibchandra Chattopadhyay[2] (1834–1889). I propose here that this slim, and otherwise seemingly purposeless and insignificant, volume is crucial to the history of Bengali travel writing, as it marks a veritable epistemic shift, ushering in a new mode of conceiving the travelling Self and writing about the same in Bengali.

Sanjibchandra[3], though not very well known outside of Bengal, was an important figure in the late 19th-century Bengali cultural milieu. He was the elder brother of the renowned Bankimchandra Chattopadhyay (1838–1894) and was from a family of colonial administrators; his father, Jadabchandra, was a deputy collector, and his younger brother, Bankimchandra, was a deputy magistrate. Sanjibchandra started his career in government service as a clerk at the Burdwan (Bardhaman) commissioner's office. His first major work was a compendious socio-

1 What appears as *Palamou* today is a collection of six essays, serialised over six issues of the journal *Bangadarshan*, from BS 1287 to 1289, from Poush 1287 to Phalgun 1289 to be precise (detailed further later). I have converted this to Common Era (CE) as 1880–1883 (December 1880 to February 1883, to be precise) and presented that as the date of original publication for this work.

Further, to simplify things for readers who may not be familiar with the Bengali calendar (BS), the dates of all Bengali works mentioned in this article have been given in CE, though the dates in the original works would invariably be given in BS. This may have resulted in some approximation, with the BS month of publication being not always known. The CE dates given here may actually be off by one year.

2 The official English spelling of his name in his lifetime, with which he published his noted English work too, was 'Sunjeeb Chunder Chatterjee', but I prefer to use 'Sanjibchandra Chattopadhyay', which would be the more acceptable transliteration today of the Bengali orthography of his name that the text in question bears.

3 I follow the accepted convention of referring to Indic authors by their first names, rather than their surnames.

historical treatise in English, *Bengal Ryots: Their Rights and Liabilities*[4]. Bankimchandra, in his biography of his elder brother that precedes a volume edited by him of some representative collected works of Sanjibchandra, says, 'On reading this book, the lieutenant governor presented him with the position of deputy magistrate' (B. Chattopadhyay 1898, 11; translation mine). He spent his first two years as a deputy magistrate in Krishnanagar. He was then posted at Palamou (currently Palamu, a district of Jharkhand) in the predominantly forested and tribal-dominated westernmost extremity of the Lower Bengal Province of the erstwhile Bengal Presidency. He recounts his experiences there almost two decades later in his travelogue *Palamou*.

While I will return to *Palamou* in a moment, to carry on with Sanjibchandra's literary credentials, he was the author of at least three novels — *Kaṇṭhamālā*[5] (1877), *Jāl Pratāpchād* (1883) and *Mādhabilatā* (1884)[6] — and several short stories and essays. Besides, he edited the monthly journal *Bhramar* from 1873 to 1876. More importantly, from 1877 to 1883, he edited *Bangadarshan*, arguably the most important Bengali literary magazine of the times, founded by Bankimchandra in 1872 and revived later by Rabindranath Tagore in 1901. What constitutes *Palamou* today was serialised over six issues of this journal (two issues in BS 1287, three issues in BS 1288 and one issue in BS 1289)[7] under the abbreviated pseudonym 'PraNāBa' (for Pramatha Nath Basu) from 1880 to 1883. The six essays were not put together in one volume in Sanjibchandra's lifetime; after his death, Bankimchandra brought out a collection of Sanjibchandra's works called *Sanjibani Sudha*, in which

---

4 See Chatterjee, Sunjeeb Chunder. 1864. *Bengal Ryots; Their Rights and Liabilities: An Elementary Treatise on the Law of Landlord and Tenant*. Calcutta: D'Rozario & Co. Available at: archive.org, 17 January 2017, https://archive.org/details/in.ernet.dli.2015.195576.

5 I have generally refrained from using diacritics to transliterate Bengali names, but for the titles of these three novels, I thought diacritics were necessary, because they could have been otherwise pronounced differently, even by the Bengali-knowing reader, leading to semantic confusion. Similarly, I have used diacritics sparingly for transliterating some titles and words later too (primarily, the diacritical *ā*, particularly when the distinction between the short and long 'a' would have been crucial) though I have mostly stuck to a common orthography.

6 These three novels are freely available at archive.org.: https://archive.org/stream/dli.bengal.10689.4681, https://archive.org/stream/in.ernet.dli.2015.457515, and https://archive.org/details/in.ernet.dli.2015.290429, respectively.

7 The six essays that constitute *Palamou* were published in the following six issues of *Bangadarshan*: BS 1287 — Poush (mid-December 1880), pp. 412–419; Phalgun (mid-February 1881), pp. 513–519; BS 1288 — Ashadh (mid-June 1881), pp. 135–139; Shraban (mid-July 1881), pp. 165–171; Ashwin (mid-September 1881), pp. 281–286; BS 1289 — Phalgun (mid-February 1883), pp. 514–517. Thus, the first five instalments of *Palamou* were published within a period of nine months, while the sixth instalment was published after a significant hiatus — seventeen months after the fifth instalment.

'Palamou' was first compiled.[8] However, this version of 'Palamou' comprised only the first five essays and not the sixth one (probably because of its temporal distance from the other five, as explained in a previous note). In a 1944 (BS Baishakh 1351) edition by Brajendranath Bandyopadhyay and Sajanikanta Das, all the six essays were collected in one volume to constitute the text of *Palamou* that we have today (S. Chattopadhyay 1944).

It is not that there was no travel writing in Bengal before *Palamou*. The *mangal-kavyas* in Bengali, composed mostly between the 15th and 18th centuries CE, include several travel accounts, but these concern the travels of imaginary characters, often to imaginary places. Bengali accounts of actual journeys conducted by real historical personages begin from the early 16th century onwards with biographies of Chaitanya Mahaprabhu (1486–1534). However, the travellers did not write these texts themselves, and thus, they may not be considered what we generally understand as travel writing. First-hand accounts of real travel in Bengali appear only in the late 18th century with accounts of pilgrimage, such as Bijayram Sen's *Tirthamangal* (c. 1769–1770) or Jaynarayan Ghoshal's *Kashi Parikrama* (c. 1792). However, all three categories stated have religious subtexts — being directly scriptural texts in praise of a deity or hagiographies of a particular saint or travel writings about visits to pilgrimage sites.

A significant body of 'secular' and 'personally experienced' travel writing by Bengalis (or people from the region that was then Bengal) can be seen in the late 18th century. Interestingly, none of the texts are in Bengali but rather in Persian or English. The first such instance may be Mirza Sheikh I'tesamuddin (c. 1730–1800) from Nadia, who travelled to England between 1765/1766 and 1769/1770 (AH 1179–1183) as munshi to Capt. Archibald Swinton, the ambassador of Shah Alam II. He wrote a travelogue about his journey to England and France, *Shegurfnama-i-Vilayet* (1784), in Persian, which was translated as *The Wonders of Vilayet* in 1827. The best-known example is of Sake Dean Mahomed (1759–1851) from Patna (then within Bengal), who wrote the now-famous first book-length work published by any Indian in English, *The Travels of Dean Mahomed* (1794). One can also mention Mirza Abu Taleb Khan (1752–1805/1806), who, though originally from Lucknow, spent most of his formative years in Murshidabad and

8 In 1898, Bankimchandra edited a collection of the late Sanjibchandra's works, under the title *Sanjibani Sudha, arthāt Sanjibchandra Chattopadhyay pranita grantha sakaler utkrishtāngsha samgraha*, in which he wrote a short biography of the author (which has already been referred to in the previous paragraph), and compiled some of Sanjibchandra's representative writings, including a truncated version of 'Palamou' (1898, 79–130).

much of his career in Calcutta (Kolkata). He travelled widely between 1799 and 1803, and his travelogue, *Masir Talib fi Bilad Afranji* (c. 1805) in Persian, was translated into English as *Travels of Mirza Abu Taleb Khan in Asia, Africa and Europe* in 1810. This tradition of people from Bengal writing travel accounts in languages other than Bengali continues into the second half of the 19th century too. Some examples are English works like Bhola Nauth Chunder's *The Travels of a Hindoo to Various Parts of Bengal and Upper India* (1860), Michael Madhusudan Dutta's account of his travel to England published in the journal *Indian Field* (1862) and Romesh Chunder Dutt's *Three Years in Europe* (1872). However, as already stated earlier, though these works are by people from Bengal, none of this was in Bengali.

'Secular' and 'personally experienced' travel writing by Bengalis in Bengali begins only in the mid-19th century with Ishwarchandra Gupta (1812–1859). He serialised his experiences of travelling through India in his newspaper, *Sambād Prabhākar*,[9] from 1854 onwards under the by-line '*bhramankāri bandhu haite prāpta*' (received from a travelling friend). Notably, Ishwarchandra had already written in praise of the railways in this paper as early as 1849, foreshadowing how 'secular' first-person travel writing in Bengali was to gain a major fillip with the introduction of the railways in Bengal and Bengalis taking up travelling on a large scale and writing about it. Though the railways started in India as early as 1837, the first passenger train service started only on 16 April 1853 between Bombay (Mumbai) and Thane. On 15 August 1854, the first passenger trains started running in Bengal between Howrah and Hooghly, with the rail network becoming widespread by the 1870s. A significant body of travel writing in Bengali centred around the railways, though not restricted to it, emerged from the mid-1850s to the late1870s. Some examples include Akshay Kumar Dutt's *Bāshpiya Upadesh* (Calcutta, 1855), Kalidas Moitra's *Bāshpiya Kal o Bhāratiya Railway* (Serampore, 1855), Azim-al-Din's *Ki Majār Kaler Gāri* (Burdwan, 1863), Kedarnath Das's *Bhāratbarsher Pratichi Digbihār* (Murshidabad, 1872), Haricharan Bandyopadhyay's *Bhraman Brittānta* (Hooghly, 1877), Baradakanta Sengupta's *Bhārat Bhraman* (Calcutta, 1877) and Priyanath Bose's *Professor Bose-r Apurba Bhraman Brittānta* (Calcutta, 1879). I have deliberately included the places of publication for all these works to show how they did not emerge from Calcutta alone but from different parts of

9 Ishwarchandra Gupta started *Sambād Prabhākar* on 20 January 1831 as a weekly but had to temporarily discontinue it after the 25 May 1832 issue, only to revive it with increased frequency as a tri-weekly from 10 August 1836 and as a daily from 14 June 1839. It thus became the first Bengali daily newspaper. Hence, secular and personal travel writing in Bengali is coeval with Bengali journalism.

Bengal, suggesting the widespread ubiquity of travel writing in Bengali from the 1850s. However, these writings are often too descriptive, lacking the personal, idiosyncratic touches that one expects of travelogues. Also, none of the above writers (barring Ishwarchandra Gupta and Akshay Kumar Dutt) are major writers.

From 1882, however, one sees a deluge of fascinating travelogues in Bengali — 'secular' in content, first-person in narrative technique and less informative and more interesting in tone — covering both India and abroad, emerging from the canonical who's who of Bengali literature. Restricting the list to the 19th century alone, one can note Rabindranath Tagore's *Europe-Prabāsir Patra* (1882) and *Europe-Yātrir Diary* (1891), Shibnath Shastri's *England-er Diary* (1888), Nabinchandra Sen's *Prabāser Patra* (1892), Debendranath Tagore's *Ātmajibani* (1894; containing accounts of his travels from 1846 onwards), Swami Vivekananda's *Paribrājak* (originally serialised in the journal *Udbodhan* in 1899) and so on. Also, women's travel writing in Bengali began in a big way: Krishnabhabini Das's *England-e Bangamahilā* (1885), Prasannamayi Devi's *Āryāvarta: Janaika Banga Mahilār Bhraman Kāhini* (1888) and numerous short pieces by Swarnakumari Devi such as 'Prayāg Yātrā' (1886), 'Darjeeling Patra' (1888) and 'Ghazipur Patra' (1889) published in the journal *Bhārati o Bālak*, and 'Samudre' (1895) and 'Nilgiri' (1896) published in the journal *Bhārati*. So, what could have changed between 1879 and 1882 to make this significant shift possible? My hypothesis is that *Palamou* (1880–1882, 1883) has facilitated this change and caused this epistemic shift. It ushered in a whole new mode of conceiving the travelling self and of writing about the same in Bengali — a whole new approach to travel writing in Bengali, as it were — and the rest of this chapter will be devoted to discussing this.

So, what exactly does *Palamou* do? Rabindranath Tagore's critical essay on Sanjibchandra's *Palamou* in 1894 (BS 1301) offers some clues. Later, he included it as the third chapter in his collection of essays on modern literature, *Adhunik Sahitya* (BS 1314), under the title 'Sanjibchandra (Palamou)' (1907). While Rabindranath discusses *Palamou* in great detail in this essay, he makes two main points about the text and its author that draws our special attention. Talking about Sanjibchandra, Rabindranath says, 'His talent had wealth but did not have homemakerliness [*grihinipanā*] [...] Sanjib is rich in talent but is not a homemaker' (Tagore 1894, 46–47; translation mine). Coupled with this non-homely disorderliness, Sanjibchandra's work is also marked by a freshness, unburdened as it is with any claim to profundity. Rabindranath further avers, 'Usually, within our race, a symptom of being wizened with knowledge [*bigyabārdhakya* (*vijñavārdhakya*)] is noticeable. [...] Sanjib's interior, however, was not inflicted with this disease. He travelled as if in a newly created world with a pair of new eyes' (48–49; translation mine). Unhomely (*unheimlich*), disorderly and unburdened with the onus of disseminating 'profound' knowledge, *Palamou* brings in, as Rabindranath hints, a wondrous and yet tentative freshness. Is this what makes the text mark a break in Bengali 'travelogy?'[10]

As Sanjibchandra, a colonial administrator and an exemplar of the Bengal Renaissance *bhadralok*, recounts his encounter with the 'wild west' of Palamou, populated by presumably alien peoples and customs, his originally distant ethnological gaze takes on relativising overtones. He self-introspectively discovers the 'Other' within himself. This is borne out in *Palamou* through an opening that is most unsure and betrays the unreliability of the author; a narratorial strategy that is full of disavowals, disclaimers and digressions; an emplotment that comprises only seemingly trivial descriptions and episodes and enshrines the quotidian; a tone that, in foregrounding the everyday, leads to a self-deprecating ironic humour that undercuts the pretentious Bengali *bhadralok* and his mores and ends up becoming a political critique of the exploitation of the tribals; an effect of the sense of wonder that withholds even that wonder; and a closure that is practically a non-closure, being just an open invitation to an abrupt and unfulfillable bacchanalia. Is this what makes *Palamou* so crucial to the history of Bengali travel writing? Is *Palamou* thus a watershed in Bengali literature, a missing link between purposive, laboriously methodical and possibly wearisome accounts of travel and a mature mode of travel writing where the writing is as free as the ideal of travelling itself? Does *Palamou* lay bare the ungraspable empty logos of travel itself, exposing a travelogy that betrays the logic of travel and casting a template for an impossible mode of travel writing that lies beyond the travelogue? Does *Palamou* provide a mould for the Bengali *bhadralok* Self to recast its officious, masculine, austere avatar and forge its not-so-self-sure version through an encounter with the Other within and without on the anvil of what only travel and travel writing can offer? These are some of the questions I wish to ask and explore here.

One can begin with the beginning of the text, which, as I have already stated, is most unsure and betrays the narrator's unreliability. Sanjibchandra starts by saying:

---

10 I use this word as 'travelogy, or the ideology of travel' in exactly the same sense in which Arup K. Chatterjee uses it. He is the founding editor of *Coldnoon: Travel Poetics (International Journal of Travel Writing)*, a wonderful journal that started in 2011 but is sadly discontinued now. See 'Philosophy: What is Travelogy'. Accessed 17 February 2022. https://coldnoon.com/history-concept/.

> A long time ago, I once went to the Palamou region. Upon my return, a couple of friends repeatedly requested me to write an account of that area, but I used to make fun of them then. Now no one requests me, and yet I have settled upon writing that account. The key issue of relevance here is age. To tell tales is the malaise of advanced years; whether anyone listens to him or not, the old man narrates. (1880–1883, 15; translation mine)[11]

With such an opening, one expects Sanjibchandra to take on the mantle of an unreliable narrator, which he unabashedly dons, saying, 'I am writing about things from a long time ago, and I can't remember everything. What I would have written had I written earlier is not necessarily what I am writing now' (1880–1883, 15). The travelogue thus presents not a coherent narrative but a series of disjointed vignettes, together comprising a *duniya* — a world that is not whole but one where the *bhadralok* recounts his awestruck, disjunctive presence within the alien wilderness. As Sanjibchandra says in the third essay:

> In the distance, all around, a boundary of hills, as if the world ends there.[…] Beyond them, the wilderness.[…] From within that, faint smoke rising slowly from one or two villages. Maybe the plaintive note of a *mādal* [a kind of drum] being played rising from some village. And, beyond all that is my tent, like a white dove sitting alone amidst the jungles, lost in thought. I would see all this unmindfully, and I used to think this is my duniya. (1880–1883, 36)

The proprietary gaze of the urban Bengali *bhadralok* — no less than the deputy magistrate of the area, appointed by the colonial administrative machinery with a possible mission of civilising this 'wild west' — flounders in the travelogue from that of the lord of all he surveys to that of one who can at best be relativistic towards what his deferred travelogy can recall.

This relativism is present throughout the text, but particularly on those rare occasions when Sanjibchandra indulges in ethnographic accounts of the tribal population of the area, only to immediately recede to relativism or digressions. For instance, in the fifth essay, he describes the marriage rituals of the Oraons. Or rather, following his characteristic style, he is not too sure if they are Oraons: 'There is a subgroup among the Kols. I don't quite recall whether they are Oraon

11 All the references to the primary source of this article are from the pdf version of the Bengali *Palamou*. See S. Chattopadhayay (1880–1883). All translations from the original Bengali to English are mine.

or something else, but their marriage customs are very old' (1880–1883, 55–56). Anyway, he tells us of the curious custom of young marriageable boys and girls of the community spending their nights together collectively in an earmarked big hut at the edge of the village. When love blossoms between a couple through this arrangement, an elaborate charade of a violent abduction and chase between the members of the couple's families is enacted, leading finally to their marriage. While this detailed two-page account is quite ethnological, it is immediately offset by a relativising comment:

> At one point of time, this sort of marriage was prevalent all over the world.[…] Even amongst the English, when the bride and the bridegroom step out of the church and board the carriage, the way that shoes are showered on them like flowers is but a remnant of this age-old custom. (57–58)

This relativism is represented even better in the best-known line from the book, the oft-quoted phrase from the second essay: '*banyerā bane sundar; shishurā mātrikroré*' [The wild are beautiful in the wilderness; infants in their mothers' laps] (29). This line has almost attained the status of a proverb in Bengali. It was uttered to articulate how the Kol tribals, the original inhabitants of the Palamou region, may not appear very good-looking from a standard perspective of beauty adopted outside of their context, but in their own habitat, they are all beautiful. While this phrase may be read as a patronising, infantilising and essentialising gesture on the author's part towards his tribal Other, in my opinion, this is symptomatic of the originally ethnological civilising gaze of the colonial administrator being converted into one of relativising self-introspection.

Apart from this comparatist relativism, Sanjibchandra also takes recourse to digressions, narratorial postponements, disavowals and foreclosures as strategies to do the same. For instance, towards the end of the second essay, once again in a rare demonstration of ethnography, he starts talking about the Asura community that also lives, alongside with but separately from the Kol and other tribal communities, in the more secluded, forested parts of the region. He digresses into a quasi-historical account of how the Asuras, who were apparently the original inhabitants of India, were defeated by the Aryan invaders and pushed off to the remote forested and mountainous regions. He also moves into a relatively lengthy comparative discussion of similar invasions by outsiders and original inhabitants being driven to extinction in other parts of the world, like in the United States of America, Canada, Australia and New Zealand (S. Chattopadhyay 1880–1883, 31–34). What is much more interesting, however, is that after inaugurating a discussion that could have been a legitimate treatise in comparative anthropology, Sanjibchandra completely withdraws from pursuing it any further, saying, 'I will discuss and debate the reason behind all this [the decline of indigenous peoples due to the advent of foreign invaders] some other time.[…] At my age, I feel like saying whatever comes to my mind; people may not like it' (34). This withholding of narratorial agency marks how the travelling authorial/authoritative subjectivity gets negotiated in *Palamou*, which will be my next point of discussion.

The narrative strategy adopted in the text is one of disavowals and disclaimers, of an underscoring of non-purposive narration and a deliberate undermining of subjectivity and the authorial Self as it travels in alien territory and attempts to document it. For instance, Sanjibchandra ends his first essay by saying:

> I will not give an account of my journey anymore; I have already troubled the readers a lot with these lines that I have written. I will not disturb them anymore. Now I do not wish to say anything apart from the core description, but if I do end up narrating one or two things that seem superfluous, it has to be interpreted as a malady of my age. (1880–1883, 24)

However, Sanjibchandra does not stick at all to his declared objective of not digressing. Having already indemnified himself on the grounds of his advanced years, he further highlights the inutile nature of his endeavour, surrendering coherent authorial subjectivity unto the altar of the reader to whom the author is apparently ethically obligated. Towards the beginning of the second essay, he says, 'Old stories linger on, increasing social capital. But no one's capital will increase through my stories because I myself have no capital. Still, I will keep on telling stories, and you keep making me forever grateful by listening to them' (35). It is, however, not a pure surrender to the reader but rather a retainment of the pointless and yet iterative narration of itineration, on the part of the travelling narrator. Here, travelogy constitutes an authorial subjectivity that has been deemed purposeless but must narrate, even at the risk of not being read. Towards the beginning of the sixth essay, the author says, 'If someone is unwilling to read "Palamou", I would tell him, "How can that be? I still have a lot more to say about Palamou"' (64).

The supreme irony — or probably the main point of the kind of subjectivity that travelogy constitutes — of this narrative imperative is that what Sanjibchandra does have to say is hardly about his journey into Palamou proper. Instead, the narrative is full of thoroughly off-tangent digressions or seemingly pointless trivia. Rather than carving out a grand informative narrative about the region the travelogue is ostensibly about or even the details of the journey, he is more interested in describing mundane things like one *ashwattha* tree growing out of a monolithic hill (S. Chattopadhyay 1880–1883, 27–28) or a wooden bell hanging from a buffalo's neck (28). In a similar vein, in the first essay, he talks about the meal he had at his host's place in Hazaribagh en route to Palamou, which had an excess of onions. He engages in a fairly long digression about whether *palāntu* and *pīyāj* — apparently two words for onion — are the same thing or not (20–21). He cites as his primary reference an almost certainly apocryphal tale of how a Hindu raja from Punjab once stopped at Medinipur on his way to a pilgrimage to Jagannath Puri and gave a discourse to the townspeople there about the differences between the two! In the fourth essay, Sanjibchandra describes how he kept staring at a beautiful young courtesan who had visited his tent one evening with an elderly gentleman to seek some alms. Here, too, he embarks on an elaborate philosophisation on *rūp* (beauty or form) — how he had encountered a similar *rūp* in a bird that he had intended to hunt but could not and in a baby goat that he had once seen abroad. He extends the discussion further to ghosts, who, being formless, adopt human bodies to articulate their *rūp* and then to trees and rivers (46–48). In the fifth essay, he, somewhat comically, digresses into how he was once defeated in an impromptu walking race by a young Englishwoman, 'the daughter of some member of the Governor General's Council', in Titagarh (55). He also describes how he had once seen a newly-wed Bengali girl feeding leftover *luchi* (a fried flatbread) to a dog the morning after her marriage (61–62).

Such instances of digression or deliberate trivialisation often lead to humour or a self-deprecating comic tone. In the first essay, upon first glimpsing hills at a distance on his way to Palamou, Sanjibchandra is reminded of a kitschy multi-coloured brick-laid model of the Gobardhan Hill that he saw at the hermitage of a small-time mendicant in his childhood (S. Chattopadhyay 1880–1883, 17). In the second essay, describing his first visit to a Kol village in a palanquin, he observes with some regret that the young boys and girls were more interested in seeing the palanquin and its bearers than the one sitting inside (30). At other times, it leads to some of the most poignant images in the text. In the third essay, the author joins a hunt for a ferocious tiger that was tormenting the local villagers and ends up seeing the tiger sleeping instead. The comicality of the whole scene — the reluctant Sanjibchandra with 'a gun slung on his shoulder, boots on his feet, and donning the coat-pantaloon' (40) — apart, the sleeping tiger is described thus:

> I went and saw that there was a huge depression like a hole or a cave at one place in the hill. At its very centre was a stone cottage, with the

> space around it like a courtyard.[...] At one end of the courtyard was the tiger, sleeping with its eyes closed like a harmless, innocent person and holding one of its beautiful paws, claws and all, next to its face as if it was a mirror. Maybe, just before going to sleep, it would have licked its paw once. (42)

The image is truly powerful. The pathos of the almost humanised sleeping tiger, which may have licked its paw and held it in front of its face like a mirror before going to sleep, being hunted the very next moment is likely to be etched in the reader's mind for a long time. Incidentally, Rabindranath also ends his essay on *Palamou* with an invocation of this very image. These trivia and digressions form the real core of *Palamou*.

Palamou is extremely disjointed and episodic in its emplotment too. As a serialised text — that too one where, though the first five instalments were published at fairly uniform intervals of a couple of months, the sixth instalment was published almost one and a half years after the fifth — one may rightly expect a certain degree of episodicity from *Palamou* but not to such a radical extent. Further, most of the episodes seem to be about trivial incidents, often not very integral to what one would expect from a functional piece of travel writing. It is impossible to recall each of the numerous episodes that constitute the plot of *Palamou*, but I choose to narrate five of the most interesting ones to give the reader a sense of how this text feels. The first episode is from the very first essay. On his way to Palamou, Sanjibchandra stops by the river Barakar, waiting to be ferried across it, and is surrounded by a group of poor children. They address him as 'saheb' and ask him for money. While such an encounter is in itself not out of place even in today's India, the narrator's choice to focus on one such child and his purposeless alms-seeking is fascinating:

> At this point, a two-year-old child came and stood with his face raised towards the sky and his palm spread before me. He did not quite know why he spread his palm. He saw everyone else do so, and he also did it. I gave a paisa in his hand. The child threw it away and held out his hand again. When another boy picked up that paisa, a big fight ensued between this latter boy and the elder sister of the former child. (S. Chattopadhyay 1880–1883, 17)

Such episodes, highlighting further the purposelessness of action, abound in the text, often coupled with elaborate observations of curious practices that have no ostensible connection to the subject at hand. For instance, a second episode that one may present here is when, again in the first essay and still on his way to Palamou, Sanjibchandra breaks his journey at a house in Hazaribagh (the same house where the digression into a discussion on onions occurred). There, the host reportedly hangs a whole bunch of bananas in the middle of the house with a piece of paper attached to it, on which a detailed account of the consumption of bananas is meticulously maintained (22). This curious practice becomes an occasion for the author to philosophise on the equal importance in life of seemingly grand and apparently petty things.

This possibility of the trivial leading to grand theorisations is illustrated even better in the third of my chosen episodes. In the second essay, now very much in Palamou, Sanjibchandra narrates an incident. One day, when he was shouting after his 'ungrateful French dog (poodle)' ('poodle' in English in the original), he noticed a strange pattern of echoes comprising long and short sounds (S. Chattopadhyay 1880–1883, 27). He then theorises how different layers of rocks can be conductors or non-conductors of sound in a display of playful, though almost certainly faux, geological knowledge. A similar instance of the trivial leading to what appear to be grand cultural revelations or 'scientific' theorisations occurs in the fourth episode too. In the third essay, Sanjibchandra describes how once, when he was watching a bumblebee and a freshly flowered vine play with each other, he suddenly heard a sound behind him — the Sanskrit sloka 'rādhe manyuṁ parihara hariḥ pādamūle tavāyam' being uttered out of nowhere. On closer inspection, he discovered that a small, nondescript pigeon or dove was making the sound in the *mandākrāntā* metre.[12] He soon observes, however, that it was not exactly the same verse but was in the same metre, and this sloka being the only verse in the mandākrāntā metre that our author knew, he initially thought the bird was singing that sloka too. This incident becomes an occasion for the author to digress at length and quote the entire quartet where this verse occurs, explaining its meaning and context (37–39). He also makes this an occasion to name Charles Darwin and theorise, in a parodic fashion, I surmise, on avian evolutionary collective memory (39)! None of this is probably done seriously; Sanjibchandra may not really be interested in enlightening the reader about some bizarre geological or evolutionary theory or even Sanskrit prosody. Rather, such theories are presented in jest, in a playful act of undercutting purposefulness. This surmise is corroborated by the fifth and final episode I want to recount. At the end of the fourth essay, his narration of an occasion when the local Kol tribals had invited him for an evening dance performance is filled

12 The mandākrāntā *chanda* is a metre commonly used in Sanskrit where each line has seventeen syllables divided into three sections: the first containing four long syllables, the second five short and one long syllable and the third a combination of seven syllables in the following order — long, short, long, long, short, long, terminal — where the length of the terminal syllable is not significant.

with extremely sensuous descriptions of the young Kol girls' practically uncovered bodies and their sexualised dance moves. However, just when the reader feels that he has caught Sanjibchandra in a weak moment of induced seriousness and sexual tension, he undercuts it all, directly addressing the reader by saying, 'If you want to read my writings, you have to bear with such delirious talk' (52). He concludes the chapter on a most inconclusive note, leaving the excited reader in the lurch: 'I could not stay on till the end of the dance; it was too cold. I could not stay long' (52). While one could cite many more episodes from the text, the sample already given should suffice.

The motive force behind this particular instance of travel writing is indeed that of articulating one's sense of incommensurable wonder at encountering an unknown world, as shown in Sanjibchandra's description in the second essay of his first glimpse of Palamou. He uses a series of images — 'when I could see Palamou from a distance, it felt like as if clouds have descended on earth' (S. Chattopadhyay 1880–1883, 25), a 'copper-hued forest […] as if covered all over with curly hair' (26) and a landscape of 'hills after hills, and after that more hills; like innumerable waves of a troubled river' (26). However, this text does this articulation not by converting this incommensurability into a systematic descriptive discourse but by making it even more chaotic. Hence, the text ends on the chaos of a bacchanalian note, the bulk of the sixth essay being devoted to the country liquor *moua* (*mahua* in its more common current Bengali orthographical form). Sanjibchandra articulates his sympathetic wonder about the liquor-drinking habits of the indigenous population of the Palamou region earlier in the narrative too, in the second essay, for instance (31). Even so, in the final essay, he really dwells on it. His long description of *moua* associates the tree and the flower that the drink is derived from with sheer chaos: the tree is not cultivated but grows in the wild and sheds its flowers naturally to the ground, where 'thousands of flies and bees flit and fly around. The entire forest resounds with their noise, as if a market has set itself up at a distance' (65). Lest we come to believe that it is the sublimity of this chaos that the author proposes as a cherished category, he undercuts that too by contrasting the harmfulness of this country liquor with foreign liquor: 'With foreign liquor one can retain both one's intoxication and liver. With moua, only one of the two stays — intoxication. The liver does not; that is why this liquor is so disparaged, so cheap' (68). In an even more comical tone, he recounts how he benefited once from *moua* because his servant confessed to stealing money from him under its intoxicating effect (67). This inconclusiveness, coupled with the bacchanalian, Dionysian celebration of an inutile, non-austere version of the Self, makes Sanjibchandra conclude his travelogue on an irreverent and inconsequential note:

> If prepared following English procedures, brandy may be distilled out of moua, but that will be a costly affair. A church father once prepared champagne out of our local *jām* [blackberries], but he could not circulate it because of lack of money. If we could export our country liquor once to England, the goal of our lives would be fulfilled, many of our internal pains would be remedied. (68)

Evidently, such a closure to this travelogue is hardly any closure at all. In its unfulfillability, to say nothing about the irrelevance of the desire itself to the narrative, this inconclusive ending simply exposes the deep irony that underlies travel writing as a means to carve out one's Self.

Needless to say, this ironic realisation of self-deprecation, as the travelling authoritative Self ventures out to encounter its Other, has immediate political overtones too. Sanjibchandra, a colonial administrator and thus part of the establishment, notices with quite some sympathy the plight of the hapless Kols in the hands of the 'Hindustani moneylenders'. In the fifth essay, there is a long account of how the poor, unlettered Kols are ensnared in debt traps by these moneylenders and exploited till their very end, with the amount being extorted at exorbitant rates (S. Chattopadhyay 1880–1883, 58–61). Sanjibchandra is scathingly critical of the system: 'The plight of the Kols is very normal. They have only one way out — running away. Many are saved by fleeing. Those who cannot flee stay bondaged to the moneylender for life' (59). He goes on to add with some racial stereotyping perhaps:

> Before the Hindustani moneylenders started residing in the area, the Kols were not so poor.[…] If Hindustani civilisation had not entered the scene, till today, the system of debt would not have arisen amongst the Kol.[…] At one point, Jewish moneylenders brought their civilised rules of moneylending to uncivilised Europe and caused a lot of damage. Now, the Hindustani moneylenders are causing similar harm to the Kols. (60–61)

That a piece of travel writing like *Palamou* would generate a possibly radical critique of the very system that the travelling Self populates is expected, but one can argue that here the critique is less directed towards the Self and more towards other others like the Hindustanis and Jews. However, the text is introspectively and self-reflexively critical of the Bengali *bhadralok* too. Right from the first essay, Sanjibchandra ironically criticises the pretentious and parochial Bengali who always thinks 'Bengalis are all good people; in Bengal, only the neighbours are evil. The neighbours are jealous, arrogant, fond of fighting, greedy, miserly, deceitful' (S. Chattopadhyay 1880–1883, 19). This self-critical, ironic glance towards one's own *bhadralok* status as a collaborator of the British who is pompously full of narratives of his own advancement and superiority gets even more sharply articulated at the end of the second essay, when he sarcastically says,

> All around, there is so much laudation about the advancement of the Bengali. The Bengali is learning English, getting titles bestowed upon him and travelling abroad. The Bengali is climbing up the ladder of civilisation. What is there to worry about the Bengali anymore? But all this is purely external. Would it not be better to investigate the internal affairs of Bengali society? I hear that the Bengali population is increasing too. Wonderful! (34)

As the gentleman, the *bhadralok*, encounters his 'uncivilised' Other without, in the course of his travels within jungles of Palamou, this ironic recasting of his officious Self leads also to a recovery of the Other within, an other linguistic register. This other language is the language of quotidian speech, of the household speech of women for instance, the register that enables one to blurt out one's inner emotions, to curse and fight if one so wishes. It is as if this everyday speech can expose the inefficacy of the official lingo of the male *bhadralok* — the gentleman's language, the *sādhu-bhāshā*. Sanjibchandra says,

> The wives of the gentry do not use the gentleman's language (sādhu-bhāshā). They say that the sadhu-bhāshā is extremely poor; you cannot curse in this language, fight in it, or express much of your thoughts in it. If this is true, may it be said with ease — to hell with sādhu-bhāshā. (S. Chattopadhyay 1880–1883, 64)

This statement is doubly ironic since Sanjibchandra writes *Palamou* in the *sādhu-bhāshā*, but this duplicity is precisely the point. Here, travel writing becomes the means of subversively and incipiently critiquing the co-ordinates of the construction of one's Self while partaking of and participating in the official means and lingo of that construction itself.

To conclude, let me briefly repeat what I have already said earlier. Sanjibchandra Chattopadhyay's *Palamou* is a curious text. It is a piece of travel writing that continuously and self-consciously subverts the very idea of purposive travel. In its deliberate digressions, circumlocutions and dealings with the trivial, the quotidian and the disruptive, it ends up deprecating the authoritative travelling and writing-about-travelling Self. As the Self of the author figure — a figure of authority in more senses than one in this instance, given that his travel described here is in his capacity as the colonial administrator of the very area he surveys

— encounters the domain of the Other in his act of travel and in writing about it, he discovers the Other within. This emergence of ironic self-critique leads the official and officious *bhadralok* to cast his self in a mould that is otherwise than self-same. I have further proposed in this essay that this ironic self-introspection and tentativeness is characteristic of the very essence of travelogy, which makes *Palamou* — an otherwise inconsequential text — a paradigmatic text of travel writing in Bengali. And, as I have hypothesised further, and let me close with it, *Palamou* (1880–1883) constitutes the veritable missing link in Bengali travel writing and Bengali travelogy, where a long history of purposeful travel writing in the language could finally graduate to the domain of a purposeless wandering — of a sheer losing and recasting the Self in travel.

References

Chattopadhyay, Bankimchandra, ed. 1898. *Sanjibani Sudha, arthāt Sanjibchandra Chattopadhyay pranita grantha sakaler utkrishtāngsha samgraha.* [In Bengali.] Part I. Calcutta: Hare Press. Accessed 29 December 2020. https://archive.org/details/in.ernet.dli.2015.317066.

Chattopadhyay, Sanjibchandra. 1880–1883 (BS 1287–1289). *Palamou.* [In Bengali.] Accessed 29 December 2020. https://www.banglabooks.in/bangla-ebooks/sanjib-chandra-chattopadhyay/palamou-by-sanjib-chandra-chattopadhyay-pdf/. Also available at https://drive.google.com/file/d/0B0kuPnq8DRkQaVlBNXpBZlJtTUk/view.

———. 1944 (BS 1351). *Palamou*, edited by Brajendranath Bandyopadhyay and Sajanikanta Das. [In Bengali.] Calcutta: Bangiya Sahitya Parishat. Accessed 29 December 2020. https://archive.org/details/Palamou.

Tagore, Rabindranath. [1894 (BS 1301)] 1907 (BS 1314). 'Sanjibchandra (Palamou)'. [In Bengali.] In *Adhunik Sahitya*, 46–57. 4th reprint Calcutta: Visva-Bharati, 1938 (BS 1345). Accessed 29 December 2020. https://archive.org/details/in.ernet.dli.2015.289292.

9

Pilgrimage Briefs: *Negotiating Faith, Aesthetics and Environment*

Jayati Gupta

A pilgrim is essentially a traveller who undertakes a journey to some sacred destination considered holy in the context of a particular religious belief system. Even outside religion, there could be secular sites that later acquire a reputation as a place to be revered. A pilgrim can very often be identified with a wanderer in quest of intangible experiences of beatitude or spirituality that can transform both the self and everyday perspectives. Metaphorically, everyone of us is a pilgrim on the path of life, and this analogy of life to a journey is ingrained in most cultures from antiquity. The 17th-century Japanese poet Bashō is well known for continuing as well as breaking with traditional or classical Japanese ways of seeing and responding to experiences and environment in his travel journal *The Narrow Road of Oku*, that documents one of the journeys that he undertook (1689) with his disciple Sora.

> *The months and days are passing wayfarers through endless ages,* and travellers too the years that come and go. Those who float their life away on boats, or meet old age plodding before a horse — they spend their days in journeying, and call the journey home. And many of those men of old too died on the journey. (Bashō 2019, 264)

This awareness of mortality, flux, divine presence and spiritual insight marks the rites of passage in pilgrimage narratives spanning an expansive spectrum of ritual practices, temporal spaces, geographical regions and ethnic denominations. Etymologically, the word *pilgrimage* can be traced back to the Latin word *peregrinatio*, equivalent to 'wandering abroad' or a journey in foreign terrain. In medieval Europe and ancient civilisations, the pilgrimage or wandering acquired a more 'sacred' connotation, if anything, to make such journeys permissible. Religions may have their different origins, histories and practices, but 'going on a pilgrimage' is an action that generates an attitude of veneration and faith about a place, a destination or a shrine. The 'pilgrimage remained a favored *image* of travel' in post-medieval and even more secular contemporary eras (Howard 1980, 3).

> It [a pilgrimage] is journey both outwards, to new, strange, dangerous places, and inwards to spiritual improvement, whether through increased self-knowledge or through the braving of physical dangers.... At one extreme, the pilgrim may pursue physical ecstasy in seeking out the place where the founder of his or her religion once lived and taught; at the other he or she may look for a miracle that offers purely physical benefits. (Barber 1991, 1)

'*Tirtha*' is the equivalent Sanskrit word for a pilgrimage, referring probably to any waterbody. Tracing its etymology reveals that the word is derived from the Sanskrit root verb *teer*, meaning 'to cross over' or 'to surpass', to which a suffix is added. So, according to the derived meaning, a *tirtha* symbolises 'trans-cosmic zones of transcendence' from where one can symbolically surpass or overcome one's actions or karma, which involves transcending to a higher stage of life (Khanna 2003, 101). Visiting a holy place is often part of ritual cleansing and purification, a pause in the tyranny of worldliness and materialism. Going on a pilgrimage is an action that can spiritually empower an ordinary individual, a *grihasthya* or householder, to tread the path towards godliness by purifying the heart and enlightening the mind.

In ancient Indian literature, beginning with the Vedas[1], we get an idea of sacred geography, the location of remote pilgrimage sites and the names of sanctified rivers, forests and mountains. In the epics, in the Mahabharata and the Puranas, the semi-historical and religious narratives, several *tirtha*s or pilgrimage routes are mentioned. There was even something in the pattern of a 'grand pilgrimage' that strung together several holy sites, often beginning from Pushkar in Rajasthan. The journey then continued along the courses of the great subcontinental rivers, the Narmada, the Sindhu (Indus) and the Ganges, before traversing the remote Himalayan regions to look for the sources of these sacred streams. Long before the arrival of colonisers in India and the mapping of the subcontinent, travel had been a part of indigenous life, and pilgrim trails were as well defined as land and sea trade routes.

Pilgrims in India traditionally travelled on foot, largely by boat and sometimes in wheeled vehicles or carts, *palki*s, *doolie*s and *jhampan*s. Occasionally, they used animals such as horses, donkeys or camels.

---

1 The dates of the four main Vedas are controversial and, according to some scholars, go back to the 5th century BCE.

To ensure their physical safety, they were often in large groups while travelling on land and water. Early pilgrimage texts or narratives written by the pilgrim are difficult to procure because most often in medieval Europe and ancient India, those who went on pilgrimage were like Geoffrey Chaucer's pilgrims[2] — 'sondry folk', 'common folk' (1986, line 25). Literacy among such pilgrims may have been minimal, and more importantly, the need to record the journey was only secondary. The site or destination and the action of going were the two primary concerns of early pilgrims. Pilgrimage as a collective activity often brings together a disparate assemblage of people of different age groups and social standing, motivated by their own individual goals. Though overtly a religious exercise or an act of profound faith, a pilgrimage was a part of popular culture and social patterns. Certainly, it is not to be constructed as a rarefied form of travel governed by esoteric religious dogma.

The withdrawal from domestic chores and daily household routine for women and from material and financial obligations for men signified the time and space allotted by a pilgrimage for spiritual well-being and introspection. The religiously inclined were initiated into a daily schedule of ritual bathing, *daan* (offerings), fasting and abstinence, worship, partaking of the *prasadam* (sanctified food), *yatra* (journey) and *pradakshina* (circumambulation)that accrued merit for salvation. In India, the location of several shrines in the spectacular northern Himalayan region, often designated as a sacred *kshetra*, the abode of the gods, led inevitably to veneration of primitive, elemental nature as the abode of the Divine.

यो देवोऽग्नौ योऽप्सु यो विश्वं भुवनमाविवेश।
य ओषधीषु यो वनस्पितषु तस्मै देवाय नमो नमः॥

Salutations to that Divinity who is in the fire, who is in the water, who is in the plants, who is in the trees, who has pervaded the whole universe.
Shevatasvatara Upanishad, Chapter 2, verse 17.
(Swami Tyagisananda, 1949)

Madhu Khanna, in her essay 'In the Flow of Modernity: Some Reflections on *Tirtha* and *Murti* in Hindu India', writes that the 'sacred geography of India is mapped around the scenic grandeur in nature. Places manifesting some specific attributes of natural beauty, are prone to be regarded as

2 The English poet Geoffrey Chaucer's *The Canterbury Tales* is a Middle English (late14th-century) collection of stories narrated by an assorted group of pilgrims who journey in spring from an inn in Southwark where they assemble to the shrine of Thomas Becket in Canterbury.

reflecting divinity in natural form' (Khanna 2003, 100). Such places could be conceptualised as the abodes of rishis or yogis, the location of myths regarding deities or sites of miracles, manifestations and revelations. Even at a more secular level, any spectacular natural scene evokes reverence and spiritual curiosity that combines religiosity and aesthetic perception.

Bankim Chandra Chattopadhyay's[3] novel *Kapalkundala* (1866) opens with a conversation between the young Nabakumar and an elderly gentleman who was a co-pilgrim returning on the same boat on a dark, foggy night of Magh[4] from a pilgrimage to Ganga-Sagar. Their boat loses its bearings, and the boatmen are clueless about the direction in which they have to navigate. An old pilgrim fretfully castigates the boatmen as he is in a particular hurry to return home and attend to material pursuits. Nabakumar tries to pacify him by remarking that he should have stayed at home if his worldly concerns were so preoccupying.

> The patriarch retorted harshly, 'I shouldn't have come? With one foot in the grave, when do you think I should be accruing merit for my salvation?'
>
> The youth replied, 'If I have understood the Shastras correctly, one can gather merit at home just as one may acquire it by going on a pilgrimage.'

The old man asked, 'So, why did you come?'

> The young man replied, 'I did tell you a while ago that I wished eagerly to catch a glimpse of the ocean, that is the reason why I came'. (Chattopadhyay 1970, 85; translation is mine)

Pilgrimage Discourses

The pilgrimage discourse is inevitably interlinked with the aesthetics of curiosity and the realisation of the concept of *saundarya* or beauty. Pilgrimage texts have no preconceived model as these emerge out of cultural practices and the forces of social change. Such texts in the late 19th and early 20th century invariably embodied changing religio-social paradigms as the assumptions of an earlier age were largely modified

3 Bankim Chandra Chattopadhyay (1838–1894) was a novelist, essayist and journalist who made a pioneering contribution to Bangla prose. He is the composer of India's national song, 'Vande Mataram'.

4 Magh in the Bengali calendar corresponds to mid-January to mid-February in the Gregorian calendar.

by secular education and more contemporary forms of travel. Surinder Bhardwaj points out that the fundamental assumptions of a religious tradition can be revealed through pilgrimage (Bhardwaj and Lochtefeld 2004). For example, he speaks of the centrality of the Hajj and the pilgrimage to Mecca as symbolically indicative of the oneness of the Divine; the Hindu pilgrimage, on the other hand, is more eclectic and incorporates an infinite variety of sites, often regional and sometimes pan-Indian, because Hinduism is more decentralised and diffuse.

This chapter seeks to examine pilgrimage narratives that open up the question of form, content and perspective — the pertinent issue being whether to consider such texts as a subgenre of the travel narrative. The earliest text chosen (1856–1857) is by Maharshi Devendranath Tagore[5], composed as an autobiography and not as a traditional pilgrimage journey to a shrine. It records the wanderings of a pilgrim soul and is centred on a very personal spiritual quest. He records in his autobiography that he 'became eager to descend into the deeper recesses of my soul in search of the Supreme Soul' (D. Tagore 2002, 105). He continues, 'I shall leave my home, never to return' (105). In the archetypal pilgrimage text, however, the return is as important as the journey. Devendranath finds spiritual peace as he meditates amidst nature and feels a oneness with pristine nature — the hills, forests and valleys in which the Divine inheres. He follows no ritual and does not seek a tangible image of God as he intuitively feels the formless Brahman in nature itself.

The three other narratives that are considered here are more intriguing: *The Master as I Saw Him* (1910), *Notes of Some Wanderings with the Swami Vivekananda* (1913) and *Kedar Nath and Badri Narayan (A Pilgrim's Diary)* (1916). Margaret Elizabeth Noble, better known as Sister Nivedita, wrote *The Master as I Saw Him* (published in 1910) as a biography. She writes of her encounter with Swami Vivekananda in 1895 on his visit to London after a tour of America and her decision to travel to India in early 1898.The biography morphs into a pilgrimage narrative in which Nivedita describes the swami's 'Wanderings in Northern India' (1910, Chap. V). She writes:

> The summer of 1898 stands out in my memory as a series of pictures, painted like old altar-pieces against a golden background of religious ardour and simplicity, and all alike glorified by the presence of one who, to us in his immediate circle, formed their central point. (Nivedita 1910, 113)

5 Devendranath Tagore (1817–1905), son of Prince Dwarakanath Tagore and father of the poet Rabindranath Tagore, was the founder of the ashram at Santiniketan. His *Autobiography* recounts his travels. The English translation of the Bangla text by Indira Devi and Satyendranath Tagore has been used here.

Curiously, Nivedita refers to no singled out *tirtha* destination but to 'wanderings' of a compatible group amidst scenes of spectacular natural beauty; the worship is not dedicated to any *murti* in the sanctum sanctorum of a shrine but focuses on the dynamic presence and discourses of a guru — of Swami Vivekananda — that was in itself a transformative experience. Nivedita was still a foreigner who had arrived in India, and the 'object-lessons' in Indian history and culture made her an eager seeker, imbibing a consciousness of indigenous history, tradition and myth.

The journey occupied a temporal span between early May and late October 1898. It traversed historical sites like Patna, the ancient ruins of Pataliputra, the riverfront of Benares (Varanasi), the nawabi luxury of Lucknow, beautiful cities and the countryside, even 'as we passed across the long stretches of the Plains, covered with fields and farms and villages' (Nivedita 1910, 115). The experience of journeying across the north-western terai was coming to terms with a deep historical consciousness of the country's past and a direct encounter with rural India's hospitable, compassionate culture. The initiation of a foreigner into the cultural nuances of an indigenous civilisation was as much of a self-transforming influence as the conversations and discourses of Vivekananda, the spiritual guru.

The other text that emerged from this sojourn, titled *Notes of Some Wanderings with the Swami Vivekananda* (1913), is an equally curious narrative that records sojourns 'in the Himalayas, at Naini-Tal and Almora; afterwards wandering here and there through Kashmir', including a visit to the sacred shrine of Amarnath (Nivedita 1913, 1). Uncharacteristically, the 'pilgrim' records in the account how 'those journeys were delightful. We were always sorry to reach a destination' (68). Nivedita describes the actual traversing of geographical space from Nainital to Almora and then again from Almora to Kathgodam: 'How beautiful the journey was! Dim, almost tropical forests, troops of monkeys and the ever-wondrous Indian night' (64). Unusually, the destination that transports one towards the goal and is a culmination of the inner pilgrimage is reflected and experienced in the journey itself — *sat-chit-ananda* (existence-consciousness-bliss), a subjective spiritual experience of reality. In the entry for 20–22 June 1898, travelling along the river Jhelum to Baramulla and towards Srinagar, Nivedita records the aesthetic experience that is identified with a form of spiritual realisation:

> We found ourselves, next day, in the midst of a beautiful valley, ringed around with snow-mountains. This is known as the Vale of Kashmir,

> but it might be more accurately described, perhaps as the Vale of Srinagar. The city of Islamabad had its own valley, high up the river, and to reach it we had to wind in and out among the mountains. The sky above was the bluest of the blue and the water-road, along which we travelled, was also, perforce, blue.
>
> Sometimes our way lay through great green tangles of lotus-leaves with a rosy dower or two, and on each side stretched the fields, in some of which, as we came, they were reaping. The whole was a symphony in blue and green and white, so exquisitely pure and vivid that for a while the response of the soul to its beauty was almost pain! (85–86)

From 29 July to 8 August 1898, the swami, who had chosen Nivedita to accompany him, visited the pilgrimage site of Amarnath, taking the Pahalgam route along with other groups of sadhus and devotees (143–153). The narrative concentrates on the rugged beauty of the terrain, documenting the arduous trek along glaciers and steep mountain trails over the dry gravel bed of the Pantajharni.[6] Pilgrim behaviour and rituals en route are reported with curiosity. Nivedita is witness to the exhilaration of the swami, trying to fathom the idiom of Hindu worship that becomes embedded in the text. Nivedita understands the euphoric experience of communion with Siva by seeing it reflected in Vivekananda after he emerges from the cave, having followed the Hindu rituals of worship offered to the ice lingam. Perceptibly, the 'ways of seeing' differ from one individual to another, and her objective account records that 'the great ice-Siva', in a niche of deepest shadow, seemed as if throned on its own base (149). A few minutes passed, and then Swami Vivekananda turned to leave the cave. To him, the heavens had opened. He had touched the feet of Siva. He said afterwards that he had to hold himself tight lest he 'should swoon away' (149).

For Vivekananda, the darshan was a life-changing vision. For his disciple Nivedita, watching her guru undergoing an internal transformation was a vicarious spiritual experience. For her, it was still the flowers and ferns blooming beside the path, the beauty of the snow-clad mountains and the dangerousness of the trek that were relevant details. Swami Vivekananda, however, predicts the future: 'You do not now understand. But you have made the pilgrimage, and it will go on

6 Though Nivedita uses this name for the river, it is the Panchtarni River near the Amarnath temple fed by five tributary streams from the glacier. She describes 'a dry, river-bed, all gravel, and through this ran five streams' in which pilgrims bathed, moving from one stream to another before entering Amarnath.

working. Causes must bring their effects. You will understand better afterwards. The effects will come' (Nivedita 1913, 151).

Sister Nivedita's *Kedar Nath and Badri Narayan: A Pilgrim's Diary* (1916) is conceptualised as a formal account of a traditional Hindu *tirthayatra* (pilgrimage).

> It is very characteristic, that while Hinduism lays great emphasis on the sacredness of the northern pilgrimage, it is yet difficult to obtain any authentic information about its details, before one starts. For this reason it seems almost obligatory upon those who perform it, that they should, if possible, publish their experiences, for the guidance of others, who are eager to undertake it. At present, there is very little that the intending traveller can make sure of, either as regards time, distances, or the accommodation available. And few things are more necessary than the frank publication of the actual diary of some pilgrim, to which all the would-be adventurous may obtain easy access. (Nivedita [1916] 1928, 2–3)

How, if at all, does a pilgrimage narrative differ from any travelogue when 'pilgrims, like any travelers, were too often distracted by the sights of that unfamiliar world, as moralists unendingly warned they would be' (Zacher 1976, 51). Does curiosity necessarily impinge on the sacred intentions of a pilgrimage? Is a pilgrim on an interior journey seeking divinity within, or is the seeker in quest of omnipotence in the environment traversed? The intersection of the discourses of faith and spirituality with that of aesthetics and environment hinges entirely on the perspective of the pilgrim-traveller.

The primary issue is the ambivalence of motive. The Puranas find an equivalence between *tirthaphala* or the fruits of a pilgrimage journey and ritual sacrifices. Yet there is nothing in a pilgrimage text *tirthakatha*, which compels us to believe that it records a ritualistic form of religious adoration *tirthamahatya*, and ecstasy that presumably forms part of the religious exercise. It is certainly not a journey in search of empirical knowledge but one that provides aesthetic satisfaction that becomes an intrinsic part of any spiritual adventure. It often has a cathartic effect on the individual's equations vis-à-vis society and the cosmos.

Wanderings of the Pilgrim Soul

Maharshi Devendranath Tagore (1817–1905) records his spiritual transformation and the growth of his soul in his *Atmajibani* (1898).

Specific sections of the narrative relate to his physical roaming and wandering for which he found sanction in the *Chhandogya Upanishad*:[7]

> य इहात्मानमिनवुद्य व्रजन्त्येतंश्च सत्यान्कामांस्तेषां सवेर्षु लोके षु कामचारो भवित॥८.१.६॥
>
> Those who wander here now, knowing the soul and her true desires, they become free to roam hereafter in all the worlds, and can pass freely from one world to another. (D. Tagore 2002, 106)

He justifies his wish to roam freely like the 'dark-blue clouds [that] brought great joy and peace' to his mind (106). This sense of release and renunciation of worldly pursuits marked his journey into the hills of Simla (Shimla). On 19 Ashwin BS 1778, roughly late August 1856, Devendranath embarked on a serendipitous boat ride to Navadwipa[8], then from there via Monghyr (Munger) to Patna and then to Benares, which took about a month and a half. He took a stagecoach from Benares to Allahabad (Prayagraj), where the carriage was hoisted on a ferry boat to be ferried across from the right bank where he had arrived. He proceeded by river from Agra to Delhi via Mathura and Vrindavan. He took a stagecoach to Umballa (Ambala), visited Lahore in a *dooly* and returned to Amritsar from where he travelled to Simla via Kalka. He traversed the mountainous interior regions from Simla on horseback or in jhampans.

Devendranath was not a pilgrim to any particular *tirthasthala*. When he was heckled by pandas[9] in Prayag, he said, 'I have not come as a pilgrim' (2002, 109) as he considered himself a wanderer on the face of this earth unattached to any single dogma. Perhaps he shared the medieval Christian idea that every Christian is a homeless traveller on earth (emphasising temporality) in search of the true destination in the otherworld. Devendranath belonged to the land-owning elite of Bengal and had reluctantly inherited the commercial interests of his father, Dwarakanath. His inclination was towards spirituality, tangibly manifest in his effort to reform Hinduism. His Tattvabodhini Sabha accepted the tenets of the Brahmo Sabha founded by Rammohan Roy, and the two *sabhas* eventually merged into the liberal Brahmo Samaj. Devendranath's restlessness of mind led him intuitively to renounce the world and set out on his travels to control the spiritual struggle and attain the perfection

---

7 The Sanskrit version is not there in the translated text I am using, where only the translation given here.

8 Nabadwip in Nadia District of West Bengal is the birthplace of Sree Chaitanya and the Bhakti Movement.

9 In north India, a panda is a Brahmin who serves as a pilgrim guide.

of the soul. This idea of spiritual restlessness transformed into physical wandering and roaming focussed on the motif of a quest — the quest for perfection, which is more than a mere aesthetic ideal.

The Hindu cultural practice of going on pilgrimages, even by women, was well entrenched in Devendranath's time. In his autobiography, Devendranath records how he 'cried bitterly' every time his grandmother 'went to Jagannath Kshetra and Brindaban', leaving him behind (2002, 1). Later, when he learnt to question religious practices, his scepticism about pilgrimage journeys or *yatra*s is recorded in his autobiography:

> There were so many people hurrying towards God — so many to the temple of Vis'wes'war, so many to the shrine of Jagannath, so many to Dwaraka and Haridwar — people without number. Everywhere the temples were filled with the presence of gods, overflowing with the rapture of devotion, ringing with the holy sounds of worship; but to me all was empty. (D. Tagore 2002, 35)

The crux of the text is not reaching any particular shrine that is replete with the myths of a specific place derived from the Sthala Puranas or the veneration of gods and goddesses enshrined in the *tirthamahatya*s. The trajectory of famed saints and rishis are often inextricably linked with particular ashrams or mutts that become *tirthasthala*s. For Devendranath, sacred sites like Benares, Prayag, Mathura, Vrindavan, Lahore and Amritsar were imbued with celestial significance, like the historical site of the Taj Mahal in Agra which, 'with its halo of beauty, seemed to have dropped on the earth from the moon' (D. Tagore 2002, 109) or the Qutb Minar outside Delhi where 'ascending the topmost turret of the Minar', he was 'enraptured to see the marvellous vast plains beneath the semicircular horizon, proclaiming the glory of the Most High' (111). On his visit to Amritsar, he delves into the history and practices of Sikhism and visits the Golden Temple 'where God is worshipped with sacred chanting' (112). His eclectic faith finds the practice of worshipping God through prayers day and night for twenty-one hours a commendable example that 'should be followed by the Brahmas' (113). Restless and distressed individuals could thus find solace and peace in prayer.

Devendranath's pilgrimage text combines the subjective/emotive perceptions, even as the mimetic representation define the physical contours of the journey. In the pilgrim narratives composed before the late 19th century, journeys were undertaken to acquire religious merit, social merit or both by visiting sacred sites. The pilgrims seem to be travelling through a neutral space that only possessed coherence because it was linked together by temples and sacred sites (Chatterjee 1995, 381). Awareness of secular history is singularly lacking in early pilgrim accounts. However, Devendranath, who was in Simla during the Sepoy Uprising of 1857, records all that happened: the British order to disarm the Gurkhas, the affront to their loyalty, the attack and defence of Simla, the terror unleashed on that peaceful settlement, the flight out of the hill station and the subsequent return. When he was passing through Cawnpore (Kanpur) in the aftermath of the massacre, he hears of the *badshah* of Delhi being taken away as a captive and remarks philosophically, 'On my way to Simla, I had seen him happy, flying kites on the Jumna sands, and on my way back I found him a captive, being led to prison. Who can tell what fate will overtake anybody in this dissolving sorrowful world?' (D. Tagore 2002, 142).

Devendranath Tagore's text hinges on the liberal tenets of Upanishadic philosophy that formed the foundation of the Brahmo religion. He discerns the hand of the Divine in all events even as the journey brought him face to face with an omnipotent presence.

> I saw that 'He is in the sky, filled with energy and immortality, the Supreme Being, all-perceiving.' This omniscient, radiant, and immortal Being pervaded all space. In the temple of the universe I saw the Lord of the universe. Nobody can place Him anywhere, nobody can make Him with the hand, He exists for ever in His own self. (D. Tagore 2002, 35–36)

Devendranath was convinced that the beauty of the universe was a manifestation of God, and the universe was his abode and temple. 'Suvishalam idam viswam brahmamandiram' (*Shloka Samgraha* 2003). In the Indian tradition, concepts of truth (*satyam*), auspiciousness (*shivam*) and beauty (*sundaram*) are inextricably intertwined in the human consciousness. The phrase 'Satyam, Shivam, Sundaram', writes Karan Singh, 'expresses beautifully a special confluence of the devotional, the erotic-sensuous, and the real' (2003, x).[10] Devendranath's narrative is, therefore, an exception. His rambles in the Himalayas are somewhat unique in that he gave a degree of attention to nature not encountered before in either pilgrim texts or travel narratives. He described the landscape and Himalayan flora with unsurpassed attention to detail and acute observation. However, Tagore's admiration for nature did not constitute an end in itself as it marked his search for a unified consciousness. His search was not for the aesthetic value of the picturesque but for a deeper meaning that lies beyond the sensuous and temporal.

10 Karan Singh makes this observation in the prefatory essay, titled 'Satyam, Shivam, Sundaram' (2003).

Describing his solitary walks in the hills around Simla, Devendranath writes:

> But the various kinds of grass and plants that grow on the hillside are very beautiful, and countless flowers bloom there in profusion. White, red, yellow, blue, and gold, blossoms of all colours, attract the eye from all directions. The mark of God's most skilful hand seemed evident in the grace and beauty of these flowers, and their stainless purity. Though these did not possess a scent equal to their beauty, another, a kind of white rose, bloomed in bunches throughout the wilderness, and made the whole forest-land fragrant with perfume. My eyes were opened, and my heart expanded, I saw the Universal Mother's hand resting on those small white blossoms. Who was there in this forest to inhale the scent of these flowers or see their beauty? Yet with loving care had she endowed them with sweet scent and loveliness, moistened them with dew, and set them upon the creeper! Her mercy and tenderness became manifest in my heart. Lord! When such is thy compassion for these little flowers, what must be the extent of Thy mercy for us? (2002, 126–127)

To view nature as a manifestation of the omnipresent and omnipotent Divine was a realisation that evoked intense spiritual experiences that were a form of enlightenment, essentially a deeply religious sentiment. He invoked the Upanishads just as he recited verses from the poet Hafiz[11]. He witnessed the majesty and magnificence of God in the 'monstrously high snow-clad mountain crest ... with head upraised like an uplifted thunderbolt' to achieve a realisation that transcended the geographical space (130).

Sojourner in the Sacred Abode

In the writings of Sister Nivedita, the perception of nature and appreciation of its beauty also evokes a reverence for the divine creator. However, the entire geographical space of the northern *tirtha* is conceptualised as a confirmation that it was indeed the sacred abode of the Hindu gods and goddess — Kailash and Manasarovar, Amarnath, Kedarnath and Badrinath.

---

11 Hafiz (literally the 'keeper'/memoriser of the Koran) refers to the Iranian lyric poet Khwāje Shams-od-Dīn Moḥammad Ḥāfeẓ-e Shīrāzī (1325–90). His Persian verses are steeped in spiritual mysticism. Devendranath could read and write Persian and read Hafiz in the original. He recited these verses to the young Rabindranath whose poetry was influenced by the tradition.

> Amongst the pines and deodars, with mountain-flowers underfoot, and hoary places of pilgrimage behind and before, it was not incredible. But we needed to drink deep for a while of the thought, that we might realise the Invisible Presence inhabiting and consecrating the holy home. (Nivedita 1928, 2)

Though Nivedita was a pilgrim-sojourner, she had the insights of an empirical, scientific observer. She was a foreigner seeking to understand the heritage of India's religious past that she endeavoured to see in continuum with a syncretic national unity. The search for an inner truth resulted in a simultaneous process of acculturation where history and tradition, reality and myth, came together. Wandering in the Himalayan region amidst forests, plains, lakes, hills, rivers and waterfalls it was a great way to attain the beatific vision and 'to read, and draw, and botanise' (1928, 51).

The intensity of aesthetic insight is imperceptibly drawn into identifying the ideal in the real. Wandering through the Vale of Kashmir or Srinagar, the valley ringed by snow-capped peaks, Nivedita communicates the deeply moving spiritual experience of encountering *saundarya*, a category of divine creativity. Beauty in nature translates as *saundarya*, a philosophical concept that is intrinsic to an object (here nature) but is received or perceived sensually. The 'aesthetic discourse of beauty is based on human creativity, not natural creation' (Dahejia 2003, 3). The subjective experience of beauty, or *sundar* as the Sanskrit adjective indicates, is a transcendent perception, and 'in its quintessential sense beauty is innate rather than created, to be discovered rather than ornamented, possessed rather than sculpted' (Dahejia 2003, 2).

Nivedita cites Vivekananda's theory about the Hindu love for nature and recounts how he pointed out — citing one example after another — that our Indian people always consecrated places of peculiar beauty and importance by making these their altars of worship (1913, 98). Therefore, the pantheistic view of nature and the human perception of natural beauty anchored spiritualism to humanism and religion to contemporary society. 'You know, we have a theory that the Universe is God's manifestation of Himself, just for fun, that the Incarnations came and lived there, "just for fun." Play, it was all play' (Nivedita 1910, 149–150). This conception of the cosmic force as inhering in the manifestation of God, whether human or natural, was the single determining factor of Upanishadic spiritualism.

Rabindranath Tagore captures this idea in his *Gitanjali*:

> When my play was with thee
> I never questioned whom thou wert...

> In the early morning thou wouldst call me from my sleep like my own comrade and lead me running from glade to glade. (2003, no. 97, 243)

Environment and Faith

Pilgrimages were occasions for social interaction or socialisation that broke class and community barriers and were a great equalising force. However, in the experience of Devendranath and Nivedita, the self-reflexive transformation takes place largely through negotiation with the natural world. Devendranath was a lone traveller, while Nivedita was in a compatible group. Her personal observations are outside the circle of *gurubhai*s, foreign disciples and the master. For Nivedita, the social learning was through emulating Vivekananda, who transgressed the boundaries of orthodox Hinduism by accepting food and water from Muslims. It was associated with the sadhus whom they met on the journey and the rural folk and boatmen whom they encountered. It was a direct lesson in humanism that underlies the eclectic nature of early Hinduism as a religion. Devendranath's narrative discovers the mystic and esoteric presence of the Eternal Being in every aspect of pristine nature as he 'used to wander about the rocky caves and enjoy the varied and marvellous beauty of the rivers and waterfalls' (D. Tagore 2002, 140). The life in nature, the whirls and currents of the river, the purity of its cool waters and its playfulness, strength and power amazed him. He learnt his lessons from every natural object, so much so that he finds the river following the commands of the 'All-ruling One' as it 'has to humble its pride and take a downward course, in order to fertilise the land, and make it yield grain' (140). The self-indulgence in a contemplative or meditative life amidst the sacred environs of the Himalayas marks a retreat from the everyday; the return is difficult but a necessary commandment to follow: 'The truth thou hast gained, the devotion and trustfulness that thou hast learnt there, go make them known to the world' (140).

Devendranath's consciousness of an all-pervading reality often amounts to a form of pantheism that pervades the topography of sacred Hindu India. The explanation offered, however, structures a realisation of a new reality:

> This universe is the outcome of perfect truth. This universe is relative truth; its Creator is the Truth of Truth, the Absolute Truth. This universe is not dream-stuff, neither is it mental illusion, but it exists in reality. The truth which has given it birth is the absolute truth, and this is relative truth. (D. Tagore 2002, Chap. XXIV, 87–88)

What Tagore interpreted as the absolute truth was perhaps central to the monotheistic Brahmo faith he initiated. The majestic Himalayas — with its rivers, falls, springs, forests and flora — and the entire region were 'infused with an inner spirituality, a space for meditation and experiencing divinity' (Banerjee and Basu 2014, 616). His spirituality inclined towards a synthesis of Vedantic Hinduism, Sufi-Islamic mysticism and Upanishadic realisation of the Atman-Brahman conjunction. His pilgrimage, therefore, converts the geographical space where he wanders into an emotionally charged spiritual arena.

For Nivedita, nature was a metaphor, a symbolic personification of the knowledge of God (the unmanifest) captured by human consciousness as 'infinite being' or 'infinite power'. This awareness of God was embedded in the 'great snow-mountains that were at once His Image and His Home. The young moon resting at night-fall above the glacier-cleft and the tossing pines, had suggested irresistibly the brow of the great God' (Nivedita 1910, 62). This Hindu idea of Siva was conceptualised by the 'spiritual intuition of man' (62). At the core of Advaita philosophy is the idea of how the absolute reality can appear as part of the phenomenal world while being the focal point of the individual consciousness. 'This personification of the unmanifesting, is necessarily succeeded by the opposite conception of God as the power behind all manifestation' (62).

The experiential aspect of Advaita philosophy involving the immanent presence of reality was more tangible than the transcendent.

Coming Home

The pilgrimage narratives considered in this chapter record journeys through sacral geographical spaces largely interiorised and spiritualised by the pilgrim. Nivedita's *Kedar Nath and Badri Narayan: A Pilgrim's Diary* connects up these northern *tirtha*s to a larger religious space that spans the subcontinent:

> The Northern Tirtha forms a great palimpsest of the history of Hinduism. Record has been written upon record. Wave has succeeded wave. And still the bond that knits these farthest points north to the farthest south, is living and unbroken, and the people stream along the pilgrim roads, in worship to testify to the fact that without the conception of India as a whole we can explain no single part or item of the Indian life. But the greatest of all synthesis is that which is written in the minds of the simple Himalayan peasantry themselves. (1928, 73–74)

This evocative reappraisal of pre-history that includes myths, legends and epic lore creates a communal space that addresses the expectations of institutionalised religion.

Through the pilgrim 'wanderings' of Devendranath and Nivedita, the spatial topography of the Himalayan regions is expanded into a transcendent cosmic realisation for the wanderers. Veneration, rather than curiosity, impacts the individualised description of the region. The 'foregrounding of the natural scenery' that 'marks ... out the secular traveller, and implicitly suggests the Himalaya as a secular space' (Banerjee and Basu 2014, 643) was a later development of the Anglo-vernacular–educated, elitist, middle-class pilgrim. A secular orientation, however, can contradict the pilgrimage text as, by and large, pilgrim sensibilities defined the textual rhetoric. Nivedita writes:

> To Indians themselves who have never before been on pilgrimage, the life of the pilgrim-roads is likely to be a revelation. Who uttered a doubt that India had a place and life for women? Certainly none who had ever seen a pilgrimage. Marching along we meet them, singly or in couples, or may be in long strings of tens and twenties, old and young mingled together. (1928, 4–5)

This may be one of the first descriptions of women pilgrims on the pilgrimage trail, of devout women having cast off their fears and inhibitions, 'telling her beads or lost in solitary thought' (5). There was an air of cheerfulness and festivity, with the women customarily decked in their jewellery. 'We are all out on a holiday together, and an air of gentle innocence and hilarity prevails, in the face of difficulties, and creates a sort of freemasonry amongst all who seek the common goal' (5).

The pilgrimage defines a shared social space comprising a collective cultural memory of a historical past and contemporary events. Devendranath captures historical monuments as markers of history, the fall of the Mughals as the transience of authority, and the Sepoy Uprising as a moral aberration. Nivedita finds justifications for geological myths and rationalises the anecdotes associated with places and shrines by delving into Shaivite and Vaishnavite, Buddhistic and Shankaracharyan influences, concluding that 'a feature of dominant religions' is that when 'fully formed they incorporate the debris of preceding systems' (1928, 86).

The dynamics of the pilgrimage texts considered here function as a dialectic of subjective perceptions and observed phenomena. The determining parameter of the aesthetic experience is the experience of beauty or *saundarya* as a concept and an ideal. Nature is an object of perception, sometimes interpreted as an ephemeral part of reality, *maya,* or considered a manifestation of the Absolute itself. The intense contemplation of the object of beauty results in a sense of bliss and serenity that draws one away from the temporal and spatial material world. The materiality of the experience, however, is embedded in the physical details of the pilgrimage, such as the spatio-temporal act of traversing the trail from one *chatti*[12] to another, interacting with fellow pilgrims or sustaining the excitement of the trek. Almost simultaneously, in these texts, the human consciousness moves from the sensuous to the super-sensuous or spiritual, thus drawing the subjective and objective fields of reality into a unified experience that merges the contentious values of aesthetics, ethics and religion.

References

Banerjee, Sandeep, and Subho Basu. 2014. 'Secularizing the Sacred, Imagining the Nation-Space: The Himalaya in Bengali Travelogues, 1856-1901'. *Modern Asian Studies* 49(3): 609–649. Accessed 19 June 2015. doi: 10.2307/24495446.

Barber, Richard. 1991. *Pilgrimages.* Woodbridge: Boydell Press.

Bashō, Matsuo. 2019. *Travels with A Writing Brush: Classical Japanese Travel Writing from the Manyoshuto Bashō.* Selected and translated by Meredith McKinney. London: Penguin Random House.

Bhardwaj, Surinder M., and James G. Lochtefeld. 2004. 'Tirtha'. In *The Hindu World*, edited by Sushil Mittal and G.R. Thursby. New York: Routledge.

Chatterjee, Kumkum. 1995. 'Nature, History and Nationalism: The Travel Narratives of a South Asian Colonial Elite'. *American Journal of Semiotics* 12 (Summer): 1–4. Special issue: 'History and Semiotics', ed. William Pencak.

Chattopadhyay, Bankim Chandra. 1970 (BS 1387). *Bankim Rachanabali.* Vol. 1. Kolkata: Sahitya Samsad.

Chaucer, Geoffrey. 1986. *The Canterbury Tales, Nine Tales and the General Prologue,* ed. V.A. Kolaveri and G. Olson. New York: Norton Critical Edition.

Dahejia, Harsha V. 2003. 'Evam Saundaryam'. In *Evam, Forum on Indian Representations,* 2:1&2, ed. Makarand Paranjape. New Delhi: Samvad India Foundation.

Howard, Donald R. 1980. *Writers and Pilgrims: Medieval Pilgrimage Narratives and their Posterity.* Berkeley: University of California Press.

Khanna, Madhu. 2003. 'In the Flow of Modernity: Some Reflections on *Tirtha* and *Murti* in Hindu India'. In *Evam, Forum on Indian Representations,* 2:1&2.

Nivedita, Sister. 1910. *The Master as I Saw Him.* London: Longman, Green and Co.

12 A *chatti* is a modest resting place for pilgrims on the route.

Nivedita, Sister. 1913. *Notes of Some Wanderings with the Swami Vivekananda*. Baghbazar, Calcutta: Udbodhan Office.

———. (1916) 1928. *Kedar Nath and Badri Narayan: A Pilgrim's Diary*. Calcutta: Udbodhan Office.

Shloka Samgraha. 2003. Kolkata: Balaswar Utkal Navavidhan Brahmo Samaj and Navavidhan Publication Committee, Kolkata.

Singh, Karan. 2003. 'Satyam, Shivam, Sundaram'. In *Evam, Forum on Indian Representations*, 2:1&2.

Swami Tyagisananda 1949. *Svetasvataropanishad*. Madras: Sri Ramakrishna Math, Mylapore.

Tagore, Devendranath. 2002. *The Autobiography of Maharshi Devendranath Tagore*. Translated from the original Bengali by Satyendranath Tagore and Indira Devi. New Delhi: Rupa & Co.

Tagore, Rabindranath. 2003. *Gitanjali*. New Delhi: UBS Publishers Distributors Pvt. Ltd. and Visva-Bharati.

Zacher, Christian. 1976. *Curiosity and Pilgrimage: The Literature of Discovery in Fourteenth Century England*. Baltimore: Johns Hopkins University Press.

10

Bangamahilār Japanyātrā (1915): *The Earliest Record of an Asian Woman's Travel to Japan*

Nandita Basu

Bangamahilār Japanyātrā (The Voyage of a Bengali Woman to Japan), published in 1915 in Bengali from Dhaka (now the capital of Bangladesh), is the earliest record of foreign travel of an Asian woman, Hariprabha Takeda, nee Mallik (1893–1973). Hariprabha was born in a Brahmo family in Dhaka. Her parents, Shashibhushan and Nagendrabala Mallik, were ardent followers of Keshab Chandra Sen (1838–1884), a celebrated social reformer who set up Nababidhan Brahmo Samaj, which was engaged in social reform as its declared agenda. The couple set up a care home in their residence for the rescued young women of Bengal. All these activities were radical measures for the social upliftment of contemporary women (Takeda [1915] 2004).

Hariprabha became acquainted with a Japanese gentleman named Wemon Takeda (?–1948), who came to Dhaka (now Bangladesh) as a fortune seeker in 1903 and worked in a soap factory. Subsequently, Hariprabha was married off to Wemon Takeda in 1907 when she was fourteen years of age. The marriage was according to the custom of the Nababidhan Brahmo Samaj, which was much simpler compared to the Hindu marriage ceremony. Four years after her marriage, Hariprabha undertook a sea voyage to Japan, her husband's land, to visit her in-laws there. *Bangamahilār Japanyātrā,* written by Hariprabha in a diary form, is the account of her travel to Japan. To understand the almost revolutionary nature of this Indian woman's travel to Japan, we need to understand the status of women, their education, and their role in Bengali society at the time. Primarily, Hariprabha's upbringing in a progressive Brahmo society made it possible for her to undertake such a voyage. The Brahmos declared themselves a separate sect distinguished from Hindus as they did not believe in idol worship and subscribed to monotheism. Moreover, unlike in Brahmo society, there was no provision of getting married to a person belonging to another religion in Hindu custom.

Bengali society in those days mainly comprised Hindus and Muslims, who were very conservative in outlook in maintaining the status quo of the society. Casteism in Hindus and fundamentalism in Muslims obstructed the progressive growth and development of the lower strata of the people and women. The social reform movement in 19th-century Bengal was mainly women-centred.

Women in most families of 19th-century Bengal were not allowed to appear before strangers. Child marriage was the order of the day; marrying off a daughter before she attained puberty used to be considered a pious act for the girl's parents. This custom was observed more strictly in wealthy and upper-caste families. The women were mostly secluded and uneducated, which made their condition wretched and unenviable. Domestic drudgery and frequent childbirths were responsible for many untimely deaths.

William Adam, a missionary, was appointed by the East India Company government then ruling in India to conduct a survey in 19th-century India about the condition of women's education. The report of that survey, called *Adam's Report* (submitted thrice between 1835 to 1838), says that some wealthy zamindars (big landowners) surreptitiously taught their daughters the three Rs so that they did not get cheated out of the family property by unscrupulous in-laws in the event of their husband's death (Adam [1838] 1941).

Women's education was initiated by social reformers such as Raja Rammohan Roy (1772–1833), Pandit Ishwar Chandra Vidyasagar (1820–1891) and a host of other Indians to reform Indian society. The colonial rulers also helped them. Roy argued very strongly in favour of women's education. Vidyasagar was instrumental in setting up women's schools in a number of places in Bengal. Moreover, the English-educated men of the 19th century were looking for educated wives who would not merely perform the roles of 'cooks' (Chakrabarty 1995) or begetters of children for maintaining the family line. So, families aspiring to good matches for their daughters were compelled to educate them under the changed circumstances of society. The Brahmo Samaj of Bengal was a pioneer in spreading women's education, first amongst their own families and then to the rest of the community. The Brahmos were much influenced by the various ideas of the Unitarian Church because they accepted monotheism.

With education, the Brahmo women started coming out from the seclusion of their homes to take up jobs as teachers, doctors and so on. For getting admissions in schools, they had to cross the threshold of the home. In the Brahmo Samaj, women were conspicuous by their tasteful dress and demeanour; whatever they did, wherever they went, the

Brahmo women displayed their cultivated manners. Unlike the Hindus, the Brahmos did not believe in the seclusion of women. They held joint prayers together with all the family members, including both men and women; sometimes, congregational prayers amongst a large group of their own sect used to take place. All these marked differences from the Hindu community specially made the Brahmo women poised and elegant.

From Hariprabha's diary, we come to know that she took her musical string instrument, *esraj*[1], along and played it during her voyage to Japan (Takeda [1915] 2004, 27). Hariprabha playing the *esraj* to keep herself grounded is of some significance as an indicator of her personality. The *esraj* was an excellent accompaniment with Brohmo-sangeet (hymn of the Brahmos sung in praise of God), transforming the songs into deeper, more penetrating experiences that sounded enchanting. The Brahmo women in Bengal were probably the first to start playing stringed musical instruments in public. Female vocalists in classical or semi-classical music were only from the *Baiji* communities. *Baiji*s were not prostitutes. They were quite accomplished in various fine arts and literature. On the whole, they enjoyed a good status in the society but were not a part of genteel domesticity. So Hariprabha's playing of this instrument (though she was playing it as an accompaniment to Brohmo-sangeet) during the voyage was a great leap forward towards the path of freedom of Indian women. The *esraj* being an ideal accompaniment to Brohmo-sangeet speaks volumes about religious syncretism because the musical instrument is associated with the Muslim community as it was developed in Arabia. As Hariprabha belonged to a Brahmo family, she possessed all the virtues of the women of that sect — education, poise and sophistication.

Her parents had progressive views and were actively involved in the upliftment of women. Her father, Shashibhushan Mallik, was an employee of the police department in undivided Bengal, posted in Dhaka. He resigned from his job to set up a rescue home for homeless women disowned by their families. The rescue home was established in their own residence in Dhaka in 1896. Initially, the home was named Dhaka Balika Uddhar Ashram (Dhaka rescue home for girls) as it was meant for sex workers only.[2] Hariprabha was brought up by progressive parents

1 Actually, *esraj* or *israj* is a central Asian string instrument. In all likelihood, the Sufis brought it to India.

2 The Malliks themselves looked after the home. The sex workers were rescued from brothels and given vocational training so that they could become self-sufficient. Some of them were reunited with their families, and some were married off too. Later on, the home was renamed as Matriniketan (Mother's Home) where homeless widows and orphan girls were also able to find a shelter. It is known that one girl belonging to this home, Snehobala (b. 1885), became a doctor later in her life. In 1908, the government took charge of Matriniketan, and it was relocated to Nimtola, Dhaka (Takeda [1915] 2004).

who worked to raise the awareness of society towards social evils. It is a measure of their involvement in the women's cause that Hariprabha and her sister Shantiprabha helped their parents look after the rescue home.

* * *

Hariprabha's decision to visit her in-laws in Japan was a bold one, the impact of which on her contemporary society is difficult to understand for the present-day reader. She was discouraged by almost all her relatives. Fear of the unknown was uppermost in their minds, including the sea voyage lasting more than a month. Not many Indian people undertook sea travel at that time. There were several injunctions against sea voyage in Hindu society in the 19th century. With the advent of British rule, some Indians started going to England, Raja Rammohan Roy being one. A pioneer in establishing the Brahmo dharma, Roy went to England in 1831, ignoring the religious diktat. Still, the Hindu society was not in favour of sea voyages. As late as 1892, the eminent writer Bankimchandra Chattopadhyay (1838–1894) wrote a letter in the Bengali journal *Hitobadi* justifying sea voyage for the Hindu people in spite of the ban on it in the scriptures (Chatterji [1954] 1969, 925–927). Although the Brahmo women rejected the purdah and were educated, until the turn of the 20th century, only a minuscule number of them went on sea voyages, and that too only to England. All these facts strongly establish how difficult and unusual it was for Hariprabha to decide to visit Japan to meet her in-laws.

Though it is often said that the women of the Tagore family in Bengal were at the forefront in the matter of women's progress, Hariprabha's journey to Japan demonstrates that hers was a pioneering effort in some respects. From the Tagore family, only Jnanadanandini Devi went to England in the 1870s. As the wife of the first Indian officer in the Indian Civil Service (ICS), she was a much more privileged woman than Hariprabha. Moreover, Jnanadanandini had some knowledge of the English language before she started for England, while Hariprabha did not know the Japanese language. India being a British colony at that time, the life and culture were fairly known to Indian people, whereas Indian acquaintance with Japanese culture and society was more limited. Also, being a Brahmo woman, Hariprabha had married a foreigner from another religion (Wemon Takeda was a Buddhist), a near unthinkable thing in those days.

For a long time, Japan was inaccessible to outsiders (Takeda [1915] 2004). Japan, under the rule of Shogun kings, shut its doors to all foreigners. However, in the 19th century, during the reign of King Mutsihoto (1868–1912), Japan saw better days as lots of reformative measures were taken to open up the country to external influences. In the history of Japan, this period is called the Meiji period, which brought a tremendous surge in the creative energy of the Japanese people. In this period, many enterprising Japanese citizens journeyed to foreign lands.

At the time of Hariprabha's marriage ceremony, none of Wemon Takeda's family members could come from Japan to Dhaka to attend the marriage. Hariprabha writes in her diary (which forms the body of her account of the voyage to Japan) that she was keen to receive the blessings of her elderly in-laws in person:

> When I got married, nobody ever thought that I shall visit Japan. No one wanted that. But I was pretty eager to visit Japan at least once though that remained a dream only. I had a longing of being blessed in person by my mother-in-law and father-in-law. After writing a letter to them, I received an answer along with their photographs, expressing mutual longing for meeting me too. And my joy knew no bounds. God has granted me that cherished desire. After receiving a series of letters from Japan, we decided to go there, but it was an uphill task. Because of our financial trouble, failing health, impending winter season in Japan, oppositions from the relatives in Dhaka and their continuous utterance of risk in taking such a long voyage — everything contributed to the fizzling out of our plan. But the ever Kind God was there to solve all the problems bothering us. (Takeda 2004, 17)

Having stayed in Japan for four months, the couple returned to Dhaka in 1912. Hariprabha was the first Asian woman to visit Japan. Before her, the Scottish explorer Isabella Lucy Bird visited Japan in 1878. Significantly, Hariprabha undertook her voyage to Japan seven months before Rabindranath Tagore did. With due respect to Tagore, Hariprabha's *Bangamahilār Japanyātrā* is far more informative about Japan than Tagore's *Japanjatri*. Tagore's *Japanjatri* speaks less of Japan since the book's focus is on something else.

Hariprabha maintained an account of her journey in her diary. It was the custom of the members of Nababidhan Brahmo Samaj to maintain a daily diary following the instruction of their leader, Keshab Chandra Sen. This practice was supposed to help the individual to keep a tab on their day-to-day activities in many ways like keeping one grounded with engagement in spiritual pursuit, to gauge one's daily engagements in social obligations and many more things. A substantial body of literature written as diaries by Brahmo women has come to light due to the efforts of subsequent researchers (Deb 1984).

Some scholars have said that the travelogue was serialised in a women's journal published in Kolkata. The same travelogue was published in the Brahmo women's magazine *Äntahpur* (1897) (Murshid 2001), which used to publish women's writings exclusively. Unconfirmed sources say that this serialised travelogue was titled *Japan Jatrir Chithi* (Deb 1984). However, the published book does not mention any of these details. Rather, it underlines that the money earned by the sale of the book will be utilised to meet the daily expenses incurred by Matriniketan, the home run by Hariprabha's parents. Hariprabha's younger sister Shantiprabha Mallik took upon herself the responsibility (Takeda [1915] 2004). At the beginning of the 20th century, when women writers were few and far between in India, Hariprabha Takeda published her book and thought of utilising the money earned for social welfare, which indicates her independence, her confidence as a writer and her enterprising nature.

* * *

In this section, we shall look at the process of identification of the Other in Japanese society by Hariprabha and also her method of negotiating that. In *Bangamahilār Japanyātrā*, we find a very keen observer in Hariprabha Takeda. She had a sensitive eye for the natural beauty of the places she visited. She also possessed a sharp sense to identify the evil customs of Indian society vis-à-vis Japanese contemporary society. Hariprabha deeply appreciated the near-total literacy, the absence of the dowry system and the free mixing of men and women (that is, lack of segregation) in workplaces in Japan. Women work everywhere in Japan, be it agricultural fields, post offices or shops. In places of entertainment, Japanese women sell the tickets and manage the crowd gathered there. They wake up at dawn and make their home tidy by cleaning the house. Then they start cooking. They light a fire in the *hibachi* (stove) and prepare tea and the entire family breakfasts together. The children leave for school by 8 am; their mothers arrange a *bento* (lunch box carrying rice, radish and some cooked vegetables) for them. Hariprabha notes that Japanese women always do work that adds some money to the family coffers. Like the works of other contemporary Bengali women travel writers (for example, Krishnabhabini Das's *England-e Bangamahilā*) (Das [1885] 1996), which describe the position of women in the land of their visit, Hariprabha also compares the social positions of Indian and Japanese women. According to her (she is a little sarcastic here in her tone), the Japanese women, unlike their Indian counterparts, do not spend the whole day in the kitchen but utilise the time for the welfare of the society. Hariprabha relates the near-total literacy in Japan with the phenomenon of women teaching their own children and shows it as a glaring difference between Indian and Japanese women. Hariprabha notes another difference between the Japanese women and their Indian counterparts. Despite their share of household drudgery like tending silk worms in family farms and extracting silk from them and husking paddy, the former still find time to dress up nicely and set their beautiful hair, which makes the Japanese women much more pleasant looking. Here, Hariprabha seems to underline the importance of women's space — that she can take a leisurely bath, make elaborate hairdos and dress elegantly. The importance of all these activities for the Japanese women is highlighted in *Bangamahilār Japanyātrā* with the implicit suggestion of a contrast with the women of her own country. She seems to discover an affinity with the Japanese women in her desires and aims.

Japanese women take public baths, that too in the nude, which must have been a huge cultural shock for Hariprabha. Even so, she had enough resilience to recognise the cultural diversities. While describing the system of public baths in Japan, Hariprabha rather appreciates it: bathing in warm water throughout the year, dipping the body in the water tub for half an hour and engaging other people for scrubbing the body. Most of these customs are absent in India and would likely have shocked and drawn criticism in Indian society. However, the narrator has not voiced any qualms about those customs, indicating Hariprabha's freedom from orthodoxy and parochialism and her ability to accept the diversity of customs in the world and appreciate the positive points of an alien society. It also reveals her feminine identity and her sensitivity and kinship as a woman with women of other cultures.

Though Hariprabha shows a remarkably positive outlook about almost everything in Japan, the land of her husband, the food in Japan could not attract her. At the beginning of the narrative, after sailing from Dhaka, Hariprabha, during her short stay in Wemon Takeda's Japanese friend's house in Kolkata, was unable to eat the food because of the excessive use of garlic. So their hostess, Mrs Simejsan, instructed her cook not to use garlic at all in the food. Hariprabha liked Japanese sticky rice as the starch is retained in the rice while cooking, which reminded her of the Bengali delicacy *fena bhat* (rice cooked retaining the starch in it). During the voyage, she even ordered plain rice with boiled potato or egg, again a Bengali delicacy. Hariprabha liked both the fragrance and the sweet taste of Japanese rice. For lunch every day, Hariprabha would look forward to rice and potato, both boiled, solving all her problems with food. Japanese green tea or *ocha*, served with lunch and dinner, has been referred to by Hariprabha Takeda as a custom of the native people. She gradually got habituated to using a spoon while taking food during her voyage. Her interest in and observation of food and cooking again indicates her feminine sensibility.

Hariprabha Takeda emphatically underlines that the Japanese way of preparing food is entirely different from the Bengali way. She mentions that Japanese people rarely use oil, clarified butter or spices while cooking vegetables, fish or meat. This appeared quite queer to her. The Japanese use a kind of liquid, *soio* (which seems to be soya sauce), in which vegetables, fish and meat are cooked or semi-cooked. In Japan, they boil the meat minimally and eat either raw dry fish or sizzled salted fish. Radish is another vegetable that is a favourite of the local people, and it is grown in abundance in Japan. People eat raw or fermented radish in Japan. Hariprabha observes that the Japanese custom is to serve food items like fish, vegetables, radish, pickled berry and a bowl of rice on a low-lying table. Individuals hold a bowl of rice in their left hand and a pair of chopsticks in their right hand while eating. Hariprabha notes that the Japanese never touch the food with their hands. In her account of Japan, Hariprabha writes in detail about the culinary delicacies and their recipes like tofu and describes sake or the native country liquor consumed by both men and women — things unknown to Indian readers.

Bangamahilār Japanyātrā can be marked as a handbook, a tourist guide for prospective travellers to Japan. Hariprabha describes everything — from picturesque aspects such as the country's landscape to the people, social customs, culinary habits, flora and fauna, religion and position of women. She tells her readers about the Japanese alphabets and pictograms, which are complicated and difficult to master. She enlightens her readers about Buddhism and Shintoism, as they are prevalent in Japan. The Buddhists cremate their dead bodies, while the people subscribing to the Shinto faith practise burials. Japanese Buddhists chant a mantra, *Namamdaut*, in front of the idol of Lord Buddha. Hariprabha says the root words behind them are '*Namu Amida-butsu*', meaning 'I adore thee, O eternal Buddha'. She also says that the underlying Sanskrit mantra is '*Namah, Amitabha Buddha*' (I salute you, Lord Amitabha Buddha). From all these accounts, her scholarly interest in Japan and the interest in everyday life is amply demonstrated. The sitting system of Japanese people by folding the lower part of the leg like *Vajrasan* (a yogic posture) proves to be a little difficult for Hariprabha, but her in-laws were so kind to her that they saw to it that nothing bothered her.

Hariprabha's travelogue resembles a tourist guide, providing many Japanese words with their meanings. Many Japanese words such as *futon* (small sitting mat), *ocha* (Japanese green tea), *othela* (big temples), *geta* (wooden slippers), *udon*, tofu, *sakena sakana*, *gomoku* (all are names of different food items) and *shokonosha* (temples dedicated to war heroes) are found in the book. The cult of hero worship has been elaborately described by her along with the yearly visit made by people to the temple (situated in Kudon, adjacent to Tokyo), dedicated to the dead heroes. She refers to the exhibition displaying the arms and ammunition used by the warriors, their photographs and their mementoes. The dress and sword of the hero of Port Arthur, General Nogi, and his wife, who committed hara-kiri, are exhibited there.

Hariprabha's mode of writing is simple and direct, betraying a genuine feeling of admiration and appreciation for an alien country. Present-day readers may feel a little astonished to see the range of curiosity of the writer who, without knowing the Japanese language, could amass so much information about the country in a visit that lasted only four months. Both emotionally and intellectually, Hariprabha made enough efforts to understand Japan. In her gesture of seeking affinity with another Asian culture without opposing it, Hariprabha suggests the non-patriarchal feminine desire to align with and accept other cultures.

* * *

From *Bangamahilār Japanyātrā*, we come to know that Hariprabha was accepted into the family of her in-laws with the utmost cordiality. Her family members, in particular, her mother-in-law, showed genuine love, care and tenderness towards Hariprabha. She also reciprocated the affection. That Hariprabha undertook her voyage is an ample indication of her profound eagerness to know her in-laws and the country of Japan. Earlier also, we referred to Hariprabha's positive attitude towards Japan, the land of her husband and his parents. Probably she inherited this positive attitude from her spiritual leaning, the teaching of the Brahmo faith. The Brahmos were committed to seeing almighty God's kind design everywhere.

Moreover, the book gives us insights into Japanese social practices like marriage ceremonies. When the marriage is fixed by the matchmaker, the bride, who is decked out in finery, starts for the house of her in-laws in a rickshaw. After reaching there, the veiled bride has to seek the blessings of the family deity along with her would-be husband. Then the couple drink sake thrice in small sips, and they serve sake to the older people assembled there. According to Hariprabha, the Japanese marriage ceremony ends here. She observes that for birth and death rituals, the Japanese do holy chanting but not during their marriages. This leads her to conclude that probably the Japanese consider marriage as simply a physical relationship. She thinks that marriage is mere fun for the Japanese people, not a spiritual bonding. This conclusion evidently implies a contrast with Indian marriages.

However, almost in the same breath, she says that there are instances when Japanese women commit hara-kiri after the death of their husbands or lead the life of a saint. Also, she mentions cases of couples committing suicide either by jumping into the sea together or committing hara-kiri if they are unable to obtain the consent of their parents for their marriage. Such acts would suggest a strong emotional attachment between couples, indicating that marital union was more than just physical. Hariprabha's statements, therefore, show a certain ambivalence.

Hariprabha also relates the drinking habits of the Japanese. In a number of places, Hariprabha refers to both Japanese men and women drinking sake together, which is a very accepted social custom there. Specifically, on celebratory occasions, it is a must. However, it seems that she was unable to accept this practice easily, for she writes, 'Frequently we had to pray to be excused when we were offered sake' (Takeda 2004, 63). By 'we,' does she mean her husband as well? Having a Brahmo background, one can understand her reservation about hard drinks because the Brahmos used to be quite conservative about that. Drinking alcohol was considered a sin by many middle-class Bengalis (Brahmos included) in the 19th and in the first quarters of the 20th century. However, although she had reservations about sake, she did not express disapprobation of the Japanese, which suggests a tolerant attitude.

A photograph of the couple embellishes the book *Bangamahilār Japanyātrā*, where Wemon Takeda appears in the attire of a Bengali gentleman, an indication of accepting the culture of his host country. Hariprabha and Wemon's behaviour suggests mutual acceptance by the husband and the wife of each other's culture, tolerance and a fulfilling relationship.

* * *

In *Bangamahilār Japanyātrā,* Hariprabha has given us glimpses of the Japanese way of life and culture. The information provided by her indicates that she might well have intended her diary to serve partially as an informal tourist guide for short-term visitors. Without visiting Japan, her readers are able to acquire some knowledge about Japan at a time when only a minuscule number of Indians had the opportunity of visiting the country. Hariprabha's comparison between Japanese and Indian women might suggest ideas about improving their plight to the latter. Her sensitive account of life in an alien country is an exemplary attempt at knowing the Other and of deconstructing the oppositional stance about Self and Other, which fulfils one of the set goals of a travelogue. When one looks back and realises that *Bangamahilār Japanyātrā* was written by a woman who had no formal education, we are struck by Hariprabha's independence, enterprising spirit, curiosity for novelty and zest for living.

The information that we have of Hariprabha's activities during the Second World War throws further light on her personality, as revealed in the travelogue. The Takedas responded to the directive issued by the Japanese government and went back to Japan during the war. After reaching Tokyo this time, the Takedas could not establish any contact with their family members because of continuous air raids. Rash Behari Bose helped Hariprabha to get the job of a radio announcer in Bengali for the makeshift radio station of the Indian National Army (INA) in Tokyo. This job helped Hariprabha to eke out a living in Japan as her husband was ill and was unable to earn anything. It was Rash Behari Bose again who arranged Hariprabha's meeting with Netaji Subhas Chandra Bose in Tokyo. He subsequently became quite well-disposed towards Hariprabha. Her relative Manju Dasgupta informs us that as a radio announcer, Hariprabha's life in Tokyo used to be quite tough. In the dead of night with frequent air raids, she had to reach the radio station with a helmet on her head. She took her passport and gold ornaments with her, hidden on her person, as she was not sure whether she would be able to return to her dwelling place again. When it became increasingly difficult for her to reach the workplace, Hariprabha started wearing her husband's pants, demonstrating how little she was hampered by conventional Bengali norms about women, dress and the like. She also wrote a book on life in Japan during the World War, titled *Juddhosomoye Japanchitro*. Hariprabha's life in Japan during the war suggests her active and daring spirit, independence, freedom from prejudices and aspirations for the freedom of the motherland. Many of these aspects of her identity are revealed in *Bangamahilār Japanyātrā*.

References

Adam, W. (1838) 1941. *Report of the State of Education in Bengal 1835 to 1838*. Edited by A.N. Basu. Calcutta: Home Deptt. Press. London: Forgotten Books.

Chakrabarty, Sambuddha. 1995. *Ondore Ontore*. [In Bengali.] Kolkata: Stri.

Chatterji, Bankim Chandra. (1954) 1969. *Bankim Rachanavali*. [In Bengali.] Part II. Edited by Jogesh Chandra Bagal. Kolkata: Sahitya Samsad.

Das, Krishnabhabini. (1885) 1996. *England-e Bangamahilā*. [In Bengali.] Edited by Damayanti Dasgupta. Kolkata: Gangchil.

Deb, Chitra. 1984. *Ontohpurer Atmokotha*. [In Bengali.] Ananda Publishers: Kolkata.

Murshid, Gulam. 2001. *Nari Progoti: Adhunikotar Obhighate Bongoromoni*. [In Bengali.] Kolkata: Naya Udyog.

Takeda, Hariprabha. (1915) 2004. *Bangamahilār Japanyātrā*. [In Bengali.] Edited by Swapan Prasanna Ray. Delhi: IMH.

Section 4

TRAVEL AND FICTION

11

India Imagined and Imaged: *'Travel to India' in Modern Japanese Fiction and Non-fiction*

M.V. Lakshmi

Travel Literature in Japan

Travel, in simple terms, means going from one place to another, covering a distance. However, when the travel is documented in a travel diary, fiction or a travelogue, it assumes unique perspectives on the land travelled to. According to Peter Hulme, 'Travellers will usually follow instincts and opportunities, rather than directions from home, and it is travellers' eccentricities and extravagances — in the literal sense of wanderings off — which have attracted many readers to the genre of travel writing' (2002, 5). Travelogues seem to have evolved from documents that provide factual information of places to commentaries and poetic expressions that describe a journey or a place visited by the writer and the emotions that a place evokes.

One aesthetic tool characteristic of the Japanese tradition of travel writing is *utamakura,* which can be literally translated as 'song pillows'. *Utamakura* are words or phrases that allude to a certain place by using a verbal image or motif. They are devices used by a writer or a poet, especially in travelogues, to help the reader to visualise the place being talked about. *Utamakura* coined by famous writers and poets tend to remain active in the readers' minds as they are reused in intertextual references made by other poets and writers when referring to the same place again in another travel account. Even though *utamakura* help as keywords to evoke images of a place, their disadvantage is that they stereotype a place by its association with a fixed set of motifs by repeated references made to it in a defined and limited way (Fessler 2004, 12).

Utamakura was conventionally a poetic tool employed in *waka* poetry and travel diaries. *Waka* is Japanese poetry, especially court poetry from the 6th to 14th century. Its characteristic feature is that it helps a poet to vividly and succinctly convey the image of a place. *Utamakura* can especially be seen in Japanese domestic travel accounts. After Japan opened its borders to the outside world in the Meiji period, Japanese people started travelling abroad, especially to the West. They found that they did not have an established *utamakura* to choose from as travel was, until then, predominantly a domestic enterprise. So they borrowed the frameworks, the motifs and the lenses with which the Westerners viewed a country. The new 'Western' *utamakura* were different from the traditional ones used in domestic travel accounts, in their allusion to artificial things as opposed to nature alone, which was typical of the traditional *utamakura* used to describe places in Japan (Fessler 2004, 16). According to Susanna Fessler, *utamakura* perform two main functions: evoking an image for the reader and inspiring and directing future travellers (15).

Interestingly, the trajectory that travel writing has taken in Japan is distinct from its Western counterpart. If one takes 'exploration' or 'discovery' as a defining feature of Western travel writing, then Japanese travel accounts depart from it, chalking a completely different path. As Meredith McKinney states,

> Places names per se play a remarkably prominent role in this literature, and their constant listing can take on an almost incantatory quality that still seems to carry in it something of the early religious potency associated with places and embodied in their names. (2019, 589)

As a result, travel writing in Japan is often instrumental in repeating or reaffirming an existing image associated with a place or building. 'For the Japanese traveller, the entire purpose of a journey was to see what had been seen, to do what had been done, to relive experiences of previous travellers, in short to experience the familiar' (Fessler 2004,17).

This chapter analyses three works, one each by Mishima Yukio and Endo Shusaku in fiction and one by Hotta Yoshie in non-fiction, to show how Japanese travel writing differs from the Western form, examining the usage of a particular set of motifs to refer to India in fiction and non-fiction. By identifying the motifs appearing in the three works, I aim to show that the authors succeeded in establishing the lexicon or *utamakura* in mainstream fiction and non-fiction about India and set up an image of India in the minds of the Japanese reader in modern Japan.

Although Western countries were the most popular travel destinations in modern Japan, India was associated with Buddhism. Many Hindu gods also found their way to Japan and were adopted into the Buddhist pantheon of gods (Chaudhuri 2003, 1). Japan and India have also shared a non-conflictual, non-imperialist and non-colonial relationship, which accounts for the cordial relations that the two nations have had throughout history. However, India's colonisation by the British and her struggle with poverty and increasing population as a developing nation after Independence were factors that could have led Japan to neglect India as a subjugated and poor third-world country. All the same, there have been works written about India, both fictional and non-fictional, by Japanese tourists, pilgrims, monks, diplomats and literary authors in the 20th century.

The two genres of fiction and travel writing have shared a close relationship. 'Many readers still hope for a literal truthfulness from travel writing that they would not expect to find in the novel, though each form has long drawn on the conventions of the other' (Hulme and Young 2002, 6). This chapter discusses the varied images pertaining to India that appear in the works and the different perspectives of the characters whose gaze defines those images.

Overview of the Works

Hojo no Umi by Mishima Yukio

Mishima Yukio's tetralogy, *Hojo no Umi* (published as *Sea of Fertility* in English), is a series of novels that travel in time and space through reincarnation. It comprises four books, namely *Haru no Yuki* (1968; translated as *Spring Snow* [1972]), *Honba* (1970; translated as *Runaway Horses* [1973]), *Akatsuki no Tera* (1970; translated as *Temple of Dawn* [1973]) and *Tenningosui* (1971; translated as *The Decay of the Angel* [197]). They are bound together by the character Honda, who appears in all four, and the theme of reincarnation.

In *Akatsuki no Tera*, the protagonist, Honda, journeys to India as a tourist, when Itsui Products, the company for which he works, presents him a pleasure trip as a token of gratitude. He plans to visit the Ajanta Caves and Benaras (Varanasi) on the Ganges, which were so far apart that he felt 'faint' (Mishima 2001, 51). The novel describes Honda's response to his India trip thus: 'Yet each attracted equally the magnetic needle of his desire for the unknown' (Mishima 2001, 52). Honda's scholarly interest in India arouses his curiosity about treatises such as *Manusmriti*, *Brihadaranyaka Upanishad* and others, which are then used in the novel to support the storehouse consciousness (*Yuishikiron)* and assert the unity of the atman and Brahma. Storehouse consciousness is the principle on which the four books of the series are built, and Honda's presence through them brings a continuity to them.

The author, Mishima, took a trip to India before writing the novel. As opposed to the route that he mentions in the story for Honda, however, Mishima travelled to Calcutta (Kolkata) in the end. The duration of his travel was half a month in 1967. Mishima starts by portraying India as a land in the realm of the 'unknown', which may be discovered in due course (2001, 52). The route that Honda follows is through Calcutta, Benaras and the Ajanta caves in Aurangabad. Honda visits Calcutta in October, when the city is bustling with preparations for the Durga Puja festival. Mishima's choice of places and themes is significant in defining the motifs associated with India in post-war Japanese literature.

The novel *Hojo no Umi* has an undercurrent of Buddhism woven into it, and Buddhist and Hindu treatises, as mentioned earlier, are integral to the story. Besides this, the theme of transmigration of the soul is woven into the plot where Honda bears witness to the 'reincarnations' of his friend Kiyoaki Matsugae in the three novels that follow.

Fukai Kawa by Endo Shusaku

Endo Shusaku's novel *Fukai Kawa* (1993)[1] revolves around a trip to India undertaken by six Japanese people. Each of them decides to visit India for unique reasons, and the trip helps them find the answers to questions with which they had been grappling. As the author mentions in an interview in '*Saishinsaku Fukai Kawa: Tamashi no Mondai, Hahanaru Kami wo motomete*', the Japanese characters travel to India 'in search of lost love', which is a translation of '*ushinawareta ai o motomete*' (Kaga and Endo 1999, 119).

Of all the Japanese characters in the novel, Enami's viewpoint gains significance because he provides an 'alternative' perspective on India, that of a resident or insider (Lakshmi 2006, 223–231), rather than that of a tourist, which somewhat represents the author's view. Enami's views on India are grounded in his experience and knowledge of the place because he has studied Indian philosophy and stayed in India for nearly four years.

Enami says, 'If you find India disgusting, then you should have chosen a pleasant tour of Europe. But since you're here in India, please make the effort to enter into this unique world' (Endo 1994, 108). Even as Enami reaffirms the 'exotic' image of India, he is simultaneously critical of the Japanese tourists for whom he is working as a guide:

> Frankly he despised the Japanese tourists he had to shuttle around.... The deeply grateful old men and women who made the rounds of

1 The novel *Fukai Kawa* was first published in 1993 as mentioned here. The edition I have referred to in translation Deep River is the 1994 edition. The original I have referred to is an edition published in 1996.

> the Buddhist relics; the college women who relished the hippie-like homeless; and the men like Numada who searched the natural environment of India for something they had lost. They always took the same souvenirs back to Japan with them: silk saris, sandalwood necklaces.... Of course, Enami never displayed his true feelings. (Endo 1994, 132)

Enami is critical of the stereotypical image of India that Japanese tourists form. The novel mentions that he returns to Japan after completing his studies in Indian philosophy. Not finding a suitable avenue to use his knowledge, he returns to India to work as a tour guide. 'In the end, I suppose I fell in love with it. Some tourists absolutely despise the place after only one visit, but then there are those who say they want to come back over and over again. I'm one of the latter' (Endo 1994, 106).

Enami attempts to show the 'real' India rather than what the Japanese tourist sees in a brief visit. Significantly, however, he cannot breakout of the process of stereotyping the country, which is followed by many modern Japanese literary writers, including Mishima. India, in this process, is typically associated with goddesses and the river Ganges.

Indo de Kangaeta Koto (*Thoughts in India*) by Hotta Yoshie

Hotta Yoshie's *Indo de Kangaeta Koto,* which may be translated as 'Thoughts in India', talks about various aspccts of India that the author encounters during his stay in the country for two months. Hotta arrives in India to participate in the first Asian Writers' Conference, held in New Delhi in 1956. *Indo de Kangaeta Koto* gives the reader a variety of perspectives on India and Japan, covering a wide range of topics based on the author's experiences and observations in the country and also his reading of Jawaharlal Nehru's *Discovery of India.*

Hotta finds India a vast country. He talks about the diversity of the people with varied appearances, the multitude of languages spoken, the expanse of space and the length of rivers such as the river Ganges, which he realises is a humongous river while on his flight to India itself. He finds many more men than women on the streets. He also compares Indian food and the natural feel of the darkness of the night with that of his own country, Japan.

Very much like the character of Honda in Mishima Yukio's *Akatsuki no Tera*, Hotta does not just observe India and Indians but also reads Nehru, Swami Vivekananda, the Gita, the Mahabharata and the *Rigveda* during his stay. Amongst these, *The Discovery of India* helps him understand how Nehru, the first prime minister, defines the image of India through the eyes of the West as a colonised nation. Hotta understands Japan's own need to aspire to model itself on the Western nations. He mentions how India's history is intertwined with that of her colonisers, the Britishers. Hotta also mentions Nehru's message of world peace and claims to understand Nehru's foreign policy. Hotta is impressed by the policy of non-alignment as a means of appeasement of conflict in the world and the Panchsheel Agreement that was to unite and help maintain peace in Asia (2009, 171).

Interestingly, Hotta does not think that India is a poor country (2009, 142). Therefore, his opinion is opposed to the stereotypical images of India. He also calls India a country of contradictions where everything exists together and finds the land 'incomprehensible' (41). For instance, although one can use the term 'Japanese people' to give a comprehensive idea of the Japanese as a nation, Indians as a whole cannot be so represented because of the complexity and variety exhibited by the numerous languages, customs, religions or even races that exist in India. He compares this variety with Japan's relatively homogeneous history or past (43). However, Hotta also seeks to find common ground between the Indians and the Japanese in some respects, such as the disconnect of Japanese and Indian youths with their past. Therefore, although the travelogue reiterates some existing stereotypes like Indians being talkative and the country's diversity, it also introduces some notions like India not being a poor nation and also Nehru's idea of world peace.

'Indian' Motifs in the Three Works

Even though the perception of India is different in each work, there is a common repository of images that the three books bring forth. Importantly, *Akatsuki no Tera, Fukai Kawa* and *Indo de Kangaeta Koto* share some views of India. The portrayals are interlinked because the authors had read the other works that were written before. It was upon reading Mishima's work that Endo Shusaku went to India, which provided the setting of his novel *Fukai Kawa*. This repetition of intertextual images to reaffirm ideas associated with India suggests how *utamakura* has been employed by modern Japanese authors to build on an existing image from an earlier text.

India finds mention in *Hojo no Umi* in various ways, which can be broadly categorised as (a) concrete images such as places and people and (b) abstract images such as concepts and treatises from India. India's presence in *Hojo no Umi* helps to validate the Buddhist concepts of transmigration and rebirth woven into the four-volume novel. The discourses on Indian philosophy that Honda refers to are manifested in India in a way. Honda witnesses the cycle of birth and death and the concepts of samsara for himself in India.

Mishima takes the reader to India through Honda's trip. In India, Honda observes, perceives and reflects on the many facets of Buddhism, life and reincarnation. As I have pointed out, Mishima had travelled to India before he wrote the novel, although his route was different from Honda's.

The goddess Kali is described in much detail in *Akatsuki no Tera*. The work mentions how Kali is a significant goddess in the Hindu pantheon of gods and is especially revered in the states of Bengal and Assam. Goddess Durga is described as one of the avatars of Goddess Kali, the latter being the more bloodthirsty and fiery of them (Mishima 2001, 52).

Kalighat in Calcutta is shown as a melting pot of people from all walks of life in huge numbers. The beggars who beg for alms and the devotees who worship the goddess all come together to this temple, which Honda visits on a rainy day. The sheer number of people who jostle in the crowds and are all there to worship the goddess Kali is a sight to behold for Honda. As Mishima describes it in the novel, in the temple's inner chamber, as though oblivious to the din and commotion surrounding her, stands the goddess Kali adorned with blood-smeared heads. She is visible in the light of flickering candles. Mishima describes further the ritual of animal sacrifice, which is carried out at a post in the temple complex for the goddess. Honda sees the temple and even compares it to the Temple of Dawn in Bangkok. Mishima's observation and keen eye for detail capture glimpses of a woman worshipping at the altar. He also describes the ritual of sacrifice at the temple with nearly clinical detail.

Unlike what he has seen or experienced in Japan till then, in India, Honda witnesses the bloody act of animal sacrifice, revolting to his Japanese sensibilities and antithetical to everything that may be perceived as holy. Yet, for the Hindus in India, it was a holy ritual. The sight of animal sacrifice, which does not evoke any reaction from the Indian people, shocks the Japanese Honda so much that the practice seems to reaffirm India in his vision as the exotic Other.

Benaras is the second stop for Honda. If Calcutta awakens Honda's senses to India, Benaras takes them to a point where he needs all his senses to perceive and comprehend the complex and myriad reality that constitutes it. Benaras is called the holy city of the Hindus, and Mishima even describes it as the 'Jerusalem of the Hindus' (2001, 58). Having researched the city's history, he depicts it as the place that receives the Ganges that flows down from the Himalayas, the residence of Lord Shiva. The city is dedicated to Shiva, the husband of Kali. After touching upon the mythological origins of the place, Mishima describes the city as a place where pilgrims from all over the country congregate. He portrays it in *Akatsuki no Tera* as '*Tengokuheno Shumon*', translated as 'the main portal to paradise' (174). He says that 'the bliss of paradise is achieved by bathing in the waters at this juncture of the five holy rivers: Ganges, Dutapapa, Krishna, Jamna and Sarasvati' (52).

Mishima quotes from the Vedas to ascertain this point. Purification by ablution is what is central to this place. He also relates how Benaras is revered as it is considered as holy as the heavens or even holier than the heavens themselves.

The Benaras that Honda encounters is a 'city of extreme filth as well as of extreme holiness' (Mishima 2001, 59). Mishima talks about the ultimate dichotomy of the place through this description in *Akatsuki no Tera*:

> Yet, Benaras was a city of extreme filth as well as of extreme holiness. On both sides of the narrow, sunless alleys stalls for fried food and cakes, astrologers, grain and flour vendors were all crowded together; and the area was filled with stench, dampness, and disease. (59)

His sketch shows the street food vendors like those of fried snacks and stalls of astrologers alongside those of food grains and a city that awakens one's senses of smell, sight and hearing. The people of the city include lepers and beggars, along with the huge numbers of pilgrims who come to the city and stay on, waiting to die in this holy land. There was disease and deformity everywhere, and a kind of repulsive holiness existed in it, as Mishima describes. The sights, sounds and smells shock Honda's senses. The response that Benaras evokes in Honda is similar to that of a Western traveller. His perception was reminiscent of an 'Oriental' perspective. One could say that Honda views India through the unique lens of a Japanese, a fellow Asian, who was at the same time influenced by the Western perspective because of his Western education. It invests the Japanese traveller with ambivalence. Japan, an Asian country herself, views India through the lens of Orientalism, being influenced by the Western gaze on India.

The portrayal of Benaras brings out the dichotomy of the place. At the same time, Mishima keeps in mind that the reaction it evokes in Honda is perhaps typical of a tourist who sees Benaras for the first time — abhorrence, shock and disbelief. In recognising the contradictions that meet his eyes, Honda takes a view similar to that of the outsider. Yet, due to Mishima's reading of Indian treatises, the portrayals help to demonstrate how, in India, cleanliness and spirituality may not be synonymous as they are in Japan. Benaras is used to build India's image as an exotic and incomprehensible Other, which is filthy in appearance but seems to hold immense value as a spiritual and religious place for the Indian people.

Mishima also describes the large number of temples in the city. Honda is taken aback to see how people, animals and even insects share the same space. He is astounded that he had gone there against all reason. For Honda, Benaras was a place where one had to 'abandon all reason' (Mishima 2001, 60).

The belief of Indians in notions of samsara, which is an eternal cycle of birth, suffering, death and rebirth and reincarnation, seemed very strong. Honda found this joy and happiness, which was because of the belief that Indians possessed in samsara, incomprehensible as a Japanese. The sight of life and death comfortably coexisting without any contradiction in a place of worship is something that is beyond comprehension to Honda's senses.

The cremation ghat — Manikarnika Ghat — is where Honda witnesses 'ultimate purification' (Mishima 2001, 52). Mishima continues to describe the rituals for men and women for cremation. The noise, chatter and activities of children and the hustle and bustle of people around, however, are not affected by the solemnity of the place. Mishima vividly describes the crackling sounds produced when the bodies are cremated. Honda is surprised that there was no sadness or remorse but only happiness. Mishima describes this inexplicable joy in the following words:

> There was no sadness. What seemed heartlessness was actually pure joy. Not only were samsara and reincarnation basic belief, but they were actually accepted as part of basic nature.... In India the source of everything that seemed heartless, was connected with a hidden, gigantic, awesome joy. Honda was afraid of grasping such delight. (67)

Unlike the other two centres of Hindu religion, the third stop that Honda takes is at Aurangabad to see the Ajanta cave paintings. The decline of Buddhism in India caused the ruin of these caves, which were rediscovered in the 19th century. Mishima explains in detail how only some of the caves of the total twenty-seven were of the age of Hinayāna Buddhism, while the majority were of the age of Mahāyāna sect of Buddhism. Honda feels destined to come to this Buddhist site after visiting the religious heartland of the Hindus in India.

After the shocking experience at Benaras, the relatively quiet place brings some peace and calm. He feels that things are normal in Ajanta compared to Benaras. Entering a space associated with Buddhism makes him happy. What he could not leave behind, however, is the noise and the sight of 'black' people bustling with activity in the tea stalls on the way to Ajanta. Nor could he escape the filth and swarms of flies.

Honda reaches Ajanta, and upon entering the first cave, he realises that it is a *chaitya*, a chapel. Mishima describes how there are four such chaityas and twenty-three *vihāras* (a monastery or place of refuge) in the ruins of Ajanta. In the misty and dark interiors of Ajanta, he sees a figure of the Buddha seated in the lotus posture and several figures of women wearing sarongs and colourful clothes, many of them holding the lotus flower in their hands.

The relative peace and calm, compared to the crowds at Benaras, relaxes Honda's senses. He experiences an emptiness, which he feels foretells that he would come upon something incredibly happy and exciting (Mishima 2001, 74–76). *Hojo no Umi* is a novel bound together by the theme of transmigration of the soul and the Buddhist concept of *alayavijnana*.[2] By bringing out the contrast between Benaras and Ajanta, the author is probably attempting to appeal to the Japanese readers for whom a Buddhist site would seem more familiar than a Hindu site of pilgrimage like Benaras. Honda's keenness in going to a 'familiar' place owing to its association with Buddhism is also a way of othering the India that Honda witnesses and experiences at Calcutta and Benaras till then in the novel. Calcutta and Benaras, associated with Hinduism, are alien to Honda; he finds affinity and comfort in Ajanta and its link with Buddhism.

India's role in the novel is significant not only because it provides a certain kind of experience for the Japanese characters but also because it induces them to reflect on treatises they have read such as the *Yuishikiron,* which is central to the tetralogy. Honda's interest in the concept of *Yuishikiron* or storehouse consciousness as defined earlier is aroused right at the beginning of the novel when the abbess of Gesshuji Temple gives a sermon on the subject. He is interested in the Gesshuji Temple and follows the *Hosso* concept of existence. The abbess's sermon impacts him so much that even though he was usually interested in the European and Western ways of thinking when it came to understanding the 'natural law', after hearing the sermon at Gesshuji, his interest and belief in Western concepts reduces.

At this juncture, he chances upon a French translation of the work *The Laws of Manu* (*Manusmriti*). What appealed to him in this work, especially when he compared it to the Roman laws, which gave utmost importance to reason, was the belief in the cosmic law of retribution, which was beyond or outside the power of reason. The *Manusmriti* was

2 As per the Nichiren Buddhist Library's definition, it is the eighth and deepest of the eight consciousnesses, so called because the results of one's actions, good or evil, are stored there as a potential force, or karmic 'seeds.' These seeds are said to sprout in the future; in other words, stored karma eventually manifests as happiness or suffering (Nichiren Daishonin, n.d.)

based on the cosmic law, which instructs humans as to the kind of life they would be allotted in their next birth based on their actions.

At Ajanta, what catches Honda's attention is the waterfalls when leaving the *vihāra*. The sound of the waterfalls cutting through the serenity is an experience that Honda describes as overwhelming. The sight of the waterfalls keeps him from going to the fifth cave. When his friend Kiyoaki said that he would meet him beneath the falls, Honda had presumed that the falls were those at Mount Miwa, but the sight of the falls at Ajanta makes him think that Kiyoaki meant the Ajanta waterfalls.

Endo, too, chose India as the site of his novel because he had read *Indo de Kangaeta Koto* and *Hojo no Umi*. However, he puts across an alternate, more 'inclusive' and accommodating way of understanding religion.

In *Akatsuki no Tera* by Mishima Yukio and *Fukai Kawa* by Endo Shusaku, India is portrayed using common motifs such as Calcutta and Benaras. Also, spirituality is interwoven with the plots in the novels. Moreover, India is employed as a trigger to reflect and ponder on Buddhist treatises in *Akatsuki no Tera* by Mishima; on religion, Christianity and the concept of coexistence in *Fukai Kawa* by Endo and on a gamut of ideas that lead to self-reflection and reflection on Japan by Hotta.

A lot of Endo Shusaku's literary works centre around the theme of coming to terms with Western Christianity and its incompatibility with Japanese sensibilities due to his own baptism at a young age. He addresses the turmoil within, of coming to terms with two very different schools of thought — monotheism, absolutism and the image of God as the father in Western Christianity as against the pantheistic, non-absolutist and maternal image of God that his Japanese heritage and religion taught him — in a large number of his works. Perhaps, the author's lifelong endeavour to find a religion suitable to a Japanese gets him finally to India and the banks of the all-encompassing river Ganges.

Tabi or 'journey' is an important theme in the plot of the novel *Fukai Kawa*. Research has referred to *Fukai Kawa* as '*tabi no monogatari*' or a story of travel because travel to India brings together totally unrelated characters (H. Endo 2000, 73–93). The conclusion of the novel does not accomplish closure but indicates that the story moves on because the novel is '*tabi no monogatari*'. In the end, we see the tourists waiting to board the bus to 'go' to the Calcutta airport.

India, the river Ganges and the city of Benaras on its banks acquire significance in the India trip that the Japanese people undertake. The author asserts that his choice of the cremation ghats of the Ganges in Benaras was influenced by Mishima Yukio's description of the cremation scene in *Akatsuki no Tera* (Kaga 1999, 118–135).

In the novel, a significant part of the story unfolds in India, which is important because the journey to India can be viewed as a journey of psychological and mental distances for each of the characters. The journey enables the travellers to transform, where they find solace and some answers to the questions within.

The characters provide various insights into their understanding and impression of India through the novel. India, for the Japanese tourists, was a means to explore answers to questions they started out with. In addition, Isobe, who is not part of the travel group, is already in India. He helps the diseased and dying on the banks of the Ganges, taking care of them and even carrying the dead to the holy river for their final journey to the other world. Mitsuko is depicted as sceptical of Otsu's faith and makes fun of it. She herself is an agnostic but is drawn to Isobe, his faith and India all the same. Numada is a writer of children's stories who believes that a myna (bird) sacrificed its life for him and goes to India to pay his respects to the bird. Kiguchi is a soldier who wants to pray for his fellow soldier who consumed human flesh under trying circumstances. Isobe comes to India urged by his wife's last words that she would be reborn. The Sanjos are a honeymooning couple.

In *Fukai Kawa*, the trip to famous Buddhist sites for a group of Japanese tourists also exposes the main characters to the experience of Hindu pilgrimage centres like Benaras. At the first briefing held for the tourists planning to visit India, the guide Enami says, much to the surprise of the tourists, 'In India today, adherents of the Hindu religion make up an overwhelming majority, followed by Muslims, while Buddhism has all but disappeared' (Endo 1994, 31). The guide builds on this image of India associated more with Hinduism, with motifs of mother goddesses and the Ganges being prominent in the novel.

The author gives us glimpses of a snake charmer, of the overpowering smells of the city and of cows and even elephants on the street — sights a Japanese tourist could expect in an Indian city. Enami explains to the group in the bus how Varanasi got its name as the point of confluence of two rivers, Varana and Asi, and how it is considered a holy place. There are brief glimpses of the Bharatmata Temple, the Banaras Hindu University (BHU) campus, the bathing sites, the Vishwanath Temple, the tiny shops along the street and the Nakshar Bhagavati Temple, which is described at length with reference to the goddess there. Goddesses are a major motif for the author, much like Mishima.

Mother figures and motifs are important in Endo's philosophy, and in India, he finds images of the 'mother' in various forms and manifestations — the river Ganges, Mother Teresa and the goddesses

Kali, Chamunda being the significant ones. These symbols influence Endo to write his work and also have a crucial role to play in the way the characters assimilate their experience of India. Enami shows the idol of Chamunda to the Japanese tourists in his briefing sessions before the Japanese group leaves for India and then at the ghats of the Ganges. In reality, though, the idol is not located in Varanasi but in a museum in Delhi. In describing the goddess Chamunda, Endo contrasts her with the Holy Mother Mary in Christianity, who is a symbol of tenderness and maternal love, by saying that Indian goddesses are 'earth-mother goddesses' who embody gentleness at times and fire and wrathfulness at others.

What started off as a tour to the major Buddhist sites becomes one in which Hindu deities and goddesses and the holy city of Varanasi find a place. Even though the place is not shown to impact all the Japanese visitors in a similar way, the goddess Chamunda leaves a lasting impression on the minds of Mitsuko and Kiguchi, in whom the goddess invokes compassion and love along with awe.

Endo Shusaku's description of places in India is more elaborate when compared to his description of people. For the most part, the description of people is generic, and Indians are described more as a group than as individuals. Not much space is given to anyone other than the prime minister, Indira Gandhi, whose assassination and the Hindu–Sikh riots that followed are mentioned.

However, other than that, the Indians described are mostly divided into two major groups: the poor and filthy diseased people found at the ghats of the river Ganges by the Japanese tourists and the rich, pompous and English-medium school-educated Indians that Numada and Mitsuko happen to meet in the city. Even though Endo seems to be enamoured by the core of what is symbolised by the river Ganges, Kali and Chamunda throughout the novel, Indian people have been referred to as 'swarms'. Sometimes, a crowd of people has been compared to a swarm of flies.

When one looks at *Indo de Kangaeta Koto*, a work of non-fiction, one perceives the difference from the two other works of fiction discussed earlier. In the former, there is no single story running through the entirety of the work. Instead, a wide range of topics is covered in the account, ranging from the author's flight to the country where he notices the expanse of the river Ganges to his observation of the Indian people, nature, the variety of languages spoken and his 'reading' through Nehru's and Vivekananda's accounts. Hotta goes back in history and realises that India was not always a poor country, even as he sees the many homeless people in Calcutta and Bombay (Mumbai).

Moreover, he seeks to establish similarities between aspects of Japan and India, although he also finds differences. As mentioned, he draws parallels between the youth of India and Japan who are both disconnected from their past. Apart from the vastness of space and the abundance of variety in every sphere of life, whether it be languages or people's appearances, food is what overwhelms his senses. His reaction is similar in this respect to the response that India evokes in Mishima and Endo. Even as Hotta understands that his experience in India may be different from that of the other two authors, what is common to the three works is how India prompts the authors to think not only about India but also about their own countries, beliefs and works that they have read. The authors have been influenced by reading the works of other authors.

More importantly, Hotta adds new motifs or *utamakura* like India's self-image, which he finds in Nehru's *Discovery of India* and other books. For instance, Hotta mentions how, in his writing, Vivekananda seeks an Indian society modelled on the West but retaining its Hindu roots.

Mishima's and Hotta's works are similar because both Honda in *Hojo no Umi* and Hotta in *Indo de Kangaeta Koto* are overwhelmed by their experiences in India. While Honda finds the sights, sounds and smells of Benaras stretching his senses to their limits, Hotta wants to escape to the Himalayas to give a rest to his *Atama* (mind) (Hotta 2009, 80). Hotta says that he doubts if the Indians themselves could grasp the enormity of the contradictions and differences that exist in India (91). His work can, perhaps, be called a journey in thoughts as much as a literal journey.

Significantly, Japanese fiction and non-fictional accounts that focus on travel to India continue with the tradition of repeating *utamakura* from earlier works while also adding new ones to it. Some places are integral to the accounts — Benaras in fiction. The two novels discussed are associated with religion and spirituality. The actual encounter between the fictional characters and India serves to reaffirm their prior impressions of the country. Hotta's observations are perhaps more varied, covering facets of the country not covered by the other two works of fiction. However, he does describe Calcutta and uses the stereotype of describing people in plurals like Mishima and Endo. His travelogue is more than a well-planned itinerary. His responses to India and perception of his experiences seem more spontaneous and on more varied themes in comparison to the two works of fiction discussed in this chapter. Hotta's chapter '*Doukutsu no Shisou*', which may be translated as 'Thoughts in the Caves', has intertextual references to E.M. Forster's *Passage to India* (2009, 180–192).

Conclusion

Through a study of motifs and images associated with India, in the three works, we see how the tradition of *utamakura* employed in fictional and non-fictional accounts reaffirm past images and introduce new ones. They reveal an interesting pattern of how the books become vehicles of self-discovery rather than exploration of the Other.

Even though 'travel' is central to the two post-war novels, the authors, Mishima Yukio and Endo Shusaku, are governed more by the images held in their minds of an 'imagined' India than those formed based on their experiences in the country alone. Moreover, the travel of Honda in *Hojo no Umi* and of the Japanese tourists in *Fukai Kawa* seems to be undertaken less to explore the land and its people and more to explore an aspect of their own inner consciousness.

Honda in *Akatsuki no Tera* and the Japanese tourists in *Fukai Kawa* could be described as tourists and pilgrims visiting India. Even though the time spent in India is limited, for Honda, prior knowledge and understanding of the essence of the philosophy of rebirth and transmigration is helped by the visit to India. The visit, which he recalls at various points in the novel, helps him to understand and comprehend the concept of samsara and *alayavijnana* — two concepts that he integrates with the main thread of the story of transmigration.

In *Fukai Kawa,* the five Japanese characters, namely Isobe, Otsu, Numada, Kiguchi and Mitsuko, had a purpose other than exploration when they journeyed to India. In addition, there was the honeymooning couple of the Sanjos. The India they visited was, perhaps, geographically a new country but one whose image was already in their minds, and this is what attracted them to come and see it for themselves. The tour guide Enami's reflections and criticism of the Japanese people show how he views India as not just a land to tour or buy souvenirs but also one that needs to be understood at a deeper level.

Honda's encounter with Hinduism and Buddhism brings forth his affinity to the latter and his abhorrence of and distance from the former. He describes the Ajanta caves as a more familiar territory than Calcutta and Benaras in his mind owing to his interest in and knowledge of Buddhism.

On the other hand, Hotta's non-fictional account of India brings him in contact with its various facets and also makes him write about the place in an unconventional way. His experiences in India make him realise how little he knows about it, and he goes on to defy the stereotypes of India as a poor nation. Hotta contrasts India's abundant past with present-day India, where a large expanse is a desert, and where droughts and floods are frequent.

> However, if one looks at the history of India, then I understand India was not always a poor country. If one looks at one of the primary industries, that is, the handloom industries, especially textile industries, one is made aware of the extent of criminal exploitation that was carried out, which is too painful to be described in words. (Hotta 2009, 142; translation mine)

While all three authors discover what they 'think about' the country India, they thereby reveal aspects of their own selves. They describe the places and their experience of them, drawing on a common pool of images — *utamakura.*

India acts as a catalyst for Honda to reflect on the many Buddhist works he has read. For the tourists, the tour guide and the characters in *Fukai Kawa,* it provides a chance to come to terms with difficult pasts or find answers to questions bothering them by offering prayers. Their witnessing the abundant nature and the motherly figures of Ganges and the goddesses Chamunda and Kali in India help them gain clarity in their thoughts and gain peace. The two fictional works help reaffirm beliefs that the characters have about India and further cement them in the readers' minds. Hotta, by contrast, offers a fresh perspective by acknowledging the influence of the colonisers on Indians while also recognising the abundance of India's past in precolonial India.

'Exploration' in the two works of fiction, especially, and, to an extent, in the non-fictional travel account is more an internal process for the authors and the characters than an external exercise of discovering new places and people. Exploration and discovery of 'self', rather than just the places visited, has been one of the characteristics of travel writing in Japan where travel was conventionally undertaken to reaffirm existing notions about a place rather than explore new ones.

References

Chaudhuri, Saroj Kumar. 2003. *Hindu Gods and Goddesses in Japan*. New Delhi: Vedams eBooks.

Daishonin, Nichiren. n.d. *Nichiren Daishonin Gosho Zenshu* [The complete works of Nichiren Daishonin]. Volume I, Glossary A. Accessed 25 August 2021. https://www.nichirenlibrary.org/en/wnd1/Glossary/A#%C4%81layaconsciousness.

Endo, Hiroshi. 2000. *nen 5 gatsu 'Ganjisu no Nagarenimukete- Fukaikawano Mitsuko to Ōtsū' -, Ferisu Jogakuin Daigaku Kokubungakukai, Tsūgō 36* [With the flow of the Ganges — Mitsuko and Otsu of Deep River] Ferris Jogakuin, Japanese Literary Society.

Endo, Shusaku. 1994. *Fukai Kawa.* Translated by Van C. Gessel. New York: New Directions Publishing.

Fessler, Sussana. 2004. *Musashino in Tuscany: Japanese Overseas Travel Literature 860-1912*. Ann Arbor: Centre for Japanese Studies, University of Michigan.

Hotta, Yoshie. 2009. *Indo de Kangaeta Koto* [Thoughts in India]. Tokyo: Iwanami Shinsho.

Hulme, Peter, and Tim Young. 2002. *The Cambridge Companion to Travel Writing*. New York: Cambridge University Press

Kaga, Otohiko. 1999. *nen 5 gatsu, tsuitachi Endō Shūsaku (taidan), 'Saishinsaku Fukai Kawa — Tamashī no Mondai', Hahanaru Kami wo motomete, Endō Shūsaku no Sekaiten. Bunyu Sha* [Endo Shusaku (Interviews), Latest work Deep River — in search of Mother Goddess, A World Exhibition of Shusaku Endo]. Bunyusha.

Lakshmi, M.V. 2006. 'India as Portrayed in Modern Japanese Literature: A study of Endo Shusaku's Deep River'. In *East Asian Literatures: An Interface with India*, edited by P.A. George, 223–231. New Delhi: Northern Book Centre.

McKinney, Meredith. 2019. *Travels with a Writing Brush: Classical Japanese Travel Writing from the Manyoshu to Basho*. London: Penguin.

Mishima, Yukio. 2001. *The Temple of Dawn*. Translated by E. Dale Saunders and Cecilia Segawa Seigle. London: Vintage. Originally published as *Akatsuki no Tera* in 1970.

12

A Tale of Two Travels: *Reading Historiography through Amitav Ghosh's* In an Antique Land

Jaya Yadav

> I could not persuade her that a place does not merely exist, that it has to be invented in one's imagination.
>
> — Amitav Ghosh (*The Shadow Lines*, 1988)

Travel writing as a genre has witnessed several transformations over time. Travelling to the East from the West became a career during the 18th century, cementing a focus on Orientalist[1] approaches to travel and trade as imperial conquest (Said 1978, 11), as well as a manner of self-fashioning, which makes separating its modes and forms from politics difficult. Reading historiography as evolving sites of intersections between different disciplines of literature, sociology and history grants a deeper insight into the process and formations of history writing, especially in today's world. Understanding literature is inextricably linked to questions of memory, knowledge and power, which become focal points to delve into the past and a critical lens to examine the present and the future.

The relationship between knowledge and power in Foucauldian terms helps deconstruct hegemonic modes of reading and understanding history (Foucault 1976). Even today, much of travel writing is embedded with discourses with an Orientalist gaze, which commodifies 'Other' regions. As history continues to be a process in a continuum, using literature as a tool to underline these questions becomes central to decoding issues of travel trade, and time. Historiographical readings based on the 'footnotes of history'[2] allow for a rewriting of history, which

1 For a seminal understanding of the use of postcolonial theory, see Said (1978).

2 Scott McClintock illustrates the use of this phrase as an overarching framework to the novel, as Ghosh's narrative stems from an actual footnote in an academic essay that mentions Ben Yiju's slave (2006).

deconstructs paradigms of the 'Western' gaze and linear postcolonial readings. Such a reading is an important methodology for Ghosh to decentre a hegemonic reading of the past and the present. *In an Antique Land* (re)examines relationships based on power through equations of labour and 'service' prior to the advent of colonialism. He points to real people who were travelling in the medieval era across North Africa and Asia without being ascribed negative connotations of more recent labels of 'slave' during that time period. Excavating such figures from history is central to Ghosh's concerns of drawing upon reading history from the margins and weaving historiography into the account of his own travels in Egypt.

It is important to (re)locate the study of *In an Antique Land (*1992) through a cartography of travel, travellers and altering landscapes prefiguring modern-day boundaries and borders. As the travellers in the novel move through different time periods, histories and geographies, it becomes important to look at various themes of language, race, gender and postcolonialism. The text becomes a site of historiography, which combines various interdisciplinary approaches to analyse travel across time, land and oceans.

In today's age, which is arguably a post-globalised one, especially after the onset of COVID-19, inequalities between different social, ethnic and class groups have become starker. The sudden rupture in travel in the past two years has prompted a critique of the power possessed by the Global North, which gained access to vaccines against the disease much faster than other parts of the world. The dichotomies in the lived realities of the citizens in the Global North and South reveal the inequalities and inaccessibility of previously colonised nations in a growing neocolonial world, where they continue to be treated as sites of resources and material gain. Reading *In an Antique Land* in the contemporary era helps unpack and delineate similar issues of agency in travel and travel writing. Who has the power and the language to write their own tale of travel as well as uncover and narrate one of the people hidden away in history?

The book is an interesting text to use to help define newer methodologies of outlining thematic concerns of postcolonialism, subaltern studies and historiography through the genre of non-fiction in the space of novel writing. The novel opens with a prologue, foregrounding issues of erasure in history and of changing demographics in the region of the Indian Ocean. It also inscribes a timeline, which acts as an overarching framework to the novel, helping the reader plot the graphs of such parallel histories, narratives and trajectories of different travellers.

In this chapter, I shall be focussing on the metamorphosing element in the (re)creation of the traveller navigating their journey through roles as narrator, administrator, anthropologist and social scientist. Ghosh draws upon the contemporary people of Egypt and occupies varying roles, at times as a foreign student and tenant and at others as a social anthropologist. The multiple voices that arise in the text help the reader to understand plural perspectives as the reader's view of different worlds and time periods constantly changes, testifying to vast networks of trade and communication across Asia and Africa in a precolonial world. The foregrounding of trade routes dating back hundreds of years before the emergence of Western imperialism establishes an alternative view of what it meant to be a traveller and presents a series of exchanges between different regions, cultures and people. An important question is how the cross-examination of the primary travellers in this text — namely, Ghosh, the Jewish merchant Ben Yiju and Bomma, his slave — potentially grants fresh insight into history and inflects present-day understandings of politics, trade and travel. Travel during the medieval era shows a remapping of global trade, with it being rerouted to the interconnected regions of North Africa and Asia.

One asks, what were the relationships between real people in the past? Do the terms assigned to them of 'slave' and 'owner' reflect more recent capitalist equations between human beings? What sort of society existed prior to colonial rule, where the well-being of a 'slave' is asked about in a letter travelling across the Indian Ocean? Do our 21st-century definitions hinder us in understanding the past in greater depth to gain insight into the nuances behind such relationships? Ghosh uses the form of the novel as a looking glass to decode the travel of precolonial traders whilst reflecting on his own position as a traveller across their intersecting journeys in Egypt and India.

Ghosh's attempt to highlight real human beings who have been relegated to the margins of history, literally and metaphorically, presents an alternative positioning of reading and understanding migration, human relations and historiography. On the first page, 'the slave of MS H.6' is introduced as part of a letter written by a merchant, Khalaf ibn Ishaq, to his friend Abraham Ben Yiju in AD 1148 (Ghosh 1992, 1).The mention gives a momentary glimpse into the past where trade between the Middle East and the southern coast of India thrived in an intricate web of interrelations and connections in motion across the vast surface of land and sea. The clear reference to a world order yet untainted by the exploits of the white man paints a stark contrast to the violent trajectory of Western interception in oceanic trade.

A peaceful and, therefore, an alternative trading world can be seen through the contents of the letter where Khalaf sends Ben Yiju 'two jars of sugar, a jar of almonds, and two bars of raisins' and 'makes a point of singling him (the slave) out and sending him "plentiful greetings"' (Ghosh 1992, 6). Textual evidence of a harmonious or, at least, a pleasant relationship comes to the surface from the letter sent to Ben Yiju, which is a distinct deviation from reading dominant forms of slavery, especially the transatlantic slave trade controlled by colonial nations later in history. This particular reference shows the reader that even today, society across the globe continues to be overshadowed by the terminology of colonisation.

The oscillating chapters in the book are an interesting tool that, on the surface, appear to be shadowing Ghosh's and Ben Yiju's footsteps. Ghosh retraces Ben Yiju's life through his footsteps, which colours his own time in Egypt as a scholar. For him, the slave mentioned in the letter becomes more essential to recover from history as his presence on paper is insignificant and does not give us many details to help Ghosh decode the slave's individual history. Importantly, Ghosh's presence as a young anthropologist in rural Egypt does not overshadow the histories of those around him. His physical and ideological space and visibility do not act as the centre of the text's narrative. His thoughts and opinions are constantly challenged by the Egyptians he interacts with, differentiating his account of travel in the region from colonial anthropologists, who had a very different agenda to perpetuate propaganda based on their 'empirical' knowledge systems.

Moreover, a close reading of and interaction with a previous world order, distanced from colonial discourses, is a crucial element in *In an Antique Land*. This chapter delineates the recurring theme of the blurring of fact and memory in the novel, which is based on Ghosh's own time and travel in Egypt over a decade as a student and young social anthropologist. The parallels and overlaps between Ghosh's time in independent Egypt and that of the slave who accompanies the Jewish merchant Ben Yiju are unravelled through different encounters with present-day Egyptians and their receptions of those who appear as 'foreigners' to them. Ghosh, in their eyes, belongs to the category of an outsider who, at times, is seen as alien-like and is unfamiliar to the locals. One can note the difference between the medieval and contemporary world, as Ben Yiju and Bomma's travels suggest that their identity is fluid, occupying different lands at times and maybe even with different modes of livelihood. The text offers insights into the evolution of the image and representation of the traveller who is not a white man and is not seeking to establish a hegemonic colonial enterprise. This shift away from Western models of writing articulates the permeable distinctions of the genre of Indian writing in English vis-à-vis the trope of the traveller. Ghosh redefines the multiplicity of genre definitions for a travelogue, as he personalises history. Here, the structure of the novel is determined not only by his movements and belief systems but also by the details of the domestic life of the Egyptians living in present-day Lataifa and Nashawy. He writes:

> The professional traders and vendors were usually the first to set up their stalls. They would begin to arrive early in the morning in their little donkey-carts, the fishmongers, the butchers, the fruit-sellers, the cloth-merchants, the watchmaker ... the amateurs would follow a little later, women for the most part, swathed heavily in black, carrying wicker baskets loaded with tomatoes, carrots and cauliflowers, depending on the season. (Ghosh 1992, 148)

Ghosh speaks the local language, Arabic; to those he interacts with, translating his experiences into English for the novel. The aim is not to replicate what the 'antique' land represents, a land fossilised in time through different colonial powers and their dogmatic views on it. Rather, it is a first-hand account of a young traveller whose purpose is to record familial history and sharpen his skills as a student of anthropology. Ghosh, the student, becomes immersed in the slave's story and, over a period of time, is able to outline his travel across the world into India. For Ghosh, the marginalised figure of Bomma is the most important figure to recover through historical investigations. (Re)discovering and remembering Bomma becomes Ghosh's parallel project in *In an Antique Land*, where he simultaneously attempts to record a people's history of Egyptians. Ghosh forms close relationships with many during his stay in Egypt, chronicling his time and inscribing their names in history through the novel.

Ghosh connects various narratives emerging from the past and present by using divisions in the book not as a point of rupture but rather, as he argues, 'joined together in a helical pattern. That was the book's formal challenge. I should explain also that neither narrative is fictional. One is based on historical sources (the Geniza documents) and the other is based on my personal experiences in Egypt' (Ghosh and Stankiewaicz 2012).[3] Tracing the journeys of the enslaved figure in Ben Yiju's life as a quest to unearth historical and anthropological findings, Ghosh, too, begins his own journey into 'this tornado of grand designs and historical destines ... a trapdoor into a vast network of foxholes where real life continues uninterrupted' (Ghosh 1992, 5). His entry into the small village of Lataifa in Egypt is marked with his appearance as alien-like as he is a foreigner

3 Ghosh's distancing from the labels of postcolonial theory is surprising to many, as he once dissociated himself from the Commonwealth Prize for his novel *The Glass Palace*, citing issues of neocolonialism.

and is often called the 'doktor from Hind' (134). Using Homi Bhabha's conceptualisation of 'Third Space', we see its ramifications in postcolonial Egypt, where Ghosh becomes the external, more powerful and privileged figure who is in the land exercising a complicated relationship with the inhabitants (Bhabha 1994). There are no distinct binaries of the oppressor in contrast to the oppressed but rather a give-and-take equation, where Ghosh's beliefs and customs make him appear a weird figure in the eyes of the residents. They incredulously ask him if people worship cows and burn their dead in India, citing their own moral and religious reasons for believing it's wrong. They ask Ghosh matter-of-factly, 'What do you do with your dead?' To their shock, Ghosh informs them that they are burnt (1992, 165). In the marketplace, shopkeepers overcharge him for vegetables, knowing that he can afford to give more money as he is a 'city dweller' (153). Other people inform him that they know about India because they remember that during the Second World War, several Indian soldiers had seemed 'so tall and dark that many of us Egyptians were afraid of them. But if you talked to them they were the most generous of all the soldiers; if you asked for a cigarette, they gave you a whole packet' (190). To this, another person says, 'That was then. Now things have changed' (190). The reference to the past here alludes to the present, highlighting changing relations between the new independent nation states of India and Egypt. Both share a colonial past that harks back to several centuries, and the reader is carried on this journey into this 'antique' land. Moreover, through the description of Egypt's terrain as 'dusty', highlighting the 'shabbiest and most derelict' parts of Nashawy with streets 'clogged with shoals of churned mud', Ghosh paints a realistic view of Egypt in contrast to its depiction in Western narratives as an 'exotic' place (86).

In light of the crisis in March 2021 when a container ship blocked the Suez Canal and closed an essential trade network passing through Egypt, understanding *In an Antique Land* becomes even more relevant to comprehend the implications of the central theme of travel in the novel. It makes the reader ask who has written the history of this land till now and in what manner. How does the geographical location of Egypt make it an important place to ensure the continuity of trade? Various people throughout history have harnessed trade through the region. Simultaneously, alongside trade, conflict, too, played a central role in reshaping Egyptian history. Egypt occupied an important position as part of the British empire during the First World War. It was an ideal strategic location for the Allies to place their armies, which significantly helped their military endeavours. Notably, a British soldier's experience of the World War was dramatically different from thousands of South Asian soldiers who served alongside them. Till today, it is difficult to locate the names and lives of the latter. The neocolonial ideologue, Britain, continues to market itself as a 'saviour'.[4] Amidst the virtual breakdown of world trade, the Suez Canal once again became a central focus in the global community. The standstill of global trade during the blockade reasserted the importance of the canal, since other sea routes around the continent of Africa would delay trade by several months and increase trading losses, as approximately 12 per cent of worldwide trade is known to pass through it daily (Das 2021).

The novel's use of intertextuality references a larger literary history, especially of the evolution of the form of the novel over time. Travel writing has historically been published on paper for literary audiences, and Ghosh's writing marks an important experiment in the overlapping genres of travelogues, memoirs, and historiographical work. This weaving of two tales leads to a multiplicity of readings and perspectives on both contemporary travels and those of the past. Ghosh's non-Orientalist passage through time helps form real connections with the people he meets in Egypt and forge unique relationships with the Egyptians. His culture shock captures the nature of postcolonial travellers who, in a world now considerably altered by the influence of colonisers and the colonial legacy, are unable to understand precolonial connections and realities at times. Nilanjana Gupta refers to these themes in her essay '*In an Antique Land*: A Counter-Narrative of Coloniality', arguing that the novel seeks to undo existing modes of continual legacies of colonialism through a unique tale.

As the narrative continues, the reader, along with Ghosh, charts out Ben Yiju and the slave Bomma's cross-continental travel, possible due to the existing trade routes on the seas. The interconnectivity of the world for Asia is not a new phenomenon. In his book *The Ocean of Churn: How the Indian Ocean Shaped Human History*, Sanjeev Sanyal highlights the in-depth maritime dimension of history and counters the dominating inland perceptions. Ghosh uses textual proofs to build upon the names and places he finds across Asia as he moves along similar paths of numerous travellers before him along similar journeys on land and sea. The 20th-century imposition of borders and arbitrary rules and visa regulations are contrasted with Ben Yiju's borderless world. In modern-day Egypt, one local has to travel to Iraq for his livelihood years after his encounter with Ghosh. He is unable to return after the onset of the war

4 A plethora of British period dramas, such as *Downton Abbey*, *The Crown*, *The Guernsey Potato Peel Pie Society* and so on, treat the World Wars and colonisation as a golden age. Their nostalgic rhetoric is popular not only in Britain but also in several other countries. Such shows glorify England and the monarchy whilst upholding problematic ideals on race, ethnicity and language.

between Iraq and Iran while his family continues to wait for him. Iraq, to the Egyptians, becomes a land of darkness, a place of violence and racism, unlike its initial days when it was a place that provided opportunities for work and upward social mobility. However, travel in the medieval era, by contrast, allowed even slaves a certain amount of freedom and relative importance.

One sees that the older voyages of the medieval era are analogous to the journeys of real people in this modern world, Ben Yiju follows a similar voyage over the sea, travelling from Egypt and Aden (Yemen) to India for trade. Travel in the pre-modern era was associated with trade, as the Indian Ocean and the Arabian Sea created a vast and intricate network of cross-cultural routes exchanging goods, ideas and people through institutions of marriage and slavery. The understanding of slavery in Ben Yiju's context remains ambiguous as history tells us he married a slave, most probably as a business alliance, whilst transgressing religious identity. Bomma acts not only as a slave but also as a coordinator to help Ben Yiju engage further and more efficiently in his trade from Mangalore (Manguluru), his place of residence in India. Bomma clearly enjoys a cordial relationship with Ben Yiju, often taking care of his business and travelling to Aden. He is called 'slave and business agent, a respected member of his household', and clearly considered as an important person to those who know of him (Ghosh 1992, 7). Ghosh challenges views on the medieval era and its people by showing an alternative relationship of two travellers who were businessmen. He articulates an unconventional understanding of the lives of two men who were together for a large part of their life.

At the same time, Ghosh also reveals the business side of their work, which aids their travels and trade. To pay his debt and fare better as a trader, Ben Yiju moves to Mangalore where he marries a local woman, Ashu. Notably, Ghosh does not shed much light on the lives of women, neither from his contemporary world nor the ancient world. One may argue that in ancient India, Ashu may not have had the agency to travel like her husband, but Ghosh does not invest much time attempting to uncover her life, unlike his commitment to his primary traveller. Ghosh remarks on the transcultural nature of this marriage, as it is Ben Yiju's second. Yiju leaves behind the marriage once he returns to Egypt after spending about two decades in Mangalore. Patriarchal norms continue to dominate the present and the past despite several marked differences in terms of transnational identities and the potential of travel in spaces not yet divided by political borders. Arguably, 'translocal' and 'global' elements permeate the pre-modern world, before such categories came to be defined in the 20th century.

Gauri Viswanathan argues that Ghosh subverts modern nationalism by looking back to a freer past as a reference point of culture, language and history. In her words, Ghosh attempts to 'break free of the conventions that install the west as a reference point for anthropological knowledge' by introducing a syncretic model of cultural exchange and identity formation (Viswanathan 1995, 19). Ghosh implicitly acknowledges the old world's syncretic nature, which is not divisible along ethnic, communal and linguistic lines as today's world is. From the letter that Ben Yiju receives, one can gauge that 'despite the merchandise it speaks of, the letter's spirit is anything but mercenary: it is lit with a warmth that Goiten's translations renders still alive and glowing' (Ghosh 1992, 7). The letter reveals the almost symbiotic relationship of Ben Yiju and Bomma as possibly two equals, if not two companions, who respected each other.

Ghosh's oeuvre in his later novels discusses issues of human warfare resulting in riots, wars and, at times, manifesting as ecological violence. In this book, the implications of a traveller's potential and power to alter the natural landscape and history are evident. Commenting on Ben Yiju's era, closely connected to the present-day Egypt that Ghosh lives in, he writes,

> The region had fared badly in the eleventh century and over a period of several decades, since well before Ben Yiju's lifetime, its merchants and traders had been moving eastwards, towards Egypt. Jews figured prominently among these migrants and those amongst them who moved to Masr generally chose to join the 'Palestinian' congregation in Babylon. Ben Yiju was thus following a well-marked trail. For the synagogue of Ben Ezra the influx of migrants from Ifriqiya was to prove providential: the newcomers proved to be the most industrious members of the community and they soon assumed its leadership, setting the pattern for the others in matters of language and culture, as well as trade and commerce. The North Africans appear to have had a particular affinity for the flourishing trade between the Mediterranean and the Indian Ocean and over a period of several centuries, the Jewish traders of Fustat counted as an integral part of the richly diverse body of merchants who were involved in the conduct of business in Asian waters. (Ghosh 1992, 38)

This historical evidence becomes the location for Ghosh to enter and exit the past and the present as he travels through time through mapping Ben Yiju's and Bomma's journey. Their paths, traversed centuries ago, are not wholly unlike his own. This inextricably interwoven and overlapping history creates a rubric that orbits the novel and provides important markers for each traveller's journey across the same region of North Africa and the Indian subcontinent.

Ghosh's cultural mapping of history in the novel undercuts Orientalist discourses and continues across the narrative, as the reader, too, travels through the pages, entering certain regions through oscillating time periods of the past and present. Their intersections shadow each other and illuminate the similarities and differences of the two overlapping travels, highlighting the multiplicity of perspectives of an age now existing in remnants through tales of the past. The emergence of the slave from Ben Yiju's letter becomes the central focus of Ghosh's later excursions as he moves deeper into Ben Yiju's journey across the ocean into India. Ghosh's own discovery of Ben Yiju's and the slave's lives unravels, as he is able to locate the slave in India and concurs from other experts that his probable name may have been 'Bomma'. As an upper-caste and upper-class Indian, Ghosh has access to certain privileged resources that allow him to live in Egypt as part of his degree at Oxford and uncover the hidden and almost invisible figure of the slave, deemed unimportant by history.

Rather, the mission to explore the trajectory of the slave's life is a problematisation of the colonial project. An unnamed figure is posited as the shadow of the 20th century-traveller, using the narrative as a site of historiography. The narrative does not chronologically record these events. Instead, it sheds light on invisible and unmarked journeys. Ghosh articulates an alternative knowledge system, moving away from rigid binaries between what is perceived as a 'discovery' by 'Western' and, therefore, 'modern' people and what are Western discourses being seen in sharp contrast to the indigenous or 'primitive' explorers who do not often occupy the narrator's role in other travelogues. Such writing has been coloured by the parameters of being a white man, extending racist tropes that have often dominated literary discourses. *Heart of Darkness* by Joseph Conrad, which uses racist themes to portray Africa as a place of darkness, is one such example of canonical literature.

The history of the travelogue, as a genre, can be traced back to Thomas More's *Utopia,* which paved the way for future texts such as Jules Verne's *From the Earth to the Moon* to become an extension of imperialist agenda. Such texts added to the belief that there were 'new found' lands to be conquered by European nations. Literature personified the discourse that the white man was the 'pioneering' figure who would 'discover' these 'new' lands, erasing the ancient history and culture of the indigenous people who had been living there for generations, especially in North America and Australia. The 'discovery' of America by Christopher Columbus led to several other expeditions towards 'new' lands, with similar narratives emerging in literature during that period.

Ghosh's *In an Antique Land* is not a simple reimagining of the colonial enterprise, nor does it seek to glorify Western notions of science. Instead, Ghosh uses 'translocal' and diasporic figures to deconstruct such narratives. The traveller is not an alien intervention used for fictionalising history. Ben Yiju and Bomma are firmly rooted in their historical backgrounds of the region. Ghosh does not represent the coloniser but rather a figure that has been (mis)placed in an intricate matrix of time, travel and history in an overarching framework of ancient civilisations of India and Egypt. Ghosh attempts to reverse this system of knowledge and power through a close reading of historiography to examine multiple, intersecting histories as part of a larger network of trade. The reader is taken on a journey of (re)discovery that continually redefines what constitutes 'modern', 'development' and 'knowledge'. Though the work is in English, one can argue that it is a form of 'writing back to the Empire' (Rushdie 1982, 1). It also undoes the power of the empire by deconstructing its popular modes of writing travelogues. Ben Yiju's travels prove the existence of precolonial travel, signifying the flow of people from various parts of the world to the South Asian coast. Ghosh writes of Ben Yiju's entrance to India through Mangalore. This port city also became a repository of his livelihood and possibly granted other migrants like him during that era a means to live and flourish in the region. The portrayal of these Asian and African journeys can be read as an alternative mode of writing.

Importantly, the participation of local communities has largely been overlooked in both fictive and non-fictive colonial accounts in history where knowledge was a linear process gathered by the colonizer subject. Here, the colonised are not passive recipients of knowledge. Instead, they also partake in indigenous methods of preserving memory, artefacts and culture. The existence of the letter that clearly mentions the slave is a prime example of this process. In Ghosh's work, the stories of the everyday life, customs and traditions, family lineage and history of the people of Nashawy and Lataifa are described,

During colonial rule, individuals and communities questioned the empire through various acts of subversion. Colonial trade, which made the imperialist conquest and the British Empire possible, was based on maritime technological advancements. The rise of colonialism was closely associated with developments made during the industrial age. The colonies and their people, too, were shareholders and participants in these developments. Ghosh uses the travelogue as a site where the reader becomes a literal and metaphorical traveller who does not follow the agenda of the white man. The process of writing this 'regular' journey emphasises narratives that act counter-hegemonic to the 'heroic' tales in history based on Western concepts of 'pioneering' in 'new' worlds.

Ghosh's experimentations with the reconstruction of time in *In an Antique Land* being cyclical and not following a linear chronology call for a comparative reading of history as histories. The fragmentation of time in the narrative invites the reader to fill these gaps with their own understanding based on the alternative forms of history presented to them on paper. Ghosh gives us glimpses of the upheavals of the World War and the Iraq–Iran War, which affect the people of Egypt drastically. By the 1980s, a new migration begins towards the Gulf nations, which helps 'modernise' Egyptian life. 'Ahmed, Shaikh Musa's son, had often talked of going to work in Iraq, he'd wanted to give his wife and children some of those things that other people had in their houses — a television set, a fridge, perhaps a washing machine' (Ghosh, 1992, 243).

The questions of this 'new' world order, connected to an old, together challenge Eurocentric understandings of the world. The travelogue becomes a medium to understand other histories, representations and misrepresentations of history that have been unquestioningly accepted as the 'truth'. One must also remember that 'truth' is a subjective viewpoint, which evolves over time. Similarly, the definitions of 'slave' have also changed over time. The narrative grants insight into a relationship between a slave and a trader not based on exploitation and dehumanisation of labour and people. The questions it raises are more than simple ones regarding science or the techniques of history retelling. The characters are globalised even if they existed several centuries ago, thus emphasising the interconnectivity of the world. Ghosh navigates through time and genre to weave in characters spread over continents in the precolonial past and the 20th century.

The colonial empire flourished due to its exploitation of the citizens of those 'antique' lands. These citizens were never given credit and are not found in the annals of history as anything but a subjugated community fit to be ruled and governed by the white man. The white man's burden and religion played a key role in perpetuating the hegemonic discourse of white, Western superiority. The text dismantles this view of power functioning vertically. Knowledge is a permeable process in which the coloniser and the colonised take an active part. No one is superior and all-knowing at any time. The locals and travellers like Ghosh as well as Ben Yiju and Bomma are characters who embody different perspectives.

The text constantly shifts the traveller's gaze, helping the reader view the world through various lenses. The past seen through the traveller's eyes serves as a looking glass to see the inflection of the present in the past. Overall, the theory of knowledge finds interesting paths in *In an Antique Land*, where the reader carries on the journey, moving beyond the traveller's existence on the pages. Ghosh, as narrator and author, symbolises new forms and styles in travel writing. He recreates the figure of the traveller as one that is always shifting to meet the emergent concerns of a postcolonial or, arguably, a neocolonial world. Ghosh's attempt to flesh out Bomma and Ben Yiju is not merely an anthropological search. The final destination is tied to uncovering Bomma's name, thereby granting him a personalised space where he emerges as a person in his own right and steps away from the label of a 'slave.' The novel symbolises the significance of the various intertwining moments of travel across time and geography. These histories of various migrations define different citizenship models of certain parts of the world. Such labels of identity, homeland and belonging are continually redefined as the travels of Ghosh, Ben Yiju and Bomma become part of historiography. Nationalism and citizenship based on newer definitions as separate and distinct nation states are ideas challenged by the lives left behind in the letter from Ben Yiju. The letter speaks to Ghosh across history and space, altering and shaping his own journey into the heartland of Egypt to across the globe. Ghosh chooses to read between the lines of the letter, identifying Bomma in the process, which emerges from the fringes to lead the voyage of the reader to various 'antique' lands. The novel becomes a historiographical project, shedding light on Bomma as the link between various worlds. The book seeks to ask how many more such people have been rendered invisible by history. As *In an Antique Land* proves, history may be renewed every day as a living process, being made and unmade with the passing of time and chronicled through writing.

References

Bhabha, Homi K. 1994. *The Location of Culture*. London and New York: Routledge.

Das, Kaustav. 2021. 'Explained: How much did Suez Canal Blockage Cost World Trade'. *India Today*, 20 March 2021. Accessed 22 March 2021. https://www.indiatoday.in/business/story/explained-how-much-did-suez-canal-blockage-cost-world-trade-1785062.

Dixon, Robert. 1996. 'Travelling in the West: The Writing of Amitav Ghosh'. *Journal of Commonwealth Literature* 31(1): 3–24.

Evenson, Norma. 1992. 'Review: *An Imperial Vision: Indian Architecture and Britain's Raj* by Thomas R. Metcalf. *The Indian Metropolis: A View toward the West*'. *Journal of the Society of Architectural Historians* 51(1): 85–87.

Foucault, Michel. 1976. *The History of Sexuality*. New York: Pantheon Books.

Gandhi, Leela. 2003. 'A Choice of Histories: Ghosh vs. Hegel in an Antique Land'. *New Literatures Review* 40: 17–32.

Ghosh, Amitav. 1992. *In an Antique Land*. New Delhi: Ravi Dayal.

———.1995. *The Calcutta Chromosome*. New Delhi: Ravi Dayal.

———.1988. *The Shadow Lines*. New Delhi: Ravi Dayal.

Ghosh, Amitav, and Damien Stankiewaicz. 2012. 'Anthropology and Fiction: An Interview with Amitav Ghosh'. *Cultural Anthropology* 27(3): 535–541. Accessed 9 December 2020. http://www.jstor.org/stable/23252412.

Gupta, Nilanjana. 1999. 'In an Antique Land: A Counter-Narrative of Coloniality'. In *The Novels of Amitav Ghosh*, edited by R.K. Dhawan, 194–201. New Delhi: Prestige Books.

Hawley, John C. 2005. *Amitav Ghosh. Contemporary Writers in English*. New Delhi, India: Foundation Books.

King, Bruce. 1994. 'In an Antique Land'. *World Literature Today* 68(2): 430.

Kumar, Vijay T. 2007. 'Postcolonial Describes You as a Negative'. *Interventions* 9(1): 99–105.

McClintock, Scott. 2006. 'Travels Outside the Empire: The Revision of Subaltern Historiography in Amitav Ghosh'. *South Asian Review* 27(2): 5–24.

Nandy, Ashis. 1983. *The Intimate Enemy: Loss and Recovery of Self Under Colonialism*. Delhi: Oxford University Press.

Historiography in Amitav Ghosh'. South Asian Review 27(2): 5–24.

Romanik, Barbara. 2005. 'Transforming the Colonial City: Science and the Practice of Dwelling in *The Calcutta Chromosome*'. *Mosaic: An Interdisciplinary Critical Journal* 38(3): 41–57. Accessed 3 December 2020. http://www.jstor.org/stable/44029669.

Rushdie, Salman. 1982. 'The Empire Writes Back with a Vengeance'. *The Times*, 3 July.

Said, Edward. 1978. *Orientalism*. New York: Pantheon Books.

Sanyal, Sanjeev. 2016. *The Ocean of Churn: How the Indian Ocean Shaped Human History*. Delhi: Penguin Random House.

Viswanathan, Gauri. 1995. 'Beyond Orientalism: Syncretism and the Politics of Knowledge'. *Stanford Humanities Review* 5(1): 19–32.

13

Narratives of Travelling Memory

Nishat Haider

> To be a traveler — and novelists are often travelers — is to be constantly reminded of the simultaneity of what is going on in the world, your world and the very different world … from which you have returned 'home'.
>
> —Susan Sontag (At the Same Time: The Novelist and Moral Reasoning)

> Travel is … an expression of the principal logic of memory: its genesis and existence through movement.
>
> —Astrid Erll (Travelling Memory)

This chapter employs an interpretive framework that arises from the recent reconceptualisation of memory that shifts the emphasis from 'the roots of memory' to 'the routes of memory' (Erll 2011, 11). It explores the possibilities and limits of analysing Qurratulain Hyder's fictional narrative *River of Fire* (originally in Urdu, *Aag ka Darya*) within the framework of approaches that privilege travelling memory with 'a focus of attention … directed towards mnemonic processes unfolding across and beyond cultures' (9). The term 'travelling memory' is 'a metaphorical shorthand, an abbreviation for the fact that in the production of cultural memory, people, media, mnemonic forms, contents, and practices are in constant, unceasing motion' (12). This chapter claims that such travel in *River of Fire* consists not only in the movement of people across spatio-temporal and sociocultural borders but also in the perpetual exchange of ideas and knowledge between individuals. Drawing on two millennia of historical memories and depicting a cast of characters that rematerialises in various incarnations and eras, the narrative of *River of Fire* maps out how the individuals and ideas travel between different spatio-temporal chronotopes, producing new cultural matrices and political contexts. Memory 'circulates, migrates, travels' (Bond et al.

2016, 1) and interacts 'multidirectionally' (Rothberg 2009) across and beyond the established socio-religious and spatio-temporal divides. In the process, memory adds new layers of signification that concentrate on the interplay between the familial and the national, the local and the global, and the regional and the transregional. Historical memory in democratic states is nudged towards what Raymond Williams calls a 'selective tradition' or 'the significant past' — how, 'from a whole possible area of past and present, certain meanings and practices are chosen for emphasis, [while] certain other meanings and practices are neglected and excluded' (1980, 39). Therefore, the narrative, as a site of travelling memories, emerges as an important medium for representing the past that extends beyond the frames of national remembrance. The travel writing critic and literary scholar Spurr observes that the 'rhetorical modes … are part of the landscape in which relations of power manifest themselves' (1993, 3). Through a close reading of *River of Fire*, the chapter seeks to unpack the signifying and mnemonic practices that encode a critical source that underscores not only travelling memory, its formation and its revision but also its remediation of asymmetrics of power inherent in the class, religious and communal divide across spatio-temporal chronotopes. I will be looking at Hyder's English transcreation of her original novel in Urdu, primarily because, as Ritu Menon claims, it is Hyder's conscious revision of a previous creation (2008, 205).

Owing to the strong motif of time in *River of Fire*, which has often been construed as being the river of time, the text can be likened to time travels across the map of memory (Palakeel 1999; Amarakeerthi 2003, Raja 2006; Oldfield 2010). In the novel, mnemonic symbols, images and icons criss-cross not only the frames of historical chronotopes but also borders of all sorts to give meanings to the events distant in time and place. The forte of *River of Fire* lies in its unique temporal shifts, characterised by journeys through time and memories. Emphasising the coexistence and free intermingling of the various epochs on social and psychological planes in India, Hyder says, 'You have to be a native, born and bred in this land to understand the synthesis and cultural richness as well as the contradictions and frictions inherent in this situation' (cited in Asaduddin 2000, 29). She does exactly that in her novel *River of Fire* by delineating the broad spatio-temporal frames of the text. In the novel, four similar stories take place in the subcontinent during different historical periods — 4th century BC, late 15th and early 16th century, end of the 18th and the whole of the 19th century and, finally, the post-Partition era. The three principal characters of the novel, Gautam Neelambar, Champak/Champa and Hari Shankar, are reincarnated in many ages. They and other characters who join them along the way, like Kamaluddin from the Sultanate period and Cyril from the time of the East India Company, flow along with the 'river of fire,' century after century, birth after birth. An enormous canvas of spatio-temporal travelling consciousness is created in the novel. As they travel through the aeons, the characters are the carriers of memory, who not only share collective images and narratives of the past but also draw on repertoires of memories and inherited habitus. Hyder organises memories temporally as acts of mental representation by which individuals locate themselves in time and distinguish themselves from the past — a 'present past' (Koselleck 2004, 254). She reminds us that this temporal shift in *River of Fire* sets up a changeable relation between the present and the past as there are multiple interpretations, which are superposed and altered by newer interpretations. Moreover, a growing critical consensus contends that interpreting the past through the normative framework of the nation obscures 'the hegemonic and often homogenizing properties of national memory regimes, occluding the ways in which memories may travel across geographical or cultural boundaries and marginalizing the experiences and histories of particular individuals or collectives' (Bond et al. 2016, 4). Hyder's narrative highlights the silence(s), elisions and prejudices inherent in national memory by exploring the ways in which diverse forms of memory, 'subject to ongoing negotiation, cross-referencing, and borrowing' (Rothberg 2009, 3), may circulate between and beyond the borders of gender, class and religion in the nation state. She variously foregrounds the 'multidirectional' (Rothberg 2009) and 'traveling' (Erll 2011) dynamics of memorative practice. This approach shifts attention from memory's static location in particular sites and objects to the dynamics through which it is articulated.

In *River of Fire*, the processes of memory travel are forms of world-making. As Hyder says, 'The entire symbol of India is the journey. The habit of always travelling, always searching' (1998, 418). Early in the narrative (*River of Fire*), there is a conversation between a Hindu prince, who has converted to Buddhism and transitorily passes as a Greek traveller, and a Hindu named Gautam, which is also the name of the Buddha:

> The stranger smiled impishly. 'Yes, I am Harius Sancarius at your service.' He bowed from the waist in an outlandish manner. Gautam was mystified then he said, 'Oh, a Yavana!' He had never seen a mleccha (a dirty foreigner) before.
>
> 'I hail from Ionia and I am in shipping,' the Greek informed him breezily. Gautam looked blank feeling like a country bumpkin. (8)

Furthermore, the prince observes:

> I have a little Cargo boat I brought from the Gulf to the River Indus. There I left it in charge of my Phoenician crew and decided to explore

> the land mass to the east. So I bought a horse from a Scythian and … may I sit down? First went up to Taxila. (9)

In this episode of the Greek traveller, that Gautam, the Hindu, has the same name as the Buddha suggests 'both a fluidity of identity and a commonality of origin for Hindus and Buddhists and the interchangeability of names/ epithets for Bactrians, Indo-Greeks, and Muslims' (Abbas 2018, 171). The most interesting word in the earlier exchange is *Yavana*, which refers to the prince who is passing as Greek. According to Romila Thapar, the term *Muslim* does not occur in Indian records of early contact with new arrivals to the country: 'The term used was either Turuska, referring to the Turks, or geographical, Yavana, or cultural, mleccha. *Yavana*, a back formation from *yona,* had been used since the first millennium B.C. for Greeks and others coming from West Asia' (Thapar 1989, 223). The term *Yavana*, derived from *Ionian*, represented 'the Hellenistic dynasties that were in control of large swathes of Afghanistan and north western India in the second century BCE' (Talbot 1995, 698). That *Yavana*, a word that was used to refer to the Greeks of Asia Minor, could later be applied to the Muslims proves to be a useful grid for understanding memory and its continual 'travels' and ongoing transformations through time and space and across social, linguistic and political borders. The travel of the word *Yavana* is perhaps most significant for it enables us to understand new constellations of memory created by their diverse inhabitants who travel from elsewhere and resettle in new places. These travelling memories are part of a continuous process whereby memories mediate between individuals across both space and time. Furthermore, the word *Yavana* 'brings Muslims into this meditation on the impossibility of historical purity and the problem of Indian authenticity right at the inception of the novel' (Abbas 2018, 169). The episode of the Greek traveller suggests routes of memory and networks or circulations of knowledge that subvert the borders that underpin them. In this regard, Astrid Erll recognises that 'much of the semantic shape that travelling memory takes on will be the result of the routes it takes in specific contexts and of the uses made by specific people with specific agendas' (2011, 15). To frame the workings of memory on the social and medial level, Hyder draws attention to the mnemonic itineraries — the migration or travel of names, images and symbols. Through the movements of memories, the 'mnemonic forms and contents are filled with new life and new meaning in changing social, temporal and local contexts' (Erll 2011, 11). Such an understanding of memory as fundamentally 'travelling memory' in *River of Fire* is backed by the sheer evidence of mnemohistory.

River of Fire presents 'pre-colonial India as a theatre of transoceanic, cross-cultural encounters' (Zaidi 2022, 56). The history of the Indian subcontinent has also been a history of travellers. Sometimes, the histories intermingle with one another to offer narratives in which memories and experiences travel across time and space. The 'idea' of India as a sociocultural entity, as Kumkum Sangari acknowledges, bears out Irfan Habib's argument that it was a product of conquest (as is evident by Mauryan emperor Asoka's inscriptions in 250 BC) and traveller's visions or a view from the outside (for instance, Alberuni's notion of India in *Kitab-ul Hind* in the 11th century) (Sangari 2003, 477; Habib 1999). Meanwhile, the effect-laden idea of India as a unique syncretic culture or a shared legacy developed from the memories of immigrants and converts (seen in Amir Khusrau's *Nuh Sipihr* [1318]). Hence, *River of Fire* becomes a significant account as it shows the intermingling of multiple travellers' narratives or travelling memories with multiple epistemologies. Hyder's mnemohistorical text becomes particularly salient because while the original Urdu version was published in 1959 after the partition of the Indian subcontinent based on religion, the English 'transcreation' by Hyder herself came out in 1998 when the Ram Mandir movement led by the Hindu right-wing political party was gaining momentum. Both periods witnessed communal strife and violent trauma. Notwithstanding the communal politics, Hyder, in *River of Fire*, challenges the narratives of divisive politics and fragmentation. As opposed to the Partition trauma narratives such as Abdullah Hussein's *Udas Naslein* (1963), Intizar Husain's *Basti* (1979) and Nasim Hijazi's *Khaaq aur Khoon* (1961), Hyder's mnemohistorical narrative represents the vivisection of the subcontinent as a phase of what Pandey calls 'aberration and as absence' (1992, 27). The subversion of the political history of the Partition is most evocatively portrayed through Hyder's recuperation of memories of personal tragedies of ordinary people like the experiences of the Gulfishan group of the late colonial period. At this juncture in the narrative, the namesakes of all the key characters scattered throughout the novel are brought collectively to depict the traumatic rupture of the subcontinent. Refraining from the representation of 'the communal orgy, accompanied by indescribable brutalities, ... [that consumed] thousands of lives in India and Pakistan' after the Partition, the narrative of *River of Fire* resonates with a nostalgia for the composite culture and the shared past of precolonial India (Pandey 1992, 30). The text 'is less focused on the violence of the partition and more on the experience of living the new form of national identity as it unfolds across the Indian landscape' (Raja 2006, 51). Thus, it also questions the paradigms of religion, ethnicity and the political state as markers of that 'national' identity (51). Hyder's fiction reorganises the ligatures of time and space to contest the mainstream history of secession and essentialist identities. To do this, she creates a sense of a syncretic past through the simultaneity of narratives featuring characters with parallel experiences in each annal of history that makes them all part of the same 'imagined community' of the nation (Anderson 1983, 26). Acknowledging the recuperation of the multiple past narratives as a mode of postcolonial resistance against hegemonising forces, Dirlik observes that if the past is constructed, so is the present (1996, 24). Hence, the very difference between the present and the past vanishes as in the natives' circular concept of time (24). Identifying this unique time of the novel as a Buddhist concept, Liyanage Amarakeerthi says that Hyder's 'choice of this time frame also has significance. It is said that Gautama Buddha's *Sasana* is to last five thousand years before the next Buddha appears. Hyder inserts her novel into this Buddhist conception of time which is itself circular' (2003, 30). Hyder's novel, moving from one historical period to the next, comes closer to the Puranic conceptualisation of history. Discussing the seamless transition of historical periods, Chatterjee says that 'myth, history, and the contemporary all become part of the same chronological sequence; one is not distinguished from another; the passage from one another, consequently, is entirely unproblematic' (1993, 80). The inescapability of the past is further reacknowledged by the reincarnations of the same characters in different eras in the novel. The names of characters repeat and re-repeat themselves in various periods of history, and there is also a recurring pattern of events. Thus, the novel ends where it began, in Shravasti. This circularity is concomitant with the Hindu Puranic concept of the *kaalachakra* or the 'wheel of time', which keeps rising and falling, pushing and hauling humanity with it. Indeed, the numerous religious systems and renunciatory faiths — Buddhist, Vedantic, Bhakti, Sufi — have meditated on the relationship between the flux of time and the transitoriness of experience. The understanding that memory travels instead of becoming inert is also a key process of memory. It becomes transformed by repetition by being put to new uses and enabling new discourses and stories.

Hyder foregrounds the 'episodic memory' of the past (Tulving 1984, 2005) and how these relate to the Self (Suddendorf and Corballis 1997; Tulving 1983; Dudai and Carruthers 2005) and the Other. She underscores the 'imaginative' capability of historical time travel in *River of Fire* as a significant means of pondering over 'complex ethical questions' of identity, memory and history (Mandler 2002, 147). The text employs narrative techniques that underscore 'remembrance as a fluid process in which commemorative tropes work to inform the representation of diverse events and traumas' beyond cultural boundaries, 'transcending — but not negating — spatial, temporal and ideational differences' (Bond and Rapson 2014, 18). Hyder's memory narrative reworks the experiences of the minoritised Other in her etchings of the trajectory of India's past. She portrays them as much persecuted (Kamaluddin), as much keen on composite culture (the nawabs of Lucknow), as much victimised by the British (Wajid Ali Shah), as much inspired by anti-British revolutionary passion (Kamal) and as much anguished by Partition (Kamal, Champa) as the Hindus believe they are. Hyder shows that there is barely any dissimilarity in the accounts of personal travails and individual harassment between the Buddhist Gautams, the Hindu Haris and the Muslim Kamals, and the Christian Cerils, whose identities memorialise the distinctive violent phases of Indian history — the pre-Muslim political turmoil, the Muslim invasion and the British colonisation, respectively. In *River of Fire*, there are many instances of tolerance as counter-narratives challenging the discourses of divisive and selective historiography: the female Muslim ruler called Razia Sultan abolishing the *jazia* (a tax levied on permanent non-Muslim subjects of a state ruled by Islamic law), Ali Jah Aliwardy's inclusion of Hindus in his ministry, the nawab wazirs of Oudh (Awadh) showing respect to the Hindu culture and the cooperation of the Hindu men for Begum Hazrat Mahal. Hyder contests the received notion of history and 'the androcentric bias of most modern national imaginings', specifically 'the assumptions behind the masculinist, heterosexual economy hitherto governing the cultural matrix through which an Indian national identity has become intelligible' (Ray 2000, 3–4).She is perhaps 'the first woman writer' who has 'annexed over twenty-five centuries of Indian History as a subject matter' and enunciated 'the grand nationalist visions of a pluralist civilization' through the memories of its women (Sangari 2003, 474). For example, she recounts the story of Razia Sultan, a female Muslim monarch who wanted to abolish the tax paid by Hindus in lieu of military service, and the story of another queen, Bibi Raji, who removes her favourite son from the throne because of his authoritarianism and declares her younger son, a musician, as the ruler. Though the female characters are not the real agents in the macro-politics throughout the two millennia period of this novel, Hyder foregrounds Bano, Champak, Nirmala, Champavati, Sujata and many other ordinary women for defying the mainstream (which is the male-stream) memories by their commitment to alternate sensibilities. In Hyder's text, the rational, the historical, the popular and the 'imaginal' knowledge(s) are not opposed to one another; they are complementary. Each of these ways of knowing the past would be inadequate without the other.

River of Fire shows how the memories that travel from the mythic past are eventually incorporated into local repertoires, how travelling memories become nativised and how contents of memory are constantly hybridised and remixed in a manner that is often extraordinary. Through its ongoing hybridisation, travelling memory engenders complex temporal phenomena such as anachronies, which 'belong to the deep history of memory and transculturality' (Erll 2011, 15), and time-space compressions (Erll and Rigney 2009). Hyder forges an evocative metonymic conflation of the Hindu mythical character Manu and the biblical Noah or the Islamic prophet Nooh in the chronotopic space of the Hindu god Lord Rama, Ayodhya. In the novel, a local Muslim man, narrating an alternative history blending myths and memory, tells Kamaluddin: 'Noah's Ark stopped at Mount Judi.... Well that was in fact, Ayodhya.... And the Hindus say they had a flood in the time of Manu. So Manu may have been Noah, for all you know' (Hyder1998, 75). Thus, the memory straddles 'established divides, it moves and travels, and it is actively transformed in the process' (Wüstenberg 2019, 371).

To stretch the metaphorical expression of travelling, since allegory is a form of travel as it involves the movement of a character through temporal borders and geopolitical sites, it can be inferred that Hyder reconstructs and re-signifies allegorical figures that circulate both within and beyond the boundaries of the Indian post-Partition moment. Furthermore, the frames of memory in the *River of Fire* also counter any assumptions about the boundedness of remembrance by showing how the local, transcultural and transnational are intertwined and what this means for the outcomes of mnemonic practice. As memory 'does not stay put, but circulates, migrates, travels; it is more and more perceived as a process' (Bond et al. 2016, 1). In so doing, memory calls into question established 'official' assumptions about the past. The blending of the biblical Noah and the Islamic prophet Nooh specifically signals a kind of hybridisation of memories that not only crosses cultural borders but also 'enables the imagining of new communities and new types of belonging' (Törnquist-Plewa 2018, 302). The most significant advantage of examining such 'hybridization produced by the layering of historical legacies that occurs in the traversal of cultural borders' is that it spotlights the power of those actors that create borders and hierarchies, particularly the State (Rothberg 2014, 130). This hybridisation entails the interrogation of the mechanisms of the reification of such hierarchies because it shows the processual nature of memory even when it is concerned with national remembering. For instance, the instructive dialectical interactions in *River of Fire* make it evident that 'the syncretic is not just secular and multi-religious, it is also the dynamic of constant change, always poised on the new, that surrenders neither to an "insider's" hegemonic assimilation nor to an "outsider's" imperious hegemony' (Sangari 2003, 477). Challenging the tendency to canonise and homogenise national memory, Hyder's *River of Fire* allows for a more fluid and processual understanding of remembering.

River of Fire frames conflicting/disputed/converging memories of entangled histories that are either borrowed from elsewhere or are co-constructed and amalgamated. Theorising 'mnemonic relationalities' that are caused by travelling memory, Erll says,

> Thus, if travel, or movement, is the fundamental dynamic of all memory, and transcultural memory — the variable mixtures of mnemo-cultural repertoires — its outcome, then 'mnemonic relationality' directs our attention towards a structuring process: towards acts of connecting and blending, co-constructions and negotiations that are necessary for bringing heterogeneous mnemonic elements into meaningful relations with one another. (2017, 6)

Thus, memory emerges as a process that links people, times, spaces, experiences and histories. The 'connective structure' of cultural memory spread over different spatio-temporal chronotopes creates linkages between the mythic, the imaginal and the social that generate changeable mnemonic assemblages (Assmann 1992). This form of remembering the past that interweaves the imaginal and imagination with everyday ordinary experience highlights the transformative potential of memories that can open up alternate epistemologies and ontology. The travelling memory in *River of Fire* implies 'a shift in perspective from migration as movement from place to place to migration as installing movement *within* place' with 'effects on place' (Aydemir and Rotas 2008, 7). The 'place' is '"thickened" as it becomes the setting of the variegated memories, imaginations, dreams, fantasies, nightmares, anticipations, and idealizations that experiences of migration, of both migrants and native inhabitants, bring into contact with each other' (7). According to the Andalusian mystic Ibn 'Arabi's use of *Khayal* or imagination, imaginal 'accords with its everyday meaning, which is closer to image than imagination. It was employed to designate mirror images, shadows, scarecrows, and everything that appears in dreams and visions' (Chittick 2008). Quilting the imaginal and memory, Hyder narrates the unbelievable conquest of Bahlol Lodhi and the fables of the prophet Suleiman as being as much a part of historiography as the actual specifics of wars for the throne of Delhi (Hyder 1998, 103). Interspersing the discursive ways of knowing (including both oral and written discourse), with the imaginal or the realm of experience and knowledge linked to dreams and visions, Hyder writes,

> Last time when Hussain Shah reached the banks of the Jamuna — it was his third and the seventh Sharqi campaign against Delhi — poor Bahlol Shah went hotfoot to the tomb of Bakhtiar Kaki in Mehrauli. He stood beside the grave of saint and prayed all night. At daybreak an unknown man came along and gave him a stick. A great many sheep have arrived at gate of Delhi, drive them away, quoth he. And Bahlol was victorious. (1998, 73)

Hyder uses memory and imaginal as valid forms of knowledge, a way of knowing the world and telling its (hi)story. Hyder's imaginal undertakes the plurality of 'subaltern' pasts built on myths and the supernatural akin to Dipesh Chakrabarty's theorisation in the context of Ranajit Guha's reading of Santal histories (Chakrabarty 2000, 112–113). For instance, in the novel, the story connecting Noah and Manu is articulated by a local Muslim man, and the story of Bibi Razia comes from a poor Persian dervish (Hyder 1998, 62). The divine intervention in Bahlol Shah's victory is articulated by the Persian dervish (73), and so on.

Although the premodern temporalities did not vanish with the colonisation of the Indian subcontinent in the 18th century to the 20th century, they instead perhaps impalpably coupled with what Partha Chatterjee calls 'the real space of modern life' where time is heterogeneous and unevenly dense (Chatterjee 2001, 402). Through the trope of travelling memories in *The River of Fire*, Hyder's imaginaire represents alternative temporalities, epistemologies and ontologies by calling our attention to its multiple mappings of becoming(s). To create a structure of experience capable of integrating history and fiction in terms of woman being a 'plural and collective unity in which the unity of destination and the differences of destinies are to be understood through each other', Hyder makes a kaleidoscopic presentation of Champa Baji (of Lucknow, Paris, London, Cambridge and Moradabad) (Ricoeur 1992, 114, 138). She merges different images of 'Champak of Shravasti standing in the corridor of time — Champak as the *Aryani* (goddess of the woods), Champavati as a Sufi allegory for Kamal and also Champajaan as the courtesan who enchants Cyril Ashley' (Kumar 2002, 91). Also, the recurring characters and their similarity in these instances, where one individual is likened to another, is a type of travel, from the Greek *metaphorein* meaning to travel, transfer or move over. Furthermore, such an extraction of spatio-temporal coordinates from the socio-historical determinations of 'woman' in *River of Fire* is motivated by Hyder's desire to construct the feminine as a spatio-temporal transposition, explicitly positioned 'as depending upon the extraction of "blocks of space-time" from the existential attributes of "women" qua a socio-historical entity' (Burchill 2010, 87). *River of Fire* is full of travels and travellers, and every traveller is literally or metaphorically entangled in a complex web of love, separation, and waiting across time and space. Still, as Kumkum Sangari proposes, it appears that in the episteme of travel, the women who mark each narrative may have signified 'home'; hence, women may have travelled less (2005). However, when Champa Ahmed refuses to put her life on hold for men, she breaks free from the shackles of female renunciation and sublimation of her previous avatars. She begins a new journey in her life. The feminine in *River of Fire* can be comprehended in terms of the Deleuzo-Guattarian concept of the 'becoming-woman'. This concept designates a perpetual process of rhizomatic deterritorialisation where all genealogies, roots, structures, beginnings and ends are renounced in support of free-floating, interlocking, nomadic subjectivities (Deleuze and Guattari 1987, 25). Deleuze and Guattari understand the process of becoming, 'a term which itself indicates heterogeneous encounters and operates by elevating ideas of difference and mutual transformation rather than the tendencies toward assimilation and identity associated with filiation' as supporting alliance (Sholtz and Carr 2019, 9). This intertwining of alliance, difference and becoming speaks to the desire for shared and mutual recognition. This process of becoming-woman is located in Hyder's female-influenced historiographic narrative in which the female protagonists are permitted to travel and move and to attain a positive sense of feminine agency. They challenge the colonial, communal and gender politics that confine them to an otherwise immutable otherness. Becoming-woman in the text is a crucial step towards the transformation of the exoticised and Orientalised Other, which is 'revolutionary' (Batra 2012, 65).

The artful narratives in *River of Fire* capture our interest and, in the process, compel a willing suspension of our conventional patterns of identification. The novel facilitates 'acts of affiliation across lines of difference' (Hirsch 2012, 21) or what Rothberg has called 'unscripted new link-ages' (2014, 133). The narrative is full of 'recurrences — of rivers, seekers, and travellers (wandering mendicants, Sufis, yogis, bhikshus), and artistic production — which repeatedly push through the layers of time' (Abbas 2018, 172). These recurrences give the novel's different periods and overall structure the quality of travelling consciousness and memory. Nation states try to maintain hegemony by producing purified monocultural memories of home or homeland, which can easily come to serve, aid and abet patriarchal, communal and majoritarian ideologies. In *River of Fire*, the 'moving testimonies' track the individual memories as they travel from one time period to another. Both meanings of 'moving' — as travel and affect — are relevant here. The 'circulatory matrix' provides a useful framework for understanding how memories travel temporally and, in the process, contribute to the construction of a 'prosthetic' (Landsberg 2004) or 'cosmopolitan' memory (Levy and Sznaider 2002) of the nation and its past. The memory travels in *River of Fire* unravel the 'processes that can be tracked within and across locations, instances, texts, narratives and events of memory' (Radstone 2011, 120). The narrative not only draws on the recognisability and power of the travelling memory schema but also actualises the schema in rather complex ways. In *River of Fire*, the travelling schemata are connective schemata in the narrativisation (Hirsch and Miller 2011, 8). In the form of travelling schemata, patterns of knowledge cut across boundaries of space, time, language or cultural communities. *River of Fire* throws the spotlight on four key characters, Gautam, Kamal, Champa and Cyril who reincarnated in different periods. Then, they all come together equally in the latter part of the narrative. The movement of one historic segment into another in the text is skilfully 'dovetailed' (Taj 2009, 199). The recurrence of the characters in the different eras transforms the subject and the narrative. In each successive story, the characters become more complex, evolved and nuanced because they are influenced by their previous personas. For instance, Champa, the main female protagonist, recurs in different avatars in the text. Initially, she is the daughter of the chief minister. Then she shows up as Champavati, the sister of a learned Brahmin of Ayodhya. Yet again, she reappears as Champajaan, a rich courtesan in Awadh. Finally, she arrives as Champa Ahmed, a social climber. Following two millennia of longing and attraction, Champa's restive spirit drifts away from Gautam, and she finally escapes the fetters of home and domesticity (Hyder 1998). Her journey across centuries can be read as a quest for self-realisation.

River of Fire is a text embedded in the layered and nuanced travelling civilisational memories that offer us the ability to grasp 'the diversity and dense affiliations of a multi-religious subcontinent' (Sangari 2005, 42). The text employs an interpretive framework arising from recent reconfigurations of memory that shift the focus to processes of travel, multidirectionality and transculturalism. Memory's movements are conveyed via different narrative strategies and thematic emphases. In *River of Fire*, dislocation, movement and the dynamics of spatio-temporal frames emerge as important underpinnings of narrative techniques or textures. Hyder's novel reconstructs India's contested past by mapping out the realms of the fantastic, the myths of collective popular consciousness and cultural memories as they travel across space and time. In the novel, Hyder constructs a synthesised past challenging not only the narratives of fragmentation in the discourse of the Partition but also the rhetoric of a separatist history through the tropes of travelling memories of the past. Hyder's efforts can be thus seen as an effort to write a history of an invisible India, a subterranean layer of the palimpsest of its history, that uses memory as an intervention in the grand 'strategy' of India's official history. Hyder uses the intrinsic flexibility of memory to seek out alternate narratives and histories and works them into the national consciousness through her narrative. As opposed to the monologic, teleological and often majoritarian 'official' texts of the past, the narrative of *River of Fire* is dialogic and less teleological, which presents different worldviews and lifeworlds. Emphasising the existence of different and irreducible interpretations of the past, Hyder shows that the past, as an effect of narrativisation, is invented and reinvented by every new narrative. The ontological pre-eminence of the imaginal in the text is also inseparably linked to an ethic of diversity and plurality.

Through the lens of the past, *River of Fire* presents a series of memory travels that unravels the ambivalence of national identity formed by the mingling of the apparently irreconcilable characteristics of the nation, such as the historical and the mythical. Beneath memory travels are the grids of love, trauma and loss that are unavoidable in the formation of the nation state. The 'entanglement' of time with memory is a condition that interlocks 'presents, pasts, and futures that retain their depths of other presents, pasts, and futures, each age bearing, altering, and maintaining the previous ones' (Mbembe 2001, 16). In *River of Fire*, the travelling memories and time flows not only refute spatio-temporal rootedness, unitary self, closed/fixed endings, singular truth claims and certain knowledge but also reveal the fissures beneath the junctures of time that offer snapshots of postcolonial conditions of being. Framing the condition of a continuity that outstrips linearity through a dazzling concert of iterations, Hyder imagines 'a past that is not singular, hegemonic, and progressive (in the style of empire itself), but rather multiple, subaltern, and heterochronic becomings' (Cooppan 2019, 411). Entangling time with memory travels is one way to represent and reconstruct its border crossings, crosshatchings and quilting. Thus, mapping the contours of the memory travels in *River of Fire* shifts the focus from tracing origins to imag(in)ing a possibility that recognises multiple, interlinked and layered histories of love and loss.

References

Abbas, Sadia. 2018. 'Neither Greek nor Indian: Space, Nation, and History in *River of Fire* and *The Mermaid Madonna*'. In *The Postcolonial Contemporary Political Imaginaries for the Global Present*, edited by Jini Kim Watson and Gary Wilder, 164–186. New York: Fordham University Press.

Amarakeerthi, Liyanage. 2003. '*River of Fire*: Critiquing the Ideology of History'. *Annual of Urdu Studies* 18: 25–44.

Anderson, Benedict. 1983. *Imagined Communities: Reflections on the Origin and Spread of Nationalism*. London: Verso.

Asaduddin, M. 2000. 'The Exiles Return: Qurratulain Hyder's Art of Fiction'. *Manushi* 119(July–August): 28–32.

Assmann, Jan. 1992. *Das kulturelle Gedächtnis: Schrift, Erinnerung und politische Identität in frühen Hochkulturen*. München: Beck.

Aydemir, Murat, and Alex Rotas. 2008. *Migratory Settings*. Amsterdam: Rodopi.

Batra, Anupa. 2012. 'Women and Becoming-Woman: Deleuze and Feminism'. In *Movements in Time: Revolution, Social Justice and Times of Change*, edited by Cecile Lawrence and Natalie Churn, 65–76. Newcastle upon Tyne: Cambridge Scholars Publishing.

Bond, L., S. Craps and P. Vermeulen. 2016. 'Introduction: Memory on the Move'. In *Memory Unbound: Tracing the Dynamics of Memory Studies*, edited by L. Bond, S. Craps and P. Vermeulen, 1–26. New York: Berghahn Publishers.

Bond, Lucy, and Jessica Rapson. 2014. Introduction to *The Transcultural Turn: Interrogating Memory Between and Beyond Borders*, edited by Lucy Bond and Jessica Rapson, 1–28. Berlin/Boston: Walter de Gruyter.

Burchill, Louise. 2010. 'Becoming-Woman: A Metamorphosis in the Present Relegating Repetition of Gendered Time to the Past'. *Time & Society* 19(1): 81–97.

Chakrabarty, Dipesh. 2000. *Provincializing Europe*. Princeton, NJ: Princeton University Press.

Chatterjee, Partha. 1993. *Nation and Its Fragments*. Princeton, NJ: Princeton University Press.

———. 2001. 'The Nation in Heterogeneous Time'. *The Indian Economic and Social History Review* 38(4): 399–418.

Chittick, William. 2008. 'Ibn Arabi'. *Stanford Encyclopedia of Philosophy*. Web. 20 August 2008. Accessed 31 January 2021. https://plato.stanford.edu/entries/ibn-arabi/.

———. 1994. *Imaginal Worlds: Ibn al-Arabi and the Problem of Religious Diversity*. Albany: State University of New York Press.

Cooppan, Vilashini. 2019. 'Time-Maps: A Field Guide to the Decolonial Imaginary'. *Critical Times* 2(3): 396–415.

Deleuze, Gilles, and Felix Guattari. 1987. *A Thousand Plateaus: Capitalism and Schizophrenia*. Translated by Brian Massumi. Minneapolis, MN: University of Minnesota Press.

Dirlik, Arif. 1996. 'The Past as Legacy and Project: Post-colonial Criticism in the Perspective of Indigenous Historicism'. *American Indian Culture and Research Journal* 20(2): 1–31.

Dudai, Y., and M. Carruthers. 2005. 'The Janus Face of Mnemosyne Memory: Some Systems in the Brain May be Better Equipped to Handle the Future Than The Past'. *Nature* 434 (567). https://doi.org/10.1038/434567a.

Erll, Astrid. 2011. 'Travelling Memory'. *Parallax* 17(4): 4–18.

Erll, Astrid. 2017. 'Travelling Memory in European Film: Towards a Morphology of Mnemonic Relationality'. *Image [&] Narrative* 18(1): 5–19.

Erll, Astrid, and Ann Rigney, eds. 2009. *Mediation, Remediation, and the Dynamics of Cultural Memory*. Berlin and New York: de Gruyter.

Habib, Irfan. 1999. 'The Envisioning of a Nation: A Defence of the Idea of India'. *Social Scientist* 27(9–10): 18–29.

Hirsch, Marianne. 2012. *The Generation of Postmemory: Writing and Visual Culture After the Holocaust*. New York: Columbia University Press.

Hirsch, Marianne, and Nancy K. Miller, eds. 2011. *Rites of Return: Diaspora Poetics and the Politics of Memory*. New York: Columbia University Press.

Husain, Intizar. 1979. *Basti*. Translated by Frances Pritchett. New Delhi: HarperCollins, 1999.

Hussein, Abdullah. (1963) 1999. *Udas Naslein* [*The Weary Generations*]. Translated by author. New Delhi: HarperCollins.

Hijazi, Naseem. 1961. *Khaak Aur Khoon*. Lahore: Jahangir Book Depot.

Hyder, Qurratulain. 1998. *River of Fire*. New Delhi: Kali for Women.

Koselleck, Reinhart. 2004 '"Neuzit": Remarks on the Semantics of Modern Concepts.' In *Futures Past: On the Semantics of Historical Time*, translated by Keith Tribe, 222–254. New York: Columbia University Press.

Kumar, Sukrita Paul. 2002. 'Beyond Partition: Turns of Centuries in *Aag Ka Darya*'. *India International Centre Quarterly* 29(2): 87–94.

Landsberg, Alison. 2004. *Prosthetic Memory: The Transformation of American Remembrance in the Age of Mass Culture*. New York: Columbia University Press.

Levy, Daniel, and Natan Sznaider. 2002. *The Holocaust and Memory in the Global Age*. Translated by Assenka Oksiloff. Philadelphia: Temple University Press.

Mandler, P. 2002. *History and National Life*. London: Profile Books.

Mbembe, Achille. 2001. *On the Postcolony*. Translated by A.M. Berrett, Murray Last, Steven Rendell and Janet Roitman. Berkeley: University of California Press.

Menon, Ritu. 2008. 'Endearing Iconoclast'. *Annual of Urdu Studies* 23: 202–205.

Oldfield, Anna C. 2010. 'Confusion in the Universe: Conflict and Narrative in Qurratulain Hyder's *River of Fire*'. *Annual of Urdu Studies* 25: 28–41.

Palakeel, Thomas. 1999. 'Experimental Novel and the Problems of Imagined History'. *Annual of Urdu Studies* 14: 293–302.

Pandey, Gyanendra. 1992. 'In Defense of the Fragment: Writing about Hindu-Muslim Riots in India Today'. *Representations* 37: 27–55.

Radstone, Susannah. 2011. 'What Place is This? Transcultural Memory and the Locations of Memory Studies'. *Transcultural Memory. Special Issue Parallax* 17(4): 109–123.

Raja, Masood Ashraf. 2006. 'Qurratulain Hyder's *River of Fire*: The Novel and the Politics of Writing Beyond the Nation-State'. *Interactions* 15(2): 49–60.

Ray, Sangeeta. 2000. *En-Gendering India: Woman and Nation in Colonial and Postcolonial Narratives*. Durham and London: Duke University Press.

Ricoeur, Paul. 1986. *Fallible Man*. New York: Fordham University Press.

———. 1992. *Oneself as Another*. Translated by Kathleen Blamey. Chicago: University of Chicago Press.

Rothberg, M. 2009. *Multidirectional Memory: Remembering the Holocaust in the Age of Decolonization*. Stanford, CA: Stanford University Press.

———. 2014. 'Multidirectional Memory in Migratory Settings: The Case of Post-Holocaust Germany'. In *Transnational Memory: Circulation, Articulation, Scales*, edited by C. de Cesari and A. Rigney, 123–146. Berlin: de Gruyter Press.

Sangari, Kumkum. 2003. 'New Nations, Old Civilizations'. *European Journal of Women's Studies* 10(4): 473–480. doi: 10.1177/13505068030104007.

———. 2005. 'The Configural Mode: *Aag ka Darya*'. In *A Wilderness of Possibilities: Urdu Studies in Transnational Perspective*, edited by Kathryn Hansen and David Lelyveld, 21–45. New York: Oxford University Press.

Sholtz, Janae, and Cheri Lynne Carr. 2019. 'Introduction: Alliances and Allies'. In *Deleuze and the Schizoanalysis of Feminism: Alliances and Allies*, edited by Janae Sholtz and Cheri Lynne Carr, 1–20. London: Bloomsbury.

Sontag, Susan. 2007. 'At the Same Time: The Novelist and Moral Reasoning'. In *At the Same Time: Essays and Speeches*, edited by Paolo Dilonardo and Anne Jump, 210–231. London: Hamilton.

Spurr, D. 1993. *The Rhetoric of Empire: Colonial Discourse in Journalism, Travel Writing, and Imperial Administration*. Durham, NC: Duke University Press.

Suddendorf, T., and M.C. Corballis. 1997. 'Mental Time Travel and the Evolution of the Human Mind'. *Genetic, Social, and General Psychology Monographs* 123: 133–167.

Taj, Nikhat. 2009. 'A Study of the Organising Principle(s) in Qurratulain Hyder's *River of Fire*'. *Indian Literature* 53.4 (252): 195–213.

Talbot, Cynthia. 1995. 'Inscribing the Other, Inscribing the Self: Hindu-Muslim Identities in Precolonial India'. *Comparative Studies in Society and History* 37(4): 692–722.

Thapar, Romila. 1989. 'Imagined Religious Communities? Ancient History and the Modern Search for a Hindu Identity.' *Modern Asian Studies* 23(2): 209–231.

Törnquist-Plewa, B. 2018. 'The Transnational Dynamics of Local Remembrance: The Jewish Past in a Former Shtetl in Poland'. *Memory Studies* 11(3): 301–314.

Tulving, E. 1983. *Elements of Episodic Memory*. Clarendon Press.

———. 1984. 'Precis of Elements of Episodic Memory'. *Behavioural and Brain Sciences* 7(2): 223–268.

———. 2005. 'Episodic Memory and Autonoesis: Uniquely human?' In *The Missing Link in Cognition: Origins of Self-reflective Consciousness*, edited by H.S. Terrace and J. Metcalfe, 3–56. Oxford University Press.

Williams, Raymond. 1980. *Problems in Materialism and Culture: Selected Essays*. London: Verso.

Wüstenberg, Jenny. 2019. 'Locating Transnational Memory'. *International Journal of Politics, Culture, and Society* 32: 371–382.

Zaidi, Nishat. 2022. 'Oceanic Encounters with The "Other" in the Age of the Empire: Late Eighteenth- and Nineteenth-Century Travel Accounts of Indian Muslims'. In *Ocean As Method: Thinking With the Maritime*, edited by Dilip M. Menon, Nishat Zaidi, Simi Malhotra and Saarah Jappie, 54–88. London and New York: Routledge.

List of Editor and Contributors

Editor

Rita Banerjee was formerly Associate Professor of English Studies at Jawaharlal Nehru University (JNU), Delhi. Currently, she is a research scholar affiliated to the Centre for Studies in Social Sciences, Calcutta. She specialised in early modern British drama and has published articles, book chapters and a monograph in early modern literature and related areas. Her current research interests include travel narratives, early modern literature, historiography, 19th- and 20th-century Bengali literature and culture, women's writings and Rabindranath Tagore. She has recently published *India in Early Modern English Travel Narratives: Protestantism, Enlightenment, and Toleration* (Brill, 2021) and an edited collection, *Cultural Histories of India: Subaltern Spaces, Peripheral Genres, and Alternate Historiography* (Routledge, 2020).

Contributors

Ajie George is Associate Professor at Stella Maris College in Chennai, India. She has been in the teaching profession for twenty-six years and has taught at the BA, MA and MPhil levels. Her doctoral research was in travel writing with reference to William Dalrymple's writing. She was involved in creating and teaching a course in travel writing at her college. She is currently researching writings by migrants to the Gulf region in the light of travel writing.

Christian Feser is Research Fellow at the Chair of British Literature and Culture at the University of Duisburg-Essen, Germany. He holds an MA from the University of Bamberg, Germany, and the City University of New York. His research interests include early modern literary networks, sociability and travel writing, and he is currently working on a PhD thesis on notions of eccentricity in the writings of Thomas Coryate.

Christoph Heyl is Chair of British Literature and Culture at the University of Duisburg-Essen, Germany. He is a Fellow of the Royal Asiatic Society, the Royal Historical Society and the Society of Antiquaries of Scotland. His research focuses on the interplay between literature and cultural history (including music, the visual arts and architecture), especially of the early modern period. He has worked on topics such as the rise of the private sphere in 18th-century London and related phenomena in literature and the visual arts, collections and collectors in 17th-century England and the literature they inspired, Hogarth's paintings and engravings, crime and crime fiction, Scottish literature and identity, the Great Fire of London and, last but not least, British perceptions of India.

Jaya Yadav is a PhD Scholar of the University of Delhi, India, working on contemporary South Asian literature. Her MPhil thesis was on Amitav Ghosh's *The Calcutta Chromosome* and the *Ibis* trilogy. She is deeply interested in the interdisciplinary aspects of literature and its role in questions of identity, history and politics. Her work also focuses on issues of class, race and gender, especially in conflict zones. She grew up in Turkmenistan, England and Nepal before relocating to India for university and continues to connect with the diaspora from these nations. She is currently a senior editor at *Strife* blog and journal, Department of War Studies, King's College, London and Assistant Professor at the Department of English, Janki Devi Memorial College in New Delhi, India.

Jayati Gupta was formerly Professor of English at West Bengal State University, Barasat, India. A large part of her teaching career was spent at the erstwhile Presidency College, Kolkata. She specialises in 18th-century literature and finds passionate scholarly interest in varied forms of travel writing. Her tenure in 2015–2017 at the National Library, Kolkata, as Tagore National Fellow for Cultural Research (Ministry of Culture, Government of India) enabled her to work on a project titled 'The Cultures of Travel in Bengal'. Her book *Travel Culture, Travel Writing and Bengali Women 1870-1940* was published in 2020 in the United Kingdom (Routledge), while the South Asia edition was published early in 2021. She is currently working on a second book on women travellers commissioned by Routledge. She currently works as visiting faculty in Adamas University, Barasat, India.

Joan-Pau Rubiés is Research Professor at ICREA (Catalan Institution for Research and Advanced Studies) and at Universitat Pompeu Fabra in Barcelona, Spain. Until 2012, he was Reader in International History at the London School of Economics. He has also been Visiting Professor at the École des Hautes Études en Sciences Sociales and at Corpus Christi Christ College, Oxford. He is currently leading a research project on ethnographies, religious missions and cultural encounters in the early modern world. A specialist of late medieval and early modern travel writing and ethnography, he has published important work on cultural encounters in South Asia and elsewhere, such as the monograph *Travel* *and Ethnology in the Renaissance: South India through European Eyes, 1250-1625* (Cambridge University Press, 2000) and the collected articles *Travellers and Cosmographers: Studies in the History of Early-Modern Travel and Ethnology* (Ashgate, Variorum, 2007). He has edited *Medieval Ethnographies. European Perceptions of the World Beyond* (Ashgate, 2009), *Voyages and Visions: Towards a Cultural History of Travel* (with Jaś Elsner) (Reaktion Books, 1999) and *Cosmopolitanism and the Enlightenment* (Cambridge University Press, forthcoming). He is currently writing a monograph titled *Europe's New Worlds: Travel Writing and the Origins of the Enlightenment, 1550-1750*, to be published by Cambridge University Press.

M.V. Lakshmi is Assistant Professor at the Centre for Japanese Studies, JNU, India, since 2002. Her doctoral thesis is on 'Changing Image of India in Modern Japanese Literature: A Study of Modern Japanese Fiction of the period 1918-2000' from JNU. Her current areas of research interest are expatriate writings on India and Japan and modern Japanese children's literature. She has co-edited the book *Japanese Language Education: A Bridge between Language and Culture* with Hideo Hosokawa and P.A. George (Northern Book Centre, 2012). Her recent publications include 'Buddhism as a Bridge to Understand India in Mishima Yukio's *Hojo no Umi* (Sea of Fertility)' in *Japanese Studies in South Asia: New Horizons* (2021) and 'Defining the Japanese Gaze on India in Postwar fiction: Analysis of Mishima Yukio's Hōjō no Umi' in the *Rupkatha Journal on Interdisciplinary Studies in Humanities* 9.3 (2017).

Nandana Dutta is Professor of English at Gauhati University, India, and holds additional charge of the Gauhati University Institute of North-East India Studies. Her specialisation is in American literature, and her areas of interest are women's studies, postcolonial theory and literature, travel writing and the discipline of English in India. Her publications include *Questions of Identity in Assam: Location, Migration, Hybridity* (SAGE, 2012), *Mothers, Daughters and Others: Representation of Women in the Folk Narratives of Assam* (edited and introduced [ABILAC, 2013]) *American Literature* (series: Literary Contexts, Orient Blackswan, 2016), *Communities of Women in Assam: Being, Doing and Thinking Together* (edited and introduced [Routledge, 2016] and essays in journals like *Interventions, Journeys, Synthesis, Commonwealth Essays and Studies, Australian Literary Studies* and *English*.

Nandita Basu has a PhD from the University of Delhi, India, and was formerly Professor of Modern Indian Languages and Literary Studies there. Her teaching career began in 1976, when she taught at Miranda House, University of Delhi. She wrote a monograph in Bengali on the writer Jyotirmoyee Devi and translated the Assamese novel *Dantal Hatir Uniye Khaoa Howda* by Mamoni Raisom Goswami into Bengali. Nandita Basu has published numerous essays, both academic and popular, on the different aspects of Bengali literature and culture. Of late, she has completed the manuscript of a critical biography of Mahasweta Devi (in Bengali). A Bengali translation of an autobiography of Pratibha Aggarwal, actress and founder of Natyoshodh, from the Hindi original, is about to be published.

Nishat Haider is Professor of English at Jamia Millia Islamia, New Delhi, India. She is the author of *Tyranny of Silences: Contemporary Indian Women's Poetry* (2010). She has served as the Director of the Institute of Women's Studies, University of Lucknow. She is the recipient of many academic awards, including the Meenakshi Mukherjee Prize (2016), C.D. Narasimhaiah Prize (2010), and Isaac Sequeira Memorial Award (2011). She has presented papers at numerous academic conferences, and her essays have been included in a variety of scholarly journals and books. She has conducted numerous conferences, seminars and workshops on gender budgeting and gender sensitisation. She has worked on various projects funded by the Ministry of Women and Child Development, United Nations Children's Fund (UNICEF), University Grants Commission (UGC) and other agencies. She has lectured extensively on subjects at the intersection of cinema, culture and gender studies. Her current research interests include postcolonial studies, translation, popular culture and gender studies.

Ranjana Mukhopadhyaya is Professor of Japanese Studies in the Department of East Asian Studies, University of Delhi, India. She has also taught at the Nagoya City University in Japan. She has bachelor's and master's degrees in Sociology and MPhil in Japanese Studies from the University of Delhi. She received her doctoral degree in Religious Studies and Japanese Studies from the University of Tokyo, Japan. She was also a Visiting Research Fellow at the International Research Center for Japanese Studies (Nichibunken), Kyoto, Japan. She is the author of a number of books and articles, in English as well as in Japanese, on Japanese Buddhism, religious studies and East Asian society and culture. Her doctoral thesis, written in Japanese and published as *Nihon no Shakai-sanka Bukkyo* (Engaged Buddhism in Japan, Toshindo Publication, Tokyo, 2005), is the recipient of two prestigious academic awards in Japan — the Japanese Association for Religious Studies

Award (2007) and the Japanese Association for Buddhist Social Welfare Studies Award (2007).

Saugata Bhaduri is Professor at the Centre for English Studies, JNU, in New Delhi, India. His areas of research interest include literary and cultural theory, popular culture studies, translation and comparative literature studies and the cultural history of colonial Bengal. His latest books are *Polycoloniality: European Transactions with Bengal from the 13th to the 19th Century* (Bloomsbury, 2020) and the forthcoming *A Critical History of Bengali Literature* (Orient Blackswan, 2022). His edited books include *Transcultural Negotiations of Gender: Studies in (Be)Longing* (Springer, 2015), *Literary Theory: An Introductory Reader* (Anthem, 2010), *Perspectives on Comparative Literature and Culture in the Age of Globalization* (Anthem, 2010), *Negotiating Glocalization* (Anthem, 2008) and *Translating Power* (Katha, 2008).

Sumit Kumar Barua is Associate Professor of Bengali at Jadavpur University, Kolkata. His research interests include modern Bengali literature, literature of Bangladesh, Buddhist literature and Tagore studies among others. Dr Barua holds a PhD in Bengali from Jadavpur University. He has been the Visiting Researcher at the Research Institute for Languages and Cultures of Asia and Africa, Tokyo University of Foreign Studies, Japan. In recent years, he has authored and edited several books, namely, *Bismrito Yatri Nichiki Kimura* (Spark, 2021), *Brahmosamaj o Bauddhasanskriti* (Chhoya, 2020), *Sishu-Kishor Patrika: Prasanga Bauddhasanskriti* (Dey's Publishing, 2021), *Kabita Singher Kabita Sangraha* (Dey's Publishing, 2019), Asha Daser *Bangla Sahitya Bauddhadharma o Sanskriti*, Vol. I and II (Chhoya, 2018) and *Kabita Singher Shrestha Galpo* (Dey's Publishing, 2021). Apart from this, he has authored several articles, mainly in Bengali, in periodicals and journals.

Index

D